P9-AGO-919

Constitution Obsolete?

Is the American Constitution Obsolete?

Edited By
Thomas J. Main

CAROLINA ACADEMIC PRESS
Durham, North Carolina

Main, Thomas J.
 Is the American constitution obsolete? / Thomas J. Main.
    p. cm.
 Includes bibliographical references.
 ISBN 978-1-59460-958-9 (alk. paper)
 1. Constitutional law--United States. 2. Judicial review--United States. 3. Slavery--
Law and legislation--United States. 4. Electoral college--United States. I. Title.

 KF4550.M255 2012
 342.7302--dc23

                                    2011052593

Carolina Academic Press
700 Kent Street
Durham, North Carolina 27701
Telephone (919) 489-7486
Fax (919) 493-5668
www.cap-press.com

Printed in the United States of America

Contents

Preface   ix

PART ONE: INTRODUCTION

Chapter 1 • Veneration and Criticism of the American Constitution   5
Thomas J. Main
   The Progressive Critique   6
   The Antifederalist Critique   9
   The Abolitionist Critique   10
   Constitutional Criticism Today   11

PART TWO: THE CONSTITUTION: PRO AND CON

Chapter 2 • Democracy and the Constitution   15
Daniel Lazare
   The Limits of Pragmatism   17
   The Political Implications   19
   End Times, Anyone?   21

Chapter 3 • We Should Preserve, Protect and Defend
          the Constitution — Not Trash It   25
Jeremy Rabkin
   Why Fix It if It's Not Broke?   26
   The Authority of the Second Best   29
   Too Much Constitutional Reform Will Undo the Constitution   31
   A Fixed Constitution Must Sometimes Be a Flexible Constitution 35
   The Most General Case for Constitutional Conservatism   37

PART THREE: RACE AND THE CONSTITUTION

Chapter 4 • Slavery's Constitution:The Creation of
          America's Covenant with Death   43
Paul Finkelman
   Slavery in the Constitutional Structure   45
   Slavery and Congressional Representation   48
   Slavery and the Executive Branch   57
   Commerce and Slavery: The Dirty Compromise   57
   Toward Sectional Harmony   65
   The Proslavery Compact   66

Chapter 5 · Planned Obsolescence? The Constitution and Slavery 69
Mark A. Graber
In the Beginning 72
Framing 72
Ratification 75
Slavery and the Northern Ratification Debates 75
Southern Ratification Conventions 77
Obsolescence Over Time 79
The Southern Perception 80
Northern Perceptions 81
Contemporary Lessons? 82

PART FOUR: THE ELECTORAL COLLEGE: END IT OR MEND IT?

Chapter 6 · Why the U.S. Needs Direct Election of the President 87
George C. Edwards III
Constitutional Consistency 88
Defending Interests 89
Attention to State Interests 92
Fragmenting the Party System 95
Preserving Federalism 98
Protecting Non-State-Based Minority Interests 100
Why Not Elect Everyone by the Same Rules? 100
Campaigns under Direct Election 101
Conclusion 102

Chapter 7 · The Electoral College: Mend It, Don't End It 105
Larry A. Sabato
The Founding of a College 106
Advantages of the Electoral College 107
Concerns with the Current Electoral College 108
Reforms That Abolish the Electoral College 109
Reforms That Mend the Electoral College... but Have
    Unintended Consequences 110
Reform Approaches That Mend the Electoral College...
    and Can Work 113

PART FIVE: THE CONSTITUTION AND GRIDLOCK

Chapter 8 · Thinking about Gridlock 121
Sanford Levinson

Chapter 9 · Does the Constitution Encourage Gridlock? 135
R. Shep Melnick
From Stalemate to Gridlock 137
Where's the Beef? 139
From Veto Points to Opportunity Points 143
Compared to What? 146

PART SIX: JUDICIAL REVIEW AND DEMOCRACY

Chapter 10 · Against Judicial Review   151
Mark Tushnet
    The Positive Component   152
    The Negative Component   154
    Justice-Related Justifications   155
    Democracy-Related Justifications   157
    Redundancy Justifications   159
    Conclusion   160

Chapter 11 · In Defense of Judicial Review   163
Stephen Macedo
    Majoritarian vs. Constitutional Conceptions of Democracy   164
    Constitutional Democracy   165
    Majoritarianism Reexamined   166
    Constitutional Democracy and Judicial Review   170
    Democracy-Enhancing Judicial Review: From Theory to Practice   172
    Judicial Review, Popular Constitutional Choice, and Global Constitutionalism   174
    Is the American Constitution Ideal?   176
    Conclusion   177

PART SEVEN: AN IMPERIAL PRESIDENCY?

Chapter 12 · The Imperial Presidency, or "Who Doesn't Belong and Why?":
        Lincoln, FDR, Bush 43 and Obama   181
Richard M. Pious
    Lincoln's Constitutional Dictatorship   184
    FDR's "Dr. Win the War" Prerogatives   188
    Surveillance Authority   191
    Status of Enemy Combatants   191
    Indefinite Detention of American Citizens   192
    Interrogation of Unlawful Combatants   193
    Military Tribunals   194
    Denial of Habeas Corpus and Counsel to American Citizens   196
    Partial Separation of Powers   197
    Partial Separation and Parallel Governance   197
    Congress and Interbranch Collaborative Frameworks   201
    Ending Judicial Evasion   202
    In sum...   204

Chapter 13 · Vindicating the Presidency in a Time of Terror   207
Marc Landy
    President and Congress   208
    Judicial Supremacy   212
    Partisanship and Foreign Policy   216
    Iran Contra   217
    The False Peace   220
    9/11, the War Metaphor and the Rebirth of Foreign Policy Partisanship   220

The War on Terror   222
Acquitting Bush   223
Coercive Interrogation   225
Conclusion   228

PART EIGHT: SUMMARY

Chapter 14 • Conclusions and Further Questions   **233**
Akhil Reed Amar
We the People   233
Remember the States   236
Remember the Amendments   238
Imagine   240

Notes   **245**

About the Authors   **291**

Index   **295**

Preface

Americans revere their Constitution but are disturbed by growing signs of political dysfunction. We have placed in the White House candidates who have not won a majority of the popular vote. In time of war and terrorism, fears of an imperial presidency persist. Gridlock prevents reform in immigration, public finance and other vital areas. An economic crisis generates fears that the system may not be able to respond effectively. Can we solve the problems we face under the current Constitution or does the 21st Century call for a new Magna Carta?

This volume had its origin in a conference to debate the strengths and weaknesses of the American Constitution sponsored by the Free Institutions Program of the City University of New York and held at Baruch College on May 4-5 2008. Contributions to the conference were organized to present the pros and cons of several important features of the Constitution. We hope that this volume will contribute to more and better discussion and understanding of the American Constitution.

Is the American Constitution Obsolete?

PART ONE

Introduction

Chapter 1

Veneration and Criticism of the American Constitution

Thomas J. Main

Why an anthology on plans to redraft the American Constitution and why now? These are good questions, ones that skeptics about change always ask when confronted with a new reform scheme. In fact one of our contributors has already used this line of attack in a review of another contributor's book. Thus, Jeremy Rabkin of George Mason Law School makes the following point in his review of Larry J. Sabato's book, *A More Perfect Constitution*: "Professor Sabato's calls for 'enlightened populism' and 'a little rebellion' might be heard with more sympathy if the country were really in dire straits." "Barring some calamity," writes Rabkin, calls for reform are not likely to receive much of a hearing.[1]

Will the present crisis of war and financial chaos count as the "dire straits" or "calamity" that is required to take constitutional reform seriously? The current situation comes closer to fulfilling such conditions than anyone could wish. Iraq certainly broaches the well-known debate about the distribution of war powers under the Constitution and raises the issue of an imperial presidency. And the so far rather faltering response to the financial crisis makes one wonder if the constitutional system doesn't in fact encourage gridlock and drift as some critics say it does.

This conference began as a review/essay on a collection of more or less recent books devoted to the theme of constitutional reform. These books included *How Democratic is the American Constitution?* by Robert Dahl; *The Frozen Republic* by Daniel Lazare; *Our Undemocratic Constitution* by Sanford Levinson; and *A More Perfect Constitution* by Larry J. Sabato. The review/essay was an outgrowth of my search for a bracing critique of the constitutional system that I could use in my introductory courses to public affairs. Reading such a text alongside of *The Federalist Papers* I have found to be an effective way to develop in students a critical appreciation of the Constitution. My thought was that a conference, similarly pairing critics and defenders of the Constitution, would also serve the end of deepening our appreciation of America's most basic political institution. And that end is the purpose of the Free Institutions Program at CUNY, which is sponsoring this conference. Pedagogical aims remain the primary object of this conference, but to them recent events have added the disturbing possibility that our present situation really does call for a rethinking of our constitutional system.

What this essay will do is look back at past efforts to reform or criticize the Constitution and put current efforts in a historical context. Such a historical overview has only infrequently been taken previously. One attempt to do so is *Rewriting the United States Constitution: An Examination of Proposals from Reconstruction to the Present* by John R. Vile. But Vile notes that the kind of accounting he undertakes has seldom been attempted. He writes of past reform proposals:

> Despite the large number of proposals, somewhat paradoxically it is (with the possible exception of those who favor proposals for a parliamentary system and/or stronger party government) difficult to identify a reform tradition if such a tradition is to be connected with a self-conscious idea that one is following in the footsteps of others. Aside from [Woodrow] Wilson, nineteenth century reformers seem to be ignored almost completely in contemporary literature.... None of the writers examined is this book has drawn on all earlier proposals and there are some twentieth-century proponents of change ... whose analysis appears to have been completely lost to modern reformers.[2]

Vile's book only partly provides the desired historical context; for while it usefully pulls together decades of proposals, it is for the most part only descriptive and does not provide much analysis of its material.

A more substantive effort to identify a reform tradition can be found in *The Case Against the Constitution: From the Antifederalists to the Present*, edited by John F. Manley and Kenneth M. Dolbeare. The editors argue that:

> ... [T]here has always been an important body of American thought that challenges or rejects this (positive) portrayal of the Constitution. It is a tradition that puts *democracy* first ... It challenges the Constitution with the basic questions: who or what interests, should be served by government, and how can control by the people be assured?[3]

This volume makes the case that there are three key moments in the history of constitutional critiques. These are (in the order they are taken up in the volume), "The Progressive Critique: Capitalism vs. Democracy," "The Antifederalist Critique: Democracy Denied," and "The Contemporary Critique: Democracy Revived?" And we can add to these moments a fourth: "The Abolitionist Critique: Democracy Compromised with Slavery." For the moment let us use this schema to organize a sketch of the critical tradition. Then we can consider alternative approaches.

The Progressive Critique

The historian Vernon Louis Parrington wrote that the "discovery of the essentially undemocratic nature of the federal Constitution [is] the chief contribution of the Progressive movement to American political thought."[4] We can consider here three main contributors to this discovery: J. Allen Smith, Charles A. Beard, and Woodrow Wilson.

J. Allen Smith was perhaps the first progressive to make the critique of the Constitution the centerpiece of his thought. According to one writer, Smith was "a main forerunner of Beard's economic interpretation."[5] Smith developed this thesis in *The Spirit of American Government*, published in 1907, just as the Progressive movement was coming to power in some states. According to Smith:

It is difficult to understand how anyone who has read the proceedings of the Federal Convention can believe that it was the intention of that body to establish a democratic government. The evidence is overwhelming that the men who sat in that convention had no faith in the wisdom or political capacity of the people.

And further, in a chapter entitled, "The Constitution a Reactionary Document":

It may be said without exaggeration that the American scheme of government was planned and set up to perpetuate the ascendency of the property-holding class in a society leavened with democratic ideas.[6]

Smith's colorful writing style and his polemical rhetoric are reminiscent of a contemporary constitutional critic, Daniel Lazare. Substantively, he also shares with Lazare an acceptance of what might be called totalitarian democracy, or perhaps, less tendentiously, unlimited democracy. Thus Smith writes:

In fact, true liberty consists, as we have seen, not in divesting the government of effective power, but in making it an instrument for the unhampered expression and prompt enforcement of public opinion.[7]

And:

We must either recognize the many as supreme, with no checks upon their authority except such as are implied in their own intelligence, sense of justice, and spirit of fair play, or we must accept the view that the ultimate authority is in the hands of the few.[8]

Or again:

The overthrow of monarchy and aristocracy necessitated a corresponding change in the idea of liberty.... In so far as government had now passed into the hands of the people there was no longer any reason to fear that it would encroach upon what they regarded as their rights.[9]

The very least that could be said of Smith's version of democracy is that "he exhibited no Actonian misgivings about the problem of power."[10]

In these passages Smith sounds very much like Lazare who writes today, in criticism of Madison, that:

[T]he notion of an 'interested and overbearing' majority, in other words one that was narrow and selfish, was a contradiction in terms since the majority's interests were synonymous with those of the public at large. Thanks to the principle of majority rule the majority *was* the public. Its interests *were* the public's interests. It could not be overbearing because if the majority was truly sovereign in a democratic society, its power was infinite and there would be no bounds for it to overstep.[11]

Another key expositor of progressive constitutional reform was Woodrow Wilson. Very interestingly for our concern in tracing the outlines of a constitutional reform tradition, Wilson argued that:

… [W]e of the present generation are in the first season of free, outspoken, unrestrained constitutional criticism. We are the first Americans to hear our own countrymen ask whether the Constitution is still adapted to serve the purposes for which it was intended; the first to entertain any serious doubts about the superiority of our institutions as compared with the systems of Europe; the first to think of remodeling the administrative machinery of the federal government; and of forcing new forms of responsibility upon Congress.[12]

Wilson was of course aware of the constitutional criticisms developed by the antifederalists but says of them that once the Constitution was adopted, "very little more is heard of the party of opposition." In any case Wilson's line of criticism in his best-known work is very different from that of the antifederalists, or from that of his progressive contemporaries. J. Allen Smith objected to the Constitution as a bulwark for the wealthy against the poor; the antifederalists objected that the Constitution did not provide enough checks on tyranny; Wilson objected to the Constitution because it contributed to the "inconvenience, slovenliness, and mismanagement of committee government." To understand Wilson's brand of constitutional criticism, therefore, we have to understand what he meant by "committee government," or by *Congressional Government*, which was the title of his most famous work.

Wilson claims that the "radical defect"[13] of separation of power, by disconnecting the president entirely from Congress, left that body without the kind of steady leadership that a prime minister provides to the legislature in a parliamentary system. Congress tries to fill this void by developing the internal structure of committees, which are largely successful at resting control of the bureaucracy from the president. According to Wilson, "That high office has fallen from its first estate of dignity because its power has waned; and its power has waned because the power of Congress has become predominant."[14] The result is "congressional government," but congressional government is bad government. Stid sums up Wilson's analysis of congressional government:

> As Congress's institutional capacity to act increased, it involved itself in more and more spheres of governmental activity. With this increased involvement came a distortion of the legislative function and a confounding of the separation of powers. Congress maladroitly sought to perform functions that Wilson held to be properly executive in nature, namely, framing legislation and supervising administration. Thus preoccupied, Congress became, at the same time, much less suited for what he saw as the appropriate legislative functions of debating the policies prepared and administered by the executive. Yet there was no stopping the congressional monolith once it had organized itself to govern.[15]

In Wilson's constitutional criticism we see another motive for reform. Most progressive critics are concerned with economic inequality; the antifederalists, as we shall see are concerned with tyranny; but Wilson's main concern is good government.

At the heart of the progressive critique of the Constitution is perhaps the most notorious constitutional critic, Charles A. Beard. Beard sums up his well-known thesis as follows:

> The members of the Philadelphia convention which drafted the Constitution were, with a few exceptions, immediately, directly, and personally interested in, and derived advantages from, the establishment of the new system.[16]

In essence, Beard followed Smith's evaluation of the Constitution as a victory of moneyed interests over democracy but backed up that conclusion with an analysis of Treasury records to document the founders' holdings and interests.

Beard's seemingly unassailable account dominated constitutional scholarship from its publication in 1913 until about 1960. In the 1950s work by Robert E. Brown, Forrest Mc-Donald, and others criticized Beard's "often crude and casual economic analysis."[17] Particularly interesting with reference to the issue of constitutional reform is Cecelia M. Kenyon's criticism of Beard. Kenyon particularly objected to the fact that the upshot of Beard's analysis had "frequently been those of simple and uncritical commitment to a theory of economic determinism.... [and] a disinclination to explore the theoretical foundations of the Constitution."[18] Kenyon's criticism of the progressive interpretation of the Constitution is particularly important to us since it directs our attention to what is supposedly the second moment in the history of constitutional criticism, the "antifederalist critique."

Kenyon's analysis of the Beardian thesis takes the apparently oblique route of examining, not the original supporters of the Constitution, but its opponents, the antifederalists. If, according to the progressives, the Constitution's elaborate structure of checks and balances, filters, and separation of powers was intended to insulate the national government from democratic forces, then we ought to find that the opponents of the Constitution objected to that structure in the name of greater democratic responsiveness. We ought to find, in other words that the antifederalists were precursors of the progressives and that their rallying cry was "Democracy Denied," as the editors of *The Case Against the Constitution* put it.

The Antifederalist Critique

Kenyon argues, however that when we listen to the opponents of the Constitution we find that "The Anti-Federalists wanted a more rigid system of separation of powers, more numerous and more effective checks and balances than the Founding Fathers had provided."[19] Kenyon directly compares the antifederalists with J. Allen Smith on the matter of checks and balances and concludes:

> There can be little doubt that the Anti-Federalists were united in their desire to put more checks on the new government.... and they would have found quite unacceptable J. Allen Smith's dictum that 'The system of checks and balances must not be confused with democracy; it is opposed to and cannot be reconciled with the theory of popular government.'[20]

Indeed, the antifederalists, who are supposedly the originators of the critical tradition, could not disagree more with Smith and his neoprogressive followers on this issue of the danger of power and democracy. The antifederalists specifically rejected Smith's thesis of unlimited democracy. Antifederalist writings are replete with warnings against the encroaching nature of power and the need to check it, even when it is in the hands of a democratic government. For example "Brutus" writes:

> Besides it is a truth confirmed by the unerring experience of ages, that every man, and every body of men invested with power are ever disposed to increase it and to acquire superiority over every thing that stands in their way.[21]

"Agrippa" agrees and explicitly rejects the idea that power is safer in the hands of a democratic government than in the hands of a king:

> The experience of all mankind has proved the prevalence of a disposition to use power wantonly. It is therefore as necessary to defend an individual against the majority in a republick as against the king in a monarchy.[22]

"John De Witt" concludes that the grasping at power by politicians can only be contained by checks and balances:

> They uniformly exercise all the powers granted to them and ninety-nine in a hundred are for grasping for more. It is this passionate thirst for power, which has produced different branches to exercise different departments and mutual checks upon those branches.[23]

This material suggests the limitations of conceiving of the antifederalists and progressives as both being expositors of the same critical tradition. Despite the claims of some neoprogressive scholars, the antifederalists expressed a much greater suspicion of political power and a stronger embrace of checks and balances than Smith and the progressives ever did.

One of the most interesting antifederalist critiques of the Constitution came from Patrick Henry and concerned the issue of slavery. Contemporary readers are familiar with the change that the Constitution did not end slavery or give Congress the power to end it. For example, Robert Dahl argues that the Constitution "neither forbade slavery nor empowered Congress to do so."[24] It is therefore striking to find that famed Virginia orator and antifederalist Patrick Henry argued against the Constitution by arguing that indeed it *would* give Congress the power to end slavery. Robin L. Einhorn sums up Henry's argument on this point:

> "Among ten thousand implied powers which they may assume," Henry threatened, "they may, if we be engaged in war, liberate every one of your slaves if they please." Nor would this danger exist only during wars. The Constitution granted the new federal government the "power of manumission." "Have they not power to provide for the general defense and welfare?" Henry asked. "May they not think that these call for the abolition of slavery? — May they not pronounce all slaves free and will they not be warranted by that power?"[25]

Whether Henry's reading of the Constitution was accurate on this point is something that will be discussed by two contributors to this conference, Paul Finkelman and Mark Graber. But now we need to take up another moment in constitutional criticism, which came with the rise of abolitionism.

The Abolitionist Critique

In 1840, James Madison's notes of the debates of the Constitutional Convention were published posthumously. Among the groups that made use of this new material were the abolitionists. For example, Wendell Phillips presented excerpts from Madison's notes to prove, as he said in the title of his book, *The Constitution a Pro-Slavery Compact*. In the introduction to this collection Phillips makes several distinct points that need to be distinguished. In making his first point, Phillips says of the Madison papers that:

> The further we explore them, the clearer becomes the fact that the Constitution was meant to be, what it has always been esteemed, a compromise between slavery and freedom.[26]

The convention debates that Phillips cites certainly prove that the Founders compromised with slavery. This indeed had an impact on how the Constitution has been evaluated. One author notes that after the use made of the Madison papers by the abolitionists, "For the next several decades the 'compromises of the constitution' over slavery were a staple of historical accounts." As a result "the Founding Fathers emerged ... as blemished political fixers, not as the saviors of the nation pictured by earlier historians."[27] This aspect of the abolitionists' constitutional criticism continues to be relevant today.

Given that the Founders compromised with slavery, then other questions present themselves. Was the compromise made with slavery so lopsided, so favorable to the slave holders, that the Constitution was in fact pro-slavery? Phillips's answer was that " ... at this time and for the last half century the Constitution of the United States has been, and still is, a pro-slavery instrument."[28] On this charge of being pro-slavery, abolitionists were divided. Phillips and followers of the abolitionist leader William Lloyd Garrison agreed with Garrison when he famously charged that the Constitution was "a covenant with death and an agreement with hell." Yet another issue was—however one evaluated the Constitution's position on slavery—could antislavery supporters take advantage of political opportunities that were available under that Constitution? Here the Garrisonians argued, as Phillips wrote, that the Constitution "ought to be immediately annulled. No abolitionist can consistently take office under it, or swear to support it."[29]

Frederick Douglass would eventually come to disagree with the Garrisonians on both these above points. Douglass would write,

> The Garrisonians ... hold the Constitution to be a slaveholding instrument, and will not cast a vote or hold office, and denounce all who vote or hold office, no matter how faithfully such persons labour to promote the abolition of slavery. I on the other hand, deny that the Constitution guarantees the right to hold property in man and believe that the way to abolish slavery in America is to vote such men into power as well as use their powers for the abolition of slavery.[30]

Again, the question of whether the Constitution is pro or antislavery is still with us and will be taken up at this conference. Today the Garrisonians' rejection of voting and office holding seems less compelling, especially given that its universal application would have kept Lincoln out of the White House. In any case, Abolitionist constitutional criticism had an impact on the progressives' interpretation of the Constitution. For while they abhorred at least parts of the Constitution, the abolitionists revered the Declaration of Independence. To them the sordid compromises of the Constitution amounted to a counterrevolution against the ideals of the Declaration. This notion of the Constitution as a counterrevolutionary repudiation of the values of the Revolution would be picked up and developed by Progressive historians. Thus, J. Allen Smith would write,

> The sweeping changes made in our form of government after the Declaration of Independence were clearly revolutionary in character.... [W]e find the democratic tendency which manifested itself with the outbreak of the Revolution giving place a few years later to the political reaction which found expression in our present Constitution.[31]

Constitutional Criticism Today

Not much needs to be said here about the critique of the Constitution today since this whole conference is already dedicated to that issue. We can however take an overview of constitutional criticism of the past to see what themes and concerns remain of interest to us.

One enduring concern of critics of the Constitution relates to the issue of democracy. Constitutional criticism forces us to address the questions of what is democracy and whether democracy needs to be balanced against other values. The antifederalists, abolitionists, and progressives all take a position on this matter. For the progressives, democracy, in the sense of the rule of the majority, is the cardinal political virtue and should be embodied in a constitution undiluted by other concerns. In J. Allen Smith, this enthusiasm reaches the point where democracy is not only the cardinal political value but the only political value. The rule of the people is to be "supreme" and "unhampered," and the democratic impulse trumps all other considerations. To a considerable extent our enthusiasm for a neoprogressive reform of the Constitution depends on whether we share the progressives' conviction that democracy is the solution to all or nearly all, political concerns.

Of course the abolitionists' antislavery agenda was an essentially democratic impulse. That goal has been achieved long ago but the abolitionists' concern for equality and racial justice are still relevant values against which the Constitution may be measured. Again, our support for constitutional reform to a certain extent depends on our judgment of how fully the nation has achieved democracy in the sense of racial equality and justice. The less successful we judge America to have been in accomplishing the abolitionists' full agenda, the more supportive we are likely to be of constitutional revisions to achieve that goal.

Although they don't use the word very much, democracy is also part of the agenda of the antifederalists in as much as they are concerned with maximizing the participation and power of what they called the "middling classes." Antifederalism was to a considerable extent an early expression of what we would call populism. And here again our position on constitutional reform is partly dependent on what we think of this democratic cum populist impulse. As one contributor to this conference, Larry J. Sabato, has noted a degree of acceptance of "enlightened populism" can result in support for constitutional reform, while skepticism about this style of politics would imply less enthusiasm for revision.

In short, we cannot decide what we think about the Constitution without deciding what we think about democracy. Such values clarification about democracy is one of the most important benefits to be had through constitutional criticism. And if democracy needs to be rethought each generation, so does each generation call for a bout of constitutional criticism.

PART TWO

The Constitution: Pro and Con

Chapter 2

Democracy and the Constitution

Daniel Lazare

In 1786, France's beleaguered monarch, Louis XVI, made a rare trip outside Versailles to visit new harbor works in Cherbourg. Wearing a freshly made scarlet coat embroidered with fleurs-de-lis, he traveled by coach to Caen where dense throngs cheered as the mayor presented him with the keys to the city. From there, he traveled on through western Normandy to Cherbourg where the reception was no less enthusiastic. The crowds, relishing the opportunity to view their king in person, seemed filled with genuine affection. "*Vive le roi*," they cried. "*Vive mon peuple*," Louis shouted in return. Artists and poets memorialized the scene in prints and engravings, and anyone who witnessed it might well have concluded that the French monarchy's run was far from over.[1] Fiscal crises might come and go, but the ties between a king and his people were as unbreakable as those between parent and child.

Three years later, with the monarchy bankrupt and the countryside swept by rioting, the unbreakable had broken beyond repair. Rather than an indication of the *ancien régime*'s strength, Cherbourg is now a reminder of how slow perceptions can be in catching up with reality. The king was still an awe-inspiring figure, and most people could no more imagine France without a monarch than without an official Catholic church. Yet it would soon be stripped of both as an entirely new type of government took the reins.

For most Americans, any comparison between their own system will seem farfetched. Where France was a monarchy, the United States thinks of itself as the world's leading democracy. Where Louis reigned by the grace of God, American presidents rule at the behest of the people. Where royal absolutism was in growing conflict with the new doctrine of popular sovereignty, the US constitutional system *is* popular sovereignty, which is to say "government of the people, by the people, for the people," to quote Lincoln's shorthand description. Hence, as long as the American people exist as a self-governing entity, the constitutional system will exist too. Canada could invade from the north, Mexico could invade from the south, or the United States could disappear into some global superstate. Short of that, we can count on the Constitution to carry on for a long time to come.

Such is the conventional wisdom. But is it true? The answer: only to the degree that the US Constitution is truly an instrument of democratic self-rule. If it is, then "we the people" have no need to go looking for alternatives. If it is not, then the time must someday come when the people jettison it for a form of government that is more fully representative.

So which is it? The place for any such inquiry to begin is at the beginning:

> We the People of the United States, in Order to form a more perfect Union, establish Justice, insure domestic Tranquility, provide for the common defense, promote the general Welfare, and secure the Blessings of Liberty to ourselves and our Posterity, do ordain and establish this Constitution for the United States of America.

This, one of the famous sentences in modern politics, would seem to meet the demands of even the most exacting democrat. The language is not entirely unambiguous, of course. Since "United States" was used as a plural noun prior to the Civil War, it is unclear whether the first seven words refer to the people separately assembled as citizens of the individual states or collectively assembled as citizens of a single nation, an important distinction, needless to say, in terms of federal-state relations. The phrase "to form a more perfect Union" is troublesome because it is ungrammatical and illogical and hence may undermine the argument as a whole. Such problems aside, the Preamble seems to advance a more or less coherent concept of popular sovereignty, one that has the people asserting their total power to modify society as they see fit "in order to ... establish justice, insure domestic tranquility," and otherwise improve their political lot. The people may pledge to limit the exercise. But since the one thing a sovereign cannot do is undo his own sovereignty, they cannot limit the power itself. Once having declared their sovereignty, they are condemned to exercise what Blackstone described as "supreme, irresistible, absolute, uncontrolled authority" in perpetuity.[2]

This is the founding principle of the US constitutional system. Articles I through IV do nothing to compromise it even though they are festooned with items like the three-fifths clause and other proslavery provisions that are repugnant to modern democracy. But if this is the best that "we the people" thought they could do in 1787, it was their sovereign right to do so. Democracy, after all, is filled with problems that the people must work their way through one step at a time. The only question is whether they have full freedom to do so, and there is nothing in the document so far to indicate that they do not.

But then the document hits a roadblock with Article V, which deals with how the Constitution may be changed. If we agree that democracy is one problem after another, then the amending clause is all important since it controls the process by which unanticipated difficulties are to be addressed. If mistakes are to be expected, the only issue, once again, is whether the article provides the people with the necessary tools to fix them. But this is where the amending clause falls flat. Reduced to its bare essentials, it states:

> The Congress, whenever two thirds of both Houses shall deem it necessary, shall propose Amendments to this Constitution ... which ... shall be valid to all Intents and Purposes, as part of this Constitution, when ratified by the Legislatures of three fourths of the several States....

Where the Preamble suggests that the people have an unqualified right to modify their political structure however they may wish, Article V says they cannot change so much as a comma without the consent of two-thirds of each house and three-fourths of the states. This means that just over one-fourth of the states can block any constitutional amendment, no matter how modest or overdue. This is a flat-out violation of majority rule, and since popular sovereignty means the sovereignty of the *preponderance* of the people, it is a flat-out violation of the Preamble. As bad as this, the immense population differences among the states make it even worse. Given the gap between a giant like California, population 36.8 million according to the latest census estimates, and a demographic midget like Wyoming, with a population of just 532,668, the three-fourths rule means that thirteen states accounting for as little as 4.4 percent of the total population can veto any change sought by the remaining 95.6. Even more astonishing is a killer clause at the end of Article V stipulating "that no State, without its Consent, shall be deprived of its equal Suffrage in the Senate." Loosely translated, this means that every last state has an unqualified right to veto any deviation from the principle of equal state representation for as long as it may wish. Even if forty-nine states agree that it is absurd that Wyoming, with just 0.2 percent of the total population, should enjoy equal representation with California, Texas, or New York, there is nothing they can do if Wyoming refuses to budge from the status quo — ever.[3]

This is not only undemocratic, but *increasingly* undemocratic. Thanks to the growth in the number of states and a long-term population shift from the agricultural interior to more urbanized coastal areas, state population differentials have steadily expanded. Where in 1790 the ratio between the most populous and the least populous state (i.e. Virginia and Delaware) was a little under twelve to one, today it is sixty-nine to one and rising. It was bad enough that four of the original thirteen states should be able to block an amendment under the three-fourths rule back at the nation's inception. But the four least populous states at the time accounted for nine percent of the US population, double the figure today. Over the course of two centuries or so, the amending clause is twice as unfair as it was originally.[4]

A system that grows more resistant to change the older it gets is not one that inspires long-term confidence. Moreover, there is no way to make the Constitution more flexible without running into the same difficulties. For the small states, their constitutional veto grows proportionally more valuable the more their population shrinks relative to the whole. Consequently, we can expect Wyoming, the Dakotas, Vermont, et al. to hold onto it all the more fiercely as time goes by, rendering change more difficult the more urgent it becomes. As Edmund Burke observed, "A state without the means of some change is without the means of its conservation."[5] If so, the United States is growing more and more bereft.

The Limits of Pragmatism

There is simply no way to smooth over the contradiction between the popular sovereignty of the Preamble and the growing encumbrances that Article V places on the power of the democratic majority. If God cannot adhere to two mutually exclusive propositions according to the medieval theologians, then neither can the Constitution.[6] Of course, a pragmatist might reply that, logical niceties aside, the adaptability that the Constitution has shown in other areas is sufficient to offset the restrictions in Article V. Consider the Supreme Court's ability to change how the Constitution is understood via judicial review. Since changing the meaning of the text means more or less changing the text itself, the result is a back-door amending process. Article V's restrictions thus wind up less onerous than it might initially appear. A problem is no longer a problem if it is easily circumvented.

But judicial interpretation has its limits. While it certainly reduces Article V's bite, it does not stop it from locking in other undemocratic features and rendering them all but untouchable. The principle of equal state representation in the Senate is the most obvious. Since California accounts for approximately twelve percent of the US population but only two out of a hundred Senate seats, it is underrepresented by a ratio of six to one. The fifty-one percent of Americans who live in the nine largest states (besides California, they are Texas, New York, Florida, Illinois, Pennsylvania, Ohio, Michigan, and Georgia) are underrepresented by a ratio of nearly three to one, while the three percent who live in the ten smallest states are overrepresented by a ratio of nearly seven to one.[7] Where a Senate majority in 1810 could be gleaned from states representing just thirty-one percent of the total population, today the figure stands at seventeen percent—another instance in which the system twice as unfair as it was two centuries ago.[8] Since forty-one votes are enough for a filibuster under current rules, senators representing as little as eleven percent of the population can bottle up any bill sought by the other eighty-nine.

There is no imaginable way that judicial review can render such imbalances less unpalatable. Of course, since Congress is prevented by Article V from tackling equal state representation head on, it could solve the problem in a more roundabout fashion by stripping the Senate of its power while leaving its membership intact. This would still require a constitutional amendment, but one that would have to be approved by two-thirds of each house and three-fourths of the states rather than all fifty. Still, it is difficult to imagine why the thirteen smallest states would go along with such a dramatic diminution of their power or, for that matter, why the Senate as a whole would as well.

Thus, we are back to square one with a Senate that grows more imbalanced and more unfixable with each passing decade. To be fair, it should be pointed out that virtually all bicameral systems feature an upper house that is less than fully representative as a gesture to rural, regional, or other special interests. But all seek to mitigate the consequences by seeing to it that real power remains with the more democratic lower chamber. Thus, Britain's House of Lords has been without any real legislative clout for close to a century, while the power of the German Bundesrat, a body composed of representatives of the *Länder*, or states, pales beside that of the Bundestag, or parliament. France has a Senate that is biased toward rural interests and has long been a stronghold of the right, but its power is similarly a shadow of that of the National Assembly. As Charles de Gaulle gloomily observed as he was about to undergo prostate surgery, "The prostate is like the Senate: useless."[9] Yet not only is the US Senate's clout fully equal to that of the House of Representatives, thanks to its "sole power to try all impeachments" (Article I, Section 3) and the advice and consent it is required to give on all treaties and major presidential appointments (Article II, Section 2), it may even be superior. It is both powerful and unrepresentative, a deadly combination.

The House is somewhat less problematic since the population differences among congressional districts do not approach those of the states. Still, Montana, which elects just one member of the House, has nearly twice as many people as Wyoming, which also elects a single member. Relative to their neighbor to the south, Montanans' votes wind up diluted nearly by half. Discrepancies like these would never be tolerated at a state or local level, but are untouchable at the federal level because the Constitution allows for no effective remedy. Although it is not terribly high on the political radar screen, it is also worth noting that the present constitutional structure locks in a system of single-member constituencies that much of the democratic world has long since discarded. Proportional representation, in which all voters choose from a single list and seats are allocated on the basis of each party's share of the total, is more equitable because it treats all votes the same regardless of where they are cast. But even though proportional representation is the rule throughout most of Europe and has even made inroads in the United Kingdom, it is all but impossible in the United States because it conflicts with an unchangeable constitutional structure. Where other countries are free to experiment with new democratic forms, the United States remains chained to one dating from the eighteenth century.

Then there is the Electoral College. Since the Constitution allocates electoral votes on the basis of each state's total congressional delegation, senators as well as representatives, the result is yet another boost for the less populous states. Wyoming winds up with three electoral votes even though it is entitled to just one, while California receives fifty-five, ten less than it would receive under some more equitable arrangement. Similarly, Texas is entitled to forty-three but receives just thirty-four, New York is entitled to thirty-four but receives just thirty-one, while Florida is also entitled to thirty-four but receives just twenty-seven. All told, the thirteen least populous states enjoy a total of forty-six electoral votes, approximately double their fair share, while the ten most populous states receive 241, approximately twelve percent less.[10]

Lopsided figures like these have a broad range of political and economic effects. Because the less populous states are predominantly rural—Delaware and Rhode Island are among the few exceptions—the extra clout they receive winds up being a boon to small-town agricultural interests. If anyone wonders why cities are so ill treated in America, this is the place to look. Small states also tend to be more racially homogeneous. Where Hispanics and nonwhites account for fifty-six percent of California's population, fifty-two percent of Texas', and forty percent of New York's, for example, they account for just thirteen percent of Wyoming's, two percent of North Dakota's, and one percent of Vermont's.[11] If a state were to artificially enhance the power of its white suburbs in this manner, it would immediately be challenged in the federal courts. But it is beyond reach at the federal level because it is constitutionally entrenched. While the United States has made significant racial progress in certain respects, its political structure remains solidly rooted in the racist past.

The Political Implications

Inequities like these are where constitutionalists and democrats part company. Where the former believes in the rule of law *über alles,* the latter believes in popular sovereignty as the supreme value. Consequently, they believe that when law no longer serves the people's interest, it should be jettisoned even if the law itself does not allow for such a drastic step. This may seem unlawful, but it's not for the simple reason that a sovereign people, as the source of all law, are incapable of an illegal act. The people are the master, while law is the servant. While the former can fire the latter, the latter cannot fire the former.

But what if the constitutionalists prevail and the people, lawful to the end, opt to remain within the confines of the present constitutional system? What will the political consequences be?

One, obviously, will be a growing sense of traditionalism. To defer to the Constitution of 1787 is to defer to the people, ideas, and historical circumstances that gave it rise. The more distant such values grow from our own, the better they will seem, i.e. smarter, more selfless, more heroic. Another consequence will be a growing tendency to see the Constitution less as an instrument or machine and more as an object of religious devotion. The harder its vagaries are to justify on practical grounds, the greater the tendency to attribute them to fate, the will of God, or some other equally nebulous concept. Even if it makes no sense for California and Wyoming to have the same number of Senate seats, the dominant attitude will be that is simply the way it's supposed to be, so what can you do? Constitutional lawyers will still argue over the meaning of specific provisions, but they will do so out of a religious devotion to the document as a whole, much like medieval clerics arguing over the precise nature of the Holy Trinity. Meanwhile, people and politics will seem more and more Lilliputian the higher the Constitution looms over society as a whole. All will seem trivial, corrupt, ineffectual, and therefore all the more dependent on an all-powerful Constitution to guide them along the way.

The process, in fact, is already far advanced. When American students read about the Scottish judge who thundered in 1793 that "[t]he British constitution is the best there ever was since the creation of the world and it is not possible to make it any better," they shake their heads. But when the American historian Clinton Rossiter writes that *The Federalist Papers* are "the most important work in political science that has ever been written, or is likely ever to be written in the United States," no one dares object.[12] The cult of the Founding Fathers grows ever more ridiculous with each passing year, yet historians pour out tome after tome. As the historian Richard Brookhiser, himself a major contributor to the cult, recently observed:

> Who cares what the founders would do? ... We do. I have heard it with my own ears. Over the past decade, I have given hundreds of talks about the founding fathers, on radio and TV, and to live audiences. Every time there is an opportunity for Q&A, there is at least one question of the form, "What would *Founder X* think about *current event*, or *living person, Y?*" No subject is too trivial, no problem too difficult. Audiences want to know what the founders would do about guns, taxes, race, the war on drugs, the war in Iraq, about Newt Gingrich, Bill Clinton, and George W. Bush.[13]

It is like wanting to know what Leif Ericsson would do about the Icelandic banking crisis. Only a people thoroughly convinced of their own inadequacy would look to a long-ago group of lawyers and slave owners for the answers to what ails them. When Republicans dared to tamper with the Senate filibuster rule in 2005, Senator Charles E. Schumer, a New York Democrat, sputtered that they were "trying to undermine the age-old checks and balances that the founding fathers placed at the center of the Constitution and the Republic"—great age apparently being synonymous with great good.[14] Referring to the view that the founders intentionally sought "to make change a slow and deliberative process," *Newsweek* magazine sagely observed: "Yes, they did, and it has served us rather well over time—not perfectly, God knows, but it has enabled us to muddle along for well over two centuries, always expanding, not contracting, individual liberty under law."[15] Amid mass surveillance due to the War on Terror and mass incarceration due to an equally ill-conceived War on Drugs (one adult in a hundred is now behind bars, the highest such rate in the world), one can only wonder how much more individual liberty has to contract before *Newsweek* finally takes notice.[16] Under criticism for steering $470 million in earmarks to his home state of Mississippi, Thad Cochran, the ranking Republican on the Senate Appropriations Committee, replied: "This is why our founding fathers gave Congress the explicit power to direct spending: so that those who are elected by the people, not bureaucrats, decide how funds are spent."[17] Caught earmarking nearly $10 million to rebuild an air traffic control tower in his home district, another Republican, Representative Dave Weldon of Florida, remarked: "I thought this was my constitutional obligation, to make sure that we're getting our fair share."[18] If the Founders say help yourself to the pork barrel, that must be the right thing to do.

The conservatism behind such statements is astounding. Since the Founders denied subsequent generations the power to work through their problems on their own, Americans have concluded that the Founders must have known what they were doing and therefore must have had the answers all along. While human knowledge has advanced on all other fronts, political philosophy, legal theory, and statecraft have apparently remained static or even regressed since the 1700s. In 1862, a brilliant constitutional analyst named Sidney George Fisher pondered the problem of how a charter of liberty could so quickly turn into its opposite. The Constitution, he decided, is actually highly constrictive because it forces Americans to submit to a document that is "to be interpreted only by itself, and to be altered only in the manner appointed by itself," a "finality" from which there is no escape. "A fixed, unchangeable Government, for a changeable, advancing people, is impossible," he wrote,[19] an idea that suddenly made sense amid the constitutional breakdown of the Civil War. But then the emergency passed, Fisher's arguments were forgotten, and the constitutional balance was restored with the Compromise of 1877. Within a few years, conditions reached the point where Grover Cleveland could assert that constitutional faith was indispensable because the Constitution is "the law of our very existence," something that Americans could not jettison without putting themselves in jeopardy. This was directly contrary to the Preamble, which says in black and white that it is the people who summoned the Constitution into existence and not the other way around. But the fact that someone like Cleveland could say something so ridiculous without being laughed out of court shows how firmly rooted such neo-Tory beliefs had become, while the fact that a modern historian would reverently quote the same statement in a 1986 academic study shows how strong it remains a century later.[20] The older the Constitution gets, the more deferential to the past Americans become. They have to. It's the law.

End Times, Anyone?

"It's worth reminding the American people that, for more than 230 years, everyone who bet against America lost money. It's a mistake to bet against this country over the long run."

Thus spoke Bill Clinton at a particularly threatening moment during the financial crisis in early 2009.[21] While one could argue that it is precisely this sort of riverboat-gambler mentality that got the United States in trouble in the first place, one must admit that the former president had a point. America's ability to dodge a bullet has been remarkable.

Still, the system has seemed at various points over the last decade to be finally nearing a *Götterdämmerung* of sorts. When the 2000 presidential election ended in an epic breakdown of the two-century-old electoral mechanisms set forth in Article II and the Twelfth Amendment, the Supreme Court, America's very own guardian council, took it upon itself to disregard the popular vote and place George W. Bush in the White House. The Sept. 11, 2001, attack on the World Trade Center generated such an outburst of xenophobia and military aggression that the rest of the world was left reeling. Soon, the United States had managed to embroil itself in not one but two wars in the Middle East with remarkably little debate on Capitol Hill—a fact that would be surprising in other countries but not in the United States where the Constitution discourages the honest airing of differences by forcing members of Congress to search for a consensus behind closed doors rather than airing their differences in public.

And then there is the global economic crisis. Conservatives will insist, of course, that the Constitution has no more to do with liar loans, mortgage-backed securities, and other toxic assets than with grain prices in Argentina. But that is more than a bit shortsighted. As a distinctly made-in-America phenomenon, the crisis arrived in mid-2007 stamped with a form of conservative populism that the system has kept alive for more than two centuries. The Constitution, for example, does not merely protect private property; thanks to the Fifth Amendment's takings clause (which stipulates that "private property [shall not] be taken for public use without just compensation"), it fairly enshrines it as a right that the people must forever assert against a tyrannical central government. Amid the politico-economic stresses of the 1970s (e.g. military defeat in Vietnam, rising crime and racial tension, stagflation, etc.), it was therefore inevitable that middle-class homeowner would respond by accusing "tax-and-spend" liberals in Washington of attempting to deprive them of their property. The upshot was the Proposition 13 tax revolt, the election of Ronald Reagan, and endless promises to restore the economy by rolling back federal power and unleashing "the miracle of the marketplace."[22] Deregulation and privatization followed, as did a long-term, government-orchestrated bull market in residential real estate beginning in the early 1990s.

The United States was not the only country subject to such pressure, but it was the one in which such pressures were most irresistible and widespread. Instead of urging quasi-governmental mortgage agencies like Fannie Mae and Freddie Mac (the Federal National Mortgage Association and the Federal Home Loan Mortgage Corporation, respectively) to proceed with caution, Democrats castigated them for not foisting more home loans on consumers who were already over their heads in debt. As Senator Jack Reed, a Rhode Island Democrat, declared in 2006: "When homes are doubling in price in every six years and incomes are increasing by a mere one percent per year, Fannie's mission is of paramount importance. In fact, Fannie and Freddie can do more, a lot more."[23] A combination of rising real-estate values and long-term income stagnation was actually a sign that the housing bubble was unsustainable. Yet a singularly mindless political class insisted that it be blown up even more.

The 2007 financial crisis was thus a combined economic and political crisis, the result of a financial system that had reached the last stage of irresponsibility and a political system that had reached the last stage of decrepitude. This is not to say that it would not have broken out had America had a different form of government. But it would have undoubtedly unfolded along very different lines.

Given all this, comparisons with eighteenth-century France may not be so inappropriate after all. The *ancien régime* suffered from a growing economic crisis that was also constitutional in origin. France was not a poor country—far from it. But because its own version of an unchangeable constitution prevented the nobility from being taxed against its will, the government was starved for revenue. A succession of financial experts—Turgot, Malesherbes, Necker, Calonne—searched for a way out of the bind, but all eventually gave up in despair. Under the theory of divine right, Louis XVI got his authority straight from God. His power was theoretically unbounded as a consequence, yet he was powerless to do anything about a recalcitrant aristocracy that refused on constitutional grounds to bow to the will of the government. It was a contradiction that would eventually prove fatal to the entire regime.

The American people are similarly powerful yet powerless, able to cast aside old constitutions like the Articles of Confederation and establish new ones in their place, yet unable to institute basic democratic reforms that, in the case of the Senate and the Electoral College, are centuries overdue. They are nominally in charge, yet are in fact prisoners of a system created in their name. Their society is in an advanced state of decay, yet they are prevented from giving it the clean sweep it plainly needs.

There is no saying how this contradiction will work itself out, just as there was no saying in the 1780s how the French would work their way through the problem of a sovereign yet nonsovereign king. Nonetheless, two things seem clear. One is that society will continue to go downhill as long as its constitutional problem go unaddressed and political democracy grows ever more crippled. The other is that some sort of rupture with the past is inevitable. If there is an iron law of history, it is that forestalling change merely guarantees that it will be all the more radical when it finally arrives. All things must come to an end, among them a superannuated system of government dating from the days of the French monarchy, the Holy Roman Empire, and the Venetian Republic. The only questions are: when, how, and what will replace it.

Chapter 3

We Should Preserve, Protect and Defend the Constitution — Not Trash It

Jeremy Rabkin

The Constitution can be amended but some advocates now urge us to go much beyond particular amendments. Their impatience with piece-meal adjustments shouts from the titles of recent books: Daniel Lazar's *The Frozen Republic*, Sanford Levinson's *Our Undemocratic Constitution*, Larry Sabato's *A More Perfect Constitution* (subtitled, *23 Proposals to Revitalize Our Constitution and Make America A Fairer Country*), to cite the most notable.[1]

I think such calls for constitutional overhaul are profoundly misguided. All or almost all changes that have been proposed might be accomplished by procedures set out in the Constitution. But I believe most would be contrary to the intentions, expectations and cautions of the Constitution's Framers. I think we should stand by the work of the Framers.

To argue against change sounds conservative. But it is somewhat misleading to call the American Founders "conservative." It is certainly misleading to suggest that our contemporary understanding of the term sums up their views. The term "conservatism" only came into general use in the mid-nineteenth century in opposition to a "liberalism" (another new term of that era) embracing a general doctrine of "progress." The Framers of the Constitution were not hostile or deeply skeptical of political progress.

Most of the Framers, after all, had been active participants in a revolution against British authority only a few years before they drafted the federal Constitution. Their Constitution could be described, at the time, as "a novelty in the political world" — as Madison acknowledged in *The Federalist Papers*. But he immediately went on to praise the generation of 1776 for having already "accomplished a revolution which had no parallel in the annals of human society" and in the state constitutions "reared the fabrics of governments which have no model on the face of the globe."

After the Constitution had been ratified, moreover, veterans of the Philadelphia Convention gladly assisted in drafting ten amendments, which came to be known as the Bill of Rights. Within another dozen years, the founding generation of statesmen embraced two further amendments, neither of which was trivial in significance.

The Eleventh Amendment prohibited suits against state governments in federal courts. Everyone understood that would allow states to repudiate their debts (or escape their immediate legal obligations to purchasers of state bonds and promissory notes). Many states did exercise this new right in the nineteenth century as others did even in the twentieth century.

The Twelfth Amendment specified separate balloting for the office of vice-president (rather than giving the office to the runner-up in the presidential balloting). It thus gave tacit endorsement to party slates and so, too, endorsed political party organization outside the Electoral College (since no one would likely run for vice-president independently). These were not mere technical adjustments.

Still, it remains true that the amending procedure makes it quite difficult to change the Constitution. Since those initial amendments, the Constitution has only been amended 15 times, averaging only one amendment every dozen years or so. It is hard to get three-fourths of the states to agree even when two-thirds in each house of Congress have already endorsed a change, as the fate of the feminist Equal Rights Amendment in the 1970s indicates. The Framers surely knew how hard it was to get three-fourths of the states to agree on change. For the Constitution itself, they provided that it would take effect when nine of the thirteen states agreed—which is less than three-fourths (though a bit more than two-thirds).

So to defend the framers work is to defend a system that is, by design, rather resistant to fundamental change. The framers were not averse to all change or perhaps even to change, per se. But they did not take for granted—as some contemporary reform advocates seem to do—that all change is for the good or that change is equivalent to progress. They hoped that the Constitution would endure as a stable framework, constraining impulsive or destructive change. If they were not simply "conservative"—in modern understandings of that term—neither were they simple populists who thought majorities of the moment should always be allowed to have their way. They thought it was "honorable" to "rest all our political experiments on the capacity of mankind for self-government"[2]—but they did not deny that their efforts were "experiments" whose outcome was not at all certain.

The Founders were not complacent about "democracy" as the answer to all questions in government. They saw that past republics had generally collapsed into anarchy or tyranny. Well into the twentieth century, Americans who cast their eyes on Latin America or Central Europe could see similar patterns unfolding. In our own time, we have seen democracy give way to a new authoritarian regime in post-Communist Russia. There are still good reasons for the cautions voiced by the framers of our Constitution. And it turns out that most Americans, even today, share that mood of caution when it comes to tampering with our fundamental charter of government.

Why Fix It if It's Not Broke?

There does not now seem to be any great clamor for constitution reform. Professor Sabato took the brave step of commissioning a survey of public reactions to his extended set of reform proposals. Only three (requiring judges to retire at age 75, limiting personal campaign contributions, strengthening congressional control over resort to war) had strong support—meaning that more than a majority (55 percent in each case) said they were "strongly in favor" of such amendments.

Five other proposals elicited more support than opposition (but not "strong support") and all the rest were disfavored. The strongest opposition was to proposals for new constitutional conventions to "bring the Constitution up to date" ("strongly opposed" by 52 percent), an amendment to make the Senate more representative ("strongly opposed" by 58 percent).[3]

Of course, people might change their minds if prominent voices joined a massive campaign for constitutional reform. But prominent figures have not shown any inclination to embrace calls for large-scale constitutional reform. Barack Obama, who made "change" the centerpiece of his 2008 presidential campaign, did not bother to broach the subject of changing the federal constitution.

Obama had taught constitutional law before becoming a US senator. He might therefore have been expected to have special understanding of constitutional obstacles to American progress—if there are serious obstacles of this kind. But President Obama remained silent about constitutional reforms, even as he unveiled an ambitious legislative agenda in the first months after his inauguration.

Certainly the United States has problems—as all countries do. That is presumably why the majority of voters in 2006 and 2008 voted for "change." But no one imagines that because the majority of voters were dissatisfied with existing policies or policy outcomes, they would have supported violent rebellion or a military coup. The problems Americans face are not *that* serious! Why suppose our problems are serious enough to justify fundamental restructuring of our fundamental law?

If there is a case for large-scale constitutional change, it ought to start with some showing that the United States has more severe problems than other countries with different (and presumably better) constitutions. It is telling that none of the recent books urging constitutional overhaul have tried to make such an argument. None, in fact, offers any sustained attention to foreign experience. Advocates for constitutional overhaul seem to have a notably self-absorbed or Amero-centric perspective on constitutional government.

Or perhaps attention to foreign experience would not help to make the case for redesigning the American Constitution. A parliamentary system may make it easier to enact government proposals into law, while the American system promotes debate, sometimes leading to compromise, often enough to policy stalemate. But if one looks at overall results, the United States does not seem to be worse off. Over the past quarter century, the American economy provided more sustained growth and much higher rates of employment and new job creation than any large state in the developed world. Even in the economic hard times that followed the 2008 financial crisis, the American economy did not perform more poorly than others and its prospects for recovery were judged somewhat more promising than most others.

It might be more on point, however, to leave economic statistics to one side and simply pose the basic political question: Are people more discontented under the American system of government? If opinion polls can be trusted, Americans are much happier with their lives than are most Europeans. Americans are among the happiest people in the developed world. At least that's what they tell pollsters.[4] Perhaps most telling, a solid majority of Americans say their own actions accounts for their success, while most Europeans tell pollsters they feel that "success in life is pretty much determined by forces outside our control."[5]

Rather than comparing actual American experience to actual results in other countries, advocates of constitutional reform appeal to very abstract claims about democracy, equality and openness to change. While ignoring actual European experience, Daniel Lazare and Sanford Levinson invoke European examples to show that constitutions elsewhere are easier to change and give voters more control over outcomes. Even at this level, however, the comparisons are more complicated than reformers acknowledge.

It's true, for example, that an American president can be elected with a clear majority of votes and then see his program blocked in Congress—as happened to President George W. Bush after the 2004 elections. In Britain, Margaret Thatcher's Tories never received a majority of votes, but (given the way votes are counted in the Britain's three-party system) held decisive majorities in Parliament and put through highly controversial changes in economic policy. In Germany, the governing Social Democratic Party was rejected by voters in 2005, after years of poor economic performance. But the Christian Democrats, who received more votes, decided after the election to take on the Socialists as their coalition partners instead of pursuing major change. Which system is more "democratic" is not so simple to determine.

Focusing on formal constitutional arrangements is particularly misleading when one takes European parliamentary systems for the comparison. When it comes to economic policy and a range of social issues, the most important decisions aren't made by national governments in Europe but by the organs of the European Union. Most policy in the European Union is made by an unelected bureaucracy (the European Commission) over which the elected EU Parliament has very little control. The Parliament has no authority over the Council of Ministers, whose members are chosen by member states and whose meetings are conducted in secret.

There are constant complaints that the European Union suffers from a "democratic deficit." Since the European Union is based on a treaty, however, constitutional change cannot even be imposed by a three-fourths majority of member states. Change in the treaty structure requires unanimous approval from member states. Thus the proposed new constitutional treaty, though endorsed by a broad majority of EU states, has been blocked by a handful of balky states.

If one looks beyond the European Union, one still sees important constraints in most other democracies. They are the sorts of constraints that would-be reformers in America should regard as "undemocratic"—if they had bothered to notice them. The United States has the Bill of Rights in its Constitution and it is difficult though not impossible to change. Other western countries have committed themselves to international human rights treaties and treaty-based organizations which are, as a formal matter, perhaps even more difficult to change.

In Europe, beyond the 27 members of the European Union, there is a wider grouping of countries—now 47—which have bound themselves to the European Convention on Human Rights. The convention is enforced by a court, whose judges are selected by member states (with one from each member state) in a process much less transparent and arguably much less democratic than the process by which federal judges are selected in the United States. The convention and its judicial system have been repeatedly reformed and amended but the process is difficult because it requires unanimous agreement from all member states. Recent proposed reforms have been endorsed by almost all other members but blocked by Russia.

It may be that Europeans are more committed to transnational structures because they are more distrustful of their domestic constitutional arrangements. It may be that Americans are more distrustful of international human rights schemes because we do have more confidence in our own Constitution. And it may be that our confidence in our Constitution is reinforced by the fact that it is time-tested and securely established—and hard to change.

At any rate, critics who think the US Constitution is insufficiently "democratic" or "open to change" are not comparing it with actual arrangements in other real-world democracies but with some abstract or imaginary model of what a true democracy should be. They ought to be asking themselves why no one else wants to embrace such a true democracy. Perhaps democracy is harder than they imagine.

The Authority of the Second Best

Arguments for constitutional reform tend to fall back on the argument that the existing Constitution frustrates the "will of the people" or is "undemocratic." After the disputed 2000 presidential election, for example, Daniel Lazare returned to his call for constitutional reform by denouncing the ultimate result—George W. Bush's selection by the Electoral College, even after Al Gore won a majority of the popular vote—as a "velvet coup."[6] Wasn't the result simply undemocratic?

The problem with democracy is that "the people" want different things. Obviously, "the people" includes many different people who may have strong disagreements with each other. But even the same people want different things. Certainly they want more than one thing. Yet even people who want most of the same things don't necessarily agree on the ranking or priority of the various things they want.

In 2000, not everyone who voted for Gore was prepared to endure a constitutional crisis to see his majority vote vindicated. So even though some die-hard majoritarians, like Daniel Lazare condemned him for it, Gore himself acquiesced to the decision of the Supreme Court rejecting his challenges to the recount system in Florida, where Bush and Gore were separated by only a few hundred votes. Despite the disputed election, George Bush's accession to the White House was, according to opinion polls, supported by the majority of Americans at the time. Bush then proved, at least for a time, a popular leader in the period of crisis following 9/11 and was given a clear majority of votes in the 2004 elections. More people, it turned out, were for stability and finality in elections than for some abstract notion of majority rule.

Meanwhile, many advocates insisted that the 2000 presidential election showed the need for fundamental reform of the Electoral College. Certainly that election called attention to problems which the Electoral College scheme can generate. But the ensuing debate also reminds us why reform is difficult—and why that is not always a bad thing.

To persuade people to undertake a major change, it is not enough to show that the status quo has problems. Life is full of problems, so every alterative to the status quo will likely have some problems, too. Even if people are discontented with existing arrangements, the challenge is to persuade people that some specific alternative is actually better. And in real life, people who agree with criticisms of the status quo may not agree on which alternative is better.

So the clamor for reforming the Electoral College died down rather quickly in the aftermath of the 2000 election. Would we be better off with "direct popular election" of the president? What if no candidate got a majority of the popular vote? What if more candidates and more parties competed, so we ended up with a "winner"—a candidate with more votes than any other—who still had less than 45 percent or even less than 40 percent of the votes cast? Would it be "democratic" to elevate that candidate to the presidency?

Or should we, as some countries do, have a separate run-off election among the top contenders? That might ensure that the winner really has been endorsed by a majority but perhaps it would encourage third, fourth and fifth party candidacies to derail the original front-runner and ensure constant recourse to such run-off contests? Would that really be more "democratic"?

If there were disputes about the vote count, would we do a recount only in a particular state, as we do now? Or would we be obliged, for the sake of consistency, to recount votes throughout the country? Would we trust federal authorities to conduct a national recount? Would we trust them to conduct state and local elections and if not, would it not be a constant source of dissension to have two different systems in place for vote counting and perhaps for voter registration?

Perhaps the most telling point about Electoral College reform is that major changes could be achieved without a constitutional amendment. The Constitution does not require states to allocate all their electoral votes in one block. If states wanted to, they could allocate their electoral votes in rough proportion to the break-down of the popular vote in that state. But of course, this would generate all sort of new objections—as, for example, nullifying the point of the contest if, in a close vote, both candidates end up receiving an equal number of electoral votes. In fact, very few states have been willing to experiment with such reforms.

If we can't agree on a better alternative, we stick with the status quo. That is not undemocratic. Perhaps it is simply rational. The same dynamic, at any rate, may explain why there is so little interest in reforming the equal representation of states in the Senate.

On its face, the equal representation of states in the Senate seems the most questionable provision in our Constitution. It means that California, whose population now exceeds 36 million, gets the same two senators as Wyoming, with barely half a million people—so voters in the latter state seem to have more than 70 times as much weight as voters in the former. The Supreme Court has held state governments in violation of the constitutional guarantee of "equal protection of the laws" when they had districts for state legislatures which varied by little more than 5 percent in population.

But if this is unfair—by some abstract rule of equality—its real world consequences are also quite uncertain. Small states tend to be rural and lean Republican. Some small states, however, like Vermont and Rhode Island are now inclined to elect left-leaning Democrats. Others, like South Dakota, have regularly elected liberal Democrats to the Senate, though usually giving their electoral votes to Republican presidential candidates.

The serious question is, what would a reapportioned Senate look like? If we allowed every state to retain its current allocation of two senators and then added extra senators to compensate larger states for extra population, we would end up with a Senate having even more members than the House of Representatives, thus forfeiting the benefits of a smaller, more deliberative body. On the other hand, if "fairness" is the overriding concern, why should a state with many senators in the new scheme—California might well claim 100 senators to put it on a per capita parity with small states—choose all of them in single, statewide ballots? Why not carve the large states into many separate Senate districts? But if we do that, what weight are we really giving to the population of each state, as such?

Then again, if we are carving up large states, why not reallocate House seats, as well? If we changed the Constitution so congressional districts did not have to remain with the boundaries of individual states, we could eliminate many disparities that now arise (as for states that have fewer voters than the average House seat or states that have almost but not quite twice as many voters as the average House seat). If we do a total nationwide redistricting, however, we would need to figure out who would be responsible for redrawing all these lines. Would we trust Congress to create its own districts?

In sum, once we reopen the questions now settled in the Constitution, a great many awkward new questions would arise. We shouldn't be surprised that politicians who have learned to compete in the current system—and even the general run of voters—are not keen to face all the possible new controversies growing out of these new questions. It may well be that after immense debate, we would discover that the current arrangements for the Senate, despite all its apparent inequity, has more support than any concrete alternative.

Reform advocates protest that Americans are too much in awe of the supposed demigods who bequeathed us such arrangements as the equal representation of states in the Senate. But other democracies have faced similar problems in reaching agreement on reform alternatives.

In Australia, there was a long campaign in the 1990s to reform the constitutional pro-vision—held over from colonial times—by which the Governor General (responsible for calling new elections) is appointed by the Queen in far-off Britain. A proposed reform plan would have given these powers to a newly designated "President of Australia," chosen by the Australian Parliament. When put to a referendum in 1999, however, the proposal was decisively repudiated by Australian voters. They may not have been sentimental about the British monarchy but they did not trust an "elected presidency" elected by politicians.[7]

Similarly, in Canada in the early 1980s, the national Parliament agreed to replace the country's mid-nineteenth century charter—formally an act of the British Parliament—with a new constitution, resting on the consent of the Canadian people. An advisory opinion of the Canadian Supreme Court cautioned that, to be consistent with established constitutional conventions, the new constitution should receive the endorsement of all ten Canadian provinces. Quebec remained opposed, however. Successive Canadian gov-ernments labored to negotiate compromises to satisfy Quebec only to find that compromises agreeable to Quebec were unacceptable to one or more of the other provinces.

The stand off was described in the 1990s as a "constitutional crisis."[8] It eventually settled into a very awkward extraconstitutional compromise. The new constitution remained in effect but the Quebec parliament regularly (and uniquely) voted to deny effect within the province to decisions of the federal Supreme Court applying the new constitution. The underlying problem was not that Quebecois were sentimental about the old constitution (the so-called "British North America Act" of the British Parliament). Quebec and the other provinces simply could not agree on a mutually acceptable alternative.[9]

If we were starting over again, probably most Americans would question the idea that states of widely differing populations should receive the same number of senators. But how many Americans want to put the country in the position of starting all over again, redrawing our Constitution from scratch? It can be quite reasonable to continue with arrangements that are no one's first choice when people don't agree on what would be better. Compared to many conceivable alternatives, most people might prefer to accept their second choice—particularly if it is at least a second choice for many others and is already in place. In an imperfect world, the second best has some claim to respect.

Too Much Constitutional Reform Will Undo the Constitution

Reform of the Senate is particularly challenging because Article V of the Constitution, which sets out the methods for making amendments, expressly constrains amending authority on this point: "no state, without its consent, shall be deprived of its equal suffrage in the Senate." It is at least arguable that this obstacle could be removed from the Constitution by ordinary amendment, requiring only three-fourths of the states to approve. After that, reform of the Senate could be imposed on the recalcitrant states, if there were fewer than thirteen of them (that is, less than one-fourth of the current 50 states). Perhaps we could make amending the Senate still easier by amending Article V to require future amendments to be ratified by only three-fifths of the states (that is, 30 rather than 38, as at present). We might also lower the threshold of congressional endorsement for future amendments to three-fifths majorities in each house (rather than two-thirds as now) or allow Congress to offer amendments approved by simple majorities.

But could we induce three-fourths of the existing states to amend the amending provisions of the Constitution in these ways? Professor Levinson, who seems to doubt that the states would give up their blocking authority, calls for a new constitutional convention, empowered to remodel the whole Constitution—including, it seems, the path to future amendments.

But would we be happy with a constitution which, being more easily amended, might well be frequently amended in the future? Perhaps new conventions would be called at regular intervals. Or a newly streamlined amending process regularly invoked. Almost certainly, if we make it easier to amend the Constitution, we will have more amendments. And very likely that will mean the Constitution will gain specific provisions on controversial social issues, from the most profound and intractable—such as abortion or same sex marriage—to the seemingly trivial, but much debated, such as flag burning or the display of religious symbols on public property. Popular policy nostrums, such as limits on government borrowing or prohibitions on certain kinds of tax exemptions, will also probably find their way into the Constitution. And successful movements to enshrine such policies in the Constitution will surely generate new campaigns to remove them or replace them with opposite provisions.

Our federal Constitution constitutes the authority from which all other federal laws flow: it is, as proclaimed in Article VI, "the supreme law of the land." If we insist on making it easy to change, we reduce the distance between the Constitution and ordinary law. That means, in turn, that we reduce the distance between supreme authority and ordinary public policy preferences.

Nobody imagines that when a new majority gains control of Congress or the presidency (or both), the new majority must conscientiously maintain the policies and priorities of the previously dominant party. But if we make the Constitution easy to change, it looks more like a legislative program. And it is hard to persuade people that the legislative program that happened to be favored by a previous majority must be faithfully maintained when opinion shifts and a new majority arises.

The more the Constitution is made to reflect the views of contemporary majorities, the less it can claim to express some broader framework or consensus, the more it looks simply like the way the current political winners try to impose their priorities on the losers. Yet reverence for the Constitution is one of the reasons losers in political competition bow to election results. We long ago agreed on how votes would be translated into offices and with what constitutional powers attaching to those offices.

At present, then, the losers in an election are not simply bowing to the strength of the latest majority. Electoral losers can still see themselves as keeping faith with the terms of political competition agreed by many generations past, political terms which, in effect, define us as a nation or a self-governing community. Patriotism can soften the sting of partisan resentment.

In this way, an established constitution can bind winners and losers in a common project. If it is too easy to change the Constitution, this binding force is weakened. Abolishing the equal representation of states in the Senate—which seems such an obvious change for reformers—illustrates the problem.

The small states consented to the Constitution only after they won this concession on the composition of the Senate—and then won an assurance that this concession would not be withdrawn in a subsequent amendment. No doubt, state loyalties are much diminished today and two centuries of experience offers ample evidence that people who happen to live in small states are not an isolated or besieged minority in the ebbs and flows of political life.

But taking away this element of our founding consensus would be a profound statement that nothing enshrined in a constitution can really be relied upon—not even in our country, which is so proud of its constitutional continuity. It would be a powerful reinforcement to the subversive thought that, with all the pieties and solemnities of constitutional discourse, even when it comes to constitutional guarantees, it's really all politics, all the way down.

Governments have, of course, broken past constitutional commitments and survived. They have also defaulted on debt and survived—but they pay a price. The United States derives many advantages from its reputation for stability. The demonstration that its constitutional commitments are unreliable would have costs, just as there would be long-term costs in repudiating obligations to repay government debt or honor federal financial guarantees.

One could counter that politics is always in the background because the force of constitutional standards rests on opinion and opinion always reflects, in some degree, the political currents of the moment. No one who reads Supreme Court opinions can doubt that politics does play a role in constitutional debate. But one of the opinions in the background—at present—is that we do have our own Constitution which remains a source of common obligation for all parties and all shades of opinion. *The Federalist Papers* put the point this way, in explaining why it would be bad to submit constitutional disputes to popular referenda—as easy and frequent recourse to amendments would, in effect, do today:

> [F]requent appeals [to current majorities] would, in great measure, deprive the government of that veneration which time bestows on everything and without which perhaps the wisest and freest governments would not possess the requisite stability. If it be true that all government rests on opinion, it is no less true that the strength of that opinion in each individual and its practical influence on his conduct depend much on the number which he supposes to have entertained the same opinion.... When the examples which fortify opinion are ancient as well as numerous, they are known to have a double effect.... [T]he most rational government will not find it a superfluous advantage to have the prejudices of the community on its side.[10]

Those who regard the composition of the Senate as a pointless anachronism might have more regard for guarantees in the Bill of Rights. These provisions were also, though a bit more indirectly, the price paid to secure the agreement of all the original states to a common national government. If we can change everything to suit the majority, why not the First Amendment? Why not guarantees of due process or constitutional protection for contracts and property?

These are not entirely hypothetical questions. In the more populist politics of Latin America, successful demagogues have frequently carried public opinion—and compliant constitutional organs—in rescinding guarantees previously given to investors or property owners. Even in contemporary Europe, the perception of new dangers has led to measures that Americans would find impossible to reconcile with constitutional traditions. In the United Kingdom, centuries of commitment to habeas corpus have been swept away in provisions for preventive detention of terror suspects, centuries of respect for free speech swept aside to accommodate demands for regulation of "hate speech."

It was hard to rally support for the old traditions after a decade of constitutional innovation, reconstituting the House of Lords to make it largely appointive, reconstituting the United Kingdom itself with Scottish self-government—and all these changes enacted by mere parliamentary action with no special procedure to guard against impulsive change. The Bush administration chose to send detainees to the Guantanamo base precisely because, even after the trauma of 9/11, it did not think it could challenge the guarantee of habeas corpus within the United States. It did not even consider cutting back on First Amendment guarantees of free speech and religious freedom within the United States.

Of course, Britain has not become a police state simply because it has curtailed some of its protections for civil liberties. The United States would not likely degenerate into chaos or tyranny simply because we made it much easier to modify longstanding constitutional commitments. But making constitutional change much easier would exact a price. It would almost certainly lead to doubts about future developments. Such doubts would worry investors and inhibit initiative, as no arbitrary government reversal or confiscatory measure could be considered entirely unthinkable in the future.

Meanwhile, British experience illustrates another complicating dynamic. British opinion may have been complacent about major changes to British constitutional norms because citizens assumed there would always be outside safeguards in the background. Basic rights could still be protected under the European Convention on Human Rights (ECHR), interpreted by a court in Strasbourg and enforced by British judges as if it were a constitution in itself.[11] But there are loopholes in this system. Apart from questions about the fidelity of British judges to the admonitions of judges in Strasbourg, Parliament retains authority to override judicial interpretations of the ECHR if it wants to insist on alternate policies.

There is, at any rate, something quite paradoxical in this whole situation. To show that contemporary Britons are masters of their own fate, the British Parliament has thrown away centuries of British constitutional tradition—and then placed itself under the tutelage of judges from Albania, Russia, Portugal and more than forty other states subscribing to the ECHR. Yet most of these judges have less personal experience with democratic government than the majority of MPs in the current UK Parliament.

Perhaps there is a general rule at work: People are bound to seek assurances of safety, even from elected governments, even from measures they generally endorse. This rule need not appeal to pronouncements of gentlemen in powdered wigs who gathered in Philadelphia in 1787. It rests on something in human nature. If people can't get security from their own constitutions, they will grasp at offers from elsewhere.

International treaty structures are unlikely to provide as much security, in fact, as a well-structured national constitution. But whatever the merits of European treaty structures (and their UN counterparts), it is very hard to pretend that restraining governments through international commitments is more democratic than restraining governments by national constitutions. Hard as it may be to change a national constitution—or a national constitutional court—it is far harder to get agreement on rewriting an international treaty with dozens of participating states, all distracted by different priorities and contending with different currents of local public opinion.

A Fixed Constitution Must Sometimes Be a Flexible Constitution

On August 8, after months of debate, the Philadelphia Convention returned to the much debated question of whether there should be a rule limiting the size of congressional districts. Madison warned that as population increased, such a rule would produce a House with too many members. Mr. Ghorum offered a vehement rejoinder: "It is not to be supposed that the Govt will last so long as to produce this effect. Can it be supposed that this vast Country including the Western territory will 150 years hence remain one nation?"[12]

Madison won the immediate point: the Constitution did not limit the size of House districts in a way that would soon have made such limitations unworkable. And he seems to have won the larger point, too. Most delegates at the Convention seemed to recognize that they were planning for a long future.

One reason we still have so much of the original Constitution is that, realizing that the future was in many ways unknowable, the founders did not try to decide too much. Today's constitutional reformers often seem to have the opposite premise: they are so confident that today's Americans know what they need, they are prepared to jettison arrangements that have lasted for centuries—and perhaps replace them with provisions that have not ever been tried. Reformers seem to think it is easy to know what reforms will prove good for us.

But this much we can say with confidence: the more issues we try to pin down with current constitutional reforms, the more we will have to change new provisions in the future. Are we so much wiser than the Founders that we can read the future better than they could? *The Federalist Papers* foresaw the danger: "A continual change, even of good measures is inconsistent with every rule of prudence and every prospect of success."[13] Apart from undermining the authority of the Constitution, as argued in the preceding section, the frequent resort to change may have the paradoxical result of making the Constitution too rigid.

Many proposed constitutional reforms play on current anxieties. The freakish result of the presidential vote in 2000 (where the winner of the electoral vote got fewer popular votes than his opponent) sparked demands for abolishing the Electoral College. In 2007, when public disaffection with the war in Iraq was at its most intense, Professor Sabato urged a new constitutional provision to limit presidential war-making powers (along with many other changes).[14] Other advocates urge new constraints or prohibitions to safeguard citizens against surveillance or to curb executive power grabs in times of emergency, as after 9/11.

But executive power is the classic area where precise rules are hard to formulate—or hard to enforce. After the Vietnam War, Congress sought to impose constraints on presidential war making with the War Powers Act, passed over President Nixon's veto. There is now near universal agreement that this measure has had little effect. Successive presidents have circumvented the spirit and sometimes the letter of its reporting requirements and triggering mechanisms. Some of the provisions are ambiguous enough or flexible enough to give presidents much discretion in applying their terms. But the measure could not have been enacted without concessions to lawmakers worried about excessive restrictions on presidential initiative. At all events, Congress has never been prepared to call a halt to ongoing or incipient military actions, in the manner contemplated by the legislation. So even where Congress has expressly withheld consent, military actions have gone forward, as with President Clinton's interventions in the Balkan wars during the 1990s. Nonetheless, President Sabato seems to think the problem can be cured by elevating the War Powers Act to constitutional status—as if its mere appearance in the Constitution assure its force.

That is not very credible. If we really expect new constitutional provisions to do better than current legislation, we would have to craft constitutional amendments that were much more detailed, with fewer loopholes or ambiguities and with something approaching automatic enforcement by courts. But the likelihood is that if we did have such a detailed measure—whether for lawmaking or intrusive security measures at home—we would soon encounter situations where presidents launched and public opinion supported (or acquiesced to) policies that seemed to exceed newly crafted constitutional barriers. Would courts enforce such provisions? They have generally been quite reticent in interfering with presidential security policies—particularly in the midst of a crisis.

The problem was again foreseen by *The Federalist Papers* (in a paper written, in fact, by Madison):

> It is in vain to oppose constitutional barriers to the impulse of self-preservation. It is worse than in vain, because it plants in the in the Constitution itself necessary usurpations of power, every precedent of which is a germ of unnecessary and multiplied repetitions.[15]

The point is not that we can never apply constitutional judgments to actions taken in a time of crisis. The point is rather that citizens (and their elected representatives) will tend to judge differently, depending on the circumstances. Presidents must know that their actions may well be challenged and perhaps harshly criticized in the aftermath of crisis—as the Bush administration learned. But that does not mean we can always formulate a precise rule in advance and expect to hold to it.

Hamilton and Madison themselves famously debated the proper understanding of executive power in the *Pacificus* and *Helvidius* pamphlets, in which Hamilton defended and Madison condemned President Washington's 1793 Proclamation of Neutrality in the war between France and its neighbors. Washington claimed authority to issue this proclamation on his own initiative, without any authorization from Congress. Hamilton's arguments in defense of this initiative have certainly been cited by presidents ever since, but the countering arguments always wait in reserve for presidents whose policies provoke public distrust and ensuing congressional resistance.

New constitutional provisions in this area may make it harder to keep future debates in reasonable focus. A general principle, such as accountability to Congress, now has considerable force in the right circumstances. Debates about undeclared wars in Korea and Vietnam chastened later presidents, so Presidents George H.W. Bush and George W. Bush were both careful to secure formal congressional authorization before committing to troops to battle in Iraq in 1991 and 2003. But smaller efforts (such as President Reagan's deployment of troops to Grenada in 1983) were undertaken without prior approval from Congress—and without protest from the public, perhaps because quick action averted larger or more protracted conflicts.

The general principle has come to be applied with exceptions, though presidents cannot be sure when it is safe to assume an exception because Congress cannot be bound by informal exceptions. Even the general principle will lose its force, however, if we come to expect all disputes to be settled by the latest amendment and debate focuses not on general principle but on lawyerly parsing of technical language in some future amendment.

What new amendments are least likely to achieve is agreement on precise lines which will actually be recognized and observed in every future crisis or future foreign conflict. When a disaster occurs that threatens American security and the president is blamed for not taking action to avert the ensuing crisis, he won't get much sympathy when he pleads that he was only following his lawyers' advice about what the new constitutional restrictions required.

There are real benefits to a system which places contending centers of power in a situation of inherent tension and lets the balance between them—as between Congress and the President—play out in response to the concrete challenges of the hour and the consequences felt in the hours afterward.

To imagine that we can plan for every contingency is not to make a more predictable system but one which may well be, in its actual effects, less predictable. There may be more law—and more uncertainty—than ever about which standards must really apply and which are mere parchment barriers, monuments to good intentions which may be disregarded in the heat of crisis.

The Most General Case for Constitutional Conservatism

The Framers' Constitution has served us reasonably well for well over two centuries. We can say that with some confidence because, after all, the basic plan has not been radically changed. Previous generations have been able to make major changes, starting with the abolition of slavery and the progressive enlargement of the right to vote. But the country endured a fierce civil war in the mid-nineteenth century, then world wars, a prolonged Cold War and a Great Depression in the twentieth century, all the while retaining the basic scheme bequeathed by the framers.

Meanwhile, the United States has become the world's greatest military and economic power, sustained more people in more material prosperity and more secure freedom than any society in all of human history. We ought to have respect for these achievements. Even enthusiasts of progress should consider the possibility that the Constitution has provided the grounding of stability and political consensus that helped make these achievements possible. Everyone must acknowledge that the Constitution has not prevented us from achieving great political success, relative to other nations and other eras.

Advocates for reform tend not to focus on real world comparisons with what other nations have achieved under differing constitutional arrangements. They tend to argue from quite abstract appeals to quite abstract standards—equality, democracy, freedom, popular sovereignty or progress. Professor Levinson protests that "structural provisions of the Constitution ... place almost insurmountable barriers in the way of any acceptable notion of democracy" and so calls for "a new constitutional convention that would feel itself legitimately empowered, and psychologically free, to do what the framers of 1787 did...."[16] Mr. Lazare stakes the claim most flamboyantly: "... modern democracy must be understood, first and foremost in terms of the positive freedom of the people as a whole to exert effective control over the whole of society. A people's freedom to reshape their entire environment is the freedom on which all others rest."[17]

One might say in response that all good things do not always fit easily together. We may all value "freedom" and "democracy" but the people's "freedom to reshape their entire environment" seems to grant majorities the power to repress any minority that affects the social environment in ways the majority finds irksome. Take that thought very far and there won't be much freedom for individuals.

We all like choice. Yet we do not always like the choices others might make. If democracy claims to decide everything, we all must pay much closer attention to politics. But what if most of us prefer to pursue private concerns? Perhaps we would do better to limit some choices to safeguard others?

A happy life may not be a life where everything is open to reconsideration. Business consultants and motivational speakers always urge clients to "focus." What it means to focus is to exclude peripheral matters from attention. Focus, then, is also a kind of discipline, a constraint on what one might otherwise prefer. Yet it is hard to succeed at anything if one is always reconsidering everything.

A lot of things we can't control, in any case. We may try to coax our children or our spouses to adjust themselves to our own priorities. But none of us chooses our parents and no family can remain together if everyone always insists on getting his or her own way. Still, most people prefer to remain with their families than completely free—and entirely isolated.

We have the luxury of taking our Constitution for granted. We ought to be grateful for that. It is hardly a thing to complain about. One might as well urge happy children to question whether their parents have really done as well by them as they might have or whether they would have been still better off with better parents. Would such questioning make anyone happier? Worrying over these questions won't help people to find confidence and contentment. It is more likely to sink them into neurotic anxiety or into depths of depression.

Critics may say the Constitution derives from the eighteenth century and after two centuries, we owe it to ourselves to rethink it. Professor Sabato assures us that "The framers left it to us ... [to] continue at regular intervals to perfect their work."[18] Professor Levinson urges a new constitutional convention to "allow 'We the People of the United States of America,' in whose name the document is ostensibly 'ordain[ed],' to examine the fit between our national aspirations ... and the particular means chosen to realize those goals."[19] So Levinson urges the need for "overcoming veneration" of compromises made in the eighteenth century. Otherwise, it seems, we will not be "We the People" but mere passive objects of decisions made long ago.

But why question the Constitution and take "the people" as a given? Our border with Canada—more precisely, the fact of the border—also derives from the eighteenth century. The leaders of the American Revolution offered to bring Canada into their new confederation. They then organized an invasion of Quebec to underscore the earnestness of the offer. Our separation from Canada was determined by the 1783 Treaty of Paris (and the 1814 Treaty of Ghent, following another failed effort to unite the United States and Canada by force in the War of 1812). No one alive today consented to these very old treaties, any more than to the Constitution of 1787. Why not rethink these old treaties, along with the Constitution? As immigration has given us a larger Hispanic minority, perhaps we should think about establishing some form of constitutional association with Mexico and Central America as well as Canada.

And why stop there? Our decisions in foreign policy, even in economic policy, can have immense and immediate implications for allies and partners throughout Europe and Asia. Why not—in the name of democracy or equality or progress—give them all some formal, constitutional mechanism of participation in our own government's decisions? Europeans have submitted to a whole range of supranational institutions. Our current Constitution probably prevents us from doing the same. But if we are rethinking the Constitution, why not go back and rethink all our traditional assumptions about ourselves and the outside world?

The more we press these questions, the dizzier we will become. Will we then be happier? Will we even make better decisions when more dazed and uncertain about who "we" are? Appeals to "democracy" or "equality" assume we can dig beneath the compromises of the Constitution to some bedrock principles on which we will all be able to agree. Advocates who argue in this way may be like explorers in northern regions who break through the permafrost in search of solid ground—only to find themselves sinking in primordial swamps below.

Our Declaration of Independence asserts our right to rebel against an abusive government. It does not burden us with the obligation to keep changing our constitutional arrangements, even when they are serving us reasonably well. We are entitled to boast of our freedoms and our capacity for self-government. We would be wise to acknowledge some sense of obligation for what has been achieved by our forebears and predecessors.

It is not due to our own merits that we find ourselves here. We might have been born into a family of serfs in medieval Europe or born into a war-ravaged village in the Congo today. We didn't ourselves make the Constitution whose blessings we enjoy. We are the "posterity"—whether by adoption or direct descent—for whom the founding generation "ordained and established" the Constitution. The sacrifices and exertions of many past generations were required to preserve that Constitution and pass it down to us. We did not ourselves struggle through a Civil War, through a Great Depression and two world wars, through a perilous Cold War and painful struggles for civil rights to preserve and extend the blessings of liberty. We should not be so quick to imagine we now have the peculiar genius to start it all over—and get it all just right.

If we do show contempt for previous generations of Americans, we must expect future generations to have as little regard for our efforts. If we are reckless, we may jeopardize for future generations the blessings of stability and continuity that were protected and preserved for us by so many previous generations. We have not had to earn our inheritance by heroic exertions but we should still feel some obligation to protect and defend the work of earlier times. We should think not only about our abstract rights but our obligation to our own "posterity"—as the Framers did.

PART THREE

RACE AND THE CONSTITUTION

Chapter 4

Slavery's Constitution: The Creation of America's Covenant with Death

Paul Finkelman

The great nineteenth-century abolitionist William Lloyd Garrison thought the Constitution was a terrible bargain between freedom and slavery. The American states were, in Garrison's words, united by a "covenant with death" and "an agreement with Hell."[1] Garrison and his followers refused to participate in American electoral politics, because to do so they would have had to support "the pro-slavery, war sanctioning Constitution of the United States." Instead, under the slogan "No Union with Slaveholders," the Garrisonians repeatedly argued for dissolution of the union.[2]

Garrisonians wanted to avoid the corruption that came from participating in a government created by the proslavery Constitution. They were also convinced that the legal protection of slavery in the Constitution made political activity not only futile, but actually counterproductive. Traditional political activity created popular support for the constitutional order, which in turn strengthened the stranglehold slavery had on America. In 1845 Wendell Phillips pointed out that since the adoption of the Constitution Americans had witnessed "the slaves trebling in numbers — slaveholders monopolizing the offices and dictating the policy of the Government — prostituting the strength and influence of the Nation to the support of slavery here and elsewhere — trampling on the rights of the free States, and making the courts of the country their tools." Phillips argued that this experience proved "that it is impossible for free and slave States to unite on any terms, without all becoming partners in the guilt and responsible for the sin of slavery."[3]

The Garrisonians argued that by participating in politics they were strengthening slavery by supporting the Union and the constitutional order. Since the political system and the Constitution were stacked in favor of slavery, it was a pointless waste of their time and money to try to fight slavery through electoral politics. The Garrisonian critique of the Constitution logically led to the conclusion that the free states should secede from the union. Garrisonians thus rallied to the slogan of "No Union with Slaveholders."

It is easy to dismiss this argument more than a century and a half after it was first made. After all, we know that secession was a reactionary, proslavery movement that failed. But, in the 1830s and 1840s the idea of a northern secession, as a way of destroying slavery, made some sense because the structure of the Constitution made emancipation by the national government impossible, while at the same time the Constitution obligated northerners to support and protect slavery. The Garrisonians understood that northern secession would ultimately undermine slavery.

The fugitive slave clause of the Constitution illustrates the Garrisonian position. This clause gave a master the right to hunt down a slave anywhere in the United States. This clause, and the federal statutes passed to enforce it, made slavery a national institution.[4] But, what would happen if the Garrisonians accomplished their goal, and the North left the Union to form a nation based on freedom instead of slavery? It would be like moving the Canadian border to the Mason-Dixon Line. Suddenly, slavery would be threatened in Kentucky and Virginia because slaves could now escape to a free country just by crossing the Ohio River.

Garrison believed that such a change in political boundaries would prove fatal to slavery. As slaves crossed the Mason-Dixon Line or the Ohio and Mississippi Rivers into freedom, slavery would be weakened in the Upper South. Committed slave owners would move further South, which would further weaken slavery in the Upper South. Eventually Delaware, Maryland, Missouri and even Kentucky might give up slavery, and seek to join the free country. Pressure on Virginia would increase. Slavery, and hundreds of thousands of slaves, would be forced into the Deep South, where whites would become a desperate minority. Ultimately the institution would fall, perhaps after a series of rebellions in a region with a huge black majority, but just as likely simply from the weight of its own isolation.

Garrisonians believed that slavery was inherently unstable, and needed force to be viable. The United States government provided that force, spending its resources to hunt fugitive slaves, and when necessary suppress rebellions. Even when rebellions were put down by the local militia, those militias were armed by the national government. The South also benefitted from the strength of the northern economy. Southerners like James Henry Hammond of South Carolina thundered that "cotton is king," and declared "No, you dare not make war on cotton. No power on earth dares make war upon it."[5] But, as the Garrisonians saw it, without the North and the proslavery Constitution, the South was little more than a prosperous producer of commodities devoid of industry and capital, lacking in population, arms, and manpower to hunt fugitive slaves and suppress rebellions. In the end, it was the proslavery bargain, and the North's contractual obligation under the Constitution to protect slavery, that made the system viable.

The Garrisonians did not necessarily see the Constitution as the result of a deliberate conspiracy of evil men; rather, they understood it to be the consequence of political give-and-take at the Convention of 1787. Indeed, before the publication of Madison's convention notes, the Garrisonians, while unhappy with the Constitutional protections of slavery, were not disunionists. Some even argued that the Constitution favored liberty. However, the publication of *The Madison Papers*, after the death of the fourth president, changed all this. Madison's papers included his extensive notes taken at the Constitutional Convention, which revealed how much slavery had influenced the writing of the Constitution. These notes convinced Garrison and his followers that the Constitution was in fact proslavery. Rev. Samuel J. May, for example, recalled that "the publication of the 'Madison Papers'… I confess, disconcerted me somewhat. I could not so easily maintain my ground in the discussions which afterwards agitated so seriously the Abolitionists themselves,—some maintaining that the Constitution was, and was intended to be, proslavery."[6]

Thus, in *The Constitution A Pro-Slavery Compact; or, Selections from the Madison Papers*, Wendell Phillips analyzed "that 'compromise,' which was made between slavery and freedom, in 1787; granting to the slaveholder distinct privileges and protection for his slave property, in return for certain commercial concessions upon his part toward the North." Using Madison's papers, Phillips argued that "the Nation at large were fully aware of this bargain at the time, and entered into it willingly and with open eyes."[7]

Phillips both exaggerated and understated the nature of the relationship between slavery and the Constitution. Some of those at the Convention "entered into" the bargain with great reservations, and many at the ratifying conventions may indeed have not seen the full extent of the "bargain." On the other hand, the bargain involved more than commerce and slavery, it concerned the very creation of the Union itself.

Other nineteenth-century antislavery leaders disagreed with the Garrisonians. Salmon P. Chase, the most successful antislavery politician, fought throughout the antebellum period to convince his colleagues, the judiciary, and northern voters that the Constitution was really antislavery. Despite his creative perseverance, Chase's efforts failed. The United States Supreme Court almost always protected slavery in the cases it heard. Likewise, almost all American presidents and their cabinet officers protected slavery in foreign and domestic politics. Perhaps most frustrating to the political abolitionists was the fact that some of their most brilliant allies in the crusade against slavery—the Garrisonians— agreed with their enemies on the meaning of the Constitution. Thus, one Liberty Party man ruefully noted after reading Wendell Phillips' pamphlet on the Constitution: "Garrison, Phillips, and Quincy; Calhoun, Rhett, and McDuffie; all harmoniously laboring to prevent such a construction of the Constitution as would abolish slavery."[8]

A careful reading of the Constitution reveals that the Garrisonians were correct: the national compact favored and protected slavery. A detailed examination of the Convention debates explains how the Constitution evolved in this way. Both the text of the Constitution and the debates surrounding it help us understand that the "more perfect Union" created by this document was in fact fundamentally imperfect.

Slavery in the Constitutional Structure

The word "slavery" appears in only one place in the Constitution—in the Thirteenth Amendment, where the institution is abolished. Throughout the main body of the Constitution, slaves are referred to as "other persons," "such persons," or in the singular as a "person held to Service or Labour." Why is this the case?

Throughout the debates the delegates talked about "blacks," "Negroes," and "slaves." But the final document avoided these terms. The change in language was clearly designed to make the Constitution more palatable to the North. In a debate over representation, William Paterson of New Jersey pointed out that under the Articles of Confederation Congress "had been ashamed to use the term 'Slaves' & had substituted a description." At the Convention few delegates expressed any shame over the word "slave," although some understood its use the final document would be impolitic. Late in the Convention the delegates from the Carolinas and Georgia vigorously demanded that the African trade remain open under the new Constitution. Gouverneur Morris of Pennsylvania, furious at this immoral compromise, suggested that the proposed clause read: the "Importation of slaves into N. Carolina, S—Carolina & Georgia" shall not be prohibited. Connecticut's Roger Sherman, who voted with the Deep South to allow the trade, objected, not only to the singling out of specific states, but also to the term slave. He declared he "liked a description better than the terms proposed, which had been declined by the old Congs & were not pleasing to some people." George Clymer of Pennsylvania "concurred" with Sherman. In the North Carolina ratifying convention James Iredell, who had been a delegate in Philadelphia, explained that "The word *slave* is not mentioned" because "the northern delegates, owing to their particular scruples on the subject of slavery, did not choose the word *slave* to be mentioned." Thus, southerners avoided the term because they did not want unnecessarily to antagonize their colleagues from the North. As long as they were assured of protection for their institution, the southerners were willing to do without the word "slave."[9]

Despite the circumlocution, slavery was sanctioned throughout the Constitution. Five provisions dealt directly with slavery:[10]

Article I, Section 2, Paragraph 3. The three-fifths clause provided for counting three-fifth of all slaves for purposes of representation in Congress. This clause also provided that, if any "direct tax" was levied on the states it could by imposed only proportionately, according to population, and that only three-fifths of all slaves would be counted in assessing what each state's contribution would be.

Article I, Section 9, Paragraph 3. Popularly known as the "slave trade clause," this provision prohibited Congress from banning the "Migration or Importation of such Persons as any of the States now existing shall think proper to admit" before the year 1808. Awkwardly phrased and designed to confuse readers, this clause prevented Congress from ending the African slave trade before 1808, but did not require Congress to ban the trade after that date. The clause was a significant exception to the general power granted to Congress to regulate all commerce.

Article I, Section 9, Paragraph 4. This clause declared any "capitation" or other "direct tax" had to take into account the three-fifths clause. It ensured that, if a head tax were ever levied, slaves would be taxed at three-fifths the rate of whites. The "direct tax" portion of this clause was redundant, because that was provided for in the three-fifths clause.

Article IV, Section 2, Paragraph 3. The fugitive slave clause prohibited the states from emancipating fugitive slaves and required that runaways be returned to their owners "on demand."

Article V. This article prohibited any amendment of the slave importation or capitation clauses before 1808.

Taken together, these five provisions gave the South a strong claim to "special treatment" for its peculiar institution. The three-fifths clause also gave the South extra political muscle — in the House of Representatives and in the Electoral College — to support that claim.

Numerous other clauses of the Constitution supplemented the five clauses that directly protected slavery. Some provisions that indirectly guarded slavery, such as the prohibition on taxing exports, were included primarily to protect the interests of slaveholders. Others, such as the guarantee of federal support to "suppress Insurrections" and the creation of the Electoral College, were written with slavery in mind, although delegates also supported them for reasons having nothing to do with slavery. The most prominent indirect protections of slavery were:

Article I, Section 8, Paragraph 15. The domestic insurrections clause empowered Congress to call "forth the Militia" to "suppress Insurrections" including slave rebellions.[11]

Article I, Section 9, Paragraph 5. This clause prohibited federal taxes on exports and thus prevented an indirect tax on slavery by taxing the staple products of slave labor, such as tobacco, rice, and eventually cotton.

Article I, Section 10, Paragraph 2. This clause prohibited the states from taxing exports or imports, thus preventing an indirect tax on the products of slave labor by a nonslaveholding state.[12]

Article II, Section 1, Paragraph 2. This clause provided for the indirect election of the president through an Electoral College based on congressional representation. This provision incorporated the three-fifths clause into the Electoral College and gave whites in slave states a disproportionate influence in the election of the president.

Article IV, Section 3, Paragraph 1. This clause allowed for the admission of new states. The delegates to the convention anticipated the admission of new slave states to the Union.

Article IV, Section 4. The domestic violence provision guaranteed the United States government would protect states from "domestic Violence," including slave rebellions.

Article V. By requiring a three-fourths majority of the states to ratify any amendment to the Constitution, this Article ensured that the slaveholding states would have a perpetual veto over any constitutional changes.[13]

Finally, some clauses did not inherently favor slavery, and were not necessarily considered to affect slavery when they were debated, but ultimately protected the institution when interpreted by the courts or implemented by Congress after the adoption of the Constitution. It would be wrong to argue that these illustrate the proslavery nature of the Constitutional Convention. However, these clauses do illustrate the way the Constitution set a proslavery tone, which enabled Congress and the courts to interpret seemingly neutral clauses in favor of slavery. Such clauses also directly challenge William W. Freehling's argument that the Framers were inherently antislavery and that "The impact of the Founding Fathers on slavery ... must be seen in the long run not in terms of what changed in the late eighteenth century but in terms of how the Revolutionary experience changed the whole American antebellum history."[14] If we look at the "long run" impact of the Constitution on "American antebellum history" we find that the following clauses were used to protect slavery, not to harm it.

Article I, Section 8, Paragraph 4. The naturalization clause allowed Congress to prohibit the naturalization of non-whites, even though it is likely that some of the new states, especially those which granted suffrage to blacks, would have also allowed foreign-born blacks to become citizens

Article I, Section 8, Paragraph 17. The federal district clause allowed Congress to regulate institutions, including slavery, in what became the national capital. Under this clause Congress allowed slavery in Washington D.C. During the Convention southerners expressed fear that the national capital would be in the North.

Article III, Section 2, Paragraph 1. The diversity jurisdiction clause limited the right to sue in federal courts to "Citizens of the different States" rather than inhabitants. This clause allowed judges to deny slaves and free blacks access to federal courts.[15]

Article IV, Section 1. The full faith and credit clause required each state to grant legal recognition to the laws and judicial proceedings of other states, thus obligating free states to recognize laws creating and protecting slavery.

Article IV, Section 2, Paragraph 1. The privileges and immunities clause required that states grant equal privileges and immunities to "citizens" of other states, however in *Dred Scott v. Sandford* (1857) the Supreme affirmed a long-standing position of the southern states that free blacks were not "citizens" under the Constitution and thus the slave states could deny privileges and immunities to northern free blacks.[16]

Article IV, Section 3, Paragraph 2. This clause allowed Congress to regulate the territories. In 1820 Congress used this clause to limit slavery in the territories, but in *Dred Scott v. Sandford* the Supreme Court ruled that the clause authorized Congress to protect slavery in the territories, but not to ban the institution.[17]

Besides specific clauses of the Constitution, the structure of the entire document ensured against emancipation by the new federal government. Because the Constitution created a government of limited powers, Congress lacked the power to interfere in the domestic institutions of the states.[18] Thus, during the ratification debates only the most fearful southern antifederalists opposed the Constitution on the grounds that it threatened slavery. Most southerners, even those who opposed the Constitution for other reasons, agreed with General Charles Cotesworth Pinckney of South Carolina, who crowed to his state's house of representatives:

> We have a security that the general government can never emancipate them, for no such authority is granted and it is admitted, on all hands, that the general government has no powers but what are expressly granted by the Constitution, and that all rights not expressed were reserved by the several states.[19]

The Constitution was not "essentially open-ended with respect to slavery," as the late Don Fehrenbacher argued. Nor is it true, as Earl Maltz has argued, that "the Constitution took no position on the basic institution of slavery."[20] On the contrary, the Constitution provided enormous protections for the peculiar institution of the South at very little cost to that region. At the Virginia ratifying convention Edmund Randolph denied the Constitution posed any threat at all to slavery. He challenged opponents of the Constitution to show, "*Where* is the part that has a tendency to the *abolition of* slavery?" He answered his own question asserting, "Were it right here to mention what passed in [the Philadelphia] convention … I might tell you" and that "*that the Southern States, even South Carolina herself, conceived this property to be secure*" and that "there was not a member of the Virginia delegation who had *the smallest suspicion of the abolition of slavery*." South Carolinians, who had already ratified the Constitution, would have agreed with Randolph. In summing up the entire Constitution, General Charles Cotesworth Pinckney, who had been one of the ablest defenders of slavery at the Convention, proudly told the South Carolina House of Representatives: "In short, considering all circumstances, we have made the best terms for the security of this species of property it was in our power to make. We would have made better if we could; but on the whole, I do not think them bad."[21]

Slavery and Congressional Representation

General Pinckney had good reason to be proud of his role in Philadelphia. Throughout the Convention Pinckney and other delegates from the Deep South tenaciously fought to protect the interests of slaveholders. In these struggles they were usually successful.

When they arrived at the Convention the delegates probably did not think slavery would be a pressing issue. Rivalries between large and small states appeared to pose the greatest obstacle to a stronger Union. The nature of representation in Congress; the power of the national government to levy taxes, regulate commerce, and pay off the nation's debts; the role of the states under a new constitution; and the power of the executive were on the agenda. Yet, as the delegates debated these issues, the importance of slavery—and the sectional differences it caused—became clear.[22] Throughout the summer of 1787 slavery emerged to complicate almost every debate. Most important by far was the way slavery figured in the lengthy debate over representation.

On May 29, Governor Edmund Randolph of Virginia proposed the series of resolutions known as the Virginia Plan. Randolph introduced these resolutions in response to the "crisis" of the nation "and the necessity of preventing the fulfillment of the prophecies of the American downfall." This plan would create an entirely new form of government in the United States. The power of the central government would be vastly enhanced at the expense of the states. The new Congress would have greater powers to tax, to secure the nation "against foreign invasion," to settle disagreements between states, and to regulate commerce.[23]

Randolph's plan called for a radical restructuring of the American government by making population the basis for representation in the national Congress. Under the Articles of Confederation, each state had one vote in Congress. By changing the basis of representation to population, Randolph's plan immediately created tensions between the large and small states at the Convention. But the plan also raised the question of whether slaves would be counted in allocating representation in the new Congress. This dilemma over counting slaves would trouble the delegates throughout the Convention.

Virginia was the most populous state in the nation, and thus Randolph had a vested interest in basing Congressional representation on population. But how that population would be counted greatly affected the potential representation of Virginia and the rest of the South. Virginia's white population, as the 1790 census would reveal, was only slightly larger than Pennsylvania's. If representation were based solely on free persons, the North would overwhelm the South.[24] But if slaves were counted equally with free persons, the Virginia delegation would be the largest, and the South would have more members of Congress than the North. The Virginians of course realized that the northern states were unlikely to support counting slaves for purposes of representation. Thus, Randolph's plan hedged the issue, declaring "that the rights of suffrage in the National Legislature ought to be proportioned to the Quotas of contribution, or to the number of free inhabitants, as the one or the other rule may seem best in different cases."[25] Randolph's avoidance of the term "slaves" by referring to "quotas of contribution" indicates the sensitivity of the subject.

Squabbling over slavery began in earnest the next day, May 30. James Madison moved to delete the term "free inhabitants" from the Randolph Plan because he felt the phrase "might occasion debates which would divert" attention "from the general question whether the principle of representation should be changed" from states to population. Madison understood that an early debate on the role of slavery in the Union might destroy the Convention before it got started. But his proposal would have left representation based solely on "quotas of contribution," and this was also unacceptable to most of the northern delegates. Madison himself agreed "that some better rule ought to be found." Alexander Hamilton then proposed that representation be based solely on the number of "free inhabitants" in each state. This proposal was also too volatile and the delegates quickly tabled it. Other attempts at compromise failed. Finally, the Delaware delegates helped put a temporary end to this divisive discussion by telling the Convention that they "were restrained by their commission from assenting to any change on the rule of suffrage," and if the body endorsed any change in representation, they would be forced to leave the Convention. The Convention, having successfully postponed this acrimonious debate, adjourned for the day.[26]

The Convention intermittently debated representation for the next two weeks, but on June 11 slavery reemerged to complicate the debate, when the Convention considered for the first time, and also approved provisionally, the three-fifths clause. Over the next three months the Convention would, on a number of occasions, redebate and reconsider the three-fifths clause before finally adopting it.[27] The evolution of the three-fifths clause during the Convention shows that the clause was not essentially a compromise over taxation and representation, as historians have traditionally claimed, and as the structure of Article I, Section 2, Paragraph 3 implies.[28] Rather, it began as a compromise between those who wanted to count slaves fully for purposes of representation and those who did not want to count slaves at all. On this crucial question the slave states won a critical victory without making any important concessions.

On June 11 Roger Sherman of Connecticut proposed that representation be based on the "numbers of free inhabitants" in each state. John Rutledge and Pierce Butler of South Carolina objected, arguing for representation according to "quotas of contribution," which had become a euphemism for counting slaves for representation.[29] James Wilson and Charles Pinckney, the younger cousin of General Charles Cotesworth Pinckney, skillfully headed off the Rutledge-Butler proposal.

Wilson proposed and Pinckney seconded a motion that ultimately became the three-fifths clause. Here for the first time was an example of cooperation between the North and the South over slavery. Significantly, Wilson was known to oppose slavery and came from a state, Pennsylvania, which had already adopted a gradual emancipation scheme. Nevertheless, harmony at the Convention was more important to Wilson than the place of slavery in the new nation. By teaming up, the nominally antislavery Pennsylvanian and the rabidly proslavery Carolinian may have hoped to undercut the antislavery sentiments of other northern delegates while also satisfying the demands of the proslavery delegates like Butler and Rutledge.[30]

Most delegates seemed to accept this proposal. However, Elbridge Gerry of Massachusetts sarcastically protested: "Blacks are property, and are used to the southward as horses and cattle to the northward; and why should their representation be increased to the southward on account of the number of slaves, than horses or oxen to the north?" Gerry believed this would be an appropriate rule for taxation, but not for representation, because under it four southern voters would have more political power than ten northern voters. He also argued that this clause would degrade freemen in the North by equating them with slaves. He wondered "Are we to enter into a Compact with Slaves?"[31] No other northerner opposed counting slaves for representation at this time.

Thus, with little debate the Convention initially accepted the three-fifths clause as a basis for representation. The clause, giving the South enormous political leverage in the nation, was accepted without any quid pro quo from the North. Application of the clause to taxation would not come until much later in the Convention. Indeed, there was no reason in mid-June to believe it would ever be applied to taxation. A brief history of the three-fifths ratio, prior to 1787, bears this out.

The ratio of three slaves to five free persons was first proposed in the Articles of Confederation Congress in 1783 as part of an overall program for the national government to raise revenue from the states. The ratio was controversial. Southerners thought it overvalued slaves, and northerners thought it undervalued them. Delegates from Virginia and South Carolina, the states with the most slaves, wanted taxation based on land values. Congress initially rejected and then later resurrected the entire package, which called for taxation based on population. Congress then sent the package to the states as an amendment to the Articles of Confederation. However, this amendment failed to achieve the necessary unanimous support of all the states, and was not added to Articles of Confederation.[32]

This history of the three-fifths clause shows there is little substance to the traditional view that the three-fifths clause "was a legacy from the Congress of 1783" or that "most northern delegates must have realized even before they arrived in Philadelphia that it would be the minimum price of southern acceptance of any new constitution." The only useful legacy of the Congress of 1783 was the numerical ratio itself, which Congress had applied only to taxation.[33] The application of the ratio to representation was an entirely new concept.

The meaning of the three-fifths clause to the delegates in Philadelphia was clear in the report of the Committee of the Whole on June 13, which stated that representation would be "in proportion to the whole number of white and other free citizens and inhabitants, of every age, sex and condition, including those bound to servitude for a term of years and three-fifths of all other persons not comprehended in the foregoing description, except Indians, not paying taxes in each State." The phrasing of the term "white and other free citizens and inhabitants" clearly implied that the "other persons" were neither white nor free.[34] By mid-June a majority in the Convention had accepted the principle that representation in the national Congress would be based on population and that three-fifths of the slave population would be added to the free population in determining representation. However, a minority of the delegates, led by those from New Jersey, were still unhappy with this plan.

On June 15 William Paterson introduced what is commonly known as the New Jersey Plan. The plan rejected congressional representation based on population and, instead, retained the system of representation then in force under the Articles of Confederation: that the states would have an equal number of delegates in the Congress. For the next fifteen days the Convention debated, without any reference to slavery, whether representation in Congress would be based on population. In most of the votes on this issue the South (except Delaware) supported population based representation. These votes were predicated on the assumption that the three-fifths clause, which had already been accepted, would be part of the basis of representation. The southern delegates also expected their region to grow faster than the North, and thus representation based on population would help them in the long run. But, even if whites did not move south, slaves could still be imported. Southerners, confident that a growing slave population would augment their representation in Congress, consistently supported population as the basis of that representation.[35]

By June 30 the Convention was at a standstill. The states in favor of population-based representation had enough votes to adopt their scheme. But if they were unable to persuade the delegates from the smaller states to acquiesce on this point, the Convention itself would fail. In the middle of this debate Madison offered a new mode of analysis for the delegates. He argued:

> [T]hat the States were divided into different interests not by their difference of size, but by other circumstances; the most material of which resulted partly from climate, but principally from their having or not having slaves. These two causes concurred in forming the great division of interests in the U. States. It did not lie between the large and small States: it lay between the Northern and Southern, and if any defensive power were necessary, it ought to be mutually given to these two interests.

So Madison proposed two branches of Congress, one in which slaves would be counted equally with free people to determine how many representatives each state would have, and one in which slaves would not be counted at all. Under this arrangement, "the Southern Scale would have the advantage in one House, and the Northern in the other." Madison made this proposal despite his reluctance to "urge any diversity of interests" among the delegates.[36]

The Convention ignored Madison's proposal. He may have offered it simply to divert attention from the heated debate between the large and small states. If this was indeed his goal, he was not immediately successful. The small states, led by Delaware, continued to express fear that they would be swallowed up by larger states if representation in the Congress were based solely on population.[37]

Subsequent debates reveal the validity of Madison's analysis that sectionalism—caused by slavery—created a major division within the Convention and the nation. Indeed, slavery continued to complicate the Convention debates long after the conflict between large and small states had evaporated. On July 2, Charles Pinckney argued that there was "a solid distinction as to interest between the southern and northern states." He noted that the Carolinas and Georgia "in their Rice and Indigo had a peculiar interest which might be sacrificed" if they did not have sufficient power in any new Congress.[38] Immediately after this speech the Convention accepted a proposal by General Charles Cotesworth Pinckney to send the entire question of representation to a committee of one delegate from each state. The Convention then adjourned until July 5.

On July 5 the committee proposed what historians have since called the Great Compromise. Under this plan representation in the lower house of the legislature would be based on population, and in the upper house the states would have an equal vote. The three-fifths clause was a part of this proposal.[39]

On July 6 the Convention once again approved the concept of representation based on population for the lower house of the Congress. The Convention then chose a five-man committee to redraft the clause. In the absence of a census this committee would also have to recommend to the Convention the number of representatives that each state would get in the First Congress. Before the Convention adjourned for the day, Charles Pinckney again raised sectional issues connected to slavery, arguing that "blacks ought to stand on an equality with whites," but he "w[oul]d.... agree to the ratio settled by Congs."[40]

Pinckney's argument here was doubly significant. First, in a debate that had nothing to do with slavery per se, Pinckney raised the issue, as if to warn the Convention not to forget the special needs of the South. Second, Pinckney made it clear that he (and presumably other southerners) thought that their acceptance of the three-fifths rule for counting slaves was a great concession.

On July 9 the committee of five reported its recommendations. Gouverneur Morris, who was on the committee, admitted that the allocations in the report were "little more than a guess." A number of delegates were dissatisfied with these guesses, because in allocating representation for the First Congress the committee had taken into account "the number of blacks and whites." This action led William Paterson to register a protest—only the second so far in the Convention—against the three-fifths clause. This was the beginning of a four-day debate over slavery and representation. Paterson declared he regarded

> [N]egroes slaves in no light but as property. They are no free agents, have no personal liberty, no faculty of acquiring property, but on the contrary are themselves property, and like other property entirely at the will of the Master.

Paterson pointedly asked, "Has a man in Virga. a number of votes in proportion to the number of his slaves?" He noted that slaves were not counted in allocating representation in southern state legislatures, and asked, "Why should they be represented in the Genl. Gov't.[?]" Finally, Paterson argued that counting slaves for purposes of representation encouraged the slave trade.[41]

In response, Madison once again proposed that representation in one house of the legislature be based on total population and the other on just the free population. Pierce Butler again argued for wealth as a basis for representation. This proposal, of course, meant that slaves would be counted equally with whites. Rufus King of Massachusetts gave unexpected support to Butler, warning that the South would not unite with the rest of the country "unless some respect were paid to their superior wealth." Furthermore, King reminded his northern colleagues that, if they expected "preferential distinctions in Commerce," they should be willing to give up something. At least at this point in the Convention, King was willing to accept the three-fifths ratio for representation.[42] Here was the beginning of a major compromise between the Deep South and the commercially oriented states of the North. At the moment, King and other northerners were offering the three-fifths clause to the South, without asking southerners for any concession in return.

This debate resulted in the appointment of yet another committee to come up with a new proposal for representation in the First Congress. This committee reported its deliberations the next day, July 10, and the Convention debated them. Like the previous committee, this one had to calculate representation in the First Congress without the benefit of a census. This allocation, which was later written into the Constitution, gave the North thirty-five seats in the First Congress while giving the South 30.[43] Not surprisingly, some delegates objected to the apportionment for their states. More important, though, was the sectional animosity that these allocations stimulated.

Almost immediately John Rutledge and Charles Cotesworth Pinckney of South Carolina moved to reduce New Hampshire's representatives from three to two. Although on the previous day Rufus King had supported Pierce Butler's demand for more southern representation, he now defended the committee's apportionment, warning that the New England states would not accept any reduction in their representation. King also endorsed Madison's analysis of sectionalism, arguing that "a difference of interests did not lie where it had hitherto been discussed, between the great and small States; but between the Southern and Eastern." King nevertheless continued to seek compromise and explicitly recognized the need "for the security of the Southern" interests. For this reason he acquiesced to the three-fifths rule and was even willing to consider "a still greater security" for the South, although he admitted he did not know what that might be. But he also asserted that "no principle would justify giving" the South "a majority" in Congress.[44]

Charles Cotesworth Pinckney responded that the South did not require "a majority of representatives, but [he] wished them to have something like an equality." Otherwise, Congress would pass commercial regulations favorable to the North, and the southern states would "be nothing more than overseers for the Northern States." Hugh Williamson of North Carolina agreed, arguing that under the present system the North would get a majority in Congress which it would never relinquish, and thus "the Southern Interest must be extremely endangered."[45]

Gouverneur Morris of Pennsylvania, who was emerging as the Convention's most vocal opponent of concessions to slavery, became the first delegate to challenge the assumption that the South was richer than the North and therefore deserved greater representation in Congress. He also argued that, in time of emergency, northerners would have to "spill their blood."[46] Madison's notes do not contain the full text of Morris's speech, but its implications are clear. Northerners would have to "spill their blood" because there were more free people in the North than in the South and because slavery made the South an unreliable ally in wartime.

After various unsuccessful attempts to reduce representation for some northern states or increase representation for some southern states, the Convention adopted an apportionment scheme for representation in the First Congress by a vote of nine to two. The negative votes did not come from the smallest states, but from the most southern.[47] The delegates from South Carolina and Georgia made their point: they must have protection for slavery or they would oppose the Constitution.

The next day, July 11, the Convention debated the provision for a census to determine future representation in Congress. Hugh Williamson of North Carolina amended the provision under consideration to explicitly include the three-fifths clause for counting slaves. Still dissatisfied with the three-fifths clause, Butler and Charles Cotesworth Pinckney of South Carolina "insisted that blacks be included in the rule of Representation, equally with the Whites," and moved to delete the three-fifths clause. Butler argued that "the labour of a slave in South Carolina was as productive and valuable as that of a freeman in Massachusetts," and since the national government "was instituted principally for the protection of property," slaves should be counted fully for representation.[48] The Convention quickly rejected the Butler-Pinckney proposal.

The defeat of the Butler-Pinckney resolution did not end the debate over slavery and representation. A motion to require Congress to take a census of all "free inhabitants" passed on a slim six-to-four vote, with four slave states voting no. The Convention then began debating the motion to count three-fifths of all slaves. King and Gorham of Massachusetts expressed reservations, and Sherman of Connecticut urged conciliation.

James Wilson of Pennsylvania, who had initially proposed the three-fifths clause, supported it on pragmatic grounds. Admitting he "did not well see on what principle the admission of blacks in the proportion of three-fifths could be explained." He asked, if slaves were citizens "why are they not admitted on an equality with White Citizens?" But, if slaves were "admitted as property" it was reasonable to ask, "Then why is not other property admitted into the computation?" But Wilson argued that these logical inconsistencies "must be overruled by the necessity of compromise." Gouverneur Morris, also representing Pennsylvania, was not so willing to sacrifice principle. Having been "reduced to the dilemma of doing injustice to the Southern States or to human nature," Morris chose the former, asserting that he "could never agree to give such encouragement to the slave trade" by allowing the slave states "a representation for their negroes." The three-fifths clause then failed, by a vote of four to six. However, this defeat was not solely the result of Morris's arguments in favor of principle: two slave states were still holding out for fully counting slaves for representation opposed the measure.[49]

The next day, July 12, the three-fifths clause was back on the floor, directly tied to taxation for the first time. The debate was the most divisive yet on slavery. Six southerners, representing Virginia, North Carolina, and South Carolina, addressed the issue. Their collective demand was clear: either give the South substantial representation for its slave population, or the South would oppose the Constitution. Randolph, who had so far avoided the debates over slavery, "lamented that such a species of property existed," but nevertheless "urged strenuously that express security ought to be provided for including slaves in the ratio of Representation." Meanwhile, the South Carolinians, as might be expected, demanded full representation for slaves, declaring themselves willing, even eager, to be taxed fully for their slaves in return for full representation for their slaves.[50] William R. Davie of North Carolina, who had been virtually silent throughout the Convention, declared "it was high time now to speak out." Davie warned that North Carolina would "never confederate" unless slaves were counted, at the very least, under a three-fifths ratio. Davie threatened that if some representation for slaves was not adopted, "the business [of the convention] was at an end."[51]

Only Gouverneur Morris was prepared to call Davie's bluff, warning that Pennsylvania would "never agree to a representation of Negroes." But he also agreed that it was "vain for the Eastern states to insist on what the Southern States will never agree to." As much as Morris wished "to form a compact for the good of America," he seemed ready to risk failure on the issue of slave representation.[52] No other northerner joined Morris on this issue. However, Oliver Ellsworth and William Samuel Johnson of Connecticut strongly supported southern interests, foreshadowing an emerging compromise between New England and the South over slavery and commerce. After a heated debate, the Convention finally adopted the three-fifths clause by a vote of six to two, with two states divided.[53]

After more than a month and a half of anguished argument, the Convention had finally resolved the issue of representation for what would become the House of Representatives. Throughout, slavery had constantly confused the issue and thwarted compromise. Sectional interests caused by slavery had emerged as a major threat to the Union. At this juncture in the Convention the smaller states still feared the larger ones; however, the northern and southern states had also come to openly distrust each other. In the last debate over representation, General Charles Cotesworth Pinckney declared he was "alarmed" over statements about slavery by northerners.[54] His alarm would soon spread to other southern delegates.

No sooner had the Convention laid to rest the issue of representation than it reemerged as part of the debate over taxation. On July 13 Elbridge Gerry proposed that, until an actual census could be taken, taxation would be based on the initial representation in the House. This seemingly reasonable proposal set the stage for a partial reopening of the debate over representation.

Reviving an earlier proposal, Hugh Williamson of North Carolina tried to cut New Hampshire's representation in the House of Representatives from three to two. Williamson argued that because New Hampshire's delegates had not yet arrived at the Convention, it was unfair to force the state to pay taxes on the basis of three representatives. This explanation fooled no one, and Williamson's maneuver failed. Next, Read of Delaware expressed the fear that Gerry's motion was a plot by the larger states to tax the smaller ones. This led Madison to reiterate his belief that "the difference of interest in the United States lay not between the large and small, but the Northern and Southern States." Madison supported Gerry's motion "because it tended to moderate the views both of the opponents and advocates for rating very high, the negroes." After three votes Gerry's motion passed. The Convention had deepened its commitment to the three-fifths clause, both for representation and for taxation.[55]

With the sense of the Convention on this issue apparently clear, Randolph moved to bring language previously used in the working document into conformity with the three-fifths clause. Earlier in the Convention the body declared that representation would be based on "wealth." Randolph now proposed substituting the wording of the three-fifths clause for the word "wealth."[56] This opened the way for yet one more debate over the three-fifths clause. This debate revealed the deep animosities that had developed between some northern and southern delegates.

Gouverneur Morris began by mocking the attempt to replace the word "wealth" with the three-fifths clause. If slaves were "property," then "the word wealth was right, and striking it out would produce the very inconsistency which it was meant to get rid of." Morris then launched into a full scale attack on southern demands. In the process he suggested that a peaceful end to the Convention, and the Union itself, might be in order. Morris asserted that, until this point in the Convention, he had believed that the distinction between northern and southern states was "heretical." Somewhat disingenuously, he declared that he "still thought the [sectional] distinction groundless." But he saw that it was "persisted in; and that the Southern Gentleman will not be satisfied unless they see the way open to their gaining a majority in the public Councils." The North naturally demanded "some defence" against this. Morris thus concluded:

> Either this distinction is fictitious or real: if fictitious let it be dismissed and let us proceed with due confidence. If it be real, instead of attempting to blend incompatible things, let us at once take a friendly leave of each other. There can be no end of demands for security if every particular interest is to be entitled to it.

Morris argued that the North had as much to fear from the South as the South had to fear from the North.[57]

South Carolina's Pierce Butler responded with equal candor: "The security the Southn. States want is that their negroes may not be taken from them which some gentlemen within or without doors, have a very good mind to do."[58] For the rest of the Convention Butler and his southern colleagues would remain vigilant in protecting this interest.

By Saturday the fourteenth, sectional tempers had cooled. The Convention now reconsidered the makeup of what would ultimately become the Senate. The small states again reiterated their fears that the large states would overwhelm them in a legislature based entirely on population. Delegates from New Jersey and Connecticut made it clear that they would not support the emerging Constitution unless there was state equality in at least one branch of the legislature. Charles Pinckney once again proposed that representation in both houses of the legislature be based on population. In supporting this motion Madison yet again argued that "the real difference of interests lay, not between the large and small but between the Northern and Southern States. The institution of slavery and its consequences formed the line of discrimination." Madison seemed particularly worried that state equality would give the North a perpetual majority in one branch of the legislature.[59]

Over Madison's protests, the equality of the states in the Senate remained part of the Constitution. On the final vote on this issue, three of the four negative votes came from the South.[60] This vote indicates that Madison was correct in asserting that sectional division was more important than the division between large and small states.

On July 16, when debate resumed over the powers of Congress, Butler and Rutledge opposed giving Congress the power to legislate where the states were "incompetent." The southerners feared this "vague" and, therefore, dangerous power, and thus four slave states supported a futile attempt to recommit this clause. This debate again illustrates that sectional fears, more than rivalries between large and small states, had emerged as the major problem for the Convention. Butler and Rutledge, after all, were fearful of what a Congress dominated by the North might do. Any vagueness in language might be used to harm slavery.[61]

The irony of the shifting sentiments of the Carolinians became clearer a day later, when Gunning Bedford offered compromise language for this clause. Bedford, of Delaware, had up to this time vociferously articulated the fears of the small states. During the debates over representation he had emphatically told him fellow delegates, "I do not gentlemen, trust you." Bedford was probably as jealous of state power, and as fearful of national power, as any man at the Convention. Yet, on this issue of the powers of Congress Bedford was not fearful and was willing to compromise, because even he saw nothing dangerous in the proposed clause, especially if it contained his compromise language. Bedford's amendment did not mollify the delegates from South Carolina and Georgia, however, who remained opposed to allowing the national government to legislate for the "general interest of the Union."[62] These Deep South delegates no doubt suspected that such language might somehow be used to harm slavery. Legislating for the "general interest" of the Union, they feared, might someday threaten the particular interest of slavery.

Slavery and the Executive Branch

The Convention was deeply divided over how the nation's chief executive should be chosen. Slavery complicated the debates on this question and partially affected their outcome. On July 17 the Convention considered, and rejected by wide margins, election by the Congress, direct election by the people, and election by the state legislatures. Significantly, the most vocal opposition to election by the people came from three southerners: Charles Pinckney, George Mason, and Hugh Williamson. While Pinckney and Mason argued against the competence of the "people," Williamson was more open about the reasons for southern opposition. He noted Virginia would not be able to elect her leaders president because "her slaves will have no suffrage."[63] The same of course would be true for the rest of the South.

For James Madison the debate over the presidency was particularly difficult. Because he believed that "concepts of right and justice were paramount expressions of majority rule,"[64] Madison instinctively favored election of the president by the people. He told the Convention that "the people at large" were "the fittest" to choose the president. But "one difficulty ... of a serious nature" made election by the people impossible. Madison noted that the "right of suffrage was much more diffusive in the Northern than the Southern States; and the latter could have no influence in the election on the score of the Negroes." In order to guarantee that the nonvoting slaves could nevertheless influence the presidential election, Madison favored the creation of the Electoral College.[65] Under this system each state was given a number of electors equal to its total congressional and senatorial representation. This meant that the three-fifths clause would help determine the outcome of presidential elections.[66] Thus, the fundamentally antidemocratic Electoral College developed, at least in part, to protect the interests of slavery.

Commerce and Slavery:
The Dirty Compromise

By late July, the Convention had hammered out the basic outline of the Constitution. On July 23 the Convention agreed to send the draft of the Constitution to a Committee of Detail. At this juncture General Charles Cotesworth Pinckney "reminded the Convention that if the Committee should fail to insert some security to the Southern States against an emancipation of slaves, and taxes on exports, he should be bound by duty to his State to vote against their Report."[67] This protest must have surprised the Convention. In the previous nine days the subject of slavery had not been directly debated; and where it had come up at all, such as in the discussion of the election of the president, the South had had its way. Now, just as the work of many weeks was about to go to a committee for what many hoped was a final redrafting, Pinckney raised new demands for the protection for slavery.

Pinckney's outburst provoked no immediate reaction. The Convention remained in session for three more days, debating, once again, how the executive should be chosen.

Finally, on July 26 the Convention adjourned until August 6, to allow the Committee of Detail to put the Convention's work into some coherent form. This five-man committee included two southerners, Rutledge and Randolph, while a third member, Oliver Ellsworth of Connecticut, consistently supported southern interests in the Convention.

The report of the Committee of Detail contained a number of provisions aimed at the protection of slavery. The new Congress could not interfere with the African slave trade and would need a two-thirds majority to pass navigation acts. The new government would be obligated to provide military support to suppress rebellions and insurrections in the states. Although Clause IV provided for representation based on "the number of inhabitants, according to the provisions herein after made," no such provisions were in fact in this draft. Thus, the committee report implied that the slaves would be counted equally with all other "inhabitants" when determining representation in Congress. The three-fifths clause was in the Committee report, but applied only to "direct" taxes and "capitation" taxes, and not to representation. The committee report also prohibited taxation of both exports and imported slaves. With the exception of a clause allowing Congress to regulate commerce by a simple majority, the draft Constitution seemed to give the South everything it wanted.[68] The Committee of Detail appeared to have taken to heart Pinckney's demand for "some security to the Southern States."

On August 7 the Convention began to debate the committee report. On the next day yet another debate over the three-fifths clause took place. Hugh Williamson moved to clarify the status of this clause by replacing the phrase "the provisions herein after made" with a direct reference to the three-fifths provision. After the Convention adopted Williamson's motion, Rufus King protested that counting slaves for representation "was a most grating circumstance," especially because the draft of the Constitution also prohibited Congress from banning the slave trade or even taxing the produce of slave labor. He thought that some provision ought to be made for ending the slave trade, but at minimum he argued that "either slaves should not be represented, or exports should be taxable."[69]

Roger Sherman, who would prove to be the Deep South's most vocal northern ally, agreed with King that the slave trade was "iniquitous" but believed that this issue should not be raised in connection with the question of representation, which had "been settled after much difficulty and deliberation." Madison, Ellsworth, and Sherman then tried to discuss other topics. But Gouverneur Morris would not let the slavery issue drop. He moved to insert the word "free" in front of the word "inhabitants" in the clause directing how representation would be determined. Believing that "much ... would depend on this point," Morris said that he could "never ... concur in upholding domestic slavery," which was "the curse of heaven on the States where it prevailed." Morris compared the "rich and noble cultivation" of the middle states with "the misery and poverty which overspread the barren wastes of Virginia, Maryland and the other [slave] states" and concluded that counting slaves for representation, when fairly explained, comes to this:

> [T]hat the inhabitant of Georgia and South Carolina who goes to the Coast of Africa, and in defiance of the most sacred laws of humanity tears away his fellow creatures from their dearest connections and damns them to the most cruel bondages, shall have more votes in a Government instituted for protection of the rights of mankind, than the Citizen of Pennsylvania or New Jersey who views with a laudable horror, so nefarious a practice.

According to Morris, the draft Constitution compelled the North "to march their militia for the defence of the Southern States; for their defence against those very slaves of whom they complain." Furthermore, the government lacked the power to levy a tax on imported slaves or on the goods they produced. Worst of all, counting slaves for representation encouraged the South to import more of them. Morris scoffed at the idea that there could ever be a direct tax, such as the three-fifths clause allowed, because it was "idle to suppose that the General Government can stretch its hand directly into the pockets of the people scattered over so vast a Country." Thus the South would get extra representation in Congress for its slaves and have to pay nothing in return. Morris declared he "would sooner submit himself to a tax for paying for all the Negroes in the United States than saddle posterity with such a Constitution."[70]

For the first time in the Convention, two northerners — King and Morris — had denounced slavery in the same debate. A third, Jonathan Dayton of New Jersey, joined them by seconding Morris's motion. Curiously, no one responded in kind to these attacks. Roger Sherman calmly answered his northern neighbors, declaring he saw no "insuperable objections" to "the admission of the Negroes into the ratio of representation." He argued "It was the freemen of the Southn. States who were in fact to be represented according to the taxes paid by them, and the Negroes are only included in the Estimate of the taxes." This response reflected claims made by delegates from South Carolina since the beginning of the Convention, that wealth as well population had to be represented in the Congress. James Wilson added that the objections by Morris and King were premature. Charles Pinckney merely indicated that he would reply "if the occasion were a proper one." The Convention then overwhelmingly rejected Morris's amendment.[71]

For the South this debate, along with the vote that followed it, was a major victory. The debate exposed many of the weaknesses of slavery; some delegates had made powerful moral and practical arguments against the institution. Yet, all the northern states except New Jersey voted with the South.

In the following week the Convention managed to avoid rancorous debates over slavery, even though sectional distrust sometimes appeared.[72] This period of calm ended on August 16, when the Convention began another debate over the powers of Congress. During a routine discussion of the power of Congress to levy taxes and duties, George Mason raised the issue of the power of Congress to tax exports. A part of the draft Constitution that had not yet been debated specifically prohibited Congress from taxing exports. Mason wanted to debate the issue out of order. He did not want to give Congress the right to levy any tax without simultaneously adopting a corresponding prohibition on export taxes. Mason "was unwilling to trust to its being done in a future article" and "professed his jealousy for the productions of the Southern or as he called them, the staple States." Sherman and Rutledge quickly reassured Mason that such a provision could be dealt with later. Mason could not, however, have been totally reassured when Gouverneur Morris declared that a prohibition on taxing exports was "radically objectionable." A number of other delegates then debated this issue. With the exception of Madison, all the southerners opposed taxing exports; all of the northerners, except those from Connecticut and Massachusetts, favored the idea.[73] The Convention then postponed the question of taxing exports.

This short debate gave hints of a developing bargain between New Englanders and delegates from the Deep South. In reassuring Mason, South Carolina's John Rutledge noted that he would vote for the commerce clause as it stood, but only "on condition that the subsequent part relating to negroes should also be agreed to."[74] Rutledge clearly equated an export tax with an attack on slavery. Delegates from Connecticut and Massachusetts indicated some support for Rutledge's position. What should be called the "dirty compromise" of the Convention was taking shape. The South Carolina delegation would support the commerce clause if New England would a support prohibition on export taxes and a protection for the slave trade. This understanding solidified during the next two weeks.

On August 21 the New England states joined the five slave states south of Delaware on three crucial votes. On the first vote all three New England states voted to defeat an amendment to the draft Constitution that would have allowed Congress, by a simple majority vote, to tax exports. During the debate over this motion Connecticut's Ellsworth argued against taxing exports because such taxes would unfairly hurt the South which produced major export crops such as "Tobo. rice and indigo." Ellsworth believed "a tax on these alone would be partial and unjust." Next, in a key five-to-six vote Connecticut joined the five slave states to defeat a proposal, made by James Madison, to allow taxes on exports by a two-thirds vote of Congress. On the final vote, to absolutely ban all export taxes, Massachusetts joined Connecticut, and the measure to prohibit export taxes, favored by the South passed, seven to four. During the debate the Virginia delegation was divided, three to two, with James Madison and George Washington unsuccessfully favoring Congressional power to tax exports.[75]

The Convention then debated a motion by Luther Martin to allow an import tax on slaves. Martin represented Maryland, a slave state, but one with a surplus of slaves, a fact that helps explain his opposition to the African trade. Rutledge opposed Martin's motion with a two-pronged attack. He first told the Convention that the "true question at present is whether the Southern States shall or shall not be parties to the Union." The implied threat of secession was clear. He then told the northern delegates that, if they would "consult their interest," they would "not oppose the increase of slaves which will increase the commodities of which they will become the carriers." Ellsworth of Connecticut agreed, refusing to debate the "morality or wisdom of slavery" and simply asserting that "what enriches a part enriches the whole." The alliance for profit between the Deep South and New England was now fully developed. Charles Pinckney then reaffirmed that South Carolina would "never receive the plan if it prohibits the slave trade."[76] Shrewdly, Pinckney equated a tax on imported slaves with a prohibition on the trade itself. On this note the Convention retired for the day.

Roger Sherman opened debate the next day by adopting a familiar pose. He declared his personal disapproval of slavery but refused to condemn it in other parts of the nation. He then argued against a prohibition of the slave trade. First, he asserted that "the public good did not require" an end to the trade. Noting that the states already had the right to import slaves, Sherman saw no point in taking a right away from the states unnecessarily because "it was expedient to have as few objections as possible" to the new Constitution. Here Sherman assumed it was necessary to defuse southern opposition to the Constitution, which might result from a ban on the slave trade, but he did not think it necessary to placate those who might oppose the Constitution if it allowed the slave trade to continue. Sherman was prepared to appease those who supported the slave trade, but he apparently was unconcerned about the strong opposition to the slave trade in his own region. Next, Sherman observed that "the abolition of slavery seemed to be going on in the U.S." If left alone, the "good sense of the several States" would soon put an end to all slavery in the country. In making this argument Sherman either confused the abolition of the slave trade with the abolition of slavery itself, or he foolishly believed that because New England and Pennsylvania had begun to abolish slavery, the rest of the nation would soon follow. Finally, revealing his priorities, Sherman urged the delegates to hurry and finish their business, noting, no doubt, that they had been in session for almost three months.[77]

George Mason of Virginia responded to Sherman with a fierce attack on the "infernal traffic" in slaves, which he blamed on "the avarice of British Merchants." Reflecting the sectional hostilities at the Convention, as well as trying to lay blame on anyone but Virginians for the problem of slavery, Mason then "lamented" that his "Eastern brethren had from a lust of gain embarked in this nefarious traffic." Mason leveled some of the strongest criticism of slavery yet heard at the Convention, declaring it an "evil" system which produced "the most pernicious effect on manners." He declared that "every master of slaves is born a petty tyrant" and warned that slavery would "bring the judgment of heaven on a Country" and ultimately produce "national calamities." Despite this apparent attack on the whole institution, Mason ended his speech by demanding only that the national government "have power to prevent the increase of slavery" by prohibiting the African trade. As Peter Wallenstein has argued, "Whatever his occasional rhetoric, George Mason was — if one must choose — proslavery, not antislavery. He acted in behalf of Virginia slaveholders, not Virginia slaves," when he opposed a continuation of the African trade.[78]

Others at the Convention understood this quite well. Mason failed to say that Virginia, like Maryland, had a surplus of slaves and did not need the African slave trade any longer. But James McHenry candidly wrote in his private notes: "That the population or increase of slaves in Virginia exceeded their calls for their services," and thus a prohibition of the slave trade "would be a monopoly" in Virginia's "favor." Under such conditions "Virginia etc. would make their own terms for such [slaves] as they might sell."[79] The "etc." no doubt included McHenry's own state of Maryland.

Ellsworth of Connecticut, adopting the same pose as Sherman, answered Mason. Because "he had never owned a slave," Ellsworth declared he "could not judge of the effects of slavery on character." However, if slavery were as wrong as Mason had suggested, merely ending the trade was insufficient. Ellsworth, of course, knew that the Virginians opposed allowing the national government to abolish slavery. Therefore, since there were many slaves in Virginia and Maryland and fewer in the Deep South, any prohibition on the trade would be "unjust towards S. Carolina and Georgia." So Ellsworth urged the Convention not to "intermeddle" in the affairs of other states.[80] The Convention had now witnessed the unusual phenomenon of a New Englander defending the slave trade against the attacks of a Virginian.

The Carolinians were of course quite capable of defending their own institution. Charles Pinckney, citing ancient Rome and Greece, declared that slavery was "justified by the example of all the world." He warned that any prohibition of the slave trade would "produce serious objections to the Constitution which he wished to see adopted."[81] His cousin, General Pinckney, also declared his support for the Constitution, but noted that his "personal influence … would be of no avail towards obtaining the assent" of his home state. He believed Virginia's opposition to the trade was more pecuniary than moral. Virginia would "gain by stopping the importations" because "her slaves will rise in value, and she has more than she wants." Prohibiting the trade would force South Carolina and Georgia "to confederate" on "unequal terms." While Virginia might gain, the nation as a whole would not. More slaves would produce more goods, and that result would help not only the South but also states involved in "the carrying trade." Seeing the slave trade solely as an economic issue, Pinckney thought it "reasonable" that imported slaves be taxed. But a prohibition of the slave trade would be "an exclusion of S. Carola from the Union." As he had made clear at the beginning of his speech, "S. Carolina and Georgia cannot do without slaves." Rutledge and Butler added similar sentiments, as did Abraham Baldwin of Georgia and Williamson of North Carolina.[82]

New England accents now supported the Southern drawls. Gerry of Massachusetts offered some conciliatory remarks, and Sherman, ever the ally of the South, declared that "it was better to let the S. States import slaves than to part with them, if they made that a sine qua non." However, in what may have been an attempt to give his remarks an antislavery tone, he argued that taxing imported slaves was morally wrong, because that "implied they were property."[83] This position undoubtedly pleased Sherman's southern allies, who did not want to pay taxes on any slaves they imported. Sherman's speech also underscored the profound support that the Carolinians and Georgians found among some New Englanders.

The reasons for cooperation between New England and the Deep South on this issue were now clear. New Englanders, involved in the "carrying trade," would profit from transporting rice and other products produced by slave labor. And the South Carolinians seemed willing to support the New Englanders' demands for Congressional power to regulate all commerce. In return, New Englanders would support the right of the Carolinas and Georgia to import the slaves they could not "do without."

On the other side of the issue only John Langdon of New Hampshire and John Dickinson of Delaware vigorously opposed allowing the slave trade to continue. Dickinson argued that the trade was "inadmissible on every principle of honor and safety." Furthermore, he was prepared to call the Carolinians' bluff on the question of Union, doubting the Deep South would reject the Constitution if the trade were prohibited. James Wilson was also skeptical of southern threats, but he did not offer any strong rebuttal. Nor did Rufus King, who only pointed out that prohibiting a tax on imported Africans was an "inequality that could not fail to strike the commercial sagacity of the Northern and middle States."[84]

The most surprising contribution to this debate came from Gouverneur Morris of Pennsylvania, who had previously been the most consistent opponent of slavery at the Convention. He suggested that the subject of commercial regulation acts and the slave trade be sent to committee. "These things may form a bargain among the Northern and Southern States," he shrewdly noted. The Convention quickly accepted his suggestion.[85]

Two days later, on August 25, the committee reported a compromise proposal; on the twenty-sixth the Convention began to debate it. The committee proposed that Congress be barred from prohibiting the African slave trade until 1800, but that in the meantime a reasonable tax could be levied on imported slaves. General Charles C. Pinckney immediately urged that the date be changed to 1808, which would be twenty years after the Constitution was ratified. Gorham of Massachusetts seconded this motion. Madison complained that this provision was "dishonorable to the National character" and to the Constitution and the "twenty years will produce all the mischief that can be apprehended from the liberty to import slaves." Nevertheless, the delegates accepted Pinckney's change by a seven-to-four vote. Three New England states, Maryland, and the three Deep South states supported Pinckney's motion.[86]

Gouverneur Morris, still resisting a continuation of the slave trade, then proposed that the clause specifically declare that the "importation of slaves" be limited to the Carolinas and Georgia. Morris wanted it known "that this part of the Constitution was a compliance with those States." Having made this motion only to embarrass supporters of the trade, Morris withdrew it. By a seven-to-four vote the Convention then adopted the slave trade provision. The three New England states once again joined Maryland and the Deep South to allow the slave trade to continue for twenty years.[87] This vote formed a key component of the "dirty compromise."

On August 28 the Convention debated what would become the privileges and immunities clause of the Constitution. Charles Cotesworth Pinckney "seemed to wish some provision should be included in favor of property in slaves," but he did not press the point, and the

Convention accepted the clause with only South Carolina voting no. Pinckney's concern was apparently over the right of masters to travel from state to state with their slaves. In fact, those states which had already passed gradual emancipation statues, like Pennsylvania, had made provisions for slave transit. Perhaps for this reason, other southern delegates did not share Pinckney's concern. This seems to have been the only time during the Convention when southerners perceived a threat to slavery, but were unable to muster the votes, or perhaps their own energies, to head it off.[88]

The Convention immediately turned to the fugitives from justice clause. Butler and Charles Pinckney attempted to amend this provision "to require fugitive slaves and servants to be delivered up like criminals." Roger Sherman sarcastically countered that he "saw no more propriety in the public seizing and surrendering a slave or servant, than a horse." James Wilson objected that this would cost the northern states money. Significantly, this opposition came from two delegates who usually sided with the South. Butler wisely "withdrew his proposition in order that some particular provision might be made apart from this article."[89]

The next day, the debates over commerce, the slave trade, and fugitive slaves were all joined to complete the "dirty compromise." In a debate over the commerce clause Charles Pinckney, the younger and more impetuous of the two cousins, moved that a two-thirds majority be required for all commercial regulations. He argued that "the power of regulating commerce was a pure concession on the part of the S. States" and that therefore the two-thirds requirement was reasonable.[90]

General C. C. Pinckney agreed that "it was the true interest of the S. States to have no regulation of commerce." But, in one of the most revealing statements of the Convention, he explained his support for a clause requiring only a simple majority for passage of commercial legislation. Pinckney said he took this position because of "their [the eastern states'] liberal conduct towards the views of South Carolina." The "views of South Carolina" concerned the slave trade. In the margins of his notes Madison made this clear. Madison wrote that Pinckney meant the permission to import slaves.

> An understanding on the two subjects of navigation and slavery, had taken place between those parts of the Union, which explains the vote on the Motion depending, as well as the language of General Pinckney and others.

Other delegates confirm this analysis. Luther Martin later reported that "the eastern States, notwithstanding their aversion to slavery, were very willing to indulge the southern States, at least with a temporary liberty to prosecute the slave trade, provided the southern States would in their turn gratify them, by laying no restriction on navigation acts; and after a very little time, the committee by a great majority, agreed on a report, by which the general government was to be prohibited from preventing the importation of slaves for a limited time, and the restrictive clause relative to navigation acts was to be omitted."[91]

Subsequent debate confirmed that New Englanders and South Carolinians had indeed struck a bargain. Butler, for example, declared that the interests of the southern and eastern states were "as different as the interests of Russia and Turkey." Nevertheless, he was "desirous of conciliating the affections of the East" and so opposed the two-thirds requirement. The Virginians, who had opposed the slave trade provisions, now supported the demand for a two-thirds requirement for commercial legislation. But they were in the minority. South Carolina joined all the northern states to defeat the motion to require a two-thirds vote to regulate commerce. The Convention then adopted the clause allowing a simple majority to regulate commerce.[92]

Immediately after this vote, Butler reintroduced the fugitive slave clause. Without debate or recorded vote, it too passed.[93] The last bargain over slavery had been made. The northerners who had opposed the fugitive slave provision only a day before were now silent.

The debates of late August reveal how willing the northern delegates—especially the New Englanders—were to support slavery and the demands of the Deep South. Some years ago William W. Freehling argued the slave trade clause was adopted to "lure Georgia and South Carolina into the Union."[94] The Convention debates, however, suggest that the Deep South did not need to be lured into the Union; the delegates from the Carolinas and Georgia were already deeply committed to the Constitution by the time the slave trade debate occurred. Moreover, the South had already won major concessions on the three-fifths clause and the prohibition on taxing exports. These were permanent features of the Constitution, unlike the slave trade provision, which would lapse in twenty years. Although some southerners talked of not joining the Union unless the slave trade were allowed, it seems unlikely they would have risked going it alone over a temporary right of importation.[95]

This prospect is even more unlikely because at the time of the Convention none of these states was actively importing slaves from Africa. This fact cuts against Professor Earl Maltz's recent contention that giving Congress the "authority to ban the importation of new slaves" would "have done serious damage to the economies of a number of southern states."[96] From 1787 until 1803 South Carolina did not import any slaves from Africa. From 1803 to 1808 South Carolina imported about 80,000 new slaves. These importations created enormous human tragedies for the individual victims of the trade—and they doubtless provided huge profits to individual importers and purchasers—but these importations did not dramatically affect the economy of South Carolina or the Deep South.

The arguments of Freehling and Maltz rest on the assumption that the states of the Deep South would have rejected the Constitution over the right to import slaves in the future when they in fact were not currently importing them. Furthermore, even without constitutional protection for the slave trade, importations from Africa would have been legal until the Congress actually took the time, and mustered the votes, to prohibit them. At no time did the Convention consider a clause flatly prohibiting the trade; the entire debate was over whether the Constitution would explicitly protect the trade. Earl Maltz writes that "under the Articles of Confederation, no federal action against the slave trade was possible; if this is the appropriate starting point then even a delayed grant of authority over the importation of slaves must be considered antislavery and nationalistic."[97] However, this analysis ignores the fact that the slave trade clause is a specific exception to the general rule giving Congress complete power to regulate all commerce *but* slave importation. In essence, the Convention granted Congress the general power to regulate *all* international commerce except the African slave trade. It is not surprising that the South Carolina delegation considered this a great victory for their special interest in slave importations.[98]

However one views the African trade, it is hard to see how anyone could assert that the fugitive slave clause was also a "lure." Added at the last possible moment, without any serious debate or discussion, this clause was a boon to the South without any quid pro quo for the North. On this vote the northern delegates either did not understand the importance of the issue or were too tired to fight it.

The August debates also reveal that the northern delegates could have had no illusions about the nature of the covenant they were forming with the South. The northern delegates could not have forgotten General C. C. Pinckney's earlier assertion that "S. Carolina and

Georgia cannot do without slaves." While the "Fathers liked to call [slavery] temporary," the evidence of the Convention shows they should have known better.[99] Throughout the Convention the delegates from the slave states made no attempt to hide the fact that they believed slavery would be a permanent part of their culture and society. No one who attended the Philadelphia Convention could have believed that slavery was "temporary" in the South.

Toward Sectional Harmony

With the adoption of the commerce clause and the fugitive slave clause, the issues of immediate concern to slave owners seemed to be settled. However, on August 30 the debate over the domestic violence clause of what became Article IV of the Constitution led to renewed conflicts over slavery. Dickinson of Delaware attempted to delete the limitation that permitted the national government to intervene to prevent violence only "on the application" of a state legislature. This change would have allowed the national government, and not the states, to determine when intervention was necessary. The Convention quickly defeated this motion, with the five slave states voting no, apparently because they did not want the national government to interfere in their domestic affairs. However, on a vote to change the wording of the clause from "domestic violence" to "insurrections," the four slave states south of Virginia voted yes, but the motion lost five to six.[100] Fear of slave insurrections no doubt motivated the South to wish for explicit protection on this matter.

The Convention now turned to the numerous proposals which had been tabled throughout the summer. North-South cooperation was quite evident through the next two weeks. Motions introduced by a delegate from one section were often seconded by one from the other. Although some patterns of sectional voting can be found in these debates, they are rare and may be more coincidental than significant.[101] Some delegates, particularly Mason of Virginia, raised sectional fears. But by this time Mason was so clearly opposed to the Constitution that he was apparently willing to make any argument to derail the work of the Convention.[102]

Even on that divisive issue — the slave trade — the sectional compromise held. On September 10, the last day of debate before the Constitution went to a final Committee of Style, John Rutledge of South Carolina noted his opposition to the amendment procedure because "the articles relating to slaves might be altered by the states not interested in that property and prejudiced against it." At Rutledge's insistence the Convention added a clause forbidding any amendment of the slave trade provision and the capitation tax provision before 1808.[103] As they had throughout the Convention, the delegates from the Deep South left almost nothing to chance in their zeal to protect slavery.

Emerging from the Committee of Style on September 14, the penultimate version of the Constitution produced further debate on issues relating to slavery and sectionalism. On September 15 an attempt to increase the representation of North Carolina in the First Congress failed, on a strictly sectional vote. Similarly, the Convention rejected an attempt to change the clause on export taxes to make it yet more favorable to the South. Here, however, Maryland and South Carolina joined the North in defeating the measure.[104] The Convention's last substantive action on slavery-related matters concerned the fugitive slave clause. The Committee of Detail had reported the clause with the language "No person legally held to service or labour in one state escaping into another shall … be discharged from such service or labour.…" The Convention substituted the term "under the laws thereof" after the word "state" for the term "legally." The delegates made this change "in compliance with the wish of some who thought the term [legal] equivocal, and favoring the idea that slavery was legal in a moral view."[105] This was a minor victory for those who were squeamish about slavery, but it had no practical effect.

The Proslavery Compact

This final compromise over the wording of the fugitive slave clause was an entirely appropriate way to end discussion of slavery at the Convention. Throughout the Convention the delegates had fought over the place of slavery in the Constitution. A few delegates had expressed moral qualms over slavery, but most of the criticism had been political and economic. Northerners opposed representation for slavery because it would give the South a political advantage; Virginians opposed the slave trade, at least in part, because it would undermine the value of their excess slaves. The initial reaction to the fugitive slave clause typified this. When Pierce Butler and Charles Pinckney first proposed it, James Wilson complained, "This would oblige the Executive of the State to do it, at public expense."[106] The costs Wilson worried about were more financial than moral.

The word "slavery" was never mentioned in the Constitution, yet its presence was felt everywhere. The new wording of the fugitive slave clause was characteristic. Fugitive slaves were called "persons owing service or Labour," and the word "legally" was omitted so as not to offend northern sensibilities. Northern delegates could return home asserting that the Constitution did not recognize the legality of slavery. In the most technical linguistic sense they were perhaps right. Southerners, on the other hand, could tell their neighbors, as General Charles Cotesworth Pinckney told his, "We have obtained a right to recover our slaves in whatever part of America they may take refuge, which is a right we had not before."[107]

Indeed, the slave states had obtained significant concessions at the Convention. Through the three-fifths clause they gained extra representation in Congress. Through the Electoral College their votes for president were far more potent than the votes of northerners. The prohibition on export taxes favored the products of slave labor. The slave trade clause guaranteed their right to import new slaves for at least twenty years. The domestic violence clause guaranteed them federal aid if they should need it to suppress a slave rebellion. The limited nature of federal power and the cumbersome amendment process guaranteed that, as long as they remained in the Union, their system of labor and race relations would remain free from national interference. On every issue at the Convention, slave owners had won major concessions from the rest of the nation, and with the exception of the commerce clause they had given up very little to win these concessions. The northern delegates had been eager for a stronger Union with a national court system and a unified commercial system. Although some had expressed concern over the justice or safety of slavery, in the end they were able to justify their compromises and ignore their qualms.

At the close of the Convention two delegates, Elbridge Gerry of Massachusetts and George Mason of Virginia, explained why they could not sign the document they had helped create. Both had a plethora of objections that included slavery-related issues. But their objections were not grounded in moral or philosophical opposition to slavery; rather, like the arguments of those delegates who ultimately supported the compromises over slavery, the objections of Gerry and Mason were practical and political. Gerry objected to the three-fifths clause because it gave the South too much political power, at the expense of New England. Mason opposed allowing the slave trade to continue, because "such importations render the United States weaker, more vulnerable, and less capable of defense."[108]

During the ratification struggles others would take more principled stands against the compromises over slavery. A New Yorker complained that the Constitution condoned "drenching the bowels of Africa in gore, for the sake of enslaving its free-born innocent inhabitants." In New Hampshire, Joshua Atherton opposed ratification because it would make all Americans "consenters to, and partakers in, the sin and guilt of this abominable traffic." A Virginian thought the slave trade provision was an "excellent clause" for "an Algerian constitution: but not so well calculated (I hope) for the latitude of America."[109]

It was more than just the slave trade that northern antifederalists feared. Three opponents of the Constitution in Massachusetts noted that the Constitution bound the states together as a "whole" and "the states" were "under obligation ... reciprocally to aid each other in defense and support of every thing to which they are entitled thereby, right or wrong." Thus, they might be called to suppress a slave revolt or in some other way defend the institution. They could not predict how slavery might entangle them in the future, but they did know that "this lust for slavery, [was] portentous of much evil in America, for the cry of innocent blood, ... hath undoubtedly reached to the Heavens, to which that cry is always directed, and will draw down upon them vengeance adequate to the enormity of the crime."[110]

The events of 1861–1865 would prove the three Massachusetts antifederalists of 1788 correct. Only after a civil war of unparalleled bloodshed and three constitutional amendments could the Union be made more perfect, by finally expunging slavery from the Constitution.

Chapter 5

Planned Obsolescence?
The Constitution and Slavery

Mark A. Graber

Americans provide two accounts of the original constitutional relationship with slavery. The first maintains that the Framers believed that slavery was a dying institution whose accommodation was peripheral to core constitutional principles. Abraham Lincoln powerfully advanced this thesis during his debates with Stephen Douglas. "[T]he way our fathers originally left the slavery question," he proclaimed, "the institution was in the course of ultimate extinction, and the public mind rested in the belief that it *was* in the course of ultimate extinction."[1] Given powerful southern opposition to immediate emancipation, a few discrete protections for human bondage were necessary. Nevertheless, such basic elements of the constitutional order as enumerated powers and the structure of the Senate were designed for other, more elevated, purposes. The alternative perspective on the Constitution and slavery insists that sectional disputes influenced the entire constitutional design. John C. Calhoun offered such an understanding of the original constitutional order in his last speech before the Senate. He praised the Framers for establishing "nearly a perfect equilibrium between the two [sections], which afforded ample means to each to protect itself against the aggression of the other."[2] On this view, constitutional protections for slavery were not limited to the three-fifths clause, the twenty-year prohibition on federal laws banning the international slavery trade, and the fugitive slave clause. Instead, the entire structure and powers of the national government were influenced by concerns with establishing a balance of sectional power sufficient to enable the slave states to prevent an unwanted national abolition.

Whether, and the extent to which, the Constitution of the United States became obsolete after slavery was abolished partly depends on which account of the framing and ratification is more accurate. If constitutional protections for slavery in 1787 were limited to a few isolated compromises that served no other purpose, then basic constitutional institutions retained their vitality after the Civil War. The Thirteenth Amendment did not undermine the design of the national legislature because, on the Lincolnian view, the national legislature was structured in particular ways for reasons entirely independent of slavery. If, however, constitutional protections for slavery were woven into the fabric of the national government, then crucial constitutional practices may have become partly anachronistic in 1865. An Electoral College Calhoun thought designed to augment the representation of slave states would seem anachronistic after abolition removed any constitutional reason for privileging southern interests.

The textual omission of "slavery" or related words might support either conception of the original relationship between human bondage and the constitutional order. Madison insisted that Framers refused to mention slavery explicitly because they would not "admit in the Constitution the idea that there could be property in men."[3] From this perspective, the Framers provided Americans with a Constitution that could govern a slaveless society without any significant revision. Joseph Story insisted that constitutional provisions must be interpreted as "guard[ing] against the doctrines and principles prevailing in the non-slaveholding States by preventing them from intermeddling with or obstructing or abolishing the rights of the owners of slaves."[4] From this perspective, the constitutional failure to mention slavery explicitly was nothing more than an accommodation to Northern squea-mishness that had no substantive impact on the principles underlying the frame of government proposed in 1787.[5]

Constitutional history apparently supports Lincoln's emphasis on the discrete nature of constitutional protections for slavery. Reconstruction Republicans, when framing and ratifying the post-Civil War amendments, did not rethink such basic constitutional practices as representation in the national legislature, judicial review, and the separation of powers, all of which are alleged by some contemporary scholars to have been ac-commodations to southern interests in 1787.[6] With the exception of Section 1 of the Fourteenth Amendment, the post-Civil War amendments dealt entirely with the abolition of slavery, particular consequences of the Civil War, or southern treatment of former slaves. Section 1, interpreted broadly, provided a national standard for citizenship and realized Madison's original hope that state governments would be constitutionally obligated to honor certain fundamental rights.[7] No constitutional provision ratified in the wake of the Civil War explicitly altered the rules for staffing the federal government, the processes for making national laws, or the balance of power among national insti-tutions.[8]

The Thirteenth, Fourteenth, and Fifteenth Amendments powerfully challenge those who insist that the Constitution of 1787 was "saturated" with protections for human bondage.[9] If the original Constitution was as proslavery as commentators from Wendell Phillips[10] to Paul Finkelman[11] allege, why did antislavery advocates propose only relatively mild constitutional changes in the wake of the Civil War? The absence of more substantial constitutional changes is particularly puzzling because several constitutional practices adopted in 1787 were likely to have prosouthern biases after 1865. State equality in the Senate provided the less populous former slave states with the same two representatives in the upper chamber of Congress as the more populous Union states. Given that the Republican Party rose to power by calling for majority rule[12] and the House of Representatives had historically had far greater northern majorities than the Senate,[13] both principle and interest might have moved Reconstruction Republicans to replace the Constitution of 1787 with a modified version of the original Virginia Plan. That proposal, rejected by the Framers, would have apportioned the House of Representatives on the basis of population, and then have House majorities elect the other members of the national government.[14] The result would have been a national government more consistent with Republican commitments to majority rule and more likely to accommodate northern interests.

The Republican willingness to maintain constitutional provisions inconsistent with their principles and interests may be explained by southern perceptions of constitutional obsolescence during the years before the Civil War. Convinced that Americans were moving in a southwestwardly direction, most members of the framing convention and almost all prominent Southern federalists assumed proportional representation in the

House of Representatives and other constitutional arrangements would guarantee that slaveholders would exercise the control over the national government necessary to protect their interests.[15] These rules for staffing the national government and making national laws malfunctioned when the northwest was settled far more rapidly than anticipated. These demographic changes gave the free states both the numbers and population necessary to control all three branches of the national government.[16] Many slaveholders responded to these unforeseen developments by proposing new constitutional arrangements that might restore the original constitutional balance of sectional power.[17] Free state citizens scoffed at southern demands for constitutional reform. They had far more reason for insisting that all sides adhere to the original constitutional bargain that every decade provided northern states with increased political advantages than for demanding constitutional reform that might further augment northern political advantages. Moreover, constitutional provisions inconsistent with Republican commitments to majoritarianism served the Republican need for legitimacy. Lincoln and his political allies could impose their minority antislavery, later racially egalitarian, vision only if dissenting northerners nevertheless perceived Republican authority as justified. The Constitution provided the foundation for that perception. By not challenging the preexisting rules for gaining office and making laws, Lincoln and his political allies assured themselves of the loyalty of such northern Democrats as Stephen Douglas, whose support played a crucial role in the initial northern war effort.

This essay uses slavery as a case study in constitutional obsolescence. First it details the different roles slavery played during the framing debates, the northern ratification debates, and the southern ratification debates. Next, this essay explains how demographic trends, which made the Constitution increasing obsolete from a southern perspective, increased northern commitments to constitutional institutions and processes. Then it discusses some contemporary lessons that might be drawn from this American experience with slavery and constitutional obsolescence. Credible commitments, history suggests, may have a tendency to become increasingly obsolete over time. Time may, however, strengthen the important legitimacy function of the constitutional design.

Constitutions become obsolete when they fail to perform distinctive constitutional functions. American efforts to accommodate slaveholders provide a window into two such functions, credible commitments and legitimacy. Constitutions, American history from 1787 to 1860 suggests, may have difficulty over time securing original commitments. Entrenched laws initially thought to provide sufficient protections for particular interests may fail to function at all or have perverse effects. Persons who make or inherit such bad constitutional bargains, slaveholders learned, are often poorly placed to renegotiate arrangements. Constitutions as legitimizing mechanisms fare better. The primary function of a constitution may be to provide a set of background rules for politics that most persons agree authorize persons who gain office by those rules to implement their political program. Republicans may not have sought to amend perceived un-Republican constitutional provisions because they preferred a constitution that their northern opponents agreed authorized rule by Republican elected officials to a constitution with more majoritarian rules for electing national officials. An Abraham Lincoln who gains office playing by preexisting rules may be seen by more people as wielding legitimate power than the first president elected under a constitution drafted and ratified by that person's supporters, even if the newer constitution is more democratic than the Constitution of 1789 and the first president elected under the regime gains a greater proportion than Lincoln of the popular vote.

In the Beginning

The original constitutional debates over slavery varied by convention and section. The persons who framed the Constitution of the United States confronted human bondage and related sectional issues during discussions over every facet of their proposed new political order. Concerns with the "peculiar institution" influenced the design of basic constitutional institutions, the nature of the powers given the national government, and specific restrictions on governing authority. Human bondage was not as pervasive a presence during the ratification conventions held in the few states where slavery had recently been abolished and other states that would soon abolish that practice. Debates north of the Mason-Dixon line over the constitutional status of slavery focused almost entirely on the provisions governing fugitive slaves, the international slave trade, and the counting of slaves during apportionment. When northern federalists and antifederalists debated the structure of the federal government, their concerns were over whether national institutions promoted the public good or an interested aristocracy. Neither *The Federalist Papers* nor any other important commentary pitched at New York, Connecticut, or Massachusetts betrayed any concern with the probable balance of power between the sections in the new regime. Slavery was, unsurprisingly, debated with more vigor and in more contexts during southern ratification conventions. Virginia and South Carolina Framers sought to assure their peers that a national government with limited, enumerated powers had no authority to pass laws promoting emancipation. In sharp contrast to their allies in Massachusetts, New York and Pennsylvania, such slave state federalists as David Ramsay and James Madison highlighted how population growth in the South was likely to give the slave states the political as well as the legal power to control the timing of any future emancipation.

Whether the Constitution became obsolete after emancipation (or before) partly depends on which convention or conventions provided the underlying foundations for national institutions. When members of the framing convention discussed slavery, they typically did so when considering provisions unaffected by the Thirteenth, Fourteenth and Fifteenth Amendments. Concerns with sectional accommodations, for example, influenced the process for selecting the president, a process that was not modified after the Civil War. When members of the ratifying conventions held in free states discussed slavery, they typically did so when considering those discrete constitutional provisions and practices that did not survive Appomattox. The Thirteenth Amendment repealed both the fugitive slave clause and the three-fifths clause of the original Constitution. Section 2 of the Thirteenth Amendment empowered the federal government to emancipate slaves within existing states, a power southern federalists in 1787 repeatedly denied could be exercised by the national legislature. The southern federalist claim that constitutional institutions provided slave states the political power necessary to control national institutions, by comparison, became obsolete long before Lincoln was elected president. The Constitution South Carolinians ratified was undermined by population shifts, not by subsequent constitutional amendments.

Framing

The persons who framed the Constitution of the United States were always conscious of the balance of power between the free and slave states. Sectional issues were on the table when specific constitutional protections for slavery were under discussion and when national institutions were being designed. Robert Weir observes, "[s]lavery was an ever-present incubus" during the Philadelphia convention, "dominating some very explicit debates and affecting questions in which the words 'slave' and 'slavery' were never mentioned."[18] The most important of these controversies was the debate over how the national legislature should be staffed. Conventional accounts insist that the Constitutional Convention during the early summer was deadlocked between large states and small states. Large states favored allocating representation by population. Small states favored allocating representation by state. James Madison perceived the conflict differently. His speech on July 14, 1787 observed, "the real difference of interests lay, not between the large & small but between the N. & Southn. States." "The institution of slavery & its consequences," he stated, "formed the line of discrimination."[19] Slaveholders championed allocated representation by population, particularly when slaves were considered as part of the population. Confident that southern territories would be settled far more rapidly than northern territories, Pierce Butler of South Carolina favored "abolishing State Legislatures" should representation "proceed on a principle favorable to the wealth as well as the numbers of free inhabitants."[20] No prominent slaveholder supported the New Jersey plan, which was drawn up by delegates from small, northern states.

The compromises over the design and powers of national institutions necessary to forge a consensus at the framing convention were as influenced by concerns with the future of human bondage as with the balance of power between larger and smaller states. Members of the framing convention structured the national government in ways they thought would guarantee a united coalition of slave states the political power necessary to determine when and whether any future emancipation would take place. When Butler insisted, "the security the Southn. States want is that their negroes may not be taken from them,"[21] the security he wanted was adequate representation in the national legislature. Hugh Williamson of North Carolina pointed out, "[t]he Southn. Interest must be extremely endangered" if "[t]he Northn. States are to have a majority in the first instance and means of perpetrating it."[22] The Great Compromise alleviated these concerns. The House of Representatives, apportioned by population, was thought to provide sufficient political support for the rapidly growing slave states. The Senate, apportioned by jurisdiction, was thought to provide sufficient political support for the more numerous free states. When the Congress was functioning as originally expected, no proposal could become law without enjoying some support in a southern-tilting branch of the national government and a northern-tilting branch of the national government.

Sectional equilibrium would be a permanent feature of American constitutional politics as long as constitutional institutions functioned and population grew as the Framers expected. Expansion would not upset constitutional arrangements. The territories as a whole could neither be fashioned in the image of the free or slave states as long as the constitutional processes for staffing national institutions and making national policy forced the sections to share power. This shared control over the governance of existing territories, the acquisition of new territories, and the admission of new states, in turn, provided practical guarantees that expansion would not threaten the original balance of power between the North and South. Having designed institutions they believed would guarantee political equilibrium between the sections, members of the framing convention felt no need to enshrine precise legal limits on congressional power to regulate slavery in the territories. Prominent delegates understood that human bondage would be prohibited in the more northern territories and permitted in the more southern territories. More specific arrangements for future territories and territorial governance were unnecessary as long as constitutional arrangements ensured that neither a united coalition of slave states nor a united coalition of free states could unilaterally dictate the course of American expansion.

The presidency and the federal judiciary were designed with slavery in mind. Madison supported the Electoral College because that institution would ensure southern "influence on the election on the score of Negroes."[23] A popular vote was objectionable, Williamson agreed, because "slaves will have no suffrage."[24] Southerners who favored proportional representation in both Houses of Congress initially favored vesting the Senate with power to appoint federal justices. Shortly after the Senate was apportioned by state, Virginians successfully moved the nomination power to the president. As Madison pointed out, allowing the Senate to select justices would "throw the appointments entirely into the hands of ye Nthern States."[25]

The Philadelphia convention's decision to enumerate national powers was also influenced by concerns with human bondage, although differences between the delegates transcended simple sectionalism. Southern representatives divided on the merits of a strong federal government with relatively amorphous powers. Madison and Charles Pinkney of South Carolina favored giving Congress supervisory power over local legislation. Both thought that "the national government shd. have the authority to negative all [state] Laws which they judge to be improper."[26] Armed with such power, they may have believed, a southern tilting national government could veto hostile free state laws. Other southern Framers, most notably Butler and Edward Rutledge, opposed the national veto. Rutledge seems to be the person most responsible for the decision to enumerate powers rather than give the federal government the power to act on all matters of national interest. He did so, historians suggest, in large part because he was concerned that a federal government with broad, undefined powers might emancipate slaves.[27]

What Rutledge and Madison shared was an understanding that basic questions about federal powers could be determined only in light of how those powers would influence slaveholding. They and other Framers entrenched particular constitutional language because they believed the words chosen would fashion the governmental arrangements that would maximize southern control over human bondage. Had those southern Framers not owned slaves or shared other sectional interests, they might well have supported very different conceptions of federal power. The decision to enumerate and the specific powers enumerated, this historical record indicates, cannot be understood without reference to perceived effects on national power to protect or abolish slavery.

The post-Civil War amendments addressed none of the major sectional issues that most excited the persons who framed the Constitution. Reconstruction Republicans did not alter representation in either the House or Senate, they did not abolish the Electoral College, and they did not return to the Senate the power to appoint federal justices. Congressional leaders after the Civil War did not see any need to rethink the original debate over enumerated powers in light of emancipation. To the extent that the Framers in 1787 choose specific constitutional institutions and processes at least in part for the purpose of providing political protections for slavery, the failure of Reconstruction to alter the staffing of the national government, the rules for making national laws, and the relationships between national institutions had the practical effect of maintaining constitutional arrangements that, from the perspective of the original constitutional order, were obsolete. Governing institutions framed in the light of slavery were left untouched with the death of human bondage.

Ratification

The persons who ratified the Constitution of the United States engaged in very different discussions about slavery in the separate state conventions. Americans from all sections were interested in the constitutional status of human bondage. Many northerners worried that the drafters made too many concessions to slavery. Southerners feared federal power to emancipate their human chattel. The ratification debates over slavery, however, placed more emphasis on discrete legal protections for human bondage and less on the basic design of national institutions than the debates in Philadelphia. Northern federalists and antifederalists disputed whether the twenty-year moratorium on federal laws banning the international slave trade promoted freedom or bondage. Southern federalists and antifederalists fought over whether such provisions as the necessary and proper clause might provide a constitutional excuse for emancipation. The balance of sectional power during the ratification debates was almost exclusively a southern concern. Slaveholding proponents of ratification assured their peers a rapidly growing South would have the representation in Congress necessary veto hostile free state proposals. Free state ratifiers rarely discussed this sectional matter.

Slavery and the Northern Ratification Debates

The Federalist Papers exemplifies how northern ratifiers discussed slavery. Madison, Hamilton, and Jay only briefly comment on human bondage in those essays, which were intended to encourage ratification in New York. *Federalist* No. 42 spends a few words noting that the federal government will have the power after 1808 to ban the international slave trade. Madison insists this was a "great point gained in favor of humanity."[28] *Federalist* No. 54 comments at greater length on the constitutional provision which treats slaves as three-fifths of a person when representation and taxation are apportioned. Madison, after considering various justifications for that provision, urges New Yorkers to consider the matter a "compromising expedient of the Constitution."[29] Northerners interested in the constitutional status of fugitive slaves would learn almost nothing from *The Federalist Papers*. Republicans reading *The Federalist Papers* after the Civil War could justifiable conclude that the Thirteenth Amendment fully excised the slavery wart from the body politic.

The Federalist Papers provides readers with no hint of the slavery debates that took place during the drafting convention. Every governing institution and practice, from the structure of the national legislature to the enumeration of powers, is defended in light of republican principles. Madison justifies state equality in the Senate as a means for achieving state influence on national politics, not as a counterbalance to a southern tilting House of Representatives. The Electoral College was justified as means for ensuring an intelligent presidential selection. "[T]he immediate election," Hamilton writes, "should be made by men most capable of analyzing the qualities adapted to the station, and acting under circumstances favourable to deliberation."[30] Madison does not repeat to a New York audience his observation during the framing convention that the Electoral College would augment the vote of slave states.

The ratification debates in the northern states largely took place within the parameters marked out by *The Federalist Papers*. When antifederalists and federalists debated whether specific provisions of the Constitution provided undue protection for slaveholding, they focused exclusively on the moratorium on prohibiting the international slave trade, the fugitive slave clause, and the three-fifths clause. Antifederalists insisted that these limits on federal power violated fundamental human rights. Federalists responded that discrete constitutional protections for slaveholding were necessary to form a national government. Some emphasized that the twenty-year moratorium implicitly acknowledged that the federal government was authorized to ban the international slave trade after 1808.[31] Most important, northern federalists treated these provisions as the crucial compromises between the free and slave state delegates at the drafting convention. The great compromise, in ratification debates held in New York, Massachusetts and neighboring jurisdictions, was between the larger and smaller states. The most important compromise over slavery that northern delegates in Philadelphia reached was the decision to yield temporary restrictions on federal power over the international slave trade for increased national authority over commerce.

Comments about the three-fifths clause aside, participants in free state debates over the Constitution almost never mentioned sectional issues when discussing the structure of national institutions or the general powers vested in the national government. Northern antifederalists complained about a federal government that would promote an aristocratic elite.[32] They did not criticize the Electoral College for augmenting the power of slaveholders. Brutus condemned the Supreme Court as a vehicle for destroying state governments.[33] He did not inform readers that justices appointed by southern tilting presidents would likely offer proslavery interpretations of ambiguous constitutional provisions or constitutional silences.

Local federalists and antifederalists were more inclined than Publius to make general comments about whether the free state representatives at the Philadelphia convention had been sufficiently antislavery. These comments, however, were rarely directed at specific constitutional institutions. William Rotch Sr., complained of a "Government, which so much favors Slavery," but pointed to no specific constitutional provision that supported his indictment.[34] The *Salem Mercury* ridiculed antifederalist pretensions, noting that "the Hon. Richard Henry Lee, Esq. of Virginia, who has written so much about the danger of losing our LIBERTY by the adoption of the New Constitution, is the master of several hundred slaves."[35] That editorial comment did not indicate how the Constitution might influence that species of property.

The northern debates over the Constitution provide good reasons for thinking that the Constitution did not become obsolete after emancipation. The only constitutional protections free state citizens perceived the Constitution as providing slaveholders either expired before the Civil War or were repealed by the Thirteenth Amendment. The twenty-year moratorium on federal laws banning the international slave trade had no legal force after 1809. The fugitive slave clause was a dead letter after 1865. Reconstruction Republicans who took *The Federalist Papers* and other cotemporaneous commentaries on the Constitution seriously would find no reason to adjust the constitutional rules for staffing the national government or making national laws. Those sources indicated that basic constitutional arrangements served legitimate purposes unrelated to either slavery or the sectional balance of power. Constitutional institutions might have become obsolete for reasons other than emancipation. The Electoral College, in particular, never functioned as Framers from all sections of the country expected. Nevertheless, judging only from the perspective provided by northern ratification debates, the post-Civil War amendments did not change underlying constitutional commitment to liberty and republicanism in ways that should have forced antislavery Americans to rethink how the federal government was staffed, enacted laws, and exercised powers. Liberty and republicanism were extended, not altered, at least as the Thirteenth, Fourteenth, and Fifteenth Amendments are read in light of *The Federalist Papers*.

An originalist might think no more analysis need be done to support the Lincolnian position that emancipation would not undermine any core constitutional practice. During the debates over the Jay Treaty, Madison forcefully asserted that constitutional meanings were imprinted by the ratification conventions, not the drafting convention. He informed the Fourth Congress,

> [W]hatever veneration might be entertained for the body of men who formed our Constitution, the sense of that body could never be regarded as the oracular guide in expounding the Constitution. As the instrument came from them, it was nothing more than the draft of a plan, nothing but a dead letter, until life and validity were breathed into it by the voice of the people, speaking through the several state conventions. If we were to look, therefore, for the meaning of the instrument beyond the face of the instrument, we must look for it, not in the General Convention, which proposed, but in the State Conventions, which accepted and ratified the Constitution.[36]

Madison was concerned with the meaning of constitutional provisions, but his analysis holds for their underlying purposes. To the extent free state citizens understood the structure of the national legislature to be a compromise between the smaller and larger states, then whether the constitution was obsolete depended on whether that compromise between Pennsylvania and New Jersey was still justified. That the persons who framed the Constitution understood the same provisions as compromises between the free and slave states had, in the words of Gilbert and Sullivan's Mikado, "nothing to do with the case." Ratifiers, not drafters, determine the purpose of constitutional arrangements, and northerners did not ratify a Constitution whose institutions were designed to protect slavery.

Problems of constitutional obsolescence nevertheless remain, even if many standard problems with discerning original understandings are ignored.[37] Slavery played a different role during southern ratification conventions, one closer but not identical to the role slavery played during the framing convention. Moreover, over time, northerners learned that the Constitution was more proslavery in practice than the ratification debates north of the Mason-Dixon line suggested. Free-state delegates who either assumed that the Senate would be a bastion of antislavery sentiment or did not give the matter much thought had every reason to rethink their constitutional commitments once population trends made clear that an unreconstructed upper chamber of Congress would privilege southern interests both before and after the Civil War.

Southern Ratification Conventions

The constitutional debates over slavery that took place during the southern ratification conventions differed in several respects from debates at both the framing convention and at northern ratifying conventions. Delegates at the Virginia and South Carolina conventions more often and more explicitly articulated needs to accommodate slaveholding than delegates at the framing and northern state conventions. Southern Framers also insisted they had gained a concession not mentioned in Philadelphia, a guarantee that the national government would not have the power to interfere with slavery in an existing state. In sharp contrast to northern federalists, slave state federalists bluntly claimed that governing institutions were structured in ways likely to privilege southern interests. The resulting slave state constitution became obsolete before rather than after emancipation.

The southern delegates at state ratifying conventions were very concerned with the status of slavery in the new republic. Participants raised questions about federal power to emancipate slaves and federal power to control the expansion of slavery. Antifederalists worried that a strong national government would deny slaveholders access to western territories and promote abolition. Federalists insisted that the South had obtained a very good constitutional bargain. Federalists in South Carolina maintained that slaveholding would thrive after ratification. David Ramsay sought to allay southern fears that the international slave trade would ever be prohibited, insisting that "[t]he more rice we make, the more business will be for [northern] shipping: their interest will therefore coincide with our's."[38] Federalists in Virginia more circumspectly claimed that slaveholders would determine the fate of human bondage in Virginia. "Even South Carolina herself," Edmund Randolph informed fellow delegates, "conceived [slave] property to be secure."[39]

Southern federalists insisted that enumerated powers provided a vital legal safeguard against abolition, a legal guarantee rarely mentioned at the framing convention or northern ratifying conventions. Charles Cotesworth Pinckney proudly informed fellow South Carolinians that "we have a security that the general government can never emancipate them, for no such authority is vested."[40] Federalists in Virginia agreed that the Constitution did not vest the national government with the legal authority to emancipate slaves. "No power," Madison bluntly declared, "is given to the General Government to interpose with respect to the property in slaves now held by the States."[41] Randolph similarly found no constitutional provision "that has a tendency to the abolition of slavery."[42]

Proponents of ratification in Virginia and South Carolina consistently commented on the balance of sectional power. Southern Federalists insisted that population trends would enable slaveholding interests to control the national government. "We shall soon out number them in as great a degree as they do us at this time," George Nicholas confidently declared at the Virginia Ratification Convention. "Therefore," he concluded, "this Government will be very shortly to our favor."[43] South Carolinians advanced similar sentiments. Edward Rutledge declared, "we should, in the course of a few years rise high in our representation, whilst other states would keep their present position."[44] Unlike the participants at the drafting convention, southern federalists did not link their beliefs about population growth to the structure of particular national institutions. Madison aside, no slaveholder pointed out likely future differences between the House and Senate when sectional issues arose. Nevertheless, southern federalists sent a clear message to their constituents that national institutions were well suited to ensure that slave state interests would always be privileged in federal councils.

From the perspective of the southern ratification debates, the 1830s presented more challenging problems of constitutional obsolescence than the 1860s. Reconstruction Republicans cured some problems with the Constitution the slave states ratified in 1791. If the original Constitution did prohibit federal laws emancipating slaves, that prohibition was repealed by the Thirteenth Amendment. Time cured others. The misplaced southern confidence in 1788 that the House of Representatives would be controlled by slaveholders hardly provided Republicans during Reconstruction with a reason for modifying what became the most northern dominated institution of the national government. The serious problem with the Constitution that slave states ratified, from the slave state perspective, occurred long before shots were fired at Fort Sumter. To the extent slaveholders correctly claimed that constitutional institutions were intended to vest a united South with at least a veto power over national legislation and that promised control depended on population moving in a southwestward direction, the Constitution became obsolete when, as was the case from the beginning of the Republic, population in the Northwest substantially outstripped population in the Southwest. The Constitution of southern federalism began malfunctioning during the first decade of the nineteenth century and had ceased to serve its original purposes by the Compromise of 1850.

Obsolescence Over Time

Constitutions become obsolete for one of two reasons.[45] First, constitutional means fail to function as expected. The Electoral College was never a deliberative body. "Extend[ing] the sphere"[46] of politics over time did more to facilitate than inhibit two party politics. Second, citizens reject original constitutional values. Jacksonians preferred a majoritarian democracy to the aristocratic republic intended by the Framers.[47] Increased social commitments to pluralism are wreaking havoc with the original understandings of the First Amendment.[48] In constitutionalism, interestingly enough, two wrongs sometimes make a right. Obsolete constitutional ends may be maintained when their original end also suffers from obsolescence. A nondeliberative Electoral College is far more consistent with the contemporary rejection of aristocratic politics than the institution intended by the Framers, even if that contemporary institution is probably inconsistent with contemporary democratic commitments.

Americans from ratification until the Civil War experienced both forms of constitutional obsolescence. Constitutional institutions failed to maintain the original framing commitment to the balance of sectional power. Many Americans rejected that constitutional end. Free-state citizens who rejected the original framing commitment to the balance of sectional power were unconcerned with the diminished constitutional capacity to generate a political leadership that would guarantee that all public policies enjoyed some support north and south of the Mason-Dixon line. Southerners perceived these same constitutional developments with horror.

Constitutional obsolescence from ratification to Reconstruction was in the eyes of the beholder. An increasing number of slaveholders over time perceived the crucial constitutional provisions as obsolete. From their perspective, basic constitutional commitments were threatened when unexpected population growth in the northwest gave free-state majorities opportunities to control the national government. Southern constitutional histories emphasized how the Framers drafted and slaveholders ratified a Constitution thought to guarantee a sectional balance of power. This account of American constitutional development treated Lincoln's election as a constitutional malfunction, an instance where constitutional means failed to promote vital constitutional ends. From the northern perspective, demographic trends had no constitutional significance. The Constitution free states ratified was indifferent on sectional control over national institutions. Lincoln felt no constitutional obligation to appeal to slave state voters if he could gain a majority of the Electoral College by other means. The fate of the original constitutional order was sealed when Lincoln and his political allies refused to so support the constitutional changes southerners thought necessary to restore the original balance of power between the sections.

The Southern Perception

Slaveholders had reason to perceive the Constitution as obsolete shortly after ratification. As settlers and immigrants moved northwestward, rather than in the expected southwesterly direction, northern state population increases easily outstripped southern state population increases.[49] These demographic developments significantly affected the balance of sectional power in the national government. Although no state below the Mason-Dixon line abandoned slavery from 1787 to 1860 and no territory in which slavery was permitted before *Dred Scott v. Sandford* became a free state, free state majorities increased in the House of Representations after every census. By 1860, less than two-fifths of the members in the lower chamber of the national government hailed from states where slavery was legal. Erroneous Southern predictions that the more northern realms of the Louisiana Purchase would remain barren for a century[50] combined with pressures to admit California as a free state eventually doomed the balance rule in the Senate. By the time Lincoln was elected to the presidency, six more Senators represented free states than slave states. These northern advantages were likely to increase in the near future as free state population continued to grow and territories north of the Missouri compromise line applied for statehood.

The precise moment the Constitution became obsolete from a southern perspective is contestable. From 1787 until 1860 Americans devised various subconstitutional means for maintaining government by bisectional consensus. Sectional balance in the Senate, a national party system that required presidential aspirants to gain southern support, and secessionist threats all created inducements for a sufficient number of free-state representations to support measures sufficiently proslavery to maintain union.[51] Congress in 1837 divided the federal judiciary into nine circuits, five of which were entirely within the slave states. Jacksonian presidents then guaranteed a Supreme Court sympathetic to southern interests by staffing that institution with one representative from each circuit. The politicians who urged federal courts to resolve whether Congress could ban slavery in the territories were well aware that a judiciary so constituted was unlikely to make decisions inconsistent with broadly shared southern constitutional understandings.

By 1860, the Constitution had become obsolete from any rational southern perspective. Members of the framing convention had designed a system for selecting the president that they believed would guarantee a chief execute who enjoyed substantial southern support. That system malfunctioned when Abraham Lincoln was elected. Lincoln gained a clear majority of the electoral votes, even though he made no effort to campaign in any state where slavery was legal. Rather than force presidential candidates to articulate national platforms, the Electoral College by the mid-nineteenth century provided a means by which antislavery candidates could gain office by appealing only to bare majorities in most, not all, of the free states. An obsolete system for selecting the president also rendered obsolete the rules for staffing the federal judiciary. As noted above, the Framers vested the president with the power to appoint Supreme Court justices in part because the president was thought likely to be more sympathetic to southern interests than the Senate. A president elected entirely by free-state votes was unlikely to prefer justices known to be sympathetic to proslavery constitutional understandings. Indeed, almost immediately after secession, Congress adjusted the federal court system in ways that, assuming the president continued to ensure that each federal circuit was represented on the Supreme Court, would guarantee an 7–2 (later 8–2) free-state majority.

Southerners recognized these constitutional failings, but lacked the power to make the necessary constitutional adjustments. John C. Calhoun's valedictory speech to the Senate asserted, "the equilibrium between the two sections, in the Government as it stood when the constitution was ratified … has been destroyed."[52] Southern moderates and northern conservatives worked feverishly during the secession winter to develop a package of constitutional amendments that might restore the original framing commitment to a balance of section power. Proposals included dividing the executive power between a free and slave state president and extending the Missouri compromise to the Pacific Ocean in order to increase the number of slave states. Southerners alleged northern violations when seceding, but the events of 1860–61 are better explained by constitutional obsolescence (from the southern perspective) than constitutional infidelity.

Northern Perceptions

The same population trends that explain southern perceptions that the Constitution was obsolete might, but did not, engender similar northern perceptions. Free-state representatives at the framing convention favored state equality in the Senate as a means for securing a national institution somewhat biased to northern interests. That protection quickly proved unnecessary. The northern fear of a House of Representatives dominated by slaveholders faded as the number of free state citizens increased. Instead, both before and immediately after the Civil War, a good case can be made that the Senate had become obsolete from the perspective of northern Framers. That branch of the national legislature, after the Mexican War, was far more likely to privilege slave state interests. The Wilmot Proviso, for example, frequently passed the House only to be defeated in the Senate. Every reason existed for thinking that an unreconstructed Senate would continue privileging southern interests after the Civil War. Republicans and northerners nevertheless seemed indifferent to the continued existence of a governing institution biased toward ex-slaveholders' constitutional visions and policy preferences. No effort was made during Reconstruction to abolish or reconstruct a Senate likely to overrepresent southern concerns.

The increased Republican and northern commitment to democratic majoritarianism provided a second reason for modifying or abandoning inherited constitutional institutions that reflected an eighteenth century commitment to a republican aristocracy. Eric Foner points out that Republicans before the Civil War placed at least as much emphasis on majority rule as human freedom.[53] Lincoln's first inaugural declared, "[a] majority, held in restraint by constitutional checks, and limitations, is the only true sovereign of a free people."[54] To a remarkable degree, these majoritarian commitments inspired antislavery northerners to make the same complaints against the Constitution as do some contemporary constitutional critics.[55] Whigs condemned the veto power.[56] Radical Republicans sought to dismantle the Supreme Court.[57] Nevertheless, once Republicans obtained control over the national government, they made no effort to alter constitutional principles that, in light of their values, seemed obsolete.

Several factors may explain why northerners did not revise the constitutional practices for staffing the national government or making national laws. As Madison had hoped, elected officials north of the Mason-Dixon line had powerful incentives to maintain the constitutional rules by which they obtained office.[58] Such states as Delaware, New Jersey, and Connecticut had no more reason in 1868 than in 1787 for supporting the Virginia Plan's proposal to apportion by population representation in all governing institutions. As Madison had also hoped, the Union was also tied together by a cult of the

Constitution.[59] Republican efforts to tinker with the Constitution, beyond measures deemed necessary to abolish the badges and incidents of slavery, would have been deemed sacrilegious. Witness the consequences when Franklin Roosevelt attacked the Supreme Court in 1936.[60]

The debates in the free-state ratifying conventions also help explain why Republicans after the Civil War retained constitutional institutions that the Framers designed in part to privilege slaveholding constitutional visions and policy preferences. As noted above, in sharp contrast to some free-state Framers, the free-state representatives at the state conventions approved a constitution whose institutions were indifferent to the national balance of power. *The Federalist Papers* described a Senate designed to promote federalism and stability, not distinctive sectional concerns. Northern attitudes toward federalism did shift between 1787 and 1868. Nevertheless, that change, as well as increased free-state commitments to majoritarianism, were not of a dimension to generate a consensus, or even a strong political movement, committed to the proposition that national institutions needed adjusting in light of the changed values of the American people.

Republicans may have recognized that their forbearances made what turned out to be a better constitutional bargain than their slaveholding counterparts. The Constitution the free states had ratified in 1787 could be improved slightly from the perspective of 1860 or 1868. Nevertheless, in the struggle for public opinion and legitimacy, antislavery proponents may have better secured their emancipatory and egalitarian goals by posing as the champion of the original constitutional order, rather than proposing wide-ranging constitutional reforms. By pledging allegiance to the Constitution as written, antislavery activists could attract to their cause those Americans who, while indifferent to slavery, venerated constitutional forms. At the very least, this commitment to playing by the constitutional rules enabled Lincoln and his political allies to retain crucial support for administration policies after secession. Stephen Douglas spent the last months of his life rallying Democrats against those states that had refused to recognize the legitimate constitutional winner of the 1860 elections.[61]

Lincoln's statements before and after the election demonstrate that he recognized the force of constitutional legitimacy. He refused to call for a constitutional amendment repealing the three-fifths clause on the ground that that constitutional provision was "in the bond" the sections had constitutionally made with each other.[62] He initially defined the Civil War as necessary to preserve constitutional forms. When addressing a Union rally in 1863, Lincoln asserted, "among free men, there can be no successful appeal from the ballot to the bullet."[63] Had Lincoln been known as a proponent of constitutional changes, these appeals might have fallen on deaf ears. Instead, they rallied the number of free-state citizens necessary to win the Civil War. Strict adherence to a slightly imperfect Constitution, Lincoln recognized, was sound political strategy. Constitutional fidelity was a means for legitimizing otherwise radical constitutional claims and policy choices. Besides, as the election of 1860 demonstrated, northerners had obtained a good constitutional deal, even if that deal might have been improved with a little more tinkering.

Contemporary Lessons?

Slavery seems a strange matter to discuss in a volume dedicated to exploring whether the Constitution of the United States is obsolete. Americans abolished slavery in 1865.

Constitutional protections for slavery were not simply obsolete after the Thirteenth Amendment was ratified. They were legal nullities. To the extent the Framers were wrong to compromise with slavery in 1787, the post-Civil War amendments corrected that error.

Or did they? On many accounts, the Constitution of 1787 is saturated with concessions to slavery. Had Americans not owned slaves, the Congress might have been apportioned differently, Americans might have a different system for electing the president, Supreme Court justices might select federal justices, federal powers might not be enumerated, and federalism might have had a different structure. Americans who complain that constitutional institutions are obsolete frequently point to such arrangements as the Electoral College, which were partly designed to privilege slaveholding interests. Indeed, judging from the framing debates, a fair case can be made that Americans for more than 150 years have been governed by institutional arrangements that were designed to provide protection for a practice that no longer existed.

The American experience with slavery illustrates some problems with constitutional obsolescence. To repeat a previous observation, constitutional obsolescence is in the eye of the beholder. Whether proportional representation became obsolete depended on whether one believed the House was supposed to represent people or be a bastion for southern interests. Whether Article V is obsolete depends on whether one believes that supermajorities, maybe superdupermajorities, ought to be required for any significant constitutional change. Recourse to the framing will not help. Different states ratified different constitutions. New Hampshire ratified a more antislavery Constitution than South Carolina. Moreover, constitutional institutions that outgrow some functions sometimes develop different functions more in line with the spirit of the times. Northern Republicans had no objection to population trends that vested them with the power to control the national executive. We do not amend Article II at present, even though presidents are not, as the Framers intended, above parties because we no longer share the original animus to two party politics.

The American experience with slavery also raises questions about the constitutional capacity to make credible commitments. Such commitments are often understood as a central purpose of constitutionalism.[64] Persons want guarantees that majorities will not abridge religious freedom, confiscate property, or free slaves. Hard-to-amend constitutional provisions are one standard means for establishing such credible commitments. The Constitution guarantees rights by entrenching constitutional protections for contracts and provisions augmenting the representation for slaveholders. The possibility exists, however, that owing to unforeseen changes, constitutional protections may lose their value. Debtors may discover new means not constitutionally prohibited for avoiding paying debts. Population increases may convert institutions thought to be conducive to slave-state interests into free-state enclaves. Should such events happen, the victims of these changes will have no constitutional recourse. Worse, the provisions their ancestors thought would lock in advantages may now provide practically unamendable boons to their rivals. To the extent we cannot predict the future, the slaveholding experience cautions, we may find that any renewed attempts to entrench credible commitments may have consequences as perverse as those provisions originally thought to protect slaveholding.

Entrenched constitutional provisions may better function to promote legitimacy than credible commitments. Candidates who win elections playing by the constitutional rules they did not create may have more legitimacy than candidates who win playing by rules of their invention. Legitimacy has limits. Witness the Civil War. On the other hand, crucial northern Democrats rallied around Lincoln precisely because they perceived Republicans as the party that had won an election fairly, as fairly was defined constitutionally. This experience might caution those who champion new constitutional arrangements. Given that no agreement exists on the best form of democratic constitutionalism, Americans may be better off retaining the old Constitution than experimenting with a new one. Professors Levinson and Amar may be correct that new constitutions may in theory be ratified by popular majorities. The question remains whether those new constitutions can be peaceably enforced.

PART FOUR

The Electoral College: End It or Mend It?

Chapter 6

Why the U.S. Needs Direct Election of the President

George C. Edwards III

Political equality lies at the core of democratic theory. Robert Dahl, the leading democratic theorist, includes equality in voting as a central standard for a democratic process: "Every member must have an equal and effective opportunity to vote, and all votes must be counted as equal."[1] Indeed, it is difficult to imagine a definition of democracy that does not include equality in voting as a central standard.

Because political equality is a central standard for democratic government, we must evaluate any current or proposed mechanism for selecting the president against it. A popular misconception is that electoral votes simply aggregate popular votes. In reality, the electoral vote regularly deviates from the popular will as expressed in the popular vote, sometimes merely in curious ways, usually by strengthening the victory margin of the popular vote leader, but at other times in such a way as to deny the presidency to the people's preferred candidate.

The percentage of electoral votes received by a candidate nationwide rarely coincides with the candidate's percentage of the national popular vote for several reasons, the most important of which is the winner-take-all (or unit-vote) system.[2] All states except Maine and Nebraska have a winner-take-all system in which they award *every* electoral vote to the candidate who receives the most popular votes in that state. In effect, the system assigns to the winner the votes of the people who voted *against* the winner.

The operation of the winner-take-all system effectively disenfranchises voters who support losing candidates in each state. In the 2000 presidential election, nearly 3 million people voted for Al Gore in Florida. Because George W. Bush won 537 more votes than Gore, however, he received all of Florida's electoral votes. A candidate can win some states by very narrow margins, lose other states by large margins (as Bush did by more than one million votes in California and New York in 2000), and so win the electoral vote while losing the popular vote. Because there is no way to aggregate votes across states, the votes for candidates who do not finish first in a state play no role in the outcome of the election.

African Americans, who are the nation's most distinctive minority group, are concentrated in the Deep South. They rarely vote for the Republican candidates who win their states. Thus, their votes are wasted because they are never aggregated across the country. It is not surprising that presidential candidates have generally ignored these voters in their campaigns.[3]

In a multi-candidate contest such as the ones in 1992, 1996, and 2000, the winner-take-all system may suppress the votes of the majority as well as the minority. In 1996, less than a majority of voters decided how the electoral votes of 26 states would be cast. In 2000, pluralities rather than majorities determined the allocation of electoral votes in 8 states, including Florida and Ohio. In each case, less than half the voters determined how all of their state's electoral votes were cast.

One result of these distorting factors is that there is typically a substantial disparity between the share of the national popular vote a candidate receives and that candidate's percentage of the electoral vote. In 1876, 1888, 2000 and, arguably, 1960,[4] the candidate who finished second in the popular vote won the election.

The unit-vote system also allows even small third parties to siphon more votes from one major-party candidate than the other and thus determine the outcome in a state.[5] For example, there is little question that Ralph Nader cost Al Gore the election in 2000.[6] Most Nader voters would have voted for Gore in the absence of a Nader candidacy. Gore lost Florida by 537 votes, while Nader received 97,488 votes in the state. (Pat Buchanan and Libertarian candidate Harry Browne received a total of only 33,899, which were more likely to go to Bush.) Similarly, Gore lost New Hampshire by 7,211 votes while Nader received 22,198 votes. (Buchanan and Browne together received 5,372 votes.)[7] Gore would have been elected if he had won either state. Thus, by taking more votes from Al Gore than from George W. Bush, Nader determined the outcome of the entire election. The results distorted the preferences of the voters, because the preferred candidate in both Florida and New Hampshire in a two-person race was Al Gore, not George W. Bush, who ultimately won the states.

If no candidate wins a majority of the electoral votes, as happened in 1800 and 1824, the House of Representatives chooses the president. Here, each state delegation receives one vote, allowing the 7 smallest states, with a population of about 5 million, to outvote the 6 largest states, with a population of about 123 million. It is virtually impossible to find any defenders of this constitutional provision, which is the most egregious violation of democratic principles in American government.

The Electoral College violates political equality. It is not a neutral counting device. Instead, it favors some citizens over others, depending solely upon the state in which they live. The Electoral College is not just an archaic mechanism for counting the votes; it is also an institution that aggregates popular votes in an inherently unequal manner.

What good reason is there to continue such a system in an advanced democratic nation in which the ideal of popular choice is the most deeply ingrained principle of government? Why should we not select the president like we select nearly every other elected official in America—with the public directly voting for candidates and the candidate who receives the most votes winning election?

Constitutional Consistency

Some defenders of the Electoral College argue that its violations of majority rule are just an example of constitutional provisions that require supermajorities to take action.[8] For example, it takes the votes of two-thirds of the senators present to ratify a treaty. The Framers designed all such provisions, however, to allow minorities to prevent an action. The Electoral College is different. It allows a minority to take an action—that is, to select the president. As such, it is the only device of its kind in the Constitution.

Defending Interests

One common justification for the Electoral College and its violations of political equality is that it protects important interests that a system of direct election by the people would overlook or even harm. Advocates argue that allocating electoral votes by state, and states casting their votes as units, ensures that presidential candidates will be attentive to and protective of states' interests, especially the interests of states with small populations. Most supporters of the Electoral College also maintain that it is an essential bulwark of both the two-party system and federalism.

On their face, such claims seem far-fetched. In practice, for example, candidates allocate proportionately more campaign stops and advertisements to competitive and large states than to small ones.[9] Because these justifications for the Electoral College are so common, however, we must investigate them more systematically. (It is illuminating—and frustrating—that advocates of the Electoral College virtually never offer systematic evidence to support their claims.)

Proponents of the view that one of the major advantages of the Electoral College is that it forces candidates to be more attentive to and protective of state interests, especially the interests of states with small populations, base their argument on the premises that (1) states have interests as states, (2) these interests require protection, and (3) interests in states with smaller populations both require and deserve special protection from federal laws.

State Interests

States do not have coherent, unified interests. Even the smallest state has substantial diversity within it. No state includes just one point of view. That is why Alaska may have a Republican governor and one or more Democratic senators, and why "conservative" states like Montana and North and South Dakota vote Republican for president but sometimes send liberal Democrats to the US Senate. As historian Jack Rakove argues, "States have no interest, as states, in the election of the president; only citizens do." He adds:

> The winner-take-all rule might make sense if states really embodied coherent, unified interests and communities, but of course they do not. What does Chicago share with Galena, except that they both are in Illinois; Palo Alto with Lodi in California; Northern Virginia with Madison's home in Orange County; or Hamilton, N.Y., with Alexander Hamilton's old haunts in lower Manhattan?[10]

James Madison, recognizing how diverse states are, opposed counting the presidential vote by state (as in the unit rule) and hoped that, at the least, votes would be counted by district within states. Disaggregating the statewide vote and allowing districts within states to support the same candidate would encourage cohesiveness in the country and counter the centrifugal tendencies of regionalism.[11] Moreover, Madison did not want candidates to make appeals to special interests. As he proclaimed at the Constitutional Convention, "Local considerations must give way to the general interest"—even on slavery.[12]

Judith Best, who is perhaps the most diligent defender of the Electoral College, recognizes that heterogeneity exists within states but nevertheless argues that the citizens of each state share a common interest in managing their state's resources, including roads, parks, schools, local taxes, and the like. True enough. She also argues that these interests are as or more important than the characteristics people in a state share with people in other states, such as race, gender, religion, and ethnicity.[13] Many women, blacks, Hispanics, farmers, and members of other groups would be surprised to hear that local roads and parks are more important to their lives than the place they occupy in the economic and social structure of the country.

Equally important, Best makes a series of either logically or empirically incorrect statements about the relation between community interests and the election of the president. First, she confuses local communities with states. Her examples are largely of local, not state, issues, even though the policies of local governments vary widely within each state. Second, she argues that the president must be responsive to state interests to be elected and that candidates must "build [the] broadest possible coalitions of local interests" to win.[14] No evidence exists to support these assertions, and Best provides none. "State interest" is a dubious concept. Best cannot offer a single example of such an interest.

Do presidents focus on local interests when building their electoral coalitions? They do not. As we will see, candidates ignore most of the country in their campaigns, and they do not focus on local interests where they do campaign. Similarly, nowhere in the vast literature on voting in presidential elections has any scholar found that voters choose candidates on the basis of their stands on state and local issues. Indeed, candidates avoid such issues because they do not want to be seen by the rest of the country as pandering to special interests. In addition, once elected, the president has little to do with the issues that Best raises as examples of the shared interests of members of communities. There is no reason, and certainly no imperative, to campaign on these issues.

The Need for Protection

The Constitution places many constraints on the actions a simple majority can take. Minorities have fundamental rights to organize, communicate, and participate in the political process. The Senate greatly overrepresents small states and, within that chamber, the filibuster is a powerful extraconstitutional tool for thwarting majorities. Moreover, more than a simple majority is required to overcome minority opposition by changing the Constitution.

With these powerful checks on simple majorities already in place do some minority rights or interests require additional protection from national majorities? If so, are these minorities concentrated in certain geographic areas? (Because it allocates electoral votes on the basis of geography, the Electoral College protects only geographically concentrated interests.) Does anything justify awarding interests in certain geographic locations — namely, small states — additional protections in the form of extra representation in the electoral system that citizens in other states do not enjoy?[15]

Two of the most important authors of the Constitution, James Wilson and James Madison, understood well both the diversity of state interests and the need to protect minorities that are embodied in the Constitution. They saw little need to confer additional power to small states through the Electoral College. "Can we forget for whom we are forming a government?" Wilson asked. "Is it for *men*, or for the imaginary beings called *States*?"[16] Madison declared that experience had shown no danger of state interests being harmed by a national majority[17] and that "the President is to act for the *people* not for *States*."[18]

Congress, whose members are elected by districts and states, is designed to be responsive to constituency interests. The president, as Madison pointed out, is supposed to take a broader view. When advocates of the Electoral College express concern that direct election of the president would suppress local interests in favor of the national interest, they are in effect endorsing a presidency that is responsive to parochial interests in a system that already offers minority interests extraordinary access to policy makers and opportunities to thwart policies they oppose.

Interestingly, supporters of the Electoral College almost never specify what geographically concentrated rights or interests need special protection through the Electoral College. They certainly have not developed a general principle to justify additional protections for some interests rather than others. Nevertheless, we can do our own analysis of the distribution of interests in the United States.

The Interests of Small States

Do the states with small populations that receive special consideration in the Electoral College have common interests to protect? In the Constitutional Convention, Madison pointed out that it was not necessary to protect small states from large ones because the large ones — Virginia, Massachusetts, and Pennsylvania — had such different economic, religious, and other interests. Their size did not constitute a common interest. Indeed, rivalry was more likely to occur among large states than coalition.[19] Madison was prescient. The great political battles of American history — in Congress and in presidential elections — have been fought by opposing ideological and economic interests, not by small states and large states.

A brief look at the 17 states with the fewest electoral votes (that is, three, four, or five) shows that they are quite diverse.[20] Maine, Vermont, New Hampshire, and Rhode Island are in New England; Delaware and West Virginia are in the Middle Atlantic region; North and South Dakota, Montana, and Nebraska are in the Great Plains; New Mexico is in the Southwest; and Nevada, Wyoming, Utah, and Idaho are in the Rocky Mountain region. Alaska and Hawaii are regions unto themselves.

Some of these states have high average levels of income and education, and others have considerably lower levels. Some are quite liberal and others are very conservative, and their policies and levels of taxation reflect these differences. Several of the states are primarily urban, but many others are rural. They represent a great diversity of core economic interests, including agriculture, mining, gambling, chemicals, tourism, and energy. Even their agricultural interests are quite diverse, ranging from grain and dairy products to hogs and sheep. In sum, small states do not share common interests. It is not surprising that their representatives do not vote as a bloc in Congress and that their citizens do not vote as a bloc for president.

Even if small states share little in common, are there some interests that occur only in states with small populations? Not many. The first interest that may come to mind is agriculture, with visions of small farmers tilling the soil of small states. But most farmers live in states with large populations. The market value of the agricultural production of California, Texas, Florida, and Illinois alone substantially exceeds that of all of the 17 smallest states combined.[21]

For that matter, agriculture does not lack for powerful champions, especially in Congress, which has taken the lead in providing benefits, principally in the form of subsidies, for agriculture. Rather than competing to give farmers more benefits, presidents of both parties have attempted to restrain congressional spending on agriculture. The Electoral College has not turned presidents into champions of rural America.

It is difficult to identify interests that are centered in a few small states. Even if we could, however, the question remains whether these few interests out of the literally thousands of interests in the United States deserve special protection. What principle would support such a view? Why should those who produce wheat and hogs have more say in electing the president than those who produce vegetables, citrus, and beef? Is not the disproportionate Senate representation of states in which wheat and hogs are produced enough to protect these interests? There is simply no evidence that interests like these deserve or require additional protection from the electoral system.

Attention to State Interests

As we have seen, a core justification for the Electoral College and its violations of political equality is that allocating electoral votes by state forces candidates to pay attention to state-based interests in general and the interests of small states in particular. In their enthusiasm for the status quo, some advocates go further and claim that under the Electoral College, "all states are 'battlegrounds'" in the presidential election.[22]

Although defenders of the Electoral College almost never specify what interests the Electoral College is protecting, they nevertheless argue that candidates would ignore these interests if the president were chosen in a direct popular election. They base this argument on the premise that candidates appeal directly to state interests and give disproportionate attention to those of small states.

Do presidential candidates focus on state-level interests in their campaigns? Do they devote a larger percentage of their campaign efforts to small states than they would if the president were elected directly? To answer these questions, we need to see what candidates actually do and whether there is evidence that the Electoral College encourages candidates to be more attentive to small states. If candidates are not more oriented to small states and the interests within them than we would expect in a system of direct election, then we have reason to reject one of the principal justifications for the Electoral College's violation of political equality.

Candidates' Speeches

One prominent way that a candidate could attend to the interests of a state is by addressing them in speeches to that state's voters. What do candidates actually say when they campaign in the various states?

The presidential election of 2000 provides an excellent test of the hypothesis that the Electoral College motivates candidates to focus on state-based interests. Because the outcome in every single state that year was crucial to the outcome of this extraordinarily close election, each candidate had the maximum incentive to appeal to state interests. Nevertheless, neither George W. Bush nor Al Gore focused on state interests in their speeches, and they certainly did not focus on small state interests.[23]

Was the presidential election of 2000 unique in this way? Apparently not. A study of the campaign speeches of Bill Clinton and Robert Dole during the 1996 campaign found that they also did not focus their speeches on local interests.[24]

Candidates' Visits

The most direct means for candidates to appeal to voters is to visit their states and address them directly.[25] Modern transportation has made it relatively easy for candidates to crisscross the nation in search of votes. Proponents of the Electoral College argue that one of its principal advantages is that it forces candidates to pay attention to small states that would otherwise be neglected in a national election and to build a broad national coalition by appealing to voters in every region.[26]

During the presidential election of 2000, only one of the seven states with three electoral votes had a visit from a presidential candidate—a single visit by Al Gore to Delaware. The six states with four electoral votes received a total of seven visits from the presidential candidates, including George W. Bush's vacation trips to Maine. Four more states had five electoral votes, and two of them had no visits from the candidates. New Mexico and West Virginia, small but highly competitive, were the two exceptions. In sum, presidential candidates did not visit eleven of the seventeen smallest states at all, and only one candidate visited two of the other 6 states.

Among the eleven states with six, seven, or eight electoral votes, Arkansas, Iowa, Oregon, and Kentucky were highly competitive, and presidential candidates paid them multiple visits. The candidates visited only one of the other seven states in this group, however—a single visit George W. Bush to Arizona. Thus, presidential candidates did not visit seventeen of the twenty-eight smallest states. Three others received a single visit from the candidate of only one party.

Vice presidential candidates' visits tell a similar story. In 2000, they visited the ten smallest states a total of only four times. Eight of the seventeen smallest states did not receive a visit from a single presidential or vice presidential candidate of either party.

Bush's and Gore's emphasis on competitive states in 2000 is not unusual.[27] In the 2004 general election, no presidential candidate visited any of the seven states with only three electoral votes, and the only visit from a vice presidential candidate came when Dick Cheney went to his home state of Wyoming. Presidential candidates did not visit twelve of the seventeen smallest states, nor did vice presidential candidates visit ten of them.

Candidates also ignored the three states with six electoral votes in 2004, except for a single vice presidential candidate visit to Arkansas. Indeed, presidential candidates appeared at campaign events in only nine of the twenty-nine smallest states during the entire general election campaign. In two of these nine states, only one candidate visited, making a single visit in each case. The presidential candidates also avoided eight of the thirteen states with ten to fifteen electoral votes.

On the other hand, the candidates lavished attention on the thirteen competitive states: New Hampshire, West Virginia, New Mexico, Nevada, Iowa, Colorado, Minnesota, Wisconsin, Missouri, Michigan, Ohio, Pennsylvania, and Florida.

In addition to its failure to encourage candidate visits to small states, the Electoral College provides incentives to ignore many larger states. In 2004, the total number of campaign visits to the highly populated states of California, Texas, New York, and Illinois for both parties' presidential and vice presidential candidates was two. One of these visits was a home state rally for George W. Bush in Texas on the last night of the campaign. New Mexico and Iowa, with a total of only twelve electoral votes, received as many visits as the other thirty of the smallest thirty-two states combined. They also received more visits than California, Texas, New York, Illinois, Michigan, and New Jersey combined.

The 2008 election followed the familiar pattern. Barack Obama campaigned in only fourteen states and John McCain went to nineteen states. Joseph Biden and Sarah Palin each campaigned in eighteen states. In others words, the candidates bypassed most states. Each of the four candidates campaigned in the competitive small states of New Mexico, Nevada, and New Hampshire. Presidential candidates Obama and McCain went to none of the fourteen other small states. Palin added a single visit to Maine and her home state of Alaska, while Biden visited Montana, West Virginia, and his home state of Delaware. In addition, with the exception of a single event by John McCain in New York (where he had to be for other reasons), none of the candidates campaigned in the four large states of California, Texas, New York, and Illinois.

Moreover, the candidates do not campaign in every region of the country. Democrats have little incentive to campaign in the heavily Republican Great Plains and Deep South, and Republicans have little incentive to visit most of Democratic New England.

In sum, the Electoral College provides no incentive for candidates to pay attention to small states and take their cases directly to their citizens. Indeed, it is difficult to imagine how presidential candidates could be *less* attentive to small states than they already are. Candidates are not fools. They go where the Electoral College makes them go, and it makes them go to competitive states, especially large competitive states. They ignore most small states; in fact, they ignore most of the country.

Candidates' Advertising

Candidates reach most voters through television advertising. Technology makes it easy to place ads in any media market in the nation at short notice. Do candidates operating under the Electoral College compensate for their lack of visits to small or noncompetitive states by advertising there?

No. In 2000, for example, advertising expenditures in each state closely tracked the number of candidate appearances in that state. Some voters were bombarded with television advertising; others saw none at all. The candidates essentially ignored twenty-six states and the District of Columbia. In doing so, they bypassed major American cities such as Phoenix, Denver, Indianapolis, Washington, Baltimore, New York, Charlotte, Houston, and Dallas/Ft. Worth. The Gore campaign also bypassed Los Angeles, San Francisco, and San Diego.[28]

Focusing advertising on competitive states is nothing new.[29] Thus, as in the case of candidate visits, the idea that the Electoral College forces candidates to take their cases to small states and build coalitions from all regions of the country is erroneous.

Presidential Primaries

Candidates do campaign in many states during the presidential primaries and caucuses. This behavior is unrelated to the Electoral College, however. The current primary system is unrelated to the Electoral College. Direct election of the president is compatible with exactly the same primary system we have now and would not diminish whatever benefits it offers. Moreover, in the period preceding the great increase in presidential primaries that began in the 1970s, candidates followed campaign strategies in the general election similar to those they have followed in recent years.

In addition, campaigning in primaries, often nearly a year before the general election, is no substitute for campaigning during the general election period. In primaries, the focus in on differentiating *within* parties, while the focus in the general election is on the more important differences between parties.

Private Pledges

Finally, an occasional desperate advocate of the Electoral College asserts that candidates make private pledges to support interests of the states in which they do not campaign. There is no evidence at all to support such an assertion. Moreover, a simple thought experiment easily reveals the weakness of such an argument. In 2008, as in every election, the candidates ignored great swaths of the country in the general election. Let us think of the sixteen states of Idaho, Utah, Wyoming, Montana, North and South Dakota, Nebraska (with the exception of one congressional district), Kansas, Oklahoma, Texas, Arkansas, Louisiana, Mississippi, Alabama, Georgia, and South Carolina. Would John McCain make private pledges in these states? Of course not. Why would he? He was going to win them anyhow. What about Barack Obama? Would he call, say Texas Republican Governor Rick Perry or Louisiana Republican Governor Bobby Jindal with private pledges? Again, certainly not. How would he benefit with the electorate from *private* pledges? Would the political leaders of these Republican states somehow secretly help the Democratic candidate? Merely asking the question shows the fundamental weakness of the whole argument.

In sum, the fundamental justification of the Electoral College—that it forces candidates to be attentive to particular state interests, especially those concentrated in small states— is based on a faulty premise. In reality, the Electoral College discourages candidates from paying attention to small states and to much of the rest of the country, as well. In 2004, neither George W. Bush nor John Kerry ran a single national television advertisement.

Fragmenting the Party System

Defenders of the Electoral College system argue that it is one of the key bulwarks of the two-party system in the U.S. and often claim that direct election would splinter the two-party system. Typically, critics base their arguments on the premise that direct election would require a runoff between the two leading candidates.[30] But it would not.

There is no need for a runoff, any more than there is for almost all other elected officials in the nation—or for the presidency under the Electoral College. Under the Electoral College, victorious presidential candidates—including, most recently, Kennedy (1960), Nixon (1968), Clinton (1992 and 1996), and George W. Bush (2000)—have received less than a majority of the national popular vote about forty percent of the time since 1824. Few have called for a runoff. In addition, there is no relation between the vote winners received and their later success in, say, dealing with Congress. Some of our strongest presidents, including Polk, Lincoln, Cleveland, Wilson, Truman, and Kennedy, received a plurality but not a majority for the popular vote.

Finally, there is no evidence at all that winning a majority in the Electoral College provides an additional element of legitimacy for new presidents who did more poorly in the popular vote. Even after two and a half years in office and the rally focused on the war on terrorism, thirty-eight percent of the public, including a majority of Democrats and half the independents, did not consider George W. Bush the legitimate winner of the 2000 presidential election.[31]

Foundations of Two-Party Systems

There are at least five broad theories explaining the existence of two-party systems. The first is the structure of the electoral system. Are officials elected in single-member districts in plurality elections or in multimember districts by proportional election? A second theory emphasizes social diversity and cleavages. Into how many interests and groups is a society divided and are these divisions reinforcing?[32] The third explanation stresses an underlying duality of interests in a society. A fourth theory is a cultural explanation that focuses on the political maturity of the citizenry and the development of a political culture that recognizes the need for compromise, the wisdom of pragmatism, and the need to avoid dogmatism. Finally, there is the social consensus theory, which traces the two parties to a broad acceptance of social, economic, and political institutions.[33]

Only the first explanation, the structure of the electoral system, is open to change in the short run, and it is this structure that has attracted the attention of opponents of direct election of the president. A half century ago, Maurice Duverger concluded that plurality election single-ballot systems are likely to produce two-party systems while proportional representation and runoff systems encourage multipartyism.[34] Since then, many other scholars have studied the impact of electoral systems on party systems and found that electoral systems influence the number of parties much as Duverger said, and that despite the importance of social structure, electoral structure has an independent impact on the number of parties.[35]

Single-member districts with plurality elections (elections with no runoffs) are winner-take-all methods of selecting officials. It is common to explain the impact of such an electoral system on the number of parties as operating through two complimentary influences. The *mechanical* effect is that in a plurality rule, single-ballot system all but the two strongest parties are underrepresented because votes for third parties do not translate into pluralities in many districts. The *psychological* factor reinforces the mechanical one in that electors do not want to waste votes by giving them to third parties, who are unlikely to win, so they vote strategically for the lesser of two evils among the major parties. Similarly, politicians do not waste their energies running as third-party candidates because they cannot win.

Is the Electoral College the basis of the two-party system? Nothing in the scholarly literature or our historical experience suggests that the Electoral College is a cause of the two-party system in America.[36] Americans fill virtually every elected office in the country by directly electing officials in single-member districts in plurality elections. This system is the real structural basis for our two-party system, not the Electoral College. In other words, we have vast experience with direct election and have not endured splintering, much less crippling, effects on the party system.

In addition, American political culture, with its pragmatism, consensus, and relative lack of reinforcing cleavages, provides the additional underpinnings for a two-party system. As Gary Cox has shown, it takes more than the absence of a runoff to create bipartisanism.[37] The Electoral College is simply irrelevant. According to Clinton Rossiter,

> The bounty of the American economy, the fluidity of American society, the remarkable unity of the American people, and, most important, the success of the

American experiment have all mitigated against the emergence of large dissenting groups that would seek satisfaction of their special needs through the formation of political parties.[38]

In addition, the institution of the presidency encourages a two-party system. According to V. O. Key,

> The Presidency, unlike a multiparty cabinet, cannot be parceled out among miniscule parties. The circumstances stimulate coalition within the electorate before the election rather than in parliament after the vote. Since no more than two parties can for long compete effectively for the Presidency, two contending groups tend to develop, each built on its constituent units in each of the 50 states.[39]

James MacGregor Burns adds that parties polarize around single executives, which force third parties to amalgamate with major parties to achieve some of their desired ends.[40]

There are other structural impediments to third parties. Federal campaign funding statutes require a third party to have obtained at least five percent of the vote in the previous presidential election to receive any funding and twenty-five percent to receive full funding. The open and permeable nature of American parties, as epitomized by the primary system, channels dissent into the two major parties and mitigates against the development of third parties. State statutes ranging from restricting ballot access to preventing primary losers from running in the general election under another party label, handicap third parties, as does the prohibition of "fusion" candidates in most states.[41] According to one of the greatest students of American political parties, Leon Epstein, state laws restricting third parties have created an "institutionalized electoral duopoly."[42]

As several scholars concluded after studying the impact of abolishing the Electoral College on the party system, there is

> [N]o reliable, convincing evidence to suggest that changing the presidential election system, in and of itself, would alter significantly the party system in a predictable manner. There are simply too many other factors that reinforce our system of two-party dominance beside Electoral College rules.[43]

The Electoral College not only does not underpin the two-party system but it also *discourages* party competition in states that do not have close partisan divisions. As we have seen, candidates simply ignore these states because votes for the candidate in the minority in them do not count toward a national total. Counting every vote, regardless of where it is cast, in a direct election would foster two-party competition on a national scale. It would provide incentives for candidates to encourage all their supporters, no matter where they lived, to go to the polls and also encourage candidates to take their campaigns to these citizens. All of this would be a boon to two-party competition.

Encouraging Third Parties

Would direct election of the president encourage third parties? Clearly not. Increased party competition would not only encourage the second party but also discourage third parties. V. O. Key found that the unity of the Democratic Party in the South was in almost direct proportion to the competition offered by Republicans. The more competition, the less splintered the Democrats.[44]

Actually, direct election would protect the country from the mischief of third parties. The Electoral College's unit rule encourages third parties, especially those with a regional base, because by winning a few states they may deny either major-party candidate a majority of the electoral vote. Winning a few states may put a third party in a position to dictate the outcome of an election by either instructing its electors to support one of the major party candidates in the Electoral College or by influencing the votes of representatives from the states that it won in a contingent election in the House. Such a result was certainly the goal of Strom Thurmond in 1948 and George Wallace in 1968. Imagine giving these racist candidates leverage to negotiate with the leading candidates before the electoral votes were officially cast.

Under direct election, there can be no deadlocks and thus, there is no incentive for regional third parties. No third party can use a few electoral votes to dictate the choice of president.

Sabato implicitly recognizes that smaller electoral units encourage third parties when he argues against allocating electoral votes by congressional district because it would lower the winner-take-all bar from the state level to the district level and thus increase the probabilities of third parties winning electoral votes.[45] However, he misses the logical extension that raising the bar from the state level to the national level also will decrease the chances of third party success.

The Electoral College has also not discouraged candidates like Ross Perot and Ralph Nader with broad but less concentrated support than regional candidates. There is substantial variation between elections, but third parties have often received a substantial percentage of the vote *under the Electoral College*,[46] large enough to encourage future candidates and sometimes large enough to affect the outcome of the election. Moreover, even without winning any states, Ralph Nader inadvertently distorted the vote and determined the outcome of the 2000 election.

To put this analysis in another way, consider two candidates, one contemplating running as a third-party candidate in a system of direct election, and the other running under the Electoral College. A potential candidate in a system of direct election risks his or her political futures by running against the official party candidate. And there is no compensation. Such a candidate can win nothing at all coming in third, even taking a significant portion of the vote. So there is little incentive to run. Under the Electoral College, however, a candidate finishing, say, third, might win some electoral votes and have leverage in determining the winner of the election. There is much more incentive for third party candidates to run under the Electoral College than under a system of direct election.

It is important that we not fall into a logical trap. It is circular reasoning to argue that direct election will produce a plethora of candidates, which will force us to have a runoff, which will encourage candidates. In fact, direct election will not produce more general election candidates than the Electoral College and there is no need for a runoff.

Preserving Federalism

Some opponents of direct popular election of the president argue that it would undermine the federal nature of the constitutional system. Defenders of the Electoral College base this assertion on the premise that the Electoral College is a key underpinning of federalism.[47] In truth, it is unclear what federalism has to do with the presidency, the one elective part of the government that is designed to represent the nation as a whole rather than as an amalgam of states and districts. Federalism is certainly an important component of the constitutional system, but is the Electoral College essential for maintaining federalism?

A Federal Principle?

The Founders did not design the Electoral College on the federal principle. The Electoral College does not enhance the power or sovereignty of the states. Moreover, the Founders expected electors to exercise their individual discretion when casting their votes. They did not expect electors to vote as part of any state bloc. No delegate at the Constitutional Convention referred to the Electoral College as an element of the federal system or even as important to the overall structure of the Constitution.

Similarly, the Founders did not regard the Electoral College as a means of implementing the Connecticut Compromise, which created a House of Representatives apportioned according to population and a Senate in which each state has two seats. The allocation of two electoral votes to each state corresponding to its Senate representation was not to further federalism. Instead, the extra votes were to serve as a corrective for large state power. The federative principle would have required that these extra electors be organized like the Senate as a separate body with an independent voice in the choice of the president.

The Electoral College was not designed to protect state interests. If it were, the Founders would have insisted that state legislatures choose electors, who would be agents of the state governments. But, they did not do so. Indeed, the Electoral College was "an anti-states-rights device," designed to keep the election of the president away from state politicians.[48]

Essential for Federalism?

Even if the Electoral College was not designed as an aspect of federalism, is it essential for preserving federalism? We have already seen that the Electoral College does not cause presidential candidates to devote attention to the states as states in general or to small states in particular. Neither the existence nor the powers and responsibilities of state governments depend in any way on the existence of the Electoral College. If it were abolished, states would have the same rights and duties they have now. Federalism is deeply embodied in congressional elections, in which two senators represent each state just because it is a state and in which members of the House are elected from districts within states. Direct election of the president would not alter these federalism-sustaining aspects of the constitutional structure. A leading expert on federalism, Neal Peirce, has said it best: "The vitality of federalism rests chiefly on the constitutionally mandated system of congressional representation and the will and capacity of state and local governments to address compelling problems, not on the hocus-pocus of an eighteenth-century vote count system."[49]

Greater National Control of the Electoral Process?

Occasionally, a defender of the Electoral College laments the prospect that direct election of the president would foster greater national control of the electoral process. But this has already occurred. The Fifteenth, Eighteenth, Nineteenth, Twenty-third,

Twenty-fourth, and Twenty-sixth Amendments to the Constitution all expanded the electorate. Federal, not state, law effectively determines who is eligible to vote now, and in the wake of the vote-counting debacle in Florida in the 2000 election, federal law dictates the rules for voter registration, voter access to the polls, counting votes, correcting voters' errors on their ballots, resolving challenges to a citizen's right to vote, and ensuring that voting systems have minimal rates of error. The federal government also provides aid to states to improve their voting machinery and registration lists.

Federal standards are here to stay—within the framework of the Electoral College. Moreover, Americans and their elected representatives overwhelmingly support these laws and constitutional amendments. If anything, the enormous disparity in ballot designs across the states, many of which are needlessly complex, makes a strong case for greater uniformity.[50] The Caltech/MIT Voting Technology Project concluded that four to six million votes were lost in the 2000 election as a result of problems with ballots, voting equipment, and registration databases.[51] As President George W. Bush said when he signed the Help America Vote Act of 2002, "The administration of elections is primarily a state and local responsibility. The fairness of all elections, however, is a national priority."[52]

Protecting Non-State-Based Minority Interests

Some observers claim that the Electoral College ensures a "proper distribution" of the vote, in which the winning candidate receives majority support across social strata, thus protecting minority interests.[53] This claim is nonsense. In 2000, George W. Bush did not win a larger percentage than Al Gore of the votes of women; African Americans, Hispanics, and Asian-Americans; voters aged 18–29 or those aged 60 or older; the poor; members of labor unions; those with less than $50,000 of household income; those with a high school education or less and those with postgraduate education; Catholics, Jews, and Muslims; liberals and moderates; urbanites; or those living in the East and West.[54]

It strains credulity to claim that Bush's vote represents concurrent majorities across the major strata of American society. What actually happened in 2000 was that the Electoral College imposed a candidate supported by white male Protestants—the dominant social group in the country—over the objections not only of a plurality of all voters but also of most "minority" interests in the country. This antidemocratic outcome is precisely the opposite of what defenders of the Electoral College claim for the system.

Why Not Elect Everyone by the Same Rules?

A common refrain by advocates of the Electoral College goes something like this: "If you insist on majority—or at least plurality—rule, why don't you insist on abolishing the Senate, in which seats are allocated to states rather than people?" The answer is straightforward. The Founders designed the Senate explicitly to represent states and the interests within them. They designed the presidency to do something quite different. The president is supposed to rise above parochial interests and represent the entire nation. Perhaps the most compelling argument that the president should be elected by direct popular vote is that the president and vice president are the only national officials in the country who represent the people as a whole and that the candidate who wins the most votes best approximates the choice of the people.

Similarly, some defenders of the Electoral College ask, "If you are so concerned that the people choose the president, what about all the nonelected judges and other officials in government? Shouldn't we elect them as well?" Of course not. It is not feasible to elect department heads and other executive officials, no matter how the president is selected. The issue is not electing additional officials. The issue is letting a plurality of voters elect the president who nominates judges and executive officials.

Campaigns under Direct Election

Some critics of direct election mistakenly argue, in the words of Sabato, that under direct election of the president "[c]andidates would be inclined to run airport 'tarmac' campaigns, jetting from population center to population center and focusing advertising dollars on large urban areas with many voters, virtually ignoring large swaths of the nation where there are relatively few voters."[55] Yet this is a myopic view, and only candidates wishing to lose the election would follow such a strategy.

We know that candidates under the Electoral College ignore most of the country, especially rural areas. Moreover, they do so because of the incentives of the system. Candidates would be much more attentive to small states and minorities with direct election than they are with the Electoral College. Because every vote counts in a direct election, candidates would have an incentive to appeal to all voters and not just those strategically located in swing states.[56] An extra vote in Massachusetts or Texas would count as much as one in Michigan or Florida.

Presidential and vice presidential candidate Robert Dole explained that under direct election, candidates also would have to pay attention to areas within states that are now ignored because they are safe for one party or the other. Thus, "the voters in the majority of States would receive greater attention and the objective of federalism would be served better."[57]

With these incentives, candidates would find it easy to spread their attention more evenly across the country. Because the cost of advertising is mainly a function of market size, it does not cost more to reach 10,000 voters in Wyoming than it does to reach 10,000 voters in a neighborhood in Queens or Los Angeles. Actually, it may cost less to reach voters in smaller communities because larger markets tend to run out of commercial time, increasing the price of advertising.[58] Politicians know this, even if advocates of the Electoral College do not. That is why, in the election of 2000, the candidates "devoted nearly as much advertising to Yakima as in Seattle, as much to Traverse City as to Flint, as much to Wausau as to Milwaukee" when they campaigned within states.[59]

Direct election of the president also would provide the incentive for candidates to encourage all of their supporters, no matter where they live, to go to the polls, because under direct election, every vote counts. Conversely, under the Electoral College, it does not matter how many votes a candidate receives in a state as long as the number of votes surpasses that which any opponent receives. The goal is to win states, not voters. As Douglas Bailey, the media manager of the 1976 Ford-Dole campaign, put it, "There is a vast population [outside urban areas], with every vote counting, that you cannot ignore in a direct election."[60]

It is possible, but by no means certain, that some candidates would find it more cost effective under direct election to mobilize votes in urban areas or to visit urban areas where they would receive free television coverage before large audiences. Such actions would do nothing to undermine the argument against the Electoral College, however. Small states cannot be worse off than they are now, because under the Electoral College, candidates rarely visit or campaign there. Direct election of the president cannot diminish campaign efforts that do not exist. Instead, direct election would provide increased incentives for candidates to campaign in most small states, as well as increased incentives to campaign in many large and medium-sized states. Direct election would disperse campaign efforts rather than deprive small states of them.

Direct election, unlike the Electoral College, thus encourages citizens to participate in elections and candidates to take their campaigns to these citizens, enhancing our civic life. It would reduce the power of sectionalism in politics and encourage candidates to focus their campaigns on the entire nation, including racial minorities. It would also reinvigorate party competition and combat voter apathy by giving candidates and parties incentives to turn out voters in states they cannot win as a whole.

Conclusion

A core justification offered by defenders of the Electoral College, and its violations of political equality, is that it is necessary to protect important interests that would be overlooked or harmed by a system of direct election of the president. Yet such claims are based on faulty premises. States — including states with small populations — do not embody coherent, unified interests and communities, and they have little need for protection. Even if they did, the Electoral College does not provide it. Contrary to the claims of its supporters, candidates do not pay attention to small states. The Electoral College actually distorts the presidential campaign so that candidates ignore many large and most small states and devote most of their attention to a few competitive states.

Rather than protecting the interests of states and minorities, the Electoral College reduces the incentives for people to vote in states that are safe for the locally dominant party's candidate. It also weakens the incentive for either the majority or minority party to attempt to persuade citizens to go to the polls and support its national ticket. Under the Electoral College it makes no sense for candidates to allocate scarce resources to states they either cannot win or are certain to win, in which case, the size of their victory is irrelevant.

Similarly, the Electoral College does not promote the two-party system. Instead, it undermines it by encouraging third parties and discouraging party competition in states where one party has a significant advantage. The Electoral College is also not a bastion of federalism. It is not based on federative principles and is not essential for the continuance of a healthy federal system. As former Senate majority leader and Republican presidential nominee Robert Dole put it, direct election is "commonsense federalism."[61]

Any proposal to reform the Electoral College must deal with its primary flaws. In an election for a national officeholder, each voter has a right to expect that he or she will stand in the same relation to the national official as every other voter. Given its many advantages for the polity, the United States should adopt direct election of the president. Only direct election of the president assures political equality. It would also do more than any alternative to strengthen the two-party system, reduce sectionalism in politics, and encourage candidates to focus their campaigns on the entire nation, including racial minorities. Direct election would combat voter apathy by giving candidates and parties incentives to turn out voters in states they cannot win as a whole. Of course, direct election would eliminate all the problems caused by the selection and voting of electors themselves.[62] Finally, direct election would not diminish benefits from the Electoral College that, as we have seen, do not exist.

There is no question that instituting direct election of the president will be difficult. Change will require amending the Constitution, a complex and time-consuming task. Although the public and many states and organizations support direct election, there are obstacles to change. Principal among them are officials who believe that their states or the members of their organizations benefit from the Electoral College. We now know that these officials are wrong. They have reached their conclusions on the basis of faulty premises. Understanding the flawed foundations of the Electoral College is the critical first step on the road to reforming the system of presidential selection. The culmination of this effort should be allowing the people to directly elect the presidents who serve them.

Chapter 7

The Electoral College: Mend It, Don't End It

Larry A. Sabato

The 2000 election cliffhanger between George W. Bush and Al Gore was only the latest crisis to beset the constitutional mechanism for the election of a president, the Electoral College. There have been other Electoral College controversies, including the presidential elections of 1800 (Thomas Jefferson, John Adams, and Aaron Burr),[1] 1824 (John Quincy Adams, Andrew Jackson, and others),[2] 1876 (Rutherford B. Hayes versus Samuel Tilden),[3] and 1888 (Grover Cleveland versus Benjamin Harrison).[4] In 1824, 1876, and 1888—just as in 2000—the popular vote winner was denied the presidency because of a contrary Electoral College vote. In 1800, 1824, and 1876—just as in 2000—there were political shenanigans of various sorts that further clouded the results.

Moreover, there have been a number of near misses in American presidential history, cases where the nation narrowly avoided great controversy in the final results. In the lifetimes of many Americans, for example, the 1968 and 1976 contests teetered on the edge. In 1968 the 46 electoral votes secured by the segregationist George Wallace of Alabama in Deep South states might well have decided the tight election between Richard Nixon (R) and Hubert Humphrey (D). In the end, Nixon edged Humphrey slightly in the popular vote and secured a modest majority in the Electoral College so that Wallace could not have determined the winner by throwing his electoral votes to one of the candidates.[5] Imagine the consequences had a race-baiter like Wallace been the one to pick a president![6] In 1976 an addition of just 11,117 votes in Ohio and 7,373 votes in Hawaii for the Republican ticket would have produced a four-year term for President Gerald Ford (R), even though Jimmy Carter (D) would have won the popular vote by a massive 1.7 million.[7] Even in a more decisive popular-vote election like 2004, when President George W. Bush won by 3 million votes nationally and an Electoral College vote of 286 to 252 over the Democrat John F. Kerry,[8] a switch of only 60 thousand votes in Ohio would have given Kerry the Buckeye State's 20 electoral votes and 272 electoral votes overall—and thus, the presidency.[9]

Many analysts and observers of American politics say that this record, and the very real potential for more mayhem in the future, calls for outright abolition of the Electoral College in the next constitutional revision.[10] But these critics ignore some important advantages of the Electoral College—which endures, albeit unloved—and deserves more respect than it gets. At the same time, the current system is inadequate to the needs of the modern republic, so a proper approach is "mend it, don't end it."

The Founding of a College

Adopted in 1789, before the establishment of political parties and before most citizens had the right to vote, the Electoral College was created for a variety of reasons—some purely political, others based upon principle. At the heart of the college was compromise, producing a republican, though undemocratic, system designed to give all states a voice in the selection of the nation's leader. The men drafting the Constitution found it very difficult to believe that a national mandate, like that naturally possessed by George Washington, would be attainable for candidates in the future. The framers wanted the Electoral College to serve as a reliable gatekeeper, a richly endowed "nominating committee" that would send the top vote-getters to the US House for a final choice, without any reliance on the will of the general public. George Mason, cited in James Madison's notes, "conceived it would be as unnatural to refer the choice of a proper character for chief Magistrate to the people, at it would, to refer a trial of colours to a blind man. The extent of the Country renders it impossible that the people can have the requisite capacity to judge."[11]

Once instituted, it did not take long for the Electoral College to stir controversy. In 1796 John Adams defeated Thomas Jefferson for the presidency by just three electoral votes, with Jefferson becoming vice president due to his second-place finish. Four years later, Jefferson ran again, against incumbent President Adams. This time around, Jefferson and his ticket mate, Aaron Burr, came out on top in the Electoral College. At that time, each elector voted for two men, and the top two vote-getters were supposed to serve as president and vice president. But the Jefferson electors had voted for both men, so Jefferson and Burr each had 73 of 138 electoral votes. While Burr had been the choice for vice president and not president, his political ambition kept him from stepping aside. It took 36 ballots in the US House of Representatives—with votes cast by state delegations as a whole, not by individual members—to select Thomas Jefferson as our third president. This fiasco prompted the Twelfth Amendment to the Constitution, which, among other provisions, requires electors to vote for presidential and vice presidential candidates separately.

More than two centuries later, despite the many controversies that have engulfed presidential elections, the Twelfth Amendment still marks the most significant change to the Electoral College in all of American history—a fact that alone suggests that some rethinking may be in order. In the 1960s, the Twenty-third Amendment granted three electoral votes to the District of Columbia. Other amendments have primarily altered the timing of the electoral vote tabulation and the way in which individual states choose to allocate their electors.[12]

Despite these small changes, the Electoral College today works much as it had since the 1800s. Each state receives a number of electors equal to the size of its delegation in the US Congress (the number of US representatives as determined by the decennial census, plus two electors for the two US senators from the state). Anyone except a federal public officeholder[13] can serve as an elector. The state political parties select their electors— usually faithful party workers—in the spring or summer of the presidential election year and submit their list to the board of election in each state. The electors appear on the ballot in November, as a slate, under the names of their party's candidates for president and vice president; we voters are actually choosing a slate of electors who are pledged to our preferred nominees for the top national offices. The electoral slate receiving a plurality of the popular vote—at least one vote more than the other electoral slates—in the November general election meets in the state capitol in early December for a formal ceremony whereby they cast their ballots for president and vice president. While pledged to their party nominees, they have the right to vote for absolutely anyone who meets the constitutional qualifications for either position (at least thirty-five years of age, natural born citizen, etc.)[14] whether the individual appeared on the ballot or not.

Those electors who do not follow their pledge are called *faithless electors*.[15] Given the considerable freedom that electors have to ignore the mandate of the voters, it is easy to understand why the political parties do their best to carefully select their elector candidates, trying to pick only the most loyal activists. Still, the parties can only hope that their electors will remain steadfast. Human beings can be unreliable and unpredictable, and an elector might be genuinely put off by a pledge made by his or her party's presidential candidate during the autumn campaign. Fortunately for the parties, there is a real stigma attached to the label of faithless elector, and anyone acquiring it can forget about a successful future career in politics.[16] In any event, the tally of the electors' ballots from the 50 state capitols is sent to the Congress, and in a simple but moving ceremony in January, the incumbent vice president—the president of the Senate—opens and reads the ballot tallies before a joint session of Congress. (In modern times, somewhat jarringly, Vice President Richard Nixon in 1961, Vice President Hubert Humphrey in 1969, and Vice President Al Gore in 2001 had to read the electoral tallies and announce their opponents, John F. Kennedy, Richard M. Nixon, and George W. Bush respectively, as having been elected president.)

As long as one presidential ticket has received an absolute majority of the electoral votes, the election is over. If no one has received a majority for president or for vice president—remember, the Twelfth Amendment requires the separate counting of ballots for each office—then the House of Representatives gathers to elect a president and the Senate to elect a vice president. An absolute majority of the House state delegations, with each delegation voting as a unit in every state—regardless of size—having a single vote, is required to elect a president, and an absolute majority of the Senate is required to elect a vice president.[17]

Whatever one thinks of its origins, development, and complicated operation, the Electoral College has become a fundamental component of our presidential selection system. Campaigns base their strategies upon it, but its impact extends far beyond presidential politics. Should the nation seriously consider altering or eliminating this system, it must carefully examine the true benefits and disadvantages of our current system versus the consequences of any reform proposals. Let's look first at the positive side of the ledger for the Electoral College.

Advantages of the Electoral College

The Electoral College has served as a stabilizing force in American politics by limiting fragmentation through the emergence of multiple parties. This benefit exists because of the winner-take-all allocation of electors in all states but Maine and Nebraska.[18] Simply put, Americans are encouraged to vote for one of the two major parties' presidential tickets so as not to "throw their vote away." Either the Democrats or the Republicans have won the presidency since the election of 1856,[19] and prior to that year, the Democrats and the Whigs had dominated presidential politics since 1836.[20] To vote for a third party or an independent candidate was to "waste" one's vote, since victory was deemed impossible for these minor contenders. Such a belief was encouraged by the two major parties, of course, but also by the system the framers created in the Electoral College, since only the top two competitors have any real chance of winning a majority of the electoral votes and therefore the White House. Thus, by pushing Americans toward the two top parties, the Electoral College can be said to forge consensus and encourage coalition building.

A two-party system, buttressed by the Electoral College, has protected the American system against the fragmentation of multiparty representation often seen in other nations, where any party securing as little as 5 percent of the national vote can find representation in the parliament. If the bar is set that low, third parties will almost certainly proliferate, and when multiple parties develop, they often do so along single-issue, ethnic, socioeconomic, religious, and regional lines. This can prove quite divisive, and especially so in a heterogeneous nation such as the United States. Also, when many small parties or factions participate independently in the process, majorities are very difficult to build, and small groups often attain disproportionate power, because they are the key to a majority, governing coalition. If small parties were suddenly able to play a continuing, major, and decisive role in presidential politics, they would likely begin to see greater success at the local, state, and national levels, perhaps changing the face of our Congress and transforming the legislatures in all of the states. Advocates of third parties would welcome this, but the United States is not Belgium or Italy, and it can be argued that the world's premier superpower cannot afford to increase its internal quarrels to the point of frequent, ungovernable destabilization.

Candidates must pay some attention to lightly populated states and regions with substantial, cumulative electoral votes, and not simply run campaigns focused entirely on large population centers that could produce a popular-vote majority. Without the Electoral College, the half of the states with the small populations would stand little chance of seeing much of the presidential candidates. Instead, the contenders would inevitably concentrate their time and travel in the top twenty urban areas, such as New York and Los Angeles, where candidates can shop for votes much more efficiently. We are one country, and would-be presidents must become acquainted with the whole of it to govern well. Waging a national campaign is one vital means to that good end.

The Electoral College undergirds federalism and reinforces the role of states in our representative democracy. The college derives its power from the various states, dampening the tyranny of the majority so feared by the founders. Although the Electoral College is arguably a ceremonial body, which convenes at the end of an election after the president-elect has been known for some time, it symbolizes the integral role the fifty states play in the American system. All matters concerning elections, from holding the primary contests to selecting electors, rest with the states, and the college underlines and augments this.

These three arguments are strong ones, but the history of the Electoral College points out some clear disadvantages, too.

Concerns with the Current Electoral College

The winner of the popular vote does not necessarily win the presidency. Admittedly, some observers do not see this as a problem, believing as the founders did that the popular vote is at best secondary to the selection of a federal president. But surely in the modern age, when virtually all other democracies around the globe choose their leaders by pure popular vote, the world's foremost democracy ought to serve as an example of majority rule. In addition, as measured by public opinion polls, most Americans now believe that the candidate with the most votes should win, and the Electoral College be damned.[21] The support of the people is essential for the success of any electoral system, after all.

When it comes to the presidency, the votes of individuals in each state do not count equally. The basis of the Electoral College (much like the foundation of the US Senate) is a far cry from "one person, one vote." This is due primarily to the allocation of two senatorial bonus electors to every state, regardless of size. So giant California receives two, and tiny Rhode Island also gets two. Several states also have excess population that does not quite merit an additional representative, and those tens or hundreds of thousands of people are discounted in the electoral count (at least until the next census). Perhaps some unfairness in allocating electors within a federal system is inevitable, but the inequity seems exaggerated in the existing arrangement. Electors, and not individual voters, pick presidents, and this fundamental fact in itself is somewhat undemocratic. The system of allocating electors adds to the undemocratic nature of the Electoral College.

Faithless electors can cast votes that do not correspond with the results of the election in their state. This is historically rare and has never played a role in deciding an election. However, one can easily imagine a situation in which a group of such electors could significantly impact a close election. This prospect is especially troubling, considering that most voters do not even know the names of the electors they choose, let alone trust in their judgment to select the president. A few examples: a Washington, D.C., elector cast a blank ballot in the extremely close contest of 2000 to protest the lack of voting rights in the District of Columbia; a West Virginia elector cast her ballot backward in 1988, picking Lloyd Bentsen for president and Michael Dukakis for vice president, a switched ticket to indicate her personal preference; a Minnesota Democratic elector did precisely the same thing in another reasonably close race, that of 2004, giving an electoral vote to John Edwards instead of John Kerry; and in 1968, a North Carolina man cast his vote for Alabama governor George Wallace instead of Richard Nixon.[22]

The college is susceptible to a tie. There are dozens of ways that the Electoral College can tie, and in this age of very tight elections, it is entirely conceivable that a tie will one day occur. In that case, the U.S. House of Representatives would select the president, but in the odd way mentioned earlier: Each state, regardless of size or population, would cast a single vote. Furthermore, if a state's House delegation tied (split evenly) between the contenders, the state's one vote for president would not be cast at all—potentially disenfranchising millions of people in the determination of the next president. This would be unfortunate for the people of any state, but imagine if the House delegations in just three states (California, Florida, and Texas) were deadlocked: Over one quarter of the nation's population would get no say in the identity of the next president. Add to this mix one other distasteful ingredient. Given the horse trading that might well ensue in the House, it is safe to predict most Americans would find this an unpalatable way to choose our chief executive. Although there is no way to say for sure how the representatives would vote, the selection of the president would likely rest in the hands of the party controlling a majority of delegations in the House of Representatives. Here again, the president chosen by the House method might easily have lost the popular party vote.

Reforms That Abolish the Electoral College

Many groups and individuals, including the League of Women Voters, most academics in the field, many members of Congress from both parties, and past presidential candidates such as the Independent John Anderson and the Democrat Michael Dukakis, insist that the Electoral College should be abolished altogether, in favor of a direct popular vote, perhaps with a runoff between the top two contenders if no candidate received at least 40 percent of the national vote.[23] Polls since the 1970s consistently show approximately 60 percent of Americans agree with this statement.[24]

At first glance, the notion of switching to a direct popular vote for president would appear to address the problems associated with the Electoral College. Most people would find it implicitly more democratic—all voters would know that their vote was counted equally—and the notion of faithless electors would be a historical footnote.

However, defenders of the Electoral College believe abolishing it would lead to fundamental change in our political system. Candidates would be inclined to run airport "tarmac" campaigns, jetting from population center to population center and focusing advertising dollars on large urban areas with many voters, virtually ignoring vast swaths of the nation where there are relatively few voters. More important, a free-for-all national direct election would certainly encourage a multiparty system. In time, the country might well see a dozen or more serious or semiserious candidates on the ballot, each pitching a big issue or basing his or her campaign on race, ethnicity, religion, region, or some other splintering characteristic. Every presidential candidate would simply hope to secure one of the runoff spots with another candidate who would be deemed less acceptable. One of the United States already has experienced the possible results, and it is a cautionary tale for the nation. In 1975 Louisiana established just such a free-for-all system for its gubernatorial contests,[25] and in a 1991 runoff for governor between the top two finishers in the first election, the state ended up with a choice between a crook, the frequently indicted former governor Edwin Edwards, and a KKK white racist, David Duke. As the famous bumper sticker of the time noted, "Vote for the Crook, It's Important." Louisianans did, to deny Duke. Edwards later went to jail after yet another corrupt term in office.[26] This is hardly the ideal model for the nation's presidential elections.

Reforms That Mend the Electoral College ... but Have Unintended Consequences

Many proposals for changing the Electoral College, without abolishing the institution, have been made over the centuries. Even James Madison had developed serious doubts about various aspects of the college by 1823 and proposed reform of it.[27] Most of these accumulated proposals are intellectually stimulating, but many are inadequate, with hidden, unintended consequences. A few are even dangerous to the American republic. Here are three such unwise plans.

Congressional District Allocation: A frequently mentioned reform proposal, district allocation of electors, has been on the table since the 1890s.[28] Under this system, electors would be apportioned one to each congressional district, with the presidential winner in each district collecting the elector, and the two extra senatorial electors going to the statewide winner. (As mentioned earlier, only Maine and Nebraska have adopted this method of elector allocation.) Interestingly, an earlier version of the Twelfth Amendment, which barely failed ratification, called for electors to be allocated by "electoral districts."[29] The states currently have the power to put the district plan into effect, just as Maine and Nebraska have done. Yet the large states have no desire to do so, since breaking up their electors would dilute the impact of their large Electoral College prizes. So a constitutional mandate would be required if this plan is to be universal.

One positive outcome of the congressional district method of assigning electors is that it might expand the campaign's playing field. Many strongly "Red" or "Blue" states have at least one congressional district that is competitive for the minority party; the large states have several each. Therefore, a Democratic presidential nominee would spend time in some Texas districts, while the Republican nominee would find his or her way to parts of New York, Illinois, and California. It would be a good thing for more states to see the candidates up close and personal during the general election. This would be a welcome antidote to the current winner-take-all system's result, whereby thirty or more states are all but decided months ahead of time and thus avoided by time-pressed candidates.

Despite this salutary effect, though, the district plan creates more problems than it solves. The impact it would have had on previous elections is mixed. Would Gore supporters who blame the Electoral College system for depriving their popular-vote winner of the presidency jump for joy if electors were counted by congressional district? Hardly. A study by the independent analyst Rhodes Cook found the winner still to be George W. Bush, with a more clear-cut 288 to 250 Electoral College win than the 271 to 266 victory he actually secured. The broader distribution of Republican votes would help all GOP presidential candidates, while Democrats might be penalized for the urban concentration of their support. Gore, for example, won all 22 Illinois electors in 2000. But under the district plan, Bush would have picked up 9 of those 22 votes.[30] Similarly, Richard Nixon would have won the 1960 presidential election if the electoral votes were allotted under the district plan.[31]

More important, this plan could alter the future dynamics of our political system in unexpected ways. Lowering the winner-take-all bar from the state level to the congressional district level might allow more parties to win electoral votes. There is great risk for our democracy in the possible fragmentation of the Electoral College, with purely sectional or highly ideological third parties and independent candidates grabbing electoral votes here and there across the map. Should this happen, probably producing no majority in the college for any candidate, the nation might be faced with the two major-party candidates engaged in postelection pandering to smaller parties in order to secure the minimum number of electoral votes for the presidency. What promises would be made, what secret deals would be concluded, to produce a college majority? Even if the major candidates were not surreptitiously engaged in these disreputable activities, many Americans would assume they were. Their suspicions would no doubt be fueled by speculative news reports and partisan attacks. With persistent questioning of the integrity of the president-elect nearly guaranteed, that helpful period known as the "honeymoon" for the nation's new leader would be difficult to achieve.

Also, imagine a multitude of Florida 2000-like disputes that could arise in any close election, as campaigns jockey for individual electoral votes by contesting tallies district by district across the nation. Every single congressional district where the candidates were separated by a thousand or fewer votes would likely be targeted, and teams of lawyers would descend on these unfortunate areas to fight over every vote. Partisan passions in these districts would be inflamed, and angry demonstrations — again, think of South Florida in 2000 — would ensue. Local, state, and federal courts would be jammed with election law cases around the nation, and judges would replace voters as the arbiters of the election results. Americans would not have much confidence in the outcome, especially since varying election law standards existing in the fifty states and thousands of localities would be applied differently from place to place

Proportional Allocation: This proposal would have each state's electoral votes divided in the same proportion as that state's popular vote, rounded to the nearest elector. This method of distributing electors presents a few benefits. Depending upon the exact method of implementation, the plan could have the effect of forcing candidates to campaign in places they currently ignore. It would certainly make decisions by the campaigns about where to stump much more complex. Unlike allocation by congressional district, this option would also boost voter enthusiasm, especially in areas that lean heavily toward one party, since everyone's vote would count in the ultimate proportional allocation of electors. (If you belong to the minority party in an area sure to vote for the majority party, you have less incentive to show up at the polls—unless proportional allocation is in effect.)

However, this approach—which could again be adopted without changing the Constitution—is even more problematic than the congressional district method because it would inevitably lead to the fragmentation of multiple parties. Every third party, whether it were organized around a charismatic individual, a hot-button issue, sectional concerns (a South-based party or a Rocky Mountain party), or some general philosophy of life (Libertarians, Greens, and so on), would have an incentive to jump into the presidential contest in at least a few states in order to grab some electoral votes. The goal would be to deny either the major-party nominee a majority of the Electoral College in order to become "the tail that wags the dog," by providing the extra electoral votes required for a majority—in exchange, of course, for a series of concessions on policy and appointments by the winner to be. Imagine the corrupt, backroom deals that could become common in the presidential elections. After all, as long as an election is reasonably close between the two majority-party candidates (as most of them are), a couple of dozen electoral votes secured by third parties would make all the difference. A proportional system of electoral vote allocation (even if there is a cutoff—say 5 percent of a state's vote, below which a party would get no electors) nearly guarantees that any muscular third party would secure some electors. Presidential elections might turn into a fearsome bazaar in the period between the November election day and the December casting of electoral votes. And if the electoral votes were made automatic, as we have recommended above, then many presidents would end up being selected by the House of Representatives (and vice presidents by the US Senate). This is not a prospect that would be welcomed by most Americans. Essentially, we would have shifted the critical choice of national leaders from the people to the Congress in quite a few election years.

As if these prospects were not enough to warn us off any system of proportional allocation of electoral votes, there are practical problems galore in determining just how many electors each party would get per state. Exactly how should popular vote percentages be converted into smaller electoral vote totals in each state? For example, in a state with three electoral votes, how would the votes split up in an election where both candidates get close to 50 percent? How would they split in an election with multiple candidates? Endless controversies and charges of unfairness would await us if we were to go down this road—which we obviously should not.

Electoral College with Superelectors: Under this third proposal, candidates would continue to compete for elections on a state-by-state, winner-take-all basis, but the winner of the national popular vote would be awarded a set of bonus electors. The historian Arthur Schlesinger Jr. suggested this reform in an editorial published in the wake of the 2000 elections.[32] Schlesinger argued that 102 electors go to the general election popular vote winner—two for each state and the District of Columbia. The major advantage of the Schlesinger system, other than guaranteeing that the popular vote winner (if clear) becomes president, would be to give voters in heavily "Red" or "Blue" states incentive to cast their ballots; even though the outcomes were clear in advance in their states, these voters would be contributing to the popular vote total for their candidate and helping him or her to win the national superelectors.

Still, the Schlesinger model would be nothing more than abolition of the Electoral College in disguise, and the substitution of a pure popular vote system. What would happen if the national vote is very close, as it was in the election of 1960, when Schlesinger's candidate, John F. Kennedy, secured a bare plurality of less than 119,000 votes out of about 70 million cast, based in large part on possibly fraudulent returns in Illinois and Texas?[33] JFK was lucky to have had a healthy Electoral College margin (303 to Richard Nixon's 219), which gave his presidency legitimacy despite the near tie in the popular vote. If the superelectors had been the difference between victory and defeat in 1960, Nixon might well have been inclined to seek a recount and to investigate possible shenanigans in the Land of Lincoln and the Lone Star State (and elsewhere). A recount in every state and locality, with the accompanying court disputes in a continental nation, would freeze the process far more than in the disputed 2000 election, when the recount was isolated to one state. Do we want the world's only superpower in crisis, with an acting president (probably the Speaker of the House of Representatives, whose direct popular mandate is limited to his or her tiny congressional district) running the United States for months or years while the election result is litigated and sorted out?

Reform Approaches That Mend the Electoral College ... and Can Work

Having made their way through this thicket of unwise reforms, diligent readers must wonder whether *any* changes can both improve the Electoral College *and* avoid the unintended consequences that have plagued the earlier proposals. In fact, there are three approaches that, together, can constitute a workable and progressive reform package.

Elimination of Faithless Electors: While faithless electors have not previously posed a serious threat to the electoral process, just one could throw a wrench into the machinery in a close election. A new Constitution must include a reform that prevents this possibility, while maintaining the party-building advantages of electors: Make the position of elector a strictly honorary one. The political parties could still offer these posts to their staunchest members, but the individuals would not need to make a trek to the statehouse (except perhaps for some sort of ceremony) and they would not cast an actual vote. Instead, each state's electoral votes would be cast automatically for the winner of the certified popular vote in the state. Surely, this is one change that cannot be very controversial. The political parties will be able to keep these prestigious patronage posts to reward loyal party activists—the honorary position of elector will remain a resume enhancer for those selected—but the nation need not worry about an illegitimate president produced by electors who arbitrarily decided to abandon their solemn pledge to back the people's candidate.

Elimination of the unit rule in the House of Representatives: The second reform, which would also be nearly universally welcomed, would apply whenever the election of a president is thrown into the U.S. House of Representatives, due to the failure of any candidate do secure a majority of electoral votes. Fortunately, this unwelcome event has only occurred twice in American history, in the presidential elections of 1800 and 1824.

Both were highly controversial contests. In 1800 the nation narrowly avoided being deprived of the signal presidency of Thomas Jefferson, and having Aaron Burr substituted instead.[34] In 1824 the machinations in the House resulting in the election of John Quincy Adams as president literally ruined Adams's one term. Having lost both the popular vote and the electoral vote to Andrew Jackson, Adams gained the White House in a "corrupt deal" with a third candidate, Henry Clay—or so Jackson insisted until his dying day. Clay's appointment as Adams's secretary of state appeared to confirm the deal. With a hostile public and many critics in Congress, Adams accomplished little during his frustrating stay in the executive branch, ending with his landslide defeat by Jackson in the election of 1828.[35] (Adams was far more successful in his second career as a crusading antislavery member of the U.S. House from Massachusetts.)

In modern times, America has faced the prospect of a nasty repeat of 1824 in several close elections (including 1968 and 2000). Most citizens are suspicious enough of Congress in good times; one can only try to imagine the deep cynicism that might be engendered should the House pick the president today. But the worse aspect of the House selection process is the unit rule, which mandates that each state shall cast one vote for president, irrespective of the state's size, with a majority of states (twenty-six) being required for the election of a chief executive. So Wyoming (population 505,887) would have the same weight as California (population 35,842,038) in selecting the occupant of the White House for four years. This news would not likely be well received in California—or in any of the populous states. (I call it "news" because 90 percent or more of the American public are unaware of this procedure, last used over 180 years ago.) Even worse, some states would not get to cast a ballot at all, since they would be deadlocked. In most cases, all it would take to produce a deadlock is an equal number of Democrats and Republicans in a state's delegation.[36]

The easiest, most sensible reform is to abolish the unit rule, and let every US representative cast a ballot as he or she sees fit—a ballot for which each member of the House will be held accountable by the constituency at the next election.[37] A good case can be made for preserving the Electoral College as a bulwark of federalism, but the House unit rule in presidential elections is federalism taken to a destructive extreme.[38] Interestingly, James Madison had perceived the antidemocratic nature of the House unit rule as early as 1823, and he urged that each member of the House should be permitted to vote individually for a presidential candidate in the case of Electoral College deadlock. As Madison wrote to his friend George Hay, the House unit rule was too "great a departure from the Republican principle of numerical equality" and was "so pregnant also with a mischievous tendency in practice, that an amendment of the Constitution on this point is justly called for by all its considerate & best friends."[39]

Growing the Electoral College: By now, it should be clear that the Electoral College serves some useful functions and ought to be preserved, especially considering the distasteful alternatives. Yet the college's status quo is not acceptable either. There is too great a chance that the popular vote winner could lose the election, and the lightly populated states have too great a cumulative edge in the Electoral College, mainly due to the automatic two senatorial bonus electoral votes allocated to each state, regardless of size.

In a previous work, I proposed that we give the ten largest states two more Senate seats each, with the next fifteen largest states gaining one additional seat. The twenty-five states with the smallest populations would not forfeit any representation and keep their current two Senate seats.[40] This reallocation of Senate seats would add electoral votes to the heavily populated states and thus help to maximize the opportunity for the popular-vote winner to capture the presidency — while preserving the wonderful college advantage of isolating recounts in close elections to one or a few states. In that sense, expanding the Senate to account for population would send two birds — both outdated constitutional pterodactyls — into well-deserved extinction. The Senate would become more representative of the electorate, and the Electoral College simultaneously would as well.

If the expansion of the Senate proves politically or constitutionally impossible, there is another sound means to accomplish the very same goal in the Electoral College.[41] The college itself could be directly enlarged, and the new electoral votes distributed among the heavily populated states to more closely reflect actual population. In addition to the 538 electoral votes currently allocated among the nation's 50 states and the District of Columbia, this proposal would give states additional electoral votes based on the percentage of the national population.

To see the practical implementation of this plan, take a look at Table 1. A state that has less than 0.5 percent of the national population would keep its current electoral vote total. But states that possess more of the country's population would be given additional electors. Each state that claims between 0.5 to 2.0 percent of the national population would receive one more elector. An additional electoral vote would also be allocated for each additional percent (rounded to the nearest percentage point) of the national population over 2.0 percent. For instance, Alabama (currently possessing nine electoral votes) has 1.5 percent of the nation's population. Since it falls between 0.5 and 2.0 percent, the state would be allotted one more electoral vote, for a total of ten electors. Florida boasts 5.9 percent of the national population, so it would get five additional electoral votes, for a total of thirty-two electors. A large majority of the fifty states (thirty-eight) would gain electoral votes in this fashion, while no state would lose any electoral votes it currently has. This should facilitate passage of the college reform, and voters in the thirty-eight states gaining electors would surely feel a sense of increased empowerment. In all, seventy-four electors would be added to the 538 in the existing Electoral College, for a total of 612. Budget hawks need not be concerned about the college's expansion since no monies are expended in the process. And the possibility of "faithless electors" would not be multiplied because electoral votes — under this new system — would be cast automatically. In fact, the political parties would have dozens more honorary posts to bestow upon their most faithful activists.

In 2004 this new version of the Electoral College would have closely paralleled President Bush's 3-million vote plurality over Democratic senator John Kerry with an electoral victory of 325 to 286. But the real test would come four years earlier. How would this system have worked in the squeaker election of 2000? It would have produced an Electoral College result that more closely reflected the popular vote. With slightly different calculations than those of 2004, due to the fact that the 1990 census allocations of electors were still in effect, the Electoral College would have produced a one-vote victory for Democrat Al Gore over Republican George W. Bush, by 306 to 305.[42] After all, Gore won the popular vote by 540,000, and I have promised that this new method will more accurately reflect the will of the people.[43]

Table 1. Growing the Electoral College in 2004

State	Population	% of National Population	Current No. of Electors	Extra Electors	Total No. of Electors
Alabama	4,525,375	1.5	9	1	10
Alaska	657,755	0.2	3		3
Arizona	5,739,879	2.0	10	1	11
Arkansas	2,750,000	0.9	6	1	7
California	35,842,038	12.2	55	11	66
Colorado	4,601,821	1.6	9	1	10
Connecticut	3,498,966	1.2	7	1	8
Delaware	830,069	0.3	3		3
District of Columbia	554,239	0.2	3		3
Florida	17,385,430	5.9	27	5	32
Georgia	8,918,129	3.0	15	2	17
Hawaii	1,262,124	0.4	4		4
Idaho	1,395,140	0.5	4		4
Illinois	12,712,016	4.3	21	3	24
Indiana	6,226,537	2.1	11	1	12
Iowa	2,952,904	1.0	7	1	8
Kansas	2,733,697	0.9	6	1	7
Kentucky	4,141,835	1.4	8	1	9
Louisiana	4,506,685	1.5	9	1	10
Maine	1,314,985	0.4	4		4
Maryland	5,561,332	1.9	10	1	11
Massachusetts	6,407,382	2.2	12	1	13
Michigan	10,104,206	3.4	17	2	19
Minnesota	5,096,546	1.7	10	1	11
Mississippi	2,900,768	1.0	6	1	7
Missouri	5,759,532	2.0	11	1	12
Montana	926,920	0.3	3		3
Nebraska	1,747,704	0.6	5	1	6
Nevada	2,332,898	0.8	5	1	6
New Hampshire	1,299,169	0.4	4		4
New Jersey	8,685,166	3.0	15	2	17
New Mexico	1,903,006	0.6	5	1	6
New York	19,280,727	6.6	31	6	37
North Carolina	8,540,468	2.9	15	2	17
North Dakota	636,308	0.2	3		3
Ohio	11,450,143	3.9	20	3	23
Oklahoma	3,523,546	1.2	7	1	8
Oregon	3,591,363	1.2	7	1	8
Pennsylvania	12,394,471	4.2	21	3	24

Rhode Island	1,079,916	0.4	4		4
South Carolina	4,197,892	1.4	8	1	9
South Dakota	770,621	0.3	3		3
Tennessee	5,893,298	2.0	11	1	12
Texas	22,471,549	7.7	34	7	41
Utah	2,420,708	0.8	5	1	6
Vermont	621,233	0.2	3		3
Virginia	7,481,332	2.5	13	2	15
Washington	6,207,046	2.1	11	1	12
West Virginia	1,812,548	0.6	5	1	6
Wisconsin	5,503,533	1.9	10	1	11
Wyoming	505,887	0.2	3		3
TOTAL	**293,656,842**	**100.0**	**538**	**74**	**612**

Source: Population totals from U.S. Census, 2004.

PART FIVE

THE CONSTITUTION AND GRIDLOCK

Chapter 8

Thinking about Gridlock

Sanford Levinson

I am truly grateful to have this opportunity to discuss the strengths and weaknesses (primarily the latter, from my perspective) of the United States Constitution with regard to whether it creates an effective government or, instead, plagues us with a system to which the term "gridlock" can be applied. The key word in the previous sentence, on which everything else rests, is "effective." There can be no doubt whatsoever that the Constitution created a system of government that functions; even I concede that we are not in a state of utter collapse. What *is* the subject of debate is whether we are well- or ill-served by aspects of the political system that was created in 1787 and remains remarkably unchanged, in substantial respects, since then, not least, of course, because of the near imperviousness to structural constitutional change created by Article V.

As University of Houston political scientist Donald Lutz has demonstrated, the United States has the most-difficult-to-amend constitution among all current constitutions in the entire world (and, one suspects, therefore, the universe).[1] I suppose that some people might in fact take pride in this fact, though I obviously do not. Indeed, I think it is a vital contributing condition to the extraordinarily depressing failure of even sophisticated Americans to think seriously of structural change. The obverse, after all, of "if it ain't broke, don't fix it," is "if it can't be fixed, then let's pretend that it isn't broken." The psychological mechanism of denial often makes sense, after all, when the prospects for change—or cure—are bleak. Better to assume the best than to sink into moroseness or even depression (a seeming concern of Professor Rabkin in his contribution to this volume). As Bobby McFerrin so memorably advised some years ago, "Don't worry, be happy."

So the obvious issue of contention between Professor Melnick and myself concerns the degree to which our political system is "broken" and, assuming that it *is* seriously defective in some respects, whether there is any plausible way to fix it. It is, I should note immediately, possible that we agree on the latter, which in many ways is a strictly empirical question, even if we vigorously disagree on the former, which, I shall argue, requires a complex mixture of empirical and normative concerns.

It is a special pleasure to be discussing such issues with Professor Melnick, whose work as a political scientist I much admire. It may be worth mentioning in this context that in the sunset years of my academic career, I find myself increasingly reverting to my original identity as a political scientist. One of my complaints about many of my colleagues in the legal academy is that arguments about American government often do not include reference to contemporary political science. Worst of all in this respect, generally speaking, are judges, especially, it appears, those who are graced appointments to the United States Supreme Court. I confess that I became increasingly ill-tempered over the years at reading judicial opinions that rely on quotations from *The Federalist Papers* or Alexis de Tocqueville to support descriptions of our political system today. There may be many valuable things to learn from reading *The Federalist Papers* or *Democracy in America,* but how American political institutions operate, for good or for ill, in the 21st century, is not one of them.

It is as if medical practitioners in the 21st century relied on textbooks written by admitted "giants in the field" some two centuries ago. "Evidence-based medicine" is, happily, on the rise; we should expect more "evidence-based" consideration of the strengths and weaknesses of basic aspects of the American political system, and one, though certainly not the only, source of such evidence is the research of political scientists like Professor Melnick. Quite obviously, I don't consider him the last word, or else I would simply concede defeat in the face of his fine chapter, but I do consider him someone well worth listening to and grappling with. Indeed, I should make clear at the outset that I scarcely disagree with everything he says. To some extent we are arguing whether the American governmental glass is half-empty or half-full. He, I believe, is the optimist, whereas, obviously, I find even a half-full glass to be unacceptably limited. (If truth be known, I am inclined to doubt that it is even half-full, though I do quickly concede that it is scarcely empty.)

This being said, and having given my encomium to evidence-based institutional evaluation, I return to my very first point about the complexities presented by defining institutions as *effective.* One might hope that the term lent itself to an exclusively *empirical* definition, so that we could define effectiveness in a way that clearly transcended any political differences among us. One would hope, for example, that conclusions of the Federal Drug Administration are based more on "scientific evidence" of "effectiveness" rather than on the basis of political ideology. Is there, for example, a discernible "liberal" or "conservative" position as to whether a particular statin is effective in lowering cholesterol, even if there may be some dispute about the overall importance of lowering cholesterol in the first place? And even adamantly antiabortion scientists, I hope, would be able to able to come to the same conclusions as their pro-choice colleagues about the "effectiveness" of a particular drug in aborting pregnancies even if the information in effect counted as "bad news" in the political contexts of the abortion wars. An absolutely crucial issue, then, is what kinds of issues can be resolved through empirical analysis, independent of one's own normative commitments, and, on the contrary, what disputes are more normative than empirical at their core.

I might take this opportunity to mention my own book *Our Undemocratic Constitution: Where the Constitution Goes Wrong (and How We the People Can Correct It),* not only as self-promotion but also as an illustration of the often inextricable joinder of empirical and normative arguments. Part of my argument is certainly intended to be the former. It is, for example, beyond doubt, as already noted, that Article V makes it unusually difficult for Americans to amend their national constitution, just as it is also undeniably true that the American legislative system is considerably more resistant to the successful passage of legislation than is the case in those systems that are parliamentary and unicameral, or even those in which one house of a bicameral legislature can overcome the opposition of the other. And even in presidential systems, it is extremely important to know whether the president has a veto power and, if so, how many votes it takes in the legislature to override a veto.[2] But agreement on these facts — or even the more controversial assertion that these features of our system merit the term "undemocratic" as a description at least if one agrees, perhaps by stipulation, to define "democracy" as requiring a certain level of immediate responsiveness to majoritarian preferences — does not entail at all that one agree as well that our "undemocratic" and "veto-point-laden" system is also *dysfunctional.*

That is almost certainly a strongly value laden term that elicits a different kind of argument that a disagreement, say, on whether it takes two-thirds of each House of Congress or merely three-fifths of the entire Congress to override a veto.

From my perspective, our Constitution makes it considerably harder than it should be for our basic institutions to respond to the exigencies that face the American polity. John Marshall once wrote that any enduring Constitution must inevitably be "adapted" in order to "respond to the various crises of human affairs."[3] He was almost certainly correct, and the challenge facing us as American citizens—and as constitutional analysts—is to determine whether our Constitution is up to the challenge or, indeed, whether it constitutes a barrier to effective responses to the crises that face us. I strongly believe the latter; Professor Melnick appears to believe that our present Constitution is up to any challenges that face it (and us) as a polity.

So how do we decide whether or not, to adopt the title of an important book by Washington veterans Thomas Mann and Norman Ornstein, Congress is "the broken branch";[4] indeed, is it possible, as we look beyond Congress, that we could find even more evidence of "breakage"? In answering such questions, though, can one look to the same kind of unequivocal, "value-free," as it were, evidence that might be brought forth if someone referred to a "broken arm" or a "broken water main," or even the more complex evidence that might support someone's description of suffering from a "broken heart"? After all, in the latter case, even if one believed that the person suffering from a broken heart should realize that she is well rid of the heel, that is not at all evidence for the proposition that she isn't suffering at the moment from something that we generally describe as the phenomenon of a broken heart. So is a broken Congress analogous to a broken arm or even a broken heart, on the one hand, or are we instead forced in effect to suspend our strictly empirical inquiries in order to engage in a very different normative inquiry? For better and, possibly, for worse, the latter is the case.

The failure to recognize this rather basic point vitiates the importance of what is undoubtedly important empirical work done by some of our leading political scientists, including that presented by Professor Melnick in his paper. I'm sure that Prof. Melnick will agree with me that probably the most important work in this context is that done by Yale political scientist David Mayhew, whose important book *Divided We Govern: Party Control, Lawmaking, and Investigations, 1946–2002*[5] is certainly the leading defense for the proposition that we have a decidedly ungridlocked government even in the circumstances where one might most expect it, i.e., "divided governments" where one party controls the executive branch and another party controls at least one house of the Congress.

It may be worth noting that one seeming attribute of such divided government is the greater frequency of congressional *oversight* over the executive that by definition is headed by the leader of the opposition party. I applaud such oversight and believe that one dysfunctionality of undivided government is precisely its general absence. This doesn't constitute gridlock as the term is generally defined, but it certainly exemplifies the failure, for example, of the Madisonian vision of "separation of powers" as set out in *Federalist* No. 51. "Ambition" simply does not "counteract ambition," at least institutionally, once the variable of party enters the scene, alas.[6] Thus there may be a strongly inverse relationship between gridlock and oversight, so that even if one agrees that undivided governments are more likely to produce significant legislation, one must also recognizes that that enhanced capacity comes at the price of diminished oversight. Any serious discussion of "constitutional obsolescence" and reparative design must take this into account.

In any event, what most perturbs me about Professor Mayhew's and Professor Melnick's otherwise superb work is the failure to pay full account to the implicit normative assumptions that are inevitably being smuggled into their rather optimistic tellings of the contemporary story of American politics. Let me make the point as clearly as possible: It is simply not enough to present what are undoubtedly true and accurate lists of what the Congress has been able to pass, even during times of divided government, when the opportunities for partisan mischief are presumably maximized, in order to prove that we are not the victims of gridlock in the contemporary American constitutional order. Those lists comprise only titles of bills and the numbers of such legislative acts, nothing more.

The real task before us is not to enumerate, but, rather, to *evaluate* the quality of the legislation. That task necessarily has a normative—perhaps one wishes to call it an ultimately *political*—dimension that doesn't fit easily with the notion of value-free social science. Yes, a divided government gave us the prescription drug bill,[7] not to mention the list of bills set forth by Professor Melnick. That is undoubtedly correct. But, with regard to the former, we could spend the rest of our time together debating whether it represented the best, or even a truly adequate, way of responding to the economic exigencies facing an increasing number of elderly (or at least late-middle-age) Americans or, rather, whether it operated primarily as a gigantic corporate welfare program to politically well-connected "big pharma." We could undoubtedly have similar debates about one of the signature achievements of President Bush's first two years, the passage, with the strong support of Democratic Sen. Edward M. Kennedy, of "No Child Left Behind" and *its* adequacy with regard to meeting the challenge that was in fact eloquently identified by President Bush. One could march through the entire litany of bills presented, by party leaders and at least some political scientists alike, as achievements of the national government and debate whether they really represented truly serious attempts to come to grips with the most serious problems facing the United States today. Yes, it's true that Congress endorsed most of President Obama's stimulus package, but only after a Republican gang-of-three was able to extort some significant cuts in trade for their willingness to refuse to join a Republican-led filibuster of the entire bill. Perhaps we didn't need the extra $100 billion or so, but if we did—and only time will tell—then this will scarcely be the achievement described by Prof. Melnick.

There is an even more serious problem presented by counting up only the bills that pass, even if we concede, for sake of argument, that at least some of them *do* represent admirable attempts to confront serious social maladies. For we must compare and contrast the rather small subset of bills that are passed against a far larger subset of bills that never had a chance of passing. I mentioned my late-in-life reversion to my original identity as a political scientist. I confess as well that I find myself returning to some of the basic political science debates of the 1960s dealing with what sorts of issues and legislation actually get on the congressional agenda and which are simply consigned to oblivion.[8] Youngsters are often taught, in so-called civics courses, "how a bill becomes a law." The more relevant lesson might well be why most bills, whatever their merits, are doomed to failure.

I might, for that matter, offer similar observations with regard to the institution of American politics that I in fact know best, the United States Supreme Court. One of the most interesting and important aspects of that court (unlike, say, courts of appeals) is that it has almost complete autonomy over its docket. As Professor Fowler Harper noted in a series of important articles in the 1940s, the cases *not* taken by the Court and the issues left unexamined by that august body are often at least as important as the cases they did take.[9] This is what makes the title of my colleague H.W. Perry's important book about the court, *Deciding to Decide*,[10] so resonant, for often the most important decision the court makes is to reject a given petition for certiorari, however meritorious it might appear to outside observers, because the court, for whatever reason, simply doesn't want to tackle the issue at that particular (or, perhaps, *any*) moment.

It was the late Alexander Bickel who coined the term "the passive virtues" for this distinctly *discretionary* aspect of the court's handiwork.[11] Bickel was happy to endorse Justice Brandeis's reminder that "not doing" was often "the most important thing we do."[12] This may well be true, though, obviously, those who are the victims of the court's procrastination may have a decidedly less optimistic view of its virtues. So even if we can all agree that Bickel identified an important empirical feature of the court's modus operandi, we should agree as well that he also sparked a debate that has not ended to this day about its *propriety*. This is not the occasion to delve further into that debate, but it is enough to note that any position one takes will inevitably be influenced by the normative views one has of the role of the Supreme Court and, for that matter, the meaning of "equal justice under law." So it is with the decisions made by Congress and presidents, passive or not, virtuous or not, to eliminate certain issues from their agenda year after year because they are too costly along some partisan dimension. (Consider the common reference to Social Security reform as the "third rail" of American politics, as is almost certainly true of proposals to raise taxes in order to meet certain environmental goals and the like.)

So any full consideration of arguments like Professors Mayher's and Melnick's should require at least equal attention to the proposals that did not get passed or, indeed, were never even seriously considered. This may well have occurred because political realists chose not to engage in what would have been described as quixotic expenditures of their inevitably scarce political time and energy. I have noted elsewhere, for example, all of the disincentives to allocating one's resources to supporting structural amendments to the Constitution. This may be only somewhat less the case with proposals for legislation that seem doomed when one considers particular features of the House or, far more likely, the Senate.

At that point one would have to determine to what extent such "legislative failures"— assuming, of course, one was willing to accord the term "failure" to such lapses—were attributable to defects in the organization of Congress (or the Constitution) that might, if reformed, lead to happier results in the future or, rather, were destined to occur for reasons having nothing to do with such institutional factors. Let me note as well that even those who believe reform is desirable, perhaps even necessary, may nonetheless choose to be decidedly non-quixotic in what they focus on. That is, there are understandable inclinations to emphasize what could be changed *without* raising any constitutional questions.

That is certainly the approach taken by Mann and Ornstein, who, for all of their genuine and merited concern about our broken Congress, are nonetheless full of good cheer inasmuch as they suggest that the cures necessary to fix the branch do not require us to confront Article V at all. The book would have been far more somber, however, if it had instead addressed those facets of Congress that are constitutionally determined. Not only would this mean that they were impervious to ordinary legislative change; it would also suggest, alas, imperviousness even to constitutional change because of the terrible hurdles to amendment erected by the framers of Article V.

It is useful in this context to consider some changes recently suggested by Professor Barbara Sinclair, another eminent student of Congress, with regard to the operations of that institution.[13] Like Professor Melnick himself, she is scarcely a naïve champion of our current legislative institutions, and she endorses the desirability of change. But she and Professor Melnick focus exclusively on a number of issues and problems that require no constitutional tinkering. It is undoubtedly true, for example, that the filibuster has become increasingly important in the Senate, where it has become simply standard-operating procedure for forty-one senators to block the consideration of bills that, by definition, have the support of a majority of the Senate (and have often handily passed the House of Representatives).[14] Jean Edward Smith recently published a blog in the *New York Times* correctly referring to the "trivialization" of the filibuster.[15] "In the entire 19th century," Smith notes, "including the struggle against slavery, fewer than two dozen filibusters were mounted." In the early 20th century, it became basically synonymous with the blockage by white Southern senators of federal civil rights legislation, though there were occasional deviations from this pattern, as with an attempt by Senate liberals in 1963 to block the passage of a federal communications act that was seen as far too friendly to AT&T. Still, Smith writes, through the administration of Lyndon B. Johnson (where the number of filibusters more than doubled from the four that occurred during Kennedy's brief presidency), "[e]xcept for exhibitionists, buffoons and white southerners determined to salvage racial segregation, the filibuster was considered off limits."

Ironically, the passage of civil rights legislation in the 1960s and 70s removed the occasion for what might be termed "classic" filibusters but led to their enhanced legitimacy precisely because they were no longer identified with unworthy goals. "Increasingly senators of all ideological persuasions began to consider the filibuster an acceptable weapon," with the Carter and Reagan administrations seeing roughly 20 filibusters per year. "Filibusters are a necessary evil," said Senator Robert Byrd of West Virginia said in 1988. "They must be tolerated lest the Senate lose its special strength and become a mere appendage to the House of Representatives." Needless to say, it is not a self-evident truth that the country would be harmed if the Senate lost "its special strength" and became more of an "appendage to the House of Representatives." It would, to be sure, require us to question the contemporary relevance of George Washington's famous "saucer that cools the tea" defense of the Senate, but, unless one is truly an ancestor worshipper, that shouldn't be a problem.

In any event, Smith describes the Clinton administration as the "years that the dam broke. In the 103rd Congress (1993–1994), 32 filibusters were employed to kill a variety of presidential initiatives ranging from campaign finance reform to grazing fees on federal land. Between 1999 and 2007, the number of Senate filibusters varied between 20 and 37 per session, a bipartisan effort." Democrats, of course, used the filibuster to block the confirmation of a number of judges nominated by President Bush, and a 2005 proposal by then-Senate Majority Leader William Frist to eliminate the filibuster with regard to judicial confirmations was described as the threat of a "'nuclear option,' evoking images of Armageddon and total destruction." For what it is worth, David Law and I have written an article, using modern game theory, to argue that the achievement of negotiated nuclear disarmament, at least if only two adversaries are involved, is in fact easier to envision than the breaking of what some consider the partisan gridlock increasingly generated by judicial nominations to almost *any* federal court. Indeed, I note that Republicans are currently (April 2009) threatening to filibuster the nomination of Dawn Johnson to head the Office of Legal Counsel within the Department of Justice, a decidedly nonlifetime but in fact very important appointment, which suggests that the partisan warfare will get far worse before it abates in some Edenic future.

According to Smith, "the routine use of the filibuster as a matter of everyday politics has transformed the Senate's legislative process from majority rule into minority tyranny." It is theoretically possible for the forty-one senators representing only the thirty-four million people who live in the twenty-one least populous states—a little more than 11 percent of the nation's population—to render irrelevant the preferences of those senators who represent the remaining 88 percent of the United States. That is, to be sure, only a theoretical possibility, for, among other things, it emphasizes only state population and totally ignores the all-important dimension of political party loyalties of the senators involved in filibusters. But it is interesting to note in this regard some recent research by an Oxford graduate student demonstrating that the propensity of large states to send Democrats to the Senate means, as a matter of fact, that Democratic filibusters are more likely to represent a majority of the actual population than is the case with Republican-led filibusters.[16]

All of this has led Norman Ornstein to write of "Our Broken Senate."[17] He notes the increasing importance not only of filibusters, but also of the perhaps even more egregious—because far less visible—practice within the Senate as honoring "holds" placed by individual senators on the consideration of presidential nominees or even substantive legislation itself. The Senate operates often under "unanimous consent" rules, which by definition allow one idiosyncratic senator to prevent legislation moving forward even if supported by overwhelming majorities. Ornstein offers as his specific example the hold placed by Oklahoma Senator Coburn, because of his refusal to join in unanimous consent, to a gun control bill that was favored by both the National Rifle Association and the Brady Campaign to Prevent Gun Violence that had passed the House of Representatives unanimously. "For months after enactment by the House, the legislation remained in limbo," Ornstein writes, "until finally limping to enactment at then end of the year—not a shining example of how government can work but instead a casualty of the way the Senate operates." Given Professor Melnick's own remarks about such holds, I am confident that he shares Ornstein's dismay. But the holds, of course, remain an important arrow in any given senator's quiver, in addition, of course, to the more collective hindrance to senatorial decision exemplified by the filibuster. I note that as I write these remarks on May 13, 2009, the *New York Times* reports that a Republican filibuster is preventing the confirmation of the number two official within the Interior Department because of the opposition of two senators from Utah and Alaska to the cancellation of oil leases by the Obama Administration.[18] Whether or not the inability of President Obama to complete the task of filling his administration counts as an example of gridlock, it is hard to see that it exemplifies the kind of functioning government we need in these parlous times. No doubt he shares some of the blame for the vacancies that exist. But practices of the Senate deserve their own scrutiny as well.

Paul Light, the leading academic expert on the staffing of the federal bureaucracy, recently wrote in the *Times* that "[t]he Senate," which is granted by the Constitution, of course, the responsibility of scrutinizing high-level presidential appointments, "has done virtually nothing, for example, to address the glacial pace of confirmations that often leads presidents to expand the White House staff as well as the number of appointees who serve without Senate approval." Indeed, according to Professor Light, President Obama "has submitted the names of nominees to the Senate relatively quickly," but he "will be lucky if the last of his nearly 500 full-time cabinet and subcabinet officers are confirmed by March 2010." Light notes that the Senate in 2004 rejected "House-sponsored reforms that would have cut the red tape that strangles the process."[19]

Still, the point is that no one has ever argued that the Constitution *requires* the possibility of filibusters or the other egregious behaviors associated with the Senate, as is true of the scourge of partisan gerrymandering that afflicts the House of Representatives and helps to encourage political trench warfare and, even if not so often, because of the rules of the House, gridlock. Indeed, some argue that filibusters are unconstitutional.[20] All one can say is that the Constitution, wisely or not, assigned to each house of Congress the power to make its own rules of procedure.[21] Those rules could obviously be changed were there but political will to do so—or a popular movement that would exact electoral retribution against senatorial mossbacks who prefer to maintain their own prerogatives regardless of the costs to the country. What political scientists must explain is why there is no movement, either within the Senate or "out-of-doors," as eighteenth-century theorists would have put it, to change such open invitations to dysfunctionality. Is there any "respectable" support for the temptations to individualized tyranny instantiated in holds?

Still, we should not confine our attention only to those things, important as they are, that *could* be changed by unilateral decision of the collective Senate. Contrast eminently malleable aspects of congressional procedures with, for example, the "hard-wired" ability, even putting the filibuster to one side, of a one-vote majority in the indefensibly, albeit constitutionally required, malapportioned Senate to kill legislation backed by perhaps hefty majorities in the House of Representatives and senators who represent by any calculation a majority of the American people. And, of course, even if the legislation is not killed outright, the compromises necessary to gain the approval of both houses of Congress might well diminish the practical importance of the legislation. There is nothing in the nature of bicameralism that requires such veto power. Many systems around the world are able to enjoy some of the genuine benefits of bicameralism without giving each of the two houses a complete veto power over the other.[22] Often, the lower, more popularly accountable house is given the ultimate power to break deadlocks.[23] Such a change in the American political system would, of course, dramatically transform the way that American politics are conducted.

But any discussion of gridlock must also include the presidential veto, another constitutional creation that gives the President of the United States, with the stroke of a pen — or, if Congress is not in session, simply by virtue of putting legislation in his "pocket" — the power to override what may be substantial, albeit not two-thirds majorities, in each house of Congress. I regard it as nothing short of bizarre that so much ink has been spilled about the ostensible countermajoritarian status of judicial review and almost none about the far more important countermajoritarianism attached to the presidential veto. The President's veto power, especially during periods of divided government, effectively transforms us into a *tricameral* political system, with the third house consisting ultimately of a single great decider. I am well aware that the institutional reality is considerably more complex, but no one familiar with American politics over the past eight years can deny the importance of the given individual who occupies the Oval Office.

Even if one wishes to justify the policy-based (as distinguished from a Constitution-based) veto by the President, there is, I think, almost literally no argument at all for the extraordinary threshold of votes in the House and the Senate required to overturn the veto. Ninety-five percent of all presidential vetoes stick. Unless one has some special reason to sanctify presidential authority, this seems to me almost self-evidently too high a success rate. And this doesn't include, of course, the far higher number of bills that are never introduced in the first place or modified beyond recognition in order to warrant the President's precious signature.

I realize that some people defend the presidential veto not only on tea-cooling grounds, but also because of the ostensible role of the President as a tribune of the entire American people, in contrast to the far more parochial Congress. There is not enough time to explore this argument in depth. Suffice it to say for now that I regard this argument as close to bogus, because of the way that another egregious feature of the Constitution, the Electoral College, structures incentives both for presidential candidates and then for elected presidents interested in re-election. Although I don't agree with every word of Professor Edwards's chapter, suffice it to say that do agree with him that we should junk the Electoral College and replace it with a national popular-vote election.[24]

It is, then, not enough to emulate the classic drunk who looks for the lost car keys under the street light (because it's easier to see there) and focus exclusively on changes that could be adopted simply through the passage of legislation because it is indeed far easier to imagine that occurring than the successful surmounting of the barriers placed in the way of reform by Article V. I obviously don't want to deny that many legislatively-possible changes *would* be highly desirable; I simply want to assert that they are only a necessary condition, and not at all a sufficient condition for the changes we need in order to have a truly effective twenty-first-century political order.

This might also be the propitious point to address Professor Melnick's very interesting point that the existence of what I view as multiple veto points can be described, again more optimistically, as providing multiple entry points for the making of public policy. There is, of course, much truth in what he says. To the extent that public policy need not be highly coordinated—indeed, *national* in scope—then I concede merit as well as truth. However, if we *do* require the kind of coordination that only policy made from the center can ultimately provide, then, once more, I am the pessimist. To be sure, this requires a precise delineation of what policies require decision making by Congress. It would be interesting to see how much Professor Melnick and I would agree or disagree on any such list, but I am confident that he cannot believe that there are no such policies that are currently being insufficiently addressed by Congress.

So this is where the long-ago debates of 1968—and, for that matter, my own actions that year in helping to found what was called the "caucus for a new political science"— remain relevant. What was wrong with the "old political science"? It was not merely that some of us were less than rapturous about some of the methodological tendencies then sweeping the profession. And, after all, contemporary political science departments are often riven by debates over the centrality of, say, rational choice theory, formal modeling, statistical analysis, or intense field study of given political institutions, as against, say, more historically focused study of the development of American (or other) political institutions—even if we set aside disputes about the comparative merits of normative, instead of so-called positive, political theory. But it would be a mistake to reduce the turmoil of four decades ago—or my criticisms now—to methodological disputation.

Far more fundamental, both then and now, is the relative complacence displayed by many political scientists (and almost everyone else) with regard to what some of us view as obvious deficiencies in the American political system. Again, one simply cannot escape the injection of normative politics into this debate. In 1968, of course, the focus was on such issues as the Vietnam War and the urban unrest sparked by the intersection of racial and class injustice. Today, we would focus on different crises, but crises there most certainly are, whatever one's politics. Those on the left might emphasize the millions of Americans without adequate health insurance or a safety net in the event of losing their jobs, not to mention concern about the actual job losses themselves. Conservatives might well be concerned about the prospective bankruptcy of the American economy should certain entitlement programs, the most important of which is probably Medicare, not be brought under some kind of effective cost-controls, not to mention the economic consequences of the various bailouts and stimuli that are offered as nostrums for the present crisis.

Many other examples could obviously be given. In any event, one cause for the rise of the broken branch debate is that Congress has proven itself incapable of generating an adequate response to practically *any* of these issues, let alone such potentially catastrophic possibilities as global warming. There is an alternative to congressional government, of course, which is the inexorable movement of power toward the executive (or occasionally, the judiciary), which acts more-or-less independently of any traditional notion of congressional authority.[25] That, to be sure, is one way that gridlocks might be broken, but for some, including myself, the cure might be worse than the disease, at least from the perspective of what is best in the vision of a "Republican Form of Government," that presumes that public deliberation and the election of representatives to Congress will in fact serve as the primary mechanism of generating the rules that bind us.

So I return to my central point: To evaluate Congress (or any other political institution) and to either define or evaluate gridlock requires adopting an inevitably *political* stance as to what constitutes success or failure. Professor Sinclair is absolutely correct, therefore, in writing that "most of us inevitably evaluate [Congress's] performance, at least in part, in terms of our own notions of what is good public policy—that is, through an ideological lens."[26] I do not know how one can have discussions of dysfunctionality, or for that matter functionality, without having some sort of baseline as to what satisfies us—what we count as a Congress that is doing its job well enough. One obviously need not share a given baseline: for all of my admiration of Professor Melnick, I suspect that we may not entirely share the same ideological preferences, and I am even more confident this is the case with regard to some of the other participants in the symposium. But might we not both agree that any evaluation requires a candid recognition of what those preferences are?

One potential preference is for a perfectly just society, one that lives up in every conceivable way to the great aspirations set out in the Preamble to the United States Constitution. It is, however, extraordinarily foolish to make such utopian demands on our political institutions. We must indeed always ask what count as *reasonable* demands. To expect to achieve utopia is obviously unreasonable, but it is equally unreasonable to be satisfied with performance that falls far short of serious confrontation with deep and real problems. Utopianism is one danger, but an equal danger is thoughtless veneration of the Constitution and acceptance of the status quo that it bequeaths us.

As I have written elsewhere, "To the extent that we continue thoughtlessly to venerate, and therefore not subject to truly critical examination, our Constitution, we are in the position of the battered wife who continues to profess the 'essential goodness' of her abusive husband."[27] One might hear the battered partner describing the batterer—usually, though not always, the husband—as not *that* bad. He gets drunk and beats up his spouse (or the children) "only" once or twice a month. Otherwise, he's often a "good father" and a "good provider." No marriage is perfect, after all, and some hard-headed (and hearted) analysts might say that the complaining spouse should be grateful for her blessings instead of dwelling on the infrequent, though admittedly indefensible, misconduct. Some of these statements might even be true. But, for better or (doubtfully) for worse, we simply have higher standards these days as to what constitutes an acceptable marriage. Being beaten up, even infrequently, or being otherwise abused, no longer meets even minimal criteria of acceptability. So we talk to victims of spousal abuse about the importance of changing things. Perhaps it will be sufficient to seek therapeutic counseling. Ultimately, though, one might encourage the envisioning of a brand new institutional reality that could be produced by slamming the door on the way out of such a dysfunctional marriage.

So let me conclude with a couple of concrete examples of the kinds of changes that I think we should be discussing if we want to make Congress a more effective institution than it currently is (or is capable of being without reform). One might begin with the Senate. My own view is that the equality of voting power of senators from Wyoming and California is absolutely illegitimate in a society that professes to take seriously the norm of one person, one vote. After all, the source of this equality of voting power in the Senate was the felt necessity by James Madison and others to submit to the extortionate demands of small states like Delaware in order to forestall an even worse evil of collapse of the Constitutional Convention and the dire consequences attending that possibility.[28] Consider only Madison's awkward attempt to defend the equal allocation of voting power in *Federalist* No. 62:

> The equality of representation in the Senate is another point, which, being evidently
> the result of compromise between the opposite pretensions of the large and the

small states, does not call for much discussion.... [I]t is superfluous to try by the standards of theory, a part of the constitution which is allowed on all hands to be the result not of theory, but 'of a spirit of amity, and that mutual deference and concession which the peculiarity of our political situation rendered indispensable.' ... A government founded on principles more consonant to the wishes of the larger states, is not likely to be obtained from the smaller states. The only option then for the former lies between the proposed government and a government still more objectionable. Under this alternative the advice of prudence must be, to embrace the lesser evil.[29]

A "lesser evil," of course, remains an evil, even if one justified by its forestalling an even worse development. Moreover, the small states were able to achieve, in Article V, a truly insurmountable barrier to any change of this allocation of voting power inasmuch as it requires unanimous consent, which is unthinkable on the part of small states faced with losing their disproportionate power in the Senate.[30] We are, altogether unfortunately, stuck with a situation that was hard to defend at its time of origin and is even less defensible today. The Senate, along with slavery, was one of the two "great compromises" that enabled the proposal and ratification of the Constitution. No one would think of praising the values undergirding chattel slavery today; one wonders exactly why the Senate is any different. Still, to suggest changing the allocation of power in the Senate would probably strike most readers as utopian, precisely because there is no good reason to believe that it is possible without a revolution, which I do not in fact advocate. So both Professor Sinclair and I—and, I suspect, Professor Melnick—agree that we "would redo the Senate if [we] could.... But that is not going to happen."[31]

But consider a proposal inspired by another contributor to our volume, University of Virginia political scientist Larry Sabato, who in his book, *A More Perfect Constitution: 23 Proposals to Revitalize Our Constitution and Make America a Fairer Country*, suggests that the number of senators be increased.[32] Sabato would also give larger states at least a bit more representation in the Senate,[33] but, as already indicated, achieving that is scarcely imaginable. But imagine a proposal consistent with equal representation: each state could have three senators instead of the present two, thus increasing the membership of the Senate by fifty. Why would anyone object to this? Consider that the last time the membership of the Senate increased was 1959, when Hawaii was added to the Union. Since then the population of the United States has increased from approximately 175 million to over 300 million.[34] Even more to the point, the actual range of issues facing the Congress of 1959 is not remotely similar to the Congress of 2009 in terms of the agenda facing the modern Congress.

The earlier Congresses did pass some important legislation, such as the federal highway bill passed during the Eisenhower Administration that transformed the country.[35] But can anyone doubt that today's Congress has an incredibly increased workload relative to that facing the 100 senators in 1959? No one fifty years ago was considering national education or medical policy, environmental policy, multi-faceted energy policy, and the conduct of foreign and military policy in an increasingly multipolar world. Generally, when an organization takes on many new onerous tasks, it hires additional workers. One can certainly be confident that the number of senatorial staff and committee aides has expanded, perhaps exponentially, since 1959. But it is not clear that this automatically translates into better informed senators, who are charged with actually having to decide and to vote; each of the present 100 senators has necessarily limited time to absorb the information produced by the most conscientious of staffs.[36] Even if one assumes a kind of division of labor among the senators, there still may be too much on the plate of any given senator. Thus the call by Sabato for an increase in the number of senators (and, he argues as well, in the House of Representatives).[37]

Still, the achievement of such a sensible change, which has no perceptible partisan tilt, would require the amendment of Article I, Section 3, which establishes that each state shall have *two* senators.[38] And, sadly, no political figure within what might be called the respectable mainstream of American politics has been willing to call for such a sensible and nonradical proposal. Why not? Even if it might indeed have some unforeseen consequences, is it really so likely that they would be sufficiently perverse to erase the benefits of having senators who might be able to spend marginally more time developing some relative expertise on vital issues of the day and thus help to counterbalance administrative agencies and entrenched bureaucracies?

Both Sabato and I bemoan the fact that *every* member of Congress is in effect a local official, responsive to the often parochial concerns or his or her constituents and therefore having no real incentive, unless contemplating a run for the presidency, to think in terms of a more general national interest. Perhaps one could add to the present Senate, whether consisting of 100 or 150 members, a number of *ex officio* members, with full voting rights, drawn, say, from former presidents and vice-presidents, speakers of the House, members of the Supreme Court, heads of the Joint Chiefs of Staff, chairs of the Federal Reserve Board, and the like. Again that would take a constitutional amendment, but I don't think it would necessarily require unanimous approval insofar as none of the new members would be viewed as "representing" a particular state.

To be sure, one might accept Akhil Reed Amar's invitation to think even more boldly by attempting to circumvent the straitjacket of Article V by passing an ordinary Article V amendment that simply defangs the Senate by removing almost all of its present powers and replacing it, assuming that we continue to believe that bicameralism is desirable, with a new institution that enjoys most of the current Senate's powers *and* is defensibly constituted. Although I doubt the likelihood of such a proposal gaining much traction in the foreseeable future, I would absolutely rejoice if it did, not least because it would generate the vital national conversation we need to have about the costs and benefits of the present Senate.

A more mundane proposal would be to eliminate our present delay between election day, in early November, and the arrival of the newly elected Congress almost two months later and, in presidential-election years, the inauguration of the winner a full two weeks later. To be sure, it used to be much worse, prior to the Twentieth Amendment in 1933. Then a new Congress did not necessarily meet until thirteen months after the election, and lame-duck congresses possessed full power for at least four full months,[39] assuming that a new President called the newly elected Congress into special session on March 4, the old inauguration day. Thus FDR's mythic 100 Days of legislative achievement were made possible only because he had called Congress into special session. Similarly, Abraham Lincoln was able to govern much like a "dictator"[40] during the first four months of the war initiated at Fort Sumter because of his unilateral decision to delay the special session of Congress until July 4, 1861.[41]

One should applaud the insight of the framers of the Twentieth Amendment in recognizing that the existing inauguration day, March 4, had become dysfunctional, and that the time of lame-duck service should be considerably shorted. Indeed, no special session has been called by a President since the ratification of the amendment. But we should recognize that the times they established seventy-five years ago are equally unsuitable for us today as the earlier times were for the generation of 1933. The United States deserves a fully-functioning and legitimate government at the earliest possible moment following elections, and our

Constitution most definitely does not provide that, especially when, as in 2008, the government in power was thoroughly and unequivocally repudiated by the electorate.

Why would anyone believe this to be desirable? "Lengthy presidential transitions rank among the oddest of America's political traditions," writes *Washington Post* columnist Jim Hoagland.[42] "In the 21st century, they are also among the most dangerous."[43] One could say this as well about the continuation of lame-duck congresses during most of the transition. One can only wonder what the costs of the present way of doing—or, more accurately, not doing—business were because of the only minimally functioning Congress that existed between November 4, 2008 and the new Congress that came into session on January 6, 2009. Would anyone *not* describe that key two months in the current economic crisis as featuring a gridlocked national government?

One might have thought that the almost self-evident dysfunctionality generated by the postelection hiatus before the newly elected officials took power would lead to suggestions for amending the Constitution to save us from such problems in the future, but that most certainly did not occur. As I have already suggested, one of the most awful parts of the Constitution is Article V, which has made constitutional change of *any* serious kind basically unthinkable because any proposals, even if completely sensible, appear doomed to fail.[44]

Thus the attraction for many—perhaps most—readers of Professor Sinclair's point that "reformers who actually want to get something done" are well advised "to concentrate on small-bore internal reforms" of Congress.[45] I can easily understand the appeal of pragmatically focusing on what might be achievable in the short term, but I fear that confining ourselves to only "small-bore" proposals will only reinforce what has often been called "the normative power of the actual." Apparently one need not be a full-blown Hegelian to believe that what is real is therefore rational and, therefore, that we do not need to subject reality to critical analysis. Political scientists have much to offer us, more, I often think, than do legal academics whose perception of what is truly important about our Constitution is sadly limited. But even after forty years, I fear that the elements of complacence fed by emphasis on the potential dangers presented by any proposals for significant deviation from the institutional status quo vitiate some of what we might otherwise learn from political science. It all depends, I suppose, on the degree to which we feel endangered by the status quo. For many of us the victory of Barack Obama is indeed a harbinger of morning in America. But we will find out, in the next few years, whether even he can surmount the institutional obstacles placed in the way of those who believe that truly significant—even radical—changes are necessary to prevent the political equivalent of driving over the cliff.

We are currently in the midst of almost society-wide discussions of the need to reorganize the basics of the American economic system, especially with regard to financial services, in order to respond adequately not only to immediate crises of 2008–09, but also to the more systemic challenges posed by globalization. No serious person of any political persuasion believes that decisions made in the 1930s, during the last Great Depression, should necessarily be treated as sacrosanct today. Similarly, anyone interested in making the United Nations more effective in the future must confront the peculiar allocation of veto power in the Security Council, which is explicable entirely by reference to the particular winners of a struggle that ended now over six decades ago. Again, no sensible person would say that because Franklin Roosevelt, Harry Truman, and their compatriots in Great Britain and the Soviet Union agreed to give France the veto power—and because no one in 1945 would have proposed giving Japan or Germany such power—that should necessarily remain unchanged in a radically different twenty-first century.

It is only with regard to the United States Constitution, drafted 220 years ago, that what I am sometimes tempted to call a "cult of stasis" stifles our imaginative faculties. What makes it even worse is that relatively few members of this cult might agree with the particular notion of "originalism" preached by, say, Justices Thomas or Scalia. Rather, it is the product of the all-too-correct perception that Article V makes amendment extraordinarily difficult if not functionally impossible. It is easier to maintain a state of resolute denial, coupled, at times, with an overemphasis on why we should be fearful of the unanticipated consequences of any proposed reforms.

This volume is itself a welcome (and still rare) manifestation of a willingness to confront the adequacy of the Constitution. My hope is that it is the harbinger of future—and widespread—public conversation about this vital topic. Will we be able to envision—and then work to bring about—necessary modifications, perhaps even genuine transformations, of our sclerotic political institutions in order to navigate the particular challenges posed by life in the twenty-first century? For me, at least, this is far more than simply an academic question.

Chapter 9

Does the Constitution Encourage Gridlock?

R. Shep Melnick

One of the most common and persistent complaints about the US Constitution is that by making legislation so hard to pass, it frequently produces political stalemate and policy gridlock. Our distinctive combination of separation of powers, bicameralism, and localistic representation creates so many veto points in the legislative process that intensely committed minorities can often thumb their noses at popular majorities and at times produce government paralysis. As Sanford Levinson puts it in his recent book, *Our Undemocratic Constitution: Where the Constitution Goes Wrong (and How We the People Can Correct It)*, "it is relatively easy these days to find a wide range of agreement that the American system is impervious to needed change."[1] Levinson attributes "Congress's inability to pass significant legislation regarding issues about which the public is legitimately worried" to "the structure of the government imposed by the Constitution."[2] Thus his call for fundamental constitutional revision. Many distinguished students of American politics have made a similar argument, ranging from Woodrow Wilson and other Progressives at the turn of the twentieth century to James McGregor Burns, Lloyd Cutler, Robert Dahl, and James Sundquist in more recent years.[3]

There can be no doubt but that the stalemate/gridlock argument captures a key feature of American government. Who could deny that our Constitution establishes an "obstacle course on Capitol Hill" that often makes it excruciatingly difficult for Congress to enact legislation on controversial issues? Those of us who teach introductory American politics classes cannot discuss the legislative process—or civil rights or welfare reform or healthcare politics or virtually anything else—without repeating ad nauseam that important legislation is almost always hard to pass. Consider the ignominious defeat of immigration legislation in 2008, Congress's continuing inability to pass legislation addressing global warming, and its failure to address the looming Social Security deficit. Most importantly, prospects for taking significant steps toward reducing our huge budget deficit remain grim. This is one reason Congress perennially receives low grades from the American public. While members of the public typically blame current members of Congress (except, of course, their own representative) rather than the design of our constitutional institutions, such persistently bad performance would seem to point to more systemic causes.

Serious critics of our Constitution recognize that they must eventually confront James Madison's defense of our complex combination of separation of powers, bicameralism, and federalism. Madison was not enamored of all features of the Constitution he helped to create—he was especially dismayed by the provision of equal representation of all states in the Senate—but he provided a sophisticated defense of the features of our system that are commonly blamed for stalemate and gridlock. First, Madison argued that the easier it is to pass legislation, the greater the "mutability of the law." The resulting "public instability" not only undermines public confidence and weakens us internationally, but gives an "unreasonable advantage" to "the sagacious, the enterprising, and the moneyed few over the industrious and uniformed mass of the people."[4] Second, by providing an opportunity for a "sober second thought," bicameralism reduces the possibility that legislation will be the product of momentary public passions. Third, by requiring very broad majorities (what today we usually call super-majorities) to enact laws, the Constitution reduces the power of majority faction. Fourth, by requiring assent to legislation by both a lower house with a short term of office and an upper house with a long term of office, the Constitution combines responsiveness to current public opinion with attention to the long-term interests of the nation. Finally, by dividing the legislature into two parts and providing the president with a veto, the Constitution prevents the legislative branch— which "necessarily predominates" in republican government—from "drawing all power into its impetuous vortex."[5] A stronger, more unified legislative body would inevitably invade the powers of the executive and judicial branches. Such concentration of power threatens judicial independence, energy in the executive, and ultimately the rights of the people. Separation of powers and bicameralism, as Justice Brandeis noted, were adopted "not to promote efficiency but to preclude the exercise of arbitrary power."[6]

Contemporary critics of the Constitution tend to diverge from Madison in two ways. First, they are less skeptical than he of simple majoritarianism. For Woodrow Wilson, Robert Dahl, and Sanford Levinson, the greatest failing of the Constitution is its failure to allow popular majorities to prevail. What about the danger of "majority faction" and "tyranny of the majority"? Certainly any contemporary law professor cannot be indifferent to the plight of politically unpopular or "discrete and insular" minorities. Their unstated assumption, I think, is that this is a job that can safely be left to the courts. Since we already have an activist judiciary, we can now tolerate an activist Congress. Let Congress do more, then let the Supreme Court invalidate those portions of the law that five of the justices consider unfair.

Second, these critics tend to assume that the dangers created by government inaction are far greater than those created by rash, premature, or intemperate action. Unlike Madison, they express no concern about the mutability of the law. Just as importantly, they tend to assume—contrary to overwhelming political science evidence—that government's mistakes can be easily remedied. We know that most government programs create constituencies that are highly organized, acutely aware of the benefits they receive from government, and strategically positioned to block substantial change. As Paul Pierson has written, "The well-documented imbalance between the way that voters react to losses and gains further enhances the political position of retrenchment opponents."[7] Delays are usually temporary; but mistakes last forever.

Consider in this regard two recent policy issues, Social Security reform and control of acid rain. We know that within a couple of decades the Social Security system will begin to run a deficit. We also know that every year we fail to raise taxes or cut benefits (or, most likely, a little of both) the problem will get harder. Our political system can justifiably be faulted for making it so difficult to broker a deal on Social Security. Score one point for the critics. Of course, parliamentary systems have not done so well on pension reform either. Partisan blame avoidance is a potent force in virtually all democratic systems.[8]

Acid rain first became a political issue in the 1970s, but it was not until 1990 that Congress enacted measures to reduce the industrial pollutions that contribute to acid rain. For many years this was considered a prime example of gridlock—just as congressional inaction on greenhouse gasses is today. But the regulatory scheme Congress eventually used to control acid rain, marketable emission rights, has proved much better at reducing pollution quickly and cheaply than the command-and-control regulation that Congress relied upon exclusively in the 1970s. In other words, delay produced much smarter government action. Moreover, just as Congress was finally passing acid rain legislation, new scientific evidence indicated that acid rain was not nearly as serious a problem as everyone had assumed. By then, though, the legislation's momentum was so great that nearly everyone ignored this inconvenient finding. Maybe a little more delay would have been advisable. The motto of those who complain of constitutionally created gridlock is "Don't just stand there, do something!" They might want to remember the line Paul Newman delivered in the film *Cool Hand Luke*: "Sometimes nothing is a real cool hand."

From Stalemate to Gridlock

Before turning to an evaluation of the evidence supporting the stalemate/gridlock argument, it is important to note how the argument has subtly changed over time. During the first third of the twentieth century, Progressives and New Dealers argued that our "horse and buggy" institutions prevented the United States from building a modern state. By this they meant constructing a generous welfare state and a national government capable of regulating large "center firms" and moderating swings in the business cycle. Although Progressives and most New Dealers showed little interest in civil rights, their successors understandably believed that the same features of our Constitution also prevented the federal government from dislodging the racial caste system in the South. Their strategy was to use a combination of presidential leadership and party government to overcome all the veto points in the legislative process. With the policy breakthroughs of 1933–35 and 1964–65, they largely succeeded. Once landmark legislation was enacted in these years, it became much easier for the president, Congress, administrative agencies, and the states to engage in incremental expansion of welfare state, regulatory, and civil rights programs. Despite divided government, the scope of federal authority grew substantially in the 1970s. "Stalemate" and "deadlock," terms so frequently used to describe congressional politics in previous decades, were briefly out of fashion.

The term "gridlock" was invented in the 1980s to describe traffic congestion so severe that cars would block multiple intersections, preventing movement in any direction. It quickly became the leading metaphor used to describe congressional politics after Ronald Reagan's initial legislative victories in 1981. Hugh Heclo has aptly described one of the chief consequences of the expansion of the government agenda in the 1960s and 1970s as "policy congestion."[9] As the government does more and more, policies intersect with one another more frequently, often pushing in different directions. Our so-called "energy policy" is a motley collection of hundreds of conflicting policies and programs, some decades old, that seek to promote and discourage, subsidize and tax various forms of energy use and production. Our welfare policy is an array of programs run by many different agencies under the jurisdiction of scores of congressional committees that is notorious for creating inconsistent rules and conflicting incentives for recipients. Much the same could be said for healthcare policy, which in turn is inextricably linked to welfare policy. Federal budget policy is the sum of the millions of decisions on spending and taxing that hundreds of governments—local, state, and national—make every year.

Gridlock captured the sense that the government could no longer manage or coordinate all the intersecting programs it had created in the preceding decades. This was particularly true for budget policy during the Reagan years. The Reagan tax cuts and military build up had created massive deficits (by pre-2001 standards), and the "obstacle course on Capitol Hill" seemed incapable of putting much of a dent in them. No longer was the complaint that Congress and the president couldn't build an extensive modern state. Now the complaint was that Congress and the president could not manage or control the massive state it had created. Especially with entitlement spending growing automatically through cost-of-living adjustments and rapidly escalating health care costs, inaction by Congress now meant an ever-larger federal budget. And indexation of tax rates meant that revenues would not rise proportionately. Now conservatives and good-government technocrats complain as much about gridlock as liberals had complained of stalemate in years gone by.

Another major change that started in the 1980s was the development of more unified, national, programmatic parties. This had long been viewed by liberals and by political scientists (the overlap between the two groups is considerable) as the most promising solution to the American disease of gridlock. The fierce partisan polarization that became so evident in early twenty-first century American politics first appeared in Congress two decades before. By the time the Republicans took control of Congress in 1995, party leadership in the House rivaled that of the period of Czar Cannon and Czar Reed nearly a century ago. Within the House most of the veto points so frequently decried for promoting stalemate were eliminated. The Speaker now controls the Rules Committee; she tells committees which bills to report; she rules the floor with an iron hand. Roll call votes on important issues followed party lines. What the majority party leadership in the House wants, it almost always gets. During the presidency of George W. Bush Republicans briefly gained control of both the House and the Senate, and rammed through Congress a series of tax cuts and a major expansion of Medicare with virtually no support from Democrats.[10]

Advocates of party government had assumed that stronger, more ideological parties would allow one dominant party to give coherent direction to the government as a whole. For better or for worse, over the long run the public was not enamored of either party, and the result was years of divided government (1981–1992, 1995–2002, 2007–2008, and 2010–??). Indeed, as soon as one party seemed to be gaining effective control of government, the voters revoked their mandate. The 2010 election was just the latest and most dramatic manifestation of this dynamic. This recurring pattern has led some analysts to conclude that American voters were "cognitive Madisonians" who wished to prevent either party from dominating. Party polarization now seemed to exacerbate gridlock, not provide a solution to it.

In the 1950s and 1960s, it was almost always liberals who complained about stalemate, and they knew what to do about it: develop a "responsible" two party system. Today nearly everyone complains about gridlock, but no one is quite sure what to do about it—other than clobber the other party in the next election. To the millions of Americans who did not share the partisan passions of activists, a "responsible two-party system" has become an oxymoron.

Where's the Beef?

Before we despair at the prospect of ever curing gridlock, it is worth asking how serious the problem is in the first place. Everyone seems to believe in gridlock. But, as Aaron Wildavsky always insisted that we ask, is it true? Looking over recent events leads me to believe that the answer is clearly "no."

Consider, for example, some of the steps the federal government took in response to the financial crisis of 2007–2008:

- In the fall of 2008 Congress passed a $700 billion financial rescue package. The Bush Administration managed to push its proposal through Congress despite massive Republican defections.

- With only tepid support from the White House, Congress bailed out—and essentially took over—Fannie Mae and Freddie Mac, adding several hundred billion dollars to the total bailout.

- A few months later the Obama Treasury Department and the Federal Reserve announced a plan that will pump an additional $1 *trillion* into the banking system. This was done by the Federal Reserve, the Treasury, and the FDIC without additional congressional authorization.

- After providing billions of dollars to keep GM and Chrysler afloat, the federal government played a central role in managing their bankruptcy and downsizing. The government suddenly became the largest stockholder in two of the nation's biggest companies.

- In the fall of 2008 Congress passed a $150 billion stimulus package—large by historical standards, if small in comparison with the $800 billion stimulus package enacted a few months later.

And this was just the beginning: the congressional effort to restructure the financial services sectors was yet to come. The United States has responded to the financial crisis much more aggressively than have parliamentary governments in Europe. Whether these policies are wise is quite unclear. But gridlock they clearly ain't.

One could respond to these remarkable events by saying that the American political system is capable of responding to emergencies, but not so good at fashioning policies that prevent such emergencies from striking in the first place. So let's look back at the first seven years of the Bush Administration. Here, it seemed, was a recipe for stalemate. The electorate was divided 50-50 in both the 2000 and 2004 elections, with George W. Bush narrowly losing the popular vote in 2000 and eking out a narrow victory in 2004. The Senate, too, was divided 50-50 in 2001, and soon shifted to the Democrats with the defection of Senator Jeffords. The Republican margin in the House after the 2000 election was only nine votes, producing the slimmest partisan margin in both houses in seventy years.[11] In the 2006 elections the Democrats regained control of both the House and the Senate, and the country returned to divided government. Animosity between the parties (and against the president) ran unusually high. But consider what Congress accomplished during these years:

- It enacted No Child Left Behind, the biggest change in federal education policy since 1965 and the most prescriptive federal education legislation ever enacted.

- It created Medicare Part D, the largest entitlement expansion since passage of Medicare and Medicaid in 1965.

- It passed the Bush Administration's tax cuts in 2001, 2003, and 2004. Together they constituted the largest tax cuts in American history.

- Despite substantial opposition from Republicans, Congress approved the McCain-Feingold campaign finance reform law, which rivals the 1974 campaign finance statute for the most important piece of legislation ever passed on the subject.

- It passed the Sarbanes-Oxley Act of 2002, which *CQ Weekly* at the time described as "the biggest increase in the regulation of publicly traded companies since the depression."[12]

- In these years Congress also extended free trade agreements to Central America, eliminated tobacco subsidies, passed several laws to limit tort litigation, and expanded federal funding for children's health insurance.

Some of these laws received bipartisan support (most notably NCLB and Sarbanes-Oxley); passage of others relied almost entirely on Republican votes (the tax cuts and Medicare Part D). While many of us consider some of these policies ill-advised and excessively partisan, no one would describe these as "do nothing" Congresses.

So far I have not even mentioned the highest priority of the Bush Administration, foreign policy and the war on terror. So let us add to the list these policy innovations of the past eight years:

- The war in Afghanistan, which was clearly authorized by legislation passed shortly after 9/11 (the bluntly named the Authorization of the Use of Military Force Act).

- The war in Iraq, which was similarly approved by Congress.

- The creation of the Department of Homeland Security.

- Enactment of the USA PATRIOT Act in 2001 and overhaul of the Federal Intelligence Surveillance Act in 2008, substantially increasing the government's ability to spy on suspected terrorists (and probably many others as well).

- The Bush Administration established the detention center in Guantanamo Bay. Congress later passed legislation banning torture, establishing military commissions to try detainees, and denying detainees held outside the US the right to file habeas corpus petitions.

- The administration announced a controversial new policy on "preventative wars."

Despite the Bush Administration's provocative arguments about the "unitary executive," most of these policies received some form of congressional approval.

Foreign and defense policy rarely come up in discussions of stalemate and gridlock. Like partisanship in days gone by, the gridlock conceit stops at the water's edge. Indeed, to the extent Professor Levinson talks about foreign policy, it is to denounce the Bush Administration for acting too aggressively and to chastise Congress for delegating too much authority to the executive:

> The problem with Congress is an institutionalized gridlock that blocks the making of timely and effective public policy. The basic problem with the presidency is the possibility that the occupant of the White House is too unconstrained and can all too easily engage in dramatic exertions of power, especially in the realm of foreign policy.[13]

He admits being considerably more "sanguine" about giving Congress far-reaching power under Article I of the Constitution than recognizing broad presidential power under Article II. Levinson explains that more people—both Americans and others—die as the result of unilateral decision making by risk-taking (and perhaps painfully ignorant) presidents who manifest basic contempt for the view that they are under a duty to take Congress seriously as a partner in the decision-making process.

Of course, President Bush and Alexander Hamilton (not to mention Abraham Lincoln, Franklin Roosevelt, and Harry Truman) would argue that there is an even greater possibility that more people—especially Americans—would die if the president was required to wait for congressional approval in emergencies. The difficult question of executive power is discussed in depth and with appropriate subtlety in the chapters by Marc Landy and Richard Pious; I have no desire either to enter that thicket or to defend the Bush Administration's theory of executive power. But it is worth noting that one of the most important characteristics of our presidential system—and one highlighted by the founders, particularly Hamilton—is that it *reduces* the prospects of stalemate and instability in foreign affairs. Any serious discussion of the American Constitution's tendency to create stalemate or gridlock needs to pay at least as much attention to foreign policy as domestic. When one looks at the sweep of American foreign policy over the course of the twentieth century—especially the pivotal role the U.S. played in defeating two vicious and expansionist totalitarian powers—I would say that our constitutional structure has served us pretty well.

When the conference that produced this volume was held in April, 2009, we did not know the fate of the Obama Administration's ambitious legislative agenda. But we now know that the record of the 111th rivals that of any Congress since the historic 89th of 1965–66. While many of these enactments are well-known, it is worth recounting them to indicate the sweep of congressional action:

- Most importantly, Congress passed a massive and controversial overhaul of the American health care system, extending coverage to 30 million Americans; imposing extensive mandates on insurance carriers, employers, and state government; creating new insurance exchanges; imposing an array of new taxes, fees, and penalties; extending drug benefits; and making significant cuts in the current Medicare program.

- A few months later Congress enacted a 1,500-page law to create a new regulatory structure for the entire financial services sector and to establish a mechanism for "winding down" failing banks and brokerage houses. According to *CQ Weekly*, the Dodd-Frank Wall Street Reform and Consumer Protection Act "touches just about every major piece of financial regulatory law of the 20th century, from the New Deal era banking and securities acts to the post-savings and loan crisis legislation of the late 1980s and early 1990s."[14] The law requires regulatory agencies, including the new Bureau of Consumer Financial Protection and Financial Stability Oversight Council, to produce 250 additional sets of regulations to govern the financial sector.

- Soon after convening, Congress passed the American Recovery and Reinvestment Act, a.k.a. the stimulus package, to pump an additional $800 billion into the slowing economy. The act included a diverse mix of tax cuts, an extension of un-employment benefits, grants to the states for infrastructure, education, and health care, and measures to encourage the development of clean energy.

- Congress passed legislation authorizing the Food and Drug Administration to regulate the content and marketing of tobacco products. It later expanded the authority of the FDA to regulate food safety.

- It made major changes in the federal student loan program, making the federal government rather than banks the direct provider of such loans. It also provided over $4.5 billion for the Obama Administration's "Race to the Top" initiative to encourage innovation in elementary and secondary education.

- It repealed Don't Ask, Don't Tell, allowing gays to serve openly in the military. It also extended the federal hate crime law to extend to crimes aimed at gay, lesbian, bisexual, or transgendered persons.

- Shortly before adjourning, the lame-duck Congress passed a compromise engineered by President Obama and Republican leaders to extend both unemployment benefits and the Bush tax cuts, to renew the estate tax, and to reduce temporarily the Social Security tax on employees.

- The lame-duck Senate also ratified a new Strategic Arms Reduction Treaty (START) with Russia to reduce the number of nuclear weapons held by both nations.

- The Senate confirmed two new Supreme Court justices, Sonia Sotomayor and Elena Kagan, both by wide margins and without the threat of a filibuster.

On top of this, the Obama Administration substantially increased our military commitment in Afghanistan, the second major American war zone "surge" in recent years. 2009–2010 were certainly years of partisan animosity, but hardly of gridlock.

To be sure, Congress failed to pass immigration legislation (or even the stripped-down "Dream Act"), and the omnibus, jerry-built climate change bill passed by the House died quietly in the Senate. It is also undeniable that Obamacare passed only by the skin of its teeth. When Scott Brown won the Senate seat that had long been held by the Senate's strongest advocate for universal health care, Edward Kennedy, the Democrats lost the crucial 60th vote for cloture. Healthcare legislation passed only because the Democrats were both lucky — the Massachusetts election came after the Senate had approved its version of the bill — and willing to employ the budget reconciliation process in a novel manner. This reminds us that while partisan polarization often leads one party to engage in obstructionism, it also impels the other party to revise the rules to counteract such obstructionism.

The Perils-of-Pauline healthcare story points to another shortcoming of the conventional gridlock narrative. Gridlock is almost always used to imply that an obstinate minority is frustrating the will of the majority. But in 2010 Obamacare was in grave danger because public opinion was turning against it. Democrats from purple districts began to sense that a vote for the bill would end their tenure in Washington. In many instances this proved to be correct. The 2010 Massachusetts Senate race became a referendum on the administration's healthcare bill. It would have been hard for Democrats to pick a more favorable forum for such a referendum: one of the most liberal and reliably Democratic states in the nation; a state in which a similar program had already been enacted; a seat formerly held by a highly popular Senator who had made universal health care his life's work; and a contest between a visible, experienced Democrat and an unknown Republican. But, of course, Scott Brown won anyway, providing the first tangible evidence of the degree of public dissatisfaction with the Democrats' plan. The next one came in 2010, when the party experienced what President Obama described as a "shellacking." If anything, the healthcare battle shows that the federal government is capable of taking dramatic action even when the public support for such action is shallow.

From Veto Points to Opportunity Points

If our Constitution creates so many veto points, how have we managed to build such a large welfare, regulatory, civil rights, penal, and national security state? A large part of the answer is that a combination of presidential leadership, party loyalty, and crisis (especially war and depression) have frequently created the supermajorities necessary to overcome the hurdles established by the Constitution. But that is not the whole picture. One of the most serious weaknesses of the stalemate/gridlock argument is that it focuses so intently not just on domestic policy, but on one small part of domestic policy, namely passage of major pieces of legislation at the national level. Lost in these all-too-abstract discussions are the daily decisions of administrators, judges, state and local officials, as well as members of Congress engaged in the quotidian business of passing appropriations, reauthorizations, and budget reconciliation bills Taken individually, these decisions might seem like small potatoes, but collectively they can produce major policy change. Critics of the Constitution overlook the enormously important fact that a political system that creates multiple veto points simultaneously creates multiple points of access for policy entrepreneurs and assorted claimants. Every veto point that can be used to block action is also an opportunity point that can be used to initiate or augment government action. As a result, American government is both more extensive and more innovative than its critics recognize.

Consider, for example, the problem of global warming. Both the Bush Administration and Congress have been repeatedly attacked for failing to take significant action to reduce carbon emissions. In 2009 the House passed a bill that combined a mishmash of regulatory requirements with a cap-and-trade program that would have had little bite for many years. Mercifully, it died in the Senate. Meanwhile, though, a number of state governments have taken steps to reduce emission of greenhouse gasses. Five years ago Barry Rabe reported that several states "have addressed the climate change issue with vigor, developing a series of reduction policies and demonstrating a level of policy sophistication that may rival the staunchest European nations supporting the Kyoto Protocol."[15] Seven northeastern states reached an accord promising to reduce power plant emissions by 10 percent by the year 2020. In the summer of 2006, California Governor Arnold Schwarzenegger signed an agreement with British Prime Minister Tony Blair to curb global warming by promoting clean-burning fuels. The governor asserted, "California will not wait for our federal government to take strong action on global warming." California has a responsibility "to be a world leader on this issue."[16]

More importantly, the Supreme Court has ordered the federal Environmental Protection Agency to regulate greenhouse gasses.[17] In response EPA issued new rules that limit carbon dioxide emissions from new and modified industrial sources. This is likely to be just the beginning of EPA's greenhouse gas regulatory initiative. Given the structure of the Clean Air Act, it is unlikely that this will be a particularly attractive, effective, or efficient form of regulation. But the worse the EPA proposal, the better the prospect for congressional action: if Congress fails to act, EPA's inevitably flawed plan becomes the default position. In early 2009 a *New York Times* article on climate change legislation noted that President Obama

> Is holding in reserve a powerful club to regulate carbon dioxide emissions through executive order. That club takes the form of Environmental Protection Agency regulation of the gases blamed for the warming of the planet, an authority granted the agency by the Supreme Court's reading of the Clean Air

Act. Administration officials consistently say they would much prefer that Congress write new legislation … but they are clearly holding it in reserve as a prod to reluctant lawmakers.[18]

We have seen this pattern play out once before: this is how the large air pollution control program called Prevention of Significant Deterioration came into being over thirty years ago.[19] Meanwhile another court decision, this one by a panel of the Second Circuit that included Sonia Sotomayor, held that federal judges could use common law nuisance suits to limit greenhouse gases.

To take another example, how did Congress manage to enact controversial legislation in 1975 guaranteeing to every disabled student a "free appropriate public education," complete with an "individualized education plan," provision of "related services," and the promise that each student would be placed in the "least restrictive environment"? The answer is that the courts acted first, suggesting (rather obliquely) that disabled students might have a constitutional right to an adequate education. This forced state governments to spend much more on special education, which led them to demand that the federal government provide the money needed to comply with this federal mandate, which led Congress to provide both more money and more federal regulation, which led to more litigation and more federal requirements, which led to state demands for even more money…. This is a vivid illustration of how separation of powers and federalism can produce not gridlock, but steady expansion of government programs.[20]

How did affirmative action—highly unpopular with the American public—become embedded in so many federal programs? Slowly, subtly, and at times surreptitiously, a long series of court decisions, agency rules, and complex legislative provisions inserted the presumption of proportional representation into federal civil rights programs.[21] How did the federal government come to set national standards for state mental institutions, schools for the developmentally disabled, nursing homes, and prisons? Largely through litigation and consent decrees negotiated by the Department of Justice. How do we explain the enactment of landmark welfare reform legislation in 1996, despite divided government and intense hostility between the parties? A big part of the story is the decision of the Bush and Clinton Administrations to grant waivers to many states, the states' innovative use of their new-found discretion, and the decision of several Republican governors to tie their ambitions to expansion of these welfare experiments.[22]

Why has the means-tested Medicaid program grown faster than the supposedly sacrosanct Medicare program? After all, the former serves the poor, while the latter provides benefits to one of the most potent political forces in American politics, the elderly. According to Lawrence Brown and Michael Sparer of the Columbia School of Public Health, part of the explanation is the shrewd incrementalism of congressional entrepreneurs such as Henry Waxman, who steadily added federal Medicaid mandates to budget reconciliation bills in the late 1980s. Even more importantly, they note, "fiscal federalism" had the dual effect of "prompting coverage expansions during good times (the feds paid most of the bill) and deterring cutbacks even in bad times (every state dollar saved meant two or three federal dollars lost.)"[23] Instead of promoting a race to the bottom, our post-New Deal "cooperative federalism" has stimulated expansion of the welfare state. This effect is not limited to health care. After studying federalism for many years, Richard Nathan has concluded that "U.S. federalism's dominant effect has been to expand the scope and spending of the social sector."[24]

David Mayhew's comprehensive examination of major congressional action since World War II found that divided government is just as productive as unified government for generating significant legislation and investigations.[25] This calls into question the standard argument about the hazards of separation of powers. Why has Congress been so much more active under divided government than we tend to assume? One part of the answer is competition and bidding-up. The classic example is the huge Social Security benefit increases and automatic cost-of-living adjustment passed in 1972. Democrats in Congress were determined to engage in the biennial Social Security credit-claiming that had served them so well for so many years. President Nixon was intent upon outdoing them just before the presidential election. This burst of legislative activism contributed to the looming Social Security deficit we now find so difficult to address. Similar competition between Democrats in Congress and Republicans in the White House produced the wildly ambitious 1970 Clean Air Act and the ambitious Americans with Disabilities Act of 1990. In 1986 a remarkable revision of the entire tax code survived the obstacle course on Capitol Hill because neither party wanted to take the blame for killing a fairer tax code with lower marginal rates.[26]

Those looking for evidence of gridlock in Washington might point to Congress's failure in 1998 to pass major legislation imposing a very large tax on tobacco products and severely limiting tobacco advertising and marketing. But soon after that legislation died in the Senate, state attorneys general throughout the country negotiated an agreement with tobacco companies that established a $250 billion tax on tobacco products—to be dispersed to state treasuries—together with unprecedented limits on advertising, sponsorships, and lobbying by tobacco companies. Having lost narrowly in one arena, anti-tobacco activists prevailed in another.[27]

When the SEC was criticized for being too lax in regulating Wall Street, another state attorney general, the now infamous Eliot Spitzer, stepped into what he perceived as a policy void. When the Obama Administration appeared too tolerant of AIG's bonuses, Spitzer's successor, New York Attorney General Andrew Cuomo, took aggressive steps to expose the miscreants. The U.S. Supreme Court recently ruled that state tort law can add a level of regulation of pharmaceuticals on top of that established by the FDA.[28] California has frequently imposed environmental standards more stringent than those of the federal government, and many other states have followed its lead. In area after area the competition and multiple avenues of access created by our Constitution provide opportunities for those who seek to expand the responsibilities of the public sector to prevail. Policy entrepreneurs have learned how to use these features of our political system to their advantage. As Congressman Henry Waxman, one of the most skilled and successful policy entrepreneurs of recent decades has put it, "Incrementalism may not get much press, but it does work."[29]

In his marvelous book *The Welfare State that Nobody Knows*, Christopher Howard convincingly argues that the American welfare state is much larger than generally recognized, largely because we provide benefits through so many programs (at least 77 separate federal programs provide assistance to the poor) and in such indirect ways (for example, loan guarantees, refundable tax credits, and tax exemptions for health care costs). Our fragmented welfare state reflects our fragmented political system. As Howard suggests, we need to understand how this fragmented system has produced a *different type* of welfare state, not simply keep repeating the mistaken claim that it has produced a *small* welfare state.[30]

Compared to What?

At the heart of all serious political analysis lies Henny Youngman's famous response to the question "How's your wife?": "Compared to what?" At one time or another we have all been frustrated or even enraged by the delays, irrationalities, and complexities of our political system. If we were starting from scratch, no one in his right mind would give Wyoming, Vermont, Rhode Island, or Alaska two seats each in the U.S. Senate. The big question is, what is the alternative? Most critics of American separation of powers and bicameralism seem to assume that the preferable alternative is parliamentary government. Not, of course, the unstable or factious multi-party, coalition government form one finds in Italy or Israel.[31] Nor would they welcome the insulated, faction-ridden, and often corrupt single-dominant-party form one finds in Japan. Rather, reformers assume that we will naturally develop the stable two- or three-party Westminster-style parliamentary government found in Britain, Australia, and (at one time, at least) Canada.

My guess is that these reformers would have a hard time convincing most Americans that the British form of government is more democratic than what we have now. Who voted for Gordon Brown to become Prime Minister? For that matter, who other than the 50,000 people who went to the polls in Sedgefield, ever voted for Tony Blair? Or the 35,000 voters in Witney who cast their ballots for David Cameron? What do you mean we can't vote in party primaries — you intend to allow party bosses to choose the party's nominees? Elections held whenever the incumbent finds it convenient? A powerful elite senior civil service without significant oversight by elected representatives? I suspect that any significant movement in that direction would provoke a populist revolt in this country. As the Canadian-British political scientist Anthony King has pointed out, Americans and Britons have much different understandings of democracy.[32]

Putting this to one side, do we have any evidence that parliamentary governments are any better at *governing*? The answer, I think, is no. There have been surprisingly few systematic efforts to address this fundamental question. The best analysis I know is presented in a Brookings volume edited by Kent Weaver and Bert Rockman. *Do Institutions Matter? Government Capabilities in the United States and Abroad* contains essays by noted policy experts comparing the capacity of a variety of western nations to deal with common problems.[33] At the risk of oversimplifying the careful analysis of Weaver, Rockman, and their collaborators, let me emphasize five of their conclusions:

1. Most importantly, their case studies "suggest that most of the governance problems of the United States are shared by all industrial democracies, most of which have similar difficulties in addressing those problems.... Problems with balancing budgets are ubiquitous. All elected (and most unelected) governments are reluctant to impose losses on pensioners. Ethnic, racial, and linguistic conflict is all too common. Particular institutional arrangements do not cause these governance problems; they are inherent in complex societies and in democratic government. Groups inevitably want more from government than government is able to provide, and they want above all else to be protected from losing ground. Therefore policy failings in the United States should not be blamed exclusively, or perhaps even mainly, on the structure of American governmental institutions."[34]

2. "The U.S. separation-of-powers system tends to cluster closely with the coalitional parliamentary regime types in terms of its associated risks and opportunities, while party government and single-party-dominant systems also tend to cluster together on most capabilities."[35] In other words if the United States was to change

its constitutional arrangements without creating disciplined national parties, we would most likely be back in the same boat.

3. "The existence of multiple veto points in the U.S. system generates a lot of policy innovation ... because the system induces policy entrepreneurship from disparate sources. The policy innovation produced in the United States system, however, tends to be at the piecemeal level of individual programs rather than comprehensive, sectorwide policies."[36]

4. "There are direct trade-offs between some institutional capabilities. Institutional arrangements whose decisionmaking attributes facilitate some capabilities tend to inhibit others. For example institutional arrangements that promote capabilities for innovation in policymaking by limiting veto points, such as party government parliamentary systems, also are likely to create risks of policy instability for exactly this reason. Institutional arrangements that increase elite cohesion tend to increase governmental capacities to set and maintain priorities and to coordinate conflicting objectives, but these arrangements are also likely to limit capabilities to represent diffuse interests."[37]

5. "The distinction between parliamentary systems and the U.S. system of checks and balances, which is often seen as a crucial influence on government effectiveness, captures only a small part of potential institutional influences on government capacity." "Second-tier institutional arrangements" such as electoral rules and norms established within legislative bodies "influence government capacity at least as much as do the separation or fusion of executive and legislative power."[38]

In short, constitutional revision is unlikely to cure much of what ails us. Eliminating bicameralism and separation of powers would most likely convert the United States into a multi-party coalitional government system. After all, for most of American history we have had weak, decentralized catch-all parties held together only by the shared desire to win the presidency. Eliminate this winner-take-all prize and our first-past-the-post electoral rules, and you seriously weaken our party system. If by some miracle we succeeded in maintaining our two party system, we might gain some coordination capacities but lose some of our sources of policy entrepreneurship and innovation.

If fundamental political change is dangerous, unlikely to produce significant benefits, and even less likely to gain public support, then it behooves us to focus instead on those "second-tier institutional arrangements" that are both important and far easier to change. Take the Senate. Please. (My last Henny Youngman joke.) Both Sanford Levinson and Robert Dahl devote a great deal of attention to the undemocratic nature of representation in the Senate. I won't dispute this—and neither did James Madison. Unfortunately, "equal Suffrage" for the states in the Senate is the only provision in the entire Constitution that *cannot* be changed. But there are a great many other things wrong with the Senate that *can* be changed relatively easily, that is, with the agreement of 51 senators. For example, today a single senator can put a "hold" on a nomination or a piece of legislation because the Senate conducts so much of its business through unanimous consent agreements. That could be changed by adopting rules closer to those of the House. The filibuster rule, too, could probably be changed by majority vote. Use of both senatorial holds and filibusters has escalated in recent years, often with serious consequences. Exercising the "nuclear option" would not be nearly so monumental a change as most senators and journalists pretend. As David Mayhew has shown, filibusters were rare before the 1970s. Not only did party leaders threaten to change the rules to make filibusters more difficult, but they made those who filibustered pay dearly for their obstinance by requiring them actually to filibuster, not just threaten to do so.[39]

In fact the Senate has recently taken small steps in this direction. In January, 2011, the Democratic and Republican leaders of the Senate agreed to limit the use of secret holds to block legislation and nominations. The Democrats also agreed to allow more amendments to be considered in return for the Republicans allowing more legislation to come to the floor. A large, bipartisan majority adopted a formal rule change that prevents senators from delaying proceedings by forcing the reading of legislation on the floor. Both parties can see the danger of allowing a few senators to control the agenda of the entire body.[40]

One more quotation from Weaver and Rockman deserves our attention:

> Governments gain some room to work around basic institutional arrangements by generating countervailing mechanisms. In a number of the case studies policy outcomes seem to be strongly influenced by institutional adaptations that directly contrasts with the limitations and risks associated with basic institutional mechanisms.[41]

Examples abound. Congressional PAYGO rules helped reduce the deficit before Republicans eliminated the mechanism in 1995. Fast track procedures have helped temper parochialism in trade legislation. So-called BRAC legislation gave Congress a way to reduce unnecessary military spending by shutting down bases even the Pentagon considered outmoded.[42] Legislation exempting budget reconciliation bills from filibusters has made the budget process somewhat more rational and majoritarian—and allowed the administration's healthcare proposal to become law. As Douglas Arnold has pointed out, a number of congressional rules shield members both from the particularistic demands of constituents and from demagoguery.[43]

In sum, I can find only three problems with the gridlock/constitutional revision argument: it is descriptively inaccurate; its suggested reforms are likely to make matters worse; and it diverts attention from more promising reforms. So if you are relatively content with the status quo, I encourage you to engage in academic debates over wholesale constitutional revision. But if you really are serious about constructive change, talk to your Senator about restricting unilateral holds and about respecting PAYGO rules.

PART SIX

Judicial Review and Democracy

Chapter 10

Against Judicial Review

Mark Tushnet

Arguments against judicial review have a positive and a negative component, although the negative component is typically emphasized and the positive one either assumed or stated only in passing. The positive component is this: As a general matter democracy requires almost definitionally that a polity's citizens be allowed to select their polity's policies (including policies respecting rights) either directly, as in referenda, or through mechanisms of representation that give them indirect but relatively proximate control over policy choice and that allow the people to substitute one policy for another without extraordinary political effort. Embedded in that sentence are a number of important qualifications, but one that is missing is something that reconciles democracy with constitutionalism understood as a set of political arrangements that ensures political stability by limiting the people's ability to alter some policy choices—those understood within the polity as basic—too easily.

The negative component is simultaneously simpler to state and more difficult to establish. Proponents of judicial review agree that it should not be justified on the basis of arguments that would authorize courts to displace policy choice across the entire range of policy, and yet they have been unable to devise justifications that satisfy that criterion. The difficulty with the negative component is that the opponent of judicial review can work through existing justifications to show that they do not satisfy the "no universal scope" criterion but cannot eliminate the possibility that some new theory—with Ptolemaic epicycles added to existing theories, for example—might do so. This chapter examines the positive and negative components of the argument.

Before getting to the argument's core, it is important to make some preliminary points about the scope of the objection to judicial review. First, the objection is to judicial displacement of *legislative* choices, or to displacement of what British constitutionalists call primary legislation.[1] Classical British constitutional theory uses the term "judicial review" to refer to court evaluation of executive or administrative action to determine whether that action was authorized by statute. Opponents of judicial review in the US sense—displacement of primary legislation—have no principled objection to that form of judicial (or *ultra vires*) review,[2] because the legislature can respond to a judicial decision finding executive or administrative action unauthorized with ordinary legislation authorizing the action.[3] Second, and related, opponents of judicial review need not object to *ultra vires* review that is intensified when a court believes that executive or administrative actions implicate constitutional values by insisting on a reasonably clear authorization for such actions, although they might be concerned that the courts might be asking for more clarity than can reasonably be expected from the legislative process or with respect to the problem at hand. Third, opponents of judicial review clearly cannot object to legislative delegations to courts of the power to displace legislation on constitutional grounds, when those delegations are revocable overall or with respect to a particular judicial decision. Such delegations are statutes no different from any other statutes imposing substantive rules, and the positive component of the argument against judicial review holds that courts must respect legislative choices. A particular implication of this preliminary point is that the opponent of judicial review can accept systems of weak-form judicial review, as I have called them, if such systems really are weak-form.[4]

The Positive Component

Opponents of judicial review present themselves as deeply committed democrats. For them, in the ordinary course of things a polity's citizens are entitled to choose whatever policies they prefer at the moment, without facing constraints on choice imposed by (unelected) judges.[5] The range of policy choice is unrestricted: The people can choose tax rates, alter structures of government, and specify which "rights" they believe people should enjoy.

Democratic policy choice can occur directly, as in referenda, or indirectly, as when the people elect representatives to a legislature, which then makes policy choices. When policy choice is made through representative bodies, the people retain the power to displace those choices, for example by overriding them in a referendum or, more important, by replacing the legislators who made choices of which the people disapprove with others who will then alter the previously chosen policies. Importantly, these mechanisms of displacement must be relatively easy, a term that cannot be defined precisely but that must mean something like this: Displacement of policy choices made by representatives is roughly no more difficult than getting representatives to adopt a new policy.[6]

Opponents of judicial review argue that judicial review by unelected judges is inconsistent with democracy so understood.[7] Decisions finding a statute unconstitutional can be overturned only by constitutional amendment or replacement of the judges with others who then overrule the prior decision. But, typically, it is more difficult to amend a constitution than it is to repeal a statute or get a new statute adopted.[8] Replacing judges ordinarily takes a long time because, for good reasons independent of the value if any of judicial review,[9] democratic polities typically ensure that their judges have tenures longer than those of their representatives. This mechanism for displacement of judicial choice is thus relatively difficult.[10]

Sometimes judicial review is defended on the quasi-democratic ground that judges are indirectly responsible to the people for the policy choices the judges make, because of front-end—that is, selection-related—mechanisms rather than the back-end ones that ensure the responsibility of elected representatives.[11] Selection mechanisms vary, and in many constitutional systems judges themselves play a significant, and often predominant, role in judicial selection. Even when judges do not play such a role, though, selection mechanisms provide a significantly weaker form of responsibility than do elections of representatives, primarily because they are not supplemented by back-end mechanisms of a strength roughly similar to that provided by the necessity for representatives to stand for reelection.

These arguments, opponents of judicial review believe, establish that judicial review by unelected judges is inconsistent with democracy as they understand it. The difficulty with these arguments, though, is that they seem to establish that constitutionalism, understood in a particular way, is inconsistent with democracy as well, because constitutionalism precludes the people from making unrestricted policy choices on what are understood to be some basic questions. Distinguishing between the democratic argument against judicial review and a democratic argument against constitutionalism is indeed difficult, but it can be done.

The starting point is the observation that democracy is compatible with a wide range of choices on the matters typically identified as basic. With respect to structures, for example, on the highest level parliamentary government and separation of powers systems can be equally democratic, as can centralized and federal systems. Or, put another way, the choices between a parliamentary system and a separation of powers system, or between centralization and federalism, are "ordinary" policy choices. So too with more specific components of government structure: Nothing central—or indeed even close to central—about democracy is implicated in the choice between allowing or prohibiting legislative vetoes, for example.

To say that the range of structural choices is wide is not to say, of course, that it is unlimited, as the classic example of a democratic election resulting in the selection of a self-perpetuating dictatorship illustrates. So, the democrat would say, democracy is compatible with constitutionalism to the extent that constitutionalism is understood to permit a wide range of choices about government structure and to rule out only those choices that can fairly be described is inconsistent with democracy according to any reasonable definition of democracy. Clearly the term "reasonable" does a lot of work here, and I will return to it shortly.

The opponent of judicial review makes the same arguments with respect to claims that constitutionalism requires that some rights-related choices be denied the people. Constitutionalism, it is said, precludes the people from adopting sharp limitations on freedom of expression (and requires some mechanism—that is, judicial review—to ensure that such limitations have no legal effect). The democratic opponent of judicial review can concede the general point, but would insist that across a wide range of choices—a much wider range than proponents of judicial review typically acknowledge—there can be reasonable disagreement about *whether* a particular form of regulation indeed limits freedom of expression.[12] The currently hot examples are campaign finance regulations and the regulation of hate speech and pornography, but the examples actually go much farther. As a law professor, for example, Robert Bork argued that the First Amendment should be interpreted to allow government regulation of speech that listeners could reasonably regard as urging them to violate the law.[13] For him, the First Amendment protected only expression merely critical of existing government policies, but not expression that reasonably could be understood as having a tendency to bring about unlawful activity. The committed democrat would agree that democratic polities could indeed choose Bork's view about the scope of freedom of expression. Again, the limit is one of reasonableness broadly understood.

A proponent of judicial review could use these points against the opponent, claiming that the opponent could not actually object on democratic grounds to judicial review devoted to enforcing the reasonableness limit on democratic choice. After all, the argument would go, choices outside the range of reasonableness destroy democracy instead of exemplifying it. And a committed democrat should welcome some way of ensuring, or even merely reducing the probability, that such choices will not be legally effective. So, for example, committed democrats should believe that *legislation* of a "militant democracy" sort—that is, legislation aimed at ensuring that political parties be themselves committed to the preservation of democracy—is not only a permissible legislative choice but is probably a desirable one.[14] Judicial enforcement of militant democracy principles should not be troubling either.

Perhaps the response to the foregoing argument lies on the border between the positive and negative components. This response is Learned Hand's: A polity that has reached the point of making a democracy-destroying choice is highly unlikely to respect a judicial decision purporting to preclude it from doing so.[15] But, one might reasonably respond, "highly unlikely" is not "never." If judicial review could be confined to this disaster-preventing role, perhaps the committed democrat would accept it. But, the negative component of the argument asserts that it cannot be so confined.[16] At this point, I believe, we may have reached the limit of the positive component of the democratic case against judicial review.[17]

Two additional points before I turn to the negative component. First, I have assumed that we know what the relevant polity is within which democratic choice is to be respected. What, though, of cases in which the very boundaries of the polity are brought into question? These cases can involve literal or metaphorical boundary drawing: literally, in cases like that of Quebec and Canada, where some people question whether they or others should be included in or excluded from the polity itself, and metaphorically, when some people say that they ought to have been included within the category "citizens entitled to vote in elections for representatives." Saying that choices made by the polity should be respected is unresponsive to the claims made in such cases. Yet, that observation is at most neutral as to the propriety of judicial review in such cases. The geographical case illustrates the difficulty: Which jurisdiction's courts, those of Canada or those Quebec, should decide the boundary-drawing question? Similarly, on what basis can we defend a decision by a white-dominated court that exclusion of blacks (say, in South Africa) from the franchise is permissible?[18]

The democrat's instinct, I think, is to say that, at least in the metaphorical case, exclusions have to be justified on moral-political grounds, which are presumably unavailable for apartheid.[19] Then, however, the final point arises. Roughly, it is this: What's so great about democracy? The democrat's answer will almost certainly sound in a moral and political theory in which respect for the autonomy of human beings plays a large role. And, of course, democrats do take positions on policy choices, supporting some and opposing others, because in their view the policies promote or are inconsistent with their foundational commitment to human autonomy. But, if a theory of human autonomy lies at the foundation of the democrat's commitment to democracy, why should not that theory be available as a basis for an institutional, not merely political, assessment of policy choices made by democratic majorities? Here too the positive component runs out, and the opponent of judicial review must invoke that aspect of the negative component that addresses the failure of justifications for judicial review predicated on human autonomy to limit judicial review to less than the entire range of policy choices in democratic polities.[20]

The Negative Component

The positive component of the argument against judicial review rests reasonably directly on ideas about the institutional characteristics of democracy. The negative component, in contrast, rests primarily on questions of relative institutional capacity. That is, the negative component begins by identifying reasons offered by defenders of judicial review for that practice, observes that proponents of judicial review contend that the proffered reason justifies judicial review with respect to some but not all public policies, and then asks whether courts and legislatures are different enough as institutions with respect to each proffered reason to justify displacement of legislative by judicial choice. The answers to the latter question typically take two forms, not always offered with respect to each reason. The opponent of judicial review can argue that legislatures are nearly as good as courts with respect to some proffered reason,[21] and that courts authorized to set aside legislation for one or a small number of reasons will inevitably overreach, meaning not that they will erroneously invoke those reasons (though they will)[22] but rather that they will fairly invoke those reasons to set aside legislation across the entire range of public policy notwithstanding the proponents' claims that the reasons justify judicial review with respect to only a subset of policy choices.

The remainder of this section classifies reasons offered in support of judicial review into three broad categories, and outlines the negative case with respect to each reason.[23]

Justice-Related Justifications

One ground frequently offered for judicial review is that constitutions use moral terms and seek to achieve justice for a nation's people.[24] Unjust legislation should be unconstitutional, but legislatures sometimes enact statutes that do not comport with the requirements of justice or political morality. Judicial review ensures compliance with the constitution by invalidating such statutes.

There are many difficulties with this argument, no matter the varying ways in which it is fleshed out. One major difficulty is that it fails to acknowledge the existence of reasonable disagreement about what justice (and the like) actually requires. The opponent of judicial review can provisionally concede that, according to some views of justice, a particular statute is unjust and therefore unconstitutional, but would often insist that it is not unjust according to some other reasonable view of justice.[25]

For example, proponents of judicial review often point out that legislators have little or no interest in protecting the rights of criminal defendants, implying that legislative regulations of criminal procedure will (often) fail the tests of justice. Actually, legislators sometimes understand that some of their constituents (or even they themselves) will indeed come into the hands of the criminal justice system and so have some, perhaps modest, electoral incentive to ensure that that system operate in some minimally fair way. But, more important, legislative policy with respect to the rights of criminal defendants ordinarily is defensible on the ground that the policy comports with a reasonable understanding of justice's requirements, which must take into account both the interests of defendants and those of law-abiding citizens who are affected by the effectiveness of the criminal justice system in identifying and punishing those who victimize the law-abiding. The classic examples are rape-shield laws, which limit the ability of criminal defendants accused of sexual assault to introduce evidence, relevant under the standards of relevance applied in the general law of evidence, regarding the complainant's past sexual history and the like. These statutes embody legislative judgments about the best accommodation of competing rights—the rights of defendants to present evidence that a jury might reasonably take into account in determining the facts and the rights of complainants/victims to personal privacy with regard to their life choices. Rape-shield laws, though, simply exemplify legislative accommodations of conflicting rights in the criminal process, including, importantly, the rights of potential victims of crime to protection from the state against criminal marauders.[26]

The examples illustrate a more general point. A particular statute might reflect a legislature's principled conclusion that the statute is consistent with, and perhaps even advances, the constitution's justice-related commitments. Judges might find different commitments in the constitution, or draw different inferences from agreed-upon principles with respect to a particular statute, but the proponent of justice-related judicial review has to offer some argument that the legislative judgment about justice is unreasonable — that is, cannot be defended on publicly disclosed reasons that a reasonable person could accept.[27]

One frequent response seems to me unavailing. It is that legislatures rarely attend to justice (and courts do so, at least more often). One might question the empirical judgment here. Legislators often defend their votes on the ground that they were voting for something that was "the right thing to do," in connection with social welfare policy and abortion policy for example, and "right" here blends "good public policy" and "advances justice properly understood." Even if the legislative critic's empirical assessment is correct, though, it is insufficient to make out the case for judicial review, I believe. The opponent of judicial review argues, I think correctly, that judges should not displace legislative decisions in the name of justice if the legislation at issue can be defended as consistent with some reasonable view of what justice requires even if no legislator actually held that view. Put another way: The justice-related reasons for judicial review authorize judicial invalidation of legislation that actually *is* unjust, but a statute supported by a reasonable view of justice's requirements is *not* unjust even if no legislator held that view.

Only a bit more plausible is the claim that legislators' orientation to election and reelection makes them less attentive to justice than judges are. The thought here seems to be something like this: Legislators interested in election and reelection focus on bringing home the bacon to their constituents, maximizing their constituents' material well-being, and the like. This focus leads them to be indifferent or even hostile to considerations of justice in making public policy. Yet, the connection between the electoral incentive, which undoubtedly exists, and indifference or hostility to justice is obscure.

Consider several substantive areas. No one could plausibly contend that legislators who respond to constituent pressures with respect to abortion or choice are indifferent to justice considerations. The legislators themselves may simply be pandering to constituents, but the constituents' views rest on deep judgments about justice. Apartheid and similar laws occur in polities where the adversely affected groups were or are disfranchised; legislative indifference to those groups results not from the electoral incentive but from its absence.[28]

The view that legislators worry only or primarily about pork and material benefits to constituents has another implication. Taking that view seriously would require a substantial revision in contemporary US constitutional law. Under that law, courts apply quite loose standards to determine the constitutionality of what they call economic legislation. But, the "pork" view of the legislative process just is that legislators are indifferent to justice considerations when they enact economic legislation. So, it would seem, the justice-related argument for judicial review would support much more aggressive judicial review of economic legislation than currently exists. And, if so, the second argument deployed in the negative component of the argument against judicial review comes into play: Courts that were serious about invalidating legislation that is unjust in their view (even if supportable by some reasonable view of justice) would end up supervising public policy across an extremely wide range.

The electoral incentive actually may contribute to legislators' ability to develop policies that are consistent with justice. Or, without regard to the electoral incentive, legislation might often be more responsive to justice considerations than are courts. Here I invert a conventional point used to support judicial review. Proponents of judicial review observe correctly that legislatures make rules that regulate a large number of specific instances whereas courts have the capacity to make case-specific judgments. A statute might be generally consistent with the requirements of justice, but its application in a particular case might be unjust. Courts have the capacity to identify these case-specific injustices and invalidate legislation "as applied."

This argument overlooks the fact that judges also make rules, through the operation of a precedent system.[29] Judges' case-specific determinations create judicially imposed precedent-based rule exceptions from legislatively adopted rules. This system of rules and exceptions might be *less* just than the legislative rules. Judges might be overly influenced by the contingent facts of a particularly appealing case, and in holding the statute unconstitutional as applied might create an overly broad precedent-based exception to the statute— "overly broad" here meaning an exception that diminishes the contribution made to justice by that statute with the exception.[30] Or, even if their judgment about justice in the particular case is accurate and their projection into a rule of the justice-related implications of the exception they craft is not problematic, the exception might be so difficult to administer that the overall contribution of the statute to achieving justice is, again, diminished.[31]

The general point raised by the preceding argument is that achieving justice in a complex society is a complex task. Perhaps legislatures, with the capacity to take a wide view of how statutes play out when implemented, are actually better at making justice-related judgments than are courts. Even if legislatures are not better than courts, the case that courts are systematically significantly better than legislatures in making justice-related judgments is much weaker than proponents of justice-related reasons for judicial review suggest.

Democracy-Related Justifications

Because the positive case against judicial review invokes democracy as its justification, a natural response is to argue that judicial review can be democracy-enhancing. So, for example, John Hart Ely's account of representation-reinforcing review—probably the best developed and almost certainly the most influential democracy-related justification for judicial review—defends judicial review when (but only when) the judges determine that rules that keep the "ins" in and the "outs" out are unconstitutional.[32] Or, more abstractly, judges should find statutes unconstitutional when their enforcement would make it more difficult for democratically constituted majorities to overturn policies of which they disapprove or to replace representatives of whom they have come to disapprove, at least when those statutes cannot be justified by showing that they do a rather good job of advancing quite important public policies. So, for example, Ely argues for stringent constitutional limitations on statutes penalizing speech critical of existing public policies that are sought to be justified on the ground that such speech has a tendency to cause some degree of law violation (prior to the statutes' repeal, if that ever occurs): That kind of speech will always have some such tendency, which in turn implies that successful efforts to penalize the speech would make it impossible for those who disagree with existing public policies to expand their circle of support by circulating critic analysis of those policies.

Democracy-related justifications are also offered to support judicial review of exclusions from the franchise and of apportionment decisions. And it is in connection with those topics that some of the difficulties with democracy-related justifications most clearly arise. In discussing the positive component of the argument against judicial review I noted that it required the opponent to specify the contours of the "democracy" to which the opponent was committed, and that the positive component in itself could not so identify those contours. The same problem affects important aspects of democracy-related justifications for judicial review.

The point here is perhaps best captured by reflecting on Chief Justice Earl Warren's observation in one of the early reapportionment cases that "legislators represent people, not trees or acres."[33] But, as Justice Felix Frankfurter correctly noted dissenting from the Court's decision finding apportionment cases justiciable, that reflects only one, albeit perhaps widely shared, view of how representation should work in a democracy. On other views, interests—"trees [and] acres"—are at least relevant to the allocation of representatives among the population. The court's apportionment decisions reinforce one contestable version of democracy, at the expense of other versions.

Similarly with respect to a rather wide range of issues. Does legislation restricting expenditures on political campaigns introduce obstacles to the operation of democracy by making it more difficult to replace incumbents, or does it eliminate obstacles to the operation of democracy by increasing the access of the relatively less well-to-do to "their" representatives, relative to the access of the wealthy? The only sensible answer is, yes and yes.[34] Democracy-related justifications have no purchase on questions that implicate the very definition of democracy, and yet those are the only questions to which democracy-related justifications purport to speak.

Or do they? Here too a question I noted earlier arises. Judicial review aimed at promoting democracy must have some implicit account of why democracy is a good thing.[35] Typically that account relies on ideas about human autonomy: Democracy is thought to be the best, or at least one of the best, means of vindicating human autonomy in a world where nonconsensual collective action must be taken to ensure either overall social or individual well-being.[36] Judicial review in the service of democracy might make sense, but, given an autonomy-based justification for democracy itself, we could reasonably think that judicial review in the service of autonomy itself would be equally defensible.[37] And, if so, democracy-related justifications for judicial review would actually justify judicial review across an enormous part of the range of public policy. Courts could obviously displace legislation dealing with abortion if they concluded that such legislation was inconsistent with the account of human autonomy that they concluded justified democracy. They could similarly displace legislation regulating contracts—the classic substantive due process problems posed in cases like *Lochner v. New York*—on the same grounds. At the very least, the suggestion made by proponents of democracy-based justifications for judicial review that their approach gives judicial review a more limited scope than do justice-based justifications seems hard to sustain.[38]

Perhaps one might support democracy-related justifications for judicial review on a seemingly narrower basis—that democracy is justified as the best means of implementing political preferences understood in the terms just identified.[39] Here the difficulty is that preferences are not primitives; they come from somewhere, and there is no defensible ground, as far as I know, for thinking it important to effectuate preferences however they have been formed. Several courses seem to me open. Consider a world in which there are what we might call respect-worthy preferences and non-respect-worthy ones. We might authorize judicial review to ensure that respect-worthy preferences are effectuated, and leave completely unregulated policies that result from non-respect-worthy ones. That, though, strikes me as bizarre, for obvious reasons. Or, we might authorize judicial review on a democracy-related basis with respect to ensuring that respect-worthy preferences are effectuated and authorize judicial review on some other basis—presumably justice-related—for policies that result from non-respect-worthy preferences. Then, though, the scope of judicial review is basically unrestricted.

Finally, we might authorize what might be called preference-cleansing judicial review (in addition to review to ensure that respect-worthy preferences are effectuated). We would have to explain what makes a preference respect-worthy, an explanation that, again, would almost certainly sound in human autonomy. Judicial review would be justified with respect to policies that obstruct a person's ability to develop respect-worthy preferences. And, once again, the scope of judicial review expands. For example, a zone of intellectual privacy seems essential for the development of respect-worthy preferences, so that my preferences are truly mine and not forced on me.[40] Defending that zone might require rather aggressive judicial review. Here too courts might be justified in identifying rights to choose with respect to abortion, on the ground that such choices have profound effects on a woman's ability to develop preferences with respect to a wide range of public policies—about work arrangements, for example—that are truly hers.[41] Egalitarians, with their concerns about material inequality, and classical republican theorists, with their concern that participants in politics not be dominated by others, could credibly argue that laws resulting in substantial material deprivations—whether such laws be statutes or common-law rules allocating property rights—deserve close judicial examination because people in straitened material circumstances cannot form political preferences that are truly theirs, that is, that are respect-worthy.[42]

In sum, democracy-related justifications for judicial review inevitably rest on contestable ideas about democracy and implicitly rely on ideas about human autonomy, and are therefore indistinguishable from justice-related justifications along the dimensions of concern to the opponent of judicial review, and they do not as their proponents contend provide the conceptual resources to limit substantially the range of public policies to which judicial review will apply.

Redundancy Justifications

A final group of justifications argue that judicial review can serve as a backstop to legislatures, which might not sufficiently attend to constitutional values when enacting statutes. These justifications typically include some skepticism about the proposition that legislatures are organized in a way that prevents the enactment of unconstitutional laws, but they need not be. All that these justifications require is that the screens in the legislative process do not leave in the sifter every possibly unconstitutional statute. So, for example, a legislature might use a committee on the constitution to evaluate the constitutionality of proposed legislation,[43] and that committee might interpose objections to a significant number of proposals, and yet, the redundancy theorist would contend, an additional judicial screen would be valuable to deal with those statutes that slip through the legislative screens.[44] How can it hurt, one might think, to give the courts the opportunity to catch constitutional errors that slip through the legislature? Indeed, how can it hurt even if courts sometimes reproduce the legislative errors and let some unconstitutional statutes take effect? Redundancy will at least reduce the number of unconstitutional statutes that are given legal effect even if it does not invalidate every such statute.

There are, of course, two kinds of judicial errors. Courts may fail to invalidate objectively unconstitutional statutes, but they may also invalidate objectively constitutional ones.[45] As Professor Fallon has written, redundancy theories rest on the proposition that constitutional errors are not symmetrical in terms of adverse effects on a polity. Without redundancy, some objectively unconstitutional statutes have legal effect because they survive all the screens in the legislative process although they should not; with redundancy, some objectively constitutional statutes are denied legal effect because the courts mistakenly screen them out. Redundancy justifications treat legislative errors as more serious than judicial ones because legislative errors lead to enforcement of unconstitutional statutes whereas judicial ones "merely" deny the public of the benefit of constitutional ones. Another way of putting the point is that enforcement of an unconstitutional statute denies someone his or her liberty, whereas failure to enforce a constitutional statute merely denies the public of the policy benefits of the statutes.

These formulations understate the costs of redundancy. Many statutes rest on legislators' judgments that they promote constitutional values or, indeed, protect constitutional rights. This is true, for example, of the rape-shield statutes mentioned earlier. Perhaps more important, it is also true of social welfare legislation that provides a social safety net to prevent people from falling into desperate material conditions. Such legislation can be justified on numerous grounds as protecting a constitutional right to material well-being, including the argument currently fashionable among proponents of social welfare rights that they are constitutionally guaranteed but are also correctly under-enforced by the courts.[46] Professor Fallon expressly and properly excludes "rights versus rights" statutes from his redundancy justification for judicial review, and in doing so quite severely restricts its scope.

Either with or without such a restriction, redundancy theories contain an asymmetry between enforcing unconstitutional laws and failing to enforce constitutional ones. This asymmetry is justifiable only because of an implicit libertarianism in the redundancy theories. For such theories, less legislation is better than more legislation. But, plainly, this reduces redundancy justifications to justice-related ones.

Opponents of judicial review can take some elements in redundancy theories into their own account of democracy. In particular, they can appreciate such theories' perception that legislatures sometimes overlook the implications of their general statutes on particular cases, and would sometimes not want the statutes to be applied as the statutes' words seemingly require. Courts can improve the legislative product by pointing out these troubling cases to the legislature and even by resolving them as the courts assume the legislatures would want them resolved—but, for the opponent of judicial review, only if the courts' decisions are readily revisable, which is to say, only if the courts are not actually exercising the power of judicial review properly understood.

Conclusion

Judicial review in the United States and, it seems, in many nations around the world, poses a problem for the practice's opponent. Whether through express constitutional authorization or through embedded practice, judicial review appears to have precisely the democratic warrant that judicial review's opponents seek. Setting policies aside seems undemocratic to judicial review's opponents, and yet citizens in democracies around the world seem largely happy with the practice. The global expansion of judicial power, as it has been labeled,[47] seems to have been accepted in the world's democracies, and to date no nation that has adopted judicial review has thereafter abandoned it.[48]

Judicial review's opponents might contend that popular acceptance of judicial review results from popular failure to understand exactly what judicial review means and does. Recently, perhaps, it has been a practice with relative small effects on important public policies. On this view, it takes a crisis of the sort the United States experienced in 1936–37 for citizens to understand why judicial review really does interfere in important ways with their ability to govern themselves.

Another possibility is more interesting, I think, and relevant to the arguments made in other chapters here. Perhaps popular "acceptance" of judicial review is more a sign of resignation to the fact that democratic majorities have been unable to eliminate a practice favored by political elites than of positive support for the practice. Opposition to judicial review would then best be understood less as a free-standing criticism of a single institutional arrangement, and more as one plank in a platform calling for reforms that would reduce elite domination of the political process.[49]

Chapter 11

In Defense of Judicial Review

Stephen Macedo

Robust or "strong"[1] judicial review—which includes the power of courts to invalidate legislation deemed to offend constitutional principles—remains a hotly contested aspect of the American constitutional order. The core problem concerns judicial review and democracy: how can it be anything other than grossly undemocratic for nine unelected judges to invalidate legislation that has been duly enacted by the elected representatives of the people? Strangely enough, this can be altogether democratic, which is why the newer democratic constitutions enacted after World War II almost uniformly embrace some form of judicial review. This chapter defends judicial review from the standpoints of principle, practice, and institutional design.

Judicial review properly conceived is, *in principle*, not only fully compatible with democracy but democracy-enhancing, at least given what I take to be an attractive conception of democracy, which is not majoritarian. Contrary to Jeremy Waldron, Mark Tushnet, and others, there is no good ground for presuming that judicial review is democratically illegitimate. Those who fasten their critical gaze on judicial review often fail to recognize the moral shortcomings of majoritarianism, and adopt an unrealistically idealized conception of legislative and electoral politics. Strong judicial review as practiced in America provides unique and important opportunities for democratic contestation, justice promotion, and the protection of minority rights.

The assessment of judicial review needs to consider not only ideal institutional theory but also the actual record: whether and to what extent *in practice* judicial review has enhanced constitutional democracy. Judicial review in the United States has a mixed record, as do the legislative and executive branches. There certainly are, however, grounds for thinking that American democracy is better off for the practice of judicial review on balance, though it is impossible to know what American politics would have been like without it. At the very least there is no warrant for crediting those critics of judicial review who confidently assert that our democracy would be better in the absence of strong judicial review. Judicial review has been a standard feature of constitutional democracies established after World War II, and courts and other remote and indirectly accountable institutions are important parts of the emerging architecture of global governance.

Finally, as concerns institutional design, I do not argue that American constitutional arrangements, including judicial review, are optimal in design. I do not know of anyone who argues that.[2] It is hard to know whether there is one best form, but for all their wisdom, it seems unlikely that the US constitutional designers would have hit on the best form at the dawn of modern constitution making and under severe political constraints. The American Constitution is now exceptionally old. Nevertheless, I am far less convinced than others that constitutional institutions are so dysfunctional as to justify a resort to the amendment process or a convention.[3] The process of constitutional amendment is very burdensome, and there are also significant costs and uncertainties involved in devising and adjusting to new constitutional arrangements. It is far from clear, indeed, that the most serious problems of American democracy—rooted as they are in inequalities of income and wealth—are amenable to constitutional reform.

So, the plan of this chapter is to defend the US Constitution against charges of obsolescence in three ways. *In principle*, as between the *majoritarian vs. constitutional* conceptions of democracy: the latter is to be preferred and judicial review is a fully respectable component of the constitutional conception of democracy. *In practice*, the actual American record with judicial review is mixed but defensible; and it is notable actual publics have confidence in courts and judicial review has become a standard feature of new constitutions. Finally, in terms of *optimal institutional design*, there are many ways to organize judicial review and the interactions of courts and legislatures. Our "antique" constitution is probably not optimal, but the fact of its continued working is a fact to be celebrated.

Majoritarian vs. Constitutional Conceptions of Democracy

Criticisms and defenses of judicial review take place against the backdrop of differing conceptions of democracy, so that is where I begin. The fundamental issue is how to understand the relationship between *judicial review and other features of constitutionalism and democracy*.

In an (otherwise) excellent article, Samuel Issacharoff says that "Constitutionalism exists in inherent tension with the democratic commitment to majority rule."[4] To the contrary: there is no democracy without constitutionalism. Democracy requires constitutional rules specifying eligibility of voters and other electoral rules, and the terms and powers of various offices. And these rules must limit the power of majorities if the system is to be regarded as democratic: at the very least, majorities must be prevented from disenfranchising and enslaving minorities. So the issue is not whether democracy needs constitutionalism but rather *which constitutional arrangements best serve democracy*?

One important question of democratic constitutional design is the timing and frequency of elections, and the relationship between the powers of various elective officials and other public officials who are also ultimately accountable to the people but only indirectly. Some say democracies ought to concentrate authority in those public officials who are directly accountable via mass public elections. The directness of the "electoral connection" seems to many to be quintessentially democratic. On this line of thinking, it would be even more democratic still to decide important questions by popular referendum. Those who favor direct decision via referenda provisions and frequent elections and short terms of office might also favor "recall" provisions that allow a majority of voters in a given "midterm" election to remove from office a currently unpopular official whose term has not yet expired.

Keeping government "close to the people" in all of these ways could help minimize what Corey Brettschneider calls the problem of false attribution, which occurs when elected representatives or others claim to represent the will or preferences of the public, but do not in fact do so.[5]

Those who identify democracy with majoritarianism often favor direct and participatory popular decision making, including devices as referenda and recall, short terms of office, and unicameralism rather than bicameralism, all in order to concentrate decision power in the people and their direct representatives. If the public or its representatives wish to delegate authority to regulatory or administrative bodies, such delegations should be easily revocable.[6]

All of this heads in the broad direction advocated by the antifederalist opponents of the US Constitution. So it might be accounted a difficulty for this view that the Constitution was submitted to the people and ratified, and overwhelming majorities of people nowadays profess support for the US Constitution's complex checks and balances, including many forms of delegated authority. Critics of the Constitution may argue that popular complacency is a further symptom of the problem: we have become lazy and stupefied by proconstitutional ideology amounting to Constitution worship, and ignorance of the alternatives (thus what the populist giveth, the populist taketh away).

The foregoing sketch captures one interpretation of the idea of democracy: a *populist and majoritarian interpretation*. On the alternative, constitutional interpretation of democracy, all power is ultimately based on authorization by the people and it is to be exercised on behalf of the people as a whole, but complex forms of checks and balances, delegation, and nonelectoral forms of accountability (including elaborate reason-giving requirements, experts and impartial bodies) are understood as ways of improving the performance of collective self-government as such.[7] Few if any constitutional democrats are in favor of getting rid of periodic mass elections: mass elections help insure that legislators and executives are held accountable to the people, and that is an important aspect of democracy. However, constitutional democrats insist that democracy can be enhanced by institutional arrangements that place elections within a wider system in which decision-making authority is frequently insulated from direct accountability to the public, in which elected officials are typically checked and limited and required to offer reasons and respond to criticisms, and in which the people as a whole are completely excluded, as Madison said, from any share of direct administration of political power.[8]

Constitutional Democracy

Constitutional democracies employ popular majority voting during particular phases of a complex process. The reason for these more complex arrangements is to better serve democratic values, properly understood. Democracy—the power of the people to rule themselves—should empower the *whole people* to rule. But since unchecked majority rule can be majority tyranny, in constitutional democracies a wide variety of constraints, authorized by supermajority requirements, are designed to check what simple majorities can do. Government becomes more rather than less democratic, when we insure that minority interests are fairly attended to and the equal rights of minorities—their basic interests—are protected. Democracy requires that the powerful are held in check by the prospect that abuses of power will be detected and publicized, which implies public access to information. Arbitrary actions of government, which could instill fear of free expression and criticism, can be limited by the rule of law (the requirement that laws be made in advance and publicized, and have a requisite generality[9]), as well as rights to free expression and press freedom. Competing public institutions, and a system of checks and balances including legislative bicameralism, politically independent courts, and administrative agencies with specialized expertise, can help insure that elected representatives and other public officials must defend their policy choices publicly against robust criticism, and that errors are identified and corrected.

Those final observations, in particular—involving the making of informed and deliberate decisions—may seem to be adding substantive criteria of "good government" to the definition of democracy. A majoritarian could reply that we should not conflate rule by the people with good government. However, at both the individual and collective levels we commonly account it a failure of self-rule if our decision making is systematically hasty and ill considered, such that we do not (either individually or collectively) *identify with and own* our decisions from one moment to the next.[10] Therefore, it does seem to me an enhancement of collective self-rule *as such* when deliberation is thorough because that helps insure that the public can *live with and own* political choices over the long haul.

The constitutional conception of democracy stands for the proposition that constitutional institutions and mechanisms can enhance the ability of the people as a whole to govern itself, on due reflection, over the long run, and on the basis of respecting the political equality of all citizens.[11] Such a conception is more complex than simpler majoritarian accounts, but it seems to me clearly normatively superior. However, since the majoritarian is unlikely to give up so easily, let us also consider problems internal to the majoritarian conception of democracy.

Majoritarianism Reexamined

Jeremy Waldron argues that "final decisions" about political questions—including individual rights and political processes themselves—should be made by majoritarian procedures.[12] Majoritarianism can be supported on a variety of grounds, but the simplest and apparently most morally basic defense is that when (equal) persons disagree about what the rules or policies should be, the fairest way of settling the disagreement is to give everyone an equal vote and the side that gets the most votes wins. Majoritarianism respects our political and moral equality (it appears) by submitting political questions to a procedure in which everyone has an equal say; no one is regarded as more competent (or worthy of having a greater say) than anyone else. Majoritarianism instantiates one straightforward understanding of the principle of political equality: equal votes for equal people and the greatest number win.[13]

Waldron admits that decisions taken via majoritarian procedures may lack legitimacy. If a majority infringes on the basic rights of a minority and thereby fails to respect their equal status, then majority rule is illegitimate. The problem, he argues, is that we disagree about the interpretation of every right or procedure that might be deployed to limit majority rule. Then the question is: whose understanding is to be preferred, that of the majority or the minority?

And so, if we ask: Why should a part of the people—even the larger part—decide for the whole? Why should the minority accept rule by the majority? And why should majorities make decisions even about "the nature and limits of majority decision making?"[14] Majoritarians have an answer: politics is characterized by pervasive disagreement, so we disagree over every standard that might be invoked to qualify or limit majority decision. As Waldron emphasizes: "it is disagreement all the way down so far as constitutional choice is concerned."[15] Since a part will always decide for the whole it is preferable that the ruling part should be the larger part.

Majorities, says Waldron, should have the final say on political questions, including the question of the procedures by which we normally decide political issues. He does not rule out reliance on complex decision procedures and he favors space for deliberation, but the majority should choose the decision procedures, and presumably those procedures should not be deeply entrenched in a way that is hard for the majority to change.

It may seem paradoxical to allow the majority to decide on the limits of majority rule. But every alternative method of decision will have the same liabilities as majority decision — persisting disagreement, and some making decisions that bind all — as well as the additional problem of privileging the "voices and votes of a few" over a greater number. Majority rule at least allows "a voice and a vote in final decision procedure to every citizen of the society," and when numbers rule, the equality of each person is (in one aspect) preserved.[16]

One problem with the foregoing defense of majoritarianism is that it seems so distant from existing political arrangements, including those often described as "majoritarian." Many actual democratic polities and associations employ majority rule in particular phases of decision making. Mass popular elections are dramatic and important moment in systems of collective self-rule, but mass elections often reward the winners of pluralities, not majorities. One thing needs to be emphasized: majority rule is merely a voting rule. Ronald Dworkin refers to it — deflatingy but appropriately — as the "head counting principle."[17] It has strengths that operate under restrictive conditions: it is a decisive voting rule when there are only two options. As everyone knows, when there are more than two options then there can be cycling of preferences such that there will be no majority winner.[18] So E.E. Schatschneider once said that "the people are a sovereign whose vocabulary is limited to two words, 'Yes' and 'No.' "[19] Majority rule cannot get us to the point at which majority decision making is possible, so it cannot be all there is to democracy.

More basically, the fundamental moral principle of democracy it is not majority rule but rather the deeper principle of the political equality of individuals.[20] Even on Waldron's account, majority rule gains its attraction as an interpretation and application of the principle of political equality. Majority rule is far from being the only, or the most appealing, interpretation of the principle of political equality: it is only one of many possible decision procedures that are consistent with the underlying principle of political equality. Other decision rules are also consistent with political equality and may be fairer and more inclusive. When it comes to elections for councils or legislative bodies, proportional representation and "multiwinner" rules can help insure that minorities get their fair share. Preferential voting can allow for more fine-grained expression of preferences. In some settings, consensus rather than majority rule is a reasonable object of deliberation.[21] Different procedures yield different accounts of what "the people" prefer, but no one procedure is clearly superior on the basis of fundamental normative principles, nor on the axioms of social choice theory.[22]

Perhaps most importantly, alternatives to majority rule might do a better job of assuring minorities that their interests will be taken into account. And indeed supermajorities might — and in the real world often *do* — prefer systems of collective self-rule in which minority interests gain special protection: we *all* might prefer that given the possibility of finding ourselves in the minority. So proponents of majoritarianism such as Waldron are simply wrong to argue that majoritarianism is, in practice, the best we can do to realize democratic values. In reality we can *and do* do better: few if any of the newer constitutional democracies embrace simple systems of unicameral parliamentary supremacy (which Waldron's principles might seem to argue for).[23]

Part of the apparent appeal of majority rule is its fairness (everyone counts for one). But under realistic conditions the choice of majority rule procedures would seem both imprudent and *unfair* from the point of view of political minorities. If majority factions develop (clusterings of voters or linkages across issues) the minority may *never* get its way via majority rule, and its fundamental interests—or rights—may be ignored.[24]

Majority rule is, finally, flawed in a way that other "aggregative" conceptions often are (such as utilitarianism). Majority rule says that the loss for the few is justified by the fact that the winners are greater in number (like utilitarianism, majoritarianism looks at social decisions as aggregation problems in which everyone counts for one). But why should the minority accept this way of looking at it? Perhaps under a system of "minorities rule" in which all groups have their turns to rule in shifting and unstable governing coalitions, the (distributive) fairness criterion is satisfied (everyone gets a fair turn to be in the majority). In politics we know there can be consistent losers ("discrete and insular minorities"[25]). Fundamental fairness requires that institutions should speak to the vulnerable perspective of minorities and not only lump the minorities in with everyone else. Fairness requires that we look at the justifiability of a political system *distributively* and not only *aggregatively*, as Charles R. Beitz has observed: that is, from representative particular points of view, and not from the point of view of everyone lumped together.

There is, finally, a global consensus that majoritarianism alone is an illegitimate basis for a political order: by itself, it fails to acknowledge and protect the fundamental interests—or human rights—of minorities. A substantial element of moral progress in the twentieth century is owed to the recognition and spread of the idea of human rights: that there are fundamental human interests that ought not be subject to political discretion, and whose infringement by domestic governments or other agencies is a matter of international concern.[26] Here is an additional ground for holding that democracy—government by the people—should not be understood in majoritarian terms if it is to designate an ideal of legitimate collective self-rule.[27]

The idea that majoritarianism is the moral core of democracy does not survive critical scrutiny. *Majoritarianism is not a uniquely authoritative decision rule in conditions of disagreement among political equals.* It has the virtue of simplicity, and it is decisive when there are two options. Majoritarianism as an ideology is a simplistic solution to the problem of collective self-rule amidst the great diversity and disagreement of modern mass societies. It is not a very promising way of taking seriously the principle of fair treatment that we should also want our politics to represent. It does not secure the equal standing of citizens. It should not be fetishized, as it too often is.

The idea of government by the people on the constitutional conception answers to several principles. One bedrock principle is the principle of the political equality of individuals.[28] What additional principles help make good on the abstract principle of political equality?

One is *inclusiveness.* The most plausible standard of political legitimacy is more *inclusive* than mere majoritarianism, as Mill argued:

> The pure idea of democracy, according to its definition, is the government of the whole people by the whole people, equally represented. Democracy as commonly conceived and hitherto practiced is the government of the whole

people by a mere majority of the people, exclusively represented. The former is synonymous with the equality of all citizens; the latter, strangely confounded with it, is a government of privilege, in favor of the numerical majority, who alone possess practically any voice in the State.[29]

The thought that collective decisions should be answerable *to all* has a venerable pedigree. It lies behind Aristotle's typology of the three correct and the three flawed or deviant regimes: in all regimes, a part rules, but in correct regimes rule is on behalf of the common good.[30] It is reflected in the ancient dictum: "What touches all ought to be approved by all." In Christopher Eisgruber's language, the goal of inclusiveness can be equated with the norm of impartiality: "[t]o qualify as democratic, a government must respond to the interests and opinions of all the people, rather than merely serving the majority, or some other faction of the people."[31]

Constitutional democracies employ various means to promote inclusive collective self-rule. One mechanism for controlling factional domination of some by others was the choice to establish representative government across an "extended republic" encompassing a large territory and a great variety of interests:

Extend the sphere, and you take in a greater variety of parties and interests; you make it less probable that a majority of the whole will have a common motive to invade the rights of other citizens; or if such a common motive exists, it will be more difficult for all who feel it to discover their own strength, and to act in unison with each other.[32]

Another device for controlling majority factions is the reservation of individual rights in a constitutional document, with a politically independent enforcement mechanism, such as is provided by judicial review. These are devices for assuring the minority that its *vital interests as political equals* will be protected against legislative encroachment: its rights to participate in politics and rights essential to the preservation of moral autonomy and agency (including rights to association and the free exercise of religion). Rights help insure political equality, given the flaws that characterize collective decision procedures.[33]

Inclusiveness may also be promoted by supermajority decision procedures, and by institutions that represent electoral constituencies in various ways.[34] The US House and Senate represent differently organized geographical constituencies, and the Senate in particular over-represents smaller states.[35] The president is selected by and is accountable to a national electorate. Legislation must pass both houses by majority vote (Senate passage may sometimes require a filibuster-proof supermajority vote) and secure the assent of the president: these institutions are not constituted so as to provide for any simple form of majority rule. They have certainly provided veto points for well-placed minority interests (partly via the committee system) and they tend to generate disagreements and debates about legislation.

So, inclusion of the whole people in the project of collective self-rule is one important democratic desiderata at which constitutional institutions aim, including via rights and impartial politically independent enforcement mechanisms.

Another is, *the value of deliberation.* We often regard decision-making procedures as having enhanced authority if they involve deliberation: if citizens and their representatives debate, respond to arguments on the other side, and discuss before reaching a decision.[36] Allowing for wide discussion can be one way of helping to insure that minority interests are taken seriously: if minority views are aired they at least might be attended to. Deliberation can also help canvass all relevant information; it can help gather and pool expertise so as to improve the quality of decisions. Whether in cases of collective or individual decision making, when decisions are made deliberately rather than hastily there is a greater chance, as I said above, that *we will own and identify with the decision over the longer term.*

Deliberation is also enhanced when the lawmaking process considers long-term interests. While constitutional institutions are often criticized for slowing down decision making and making change excessively difficult, the very difficulty of changing law can be an inducement to reflection and impartiality. As Adrian Vermeule emphasizes, knowledge that we will live with the consequences of a decision over the long term can act as a "veil mechanism" — similar to Rawls's "veil of ignorance" — while someone else's ox is gored today or tomorrow, I may be in their position at some point in an uncertain future.

So, on the constitutional conception, we have at least three basic features — three sets of values — that we want to realize in practice, and that we can understand as regulative principles of democracy: *political equality, inclusiveness (including rights protection and faction control), and deliberateness.*[37] Political equality is a "hard constraint": every adult citizen should be respected as an equal by the political system. But political equality is subject to interpretation: it does not require majority rule and it may be furthered by constitutional institutions.[38] *Inclusiveness*: everyone's basic interests should be respected and the law should take into account the interests of all; in practice this stands for institutional mechanisms designed to protect minority rights and control factions. Reflectiveness or *deliberateness*: reasons should accompany power, reasons that have been articulated and tested in public debate and by high standards of expert scrutiny.

Within the complex scheme of American constitutional democracy, majority rule procedures are sometimes employed. And indeed, mass elections are splendid and dramatic democratic moments. But we should not allow the razzle dazzle of elections to obscure the fact that the employment of majority decision rules within particular phases of decisions does not make the American system of government majoritarian.[39]

Democracy is best understood as a complex form of collective self-rule: constitutional self-government is the large canvass across which the people of the United States govern themselves. To focus on particular aspects of this canvass — even those aspects which are notable for their participatory features — is to mistake a part of the process for the complex whole of democracy.

Oddly, even the warmest supporters of the idea of majoritarianism often seem half-hearted. In his most recent criticisms of judicial review, Jeremy Waldron — the leading philosophical defender of majoritarianism — does not rely on majoritarian premises.[40]

Constitutional Democracy and Judicial Review

In many conventional accounts, "democratic" politics is identified only with the parts of this system that involve mass elections, or the activities of those institutions that operate on the basis of a direct electoral connection. Hence, the tendency to view the court as an antidemocratic institution. Once we recognize the superiority of the constitutional as opposed to the majoritarian conception of democracy, the case against democracy as a matter of basic principle dissolves (I would say), or at least weakens considerably. At its core, democracy is concerned with providing institutions to enable a people to rule itself over the course of time. Under the conditions of modern mass democracy, this is an enormously ambitious undertaking. Those who consider the vast scale and diversity of modern democracies have often doubted that it is possible. The office of modern citizenship is not, moreover, designed to elicit a high level of sustained attention and conscientiousness. As Schumpeter famously observed, being one among tens of millions of citizens is like being a member of an enormous and unwieldy committee: you don't have a strong incentive to do your homework for the meetings. That observation is no insult to citizens, it is simply a dose of realism about the circumstances that citizens face. Much political science has sought to plumb the depths of citizen ignorance.[41]

So it is astonishing that modern democracy works at all. It works in part because constitutional institutions involve many forms of accountability beyond periodic mass elections.

The system of checks and balances—the cornerstone of our constitutional system— should not be viewed solely as a check on majority tyranny but as a positive mechanism to encourage discussion and deliberation among different governmental entities and between institutions and segments of the public. By ensuring a variety of different access points to the political system, such constitutional institutions can help to ensure that the perspectives and interests of all citizens (rather than a mere majority of them) can be taken into account before any given policy is enacted. Senators' six-year terms and reeligibility should allow them to concern themselves with the long-term interests of the people, rather than the short term whims and passions. And there is some evidence that senators behave differently from members of the House.[42] By encouraging such horizontal and vertical deliberation, the constitutional system increases the likelihood that policies will reflect the deliberate sense of the community as a whole.

I agree with Dworkin, Eisgruber, and others that the Supreme Court can itself be seen as a representative institution. The small size and consequent high visibility of the high court and the justices' need to justify their decisions in reasoned opinions help to concentrate their responsibility for reasoned judgment. The secure tenure of Supreme Court justices, their independence from periodic electoral accountability, and the fact that justices are at the summit of their profession and do not need to worry about earning a living when out of office, can all help promote the justices' impartiality.[43] Institutional design thus helps make the justices well placed to reflect on principles of justice on behalf of the American people.

Judicial review most clearly supports constitutional democracy when it is conceived as playing the sort of "representation-reinforcing" function that Ely assigned to the institution.[44] Nevertheless, I agree with James E. Fleming and Corey Brettschneider (among others) who argue that the best understanding of the role of the court is as protector of the personal autonomy of citizens to make important personal decisions, in addition to protecting their political liberties and equal civic standing.[45]

One frequently hears that judicial review in the United States is undemocratic because it assigns final authority to determine the constitutionality of legislation to a small cadre of "unelected and unaccountable" judges, but the charge is untrue.[46] Judicial review is not to be confused with judicial supremacy or finality. Elected officials and citizens should also interpret the constitution and act on their interpretations in appropriate ways. I agree with those who would promote the interpretive capacities of citizens and elected officials, but there is no good reason to think that that agenda requires (or will be advanced by) curbing the interpretive role of the courts.[47] Dworkin emphasizes the potential for courts to infuse a measure of principled considerations into ordinary politics.[48]

I should emphasize that this is all by way of defending the legitimacy of the overall US constitutional conception on the basis of democratic values. I am not arguing that the working system is perfect from a democratic standpoint. The American system has been charged with having too many veto points, making it too easy for special interest minorities to block needed legislative change. Such charges may well have merit. Some measure of "status quo bias" may be accepted on the grounds that people plan around and come to rely upon existing legal arrangements. In addition, when change is difficult and there is, as a consequence, a prospect that we will have to live under proposed reforms over some extended period, that extended temporal horizon may, as Adrian Vermeule emphasizes, act as a kind of "veil mechanism" to promote greater impartiality.[49] For all that, it still may be the case that legislative change is too difficult in the American system.

There are, moreover, a variety of ways of structuring the interactions among courts and legislatures, and there may be arrangements that are better than the American model when it comes to promoting consideration of constitutional principles throughout our politics, including in legislatures.

Democracy-Enhancing Judicial Review: From Theory to Practice

So far I have argued that judicial review is defensible in theory, but its assessment must also consider the practice. How has the institution worked in practice? Does judicial review in practice approximate its "ideal description?"[50] These are difficult questions to answer.

The most obvious thing to be said about the American practice of judicial review—whether understood from the standpoint of democracy or justice—is that the record is mixed. We can celebrate cases like *Brown vs. Board of Education*, deplore cases like *Dred Scott v. Sanford*, and argue about the merits of cases like *Roe v. Wade*. The examples in each category can be multiplied many times over. I will not attempt a systematic tally, but will simply offer a few observations.

I agree with Tushnet's assessment of many of the court's mistakes. I think he is right for example to criticize the court's judgment that money is a form of constitutionally protected speech. And certainly the court has sometimes failed to adequately defer to reasonable disagreement: the fact that reasonable people defend the alternative point of view. Constitutional limits on legislative deliberation should indeed be sensitive to the question of whether a reasonable case can be made for various sides of the issue at hand.

But on that standard (absence of reasonable disagreement), one could argue (as I would) that the court got it right in *Lawrence v. Texas*, and that it should find (as a matter of principle) that disallowing same-sex marriage is a violation of constitutional equality. Obviously, prudence might suggest an exercise of Bickel's "passive virtues" here, at least for a time; *Goodridge* seemed to me overreaching, and the predictable political backlash furnished a case for incrementalism, by requiring civil unions, as was the case in Vermont. On the other hand, there is an argument that the controversies promoted by the courts have been educative. Certainly, the issue of same-sex marriage was thrust into public debate sooner than otherwise as a consequence of the litigation in Massachusetts and elsewhere. There seems to have been little backlash against the recent Iowa decision.

Obviously, Gerald Rosenberger's arguments need to be taken seriously. The question of whether litigation strategies make sense for social movements seeking more equal treatment or other reforms — civil rights, abortion rights, gay rights — seems to me hard to answer. It is hard to do counterfactual history. With respect to *Brown vs. Board of Education*, Michael Klarman argues that the decision did more to mobilize Southern white opposition than it did to encourage civil rights protest, and that it was the resulting violence that led to civil rights legislation in the 1960s.[51] There is no doubt that constitutional change is complex, and political mobilization is crucial.

It would also be important here to consider that recent scholarship — by Mark Graber, Keith Whittington, and others — arguing that some cases that are widely regarded as countermajoritarian and mistaken — such as *Dred Scott* — might more accurately be seen as reflections of the dominant party coalition of the time. More broadly, Whittington has argued that the relationship between the courts and other political actors is complex, and executives and legislatures often have reasons for supporting judicial action ("Courts can build authority by specializing in the type of issues that complement the agenda of other political actors"[52]).

I am not going to try and offer an overall assessment of the historical record — a task well beyond the scope of this paper. I would like to see the court play Ely's "channel clearing" and "representation reinforcing" roles vigorously, but that could well be a very expansive role (as Tushnet has observed) and one that would be fraught with controversy. Representation reinforcement could include a substantive right to equitable education funding, and any number of other things. But the court has sometimes played its role well.

Stephen Ansolobehere and Jack Snyder provide evidence to support Chief Justice Warren's observation that the reapportionment cases — *Baker* and *Reynolds* — may have been the most important decisions of his tenure. As Ansolobehere and Snyder put it, "reapportionment reshaped who gets what from government and made for a more equitable division of public expenditures on schools, hospitals, roads, and other essential services. It also shifted the balance among competing ideologies or public philosophies.... Equalization of votes resulted in the equalization of political power for geographic areas of the country." They argue that there were substantial consequences in terms of public spending and social services. The title of their book expresses their overall assessment: *The End of Inequality: One Person, One Vote and the Transformation of American Politics.* And these aren't dreamy-eyed theorists, they are tough-minded empiricists.[53]

Courts can play an important role in protecting the values of due process and the rights of the accused, and this can be especially important when (as is often the case) accused persons are also poor or members of unpopular minorities, or in times of emergency. There is reason to think that individual rights and democratic equality have suffered in the US in the course of the war on terror on account of the Supreme Court's relative inaction and deferential attitude toward the executive branch. It is not only that court decisions can themselves help protect individual rights, but also that they can help energize congressional action.[54]

If the theory of judicial review is sound from the standpoint of democratic principles, the practice of judicial review in the American case also permits a defense, though not one that is beyond contestation. There is no question that the American record is a mixed bag, but I join those who assert that, on balance, the Supreme Court has contributed to the promotion of justice and democracy in America.[55]

Leaving specific cases aside, it is worth noting that public confidence in the Supreme Court typically registers as considerably higher than the executive branch or Congress.

In 2007, *Real Clear Politics* calculated President Bush's approval rating at 31 percent. Congress came in even lower, at 25. But a Gallup poll found that 51 percent of Americans approved of the performance of the Supreme Court.[56] Moreover, it is well known that political party elites have become polarized: with Republican leaders defending positions far to the right and Democratic leaders far to the left of the median voter. Morris Fiorina and others have shown that American public opinion still tends to be clustered toward the middle.[57]

Let us turn from the American record to consider the popularity of constitutionalism and judicial review among post-World War II democracies.

Judicial Review, Popular Constitutional Choice, and Global Constitutionalism

As Issacharoff puts it, "all of the newly emerging democracies of the late twentieth century have opted for some form of written constitution and adopted some form of constitutionally based judicial review." Issacharoff in particular emphasizes the ways in which constitutionalism and judicial review can help secure "legitimacy for the exercise of political power in fractured societies" — that is — those "characterized by deep racial, ethnic, or religious animosities in which cross-racial, ethnic, and religious political institutions do not exist."[58] Legitimacy here stands for securing the trustful participation, or at least acquiescence, of all groups in the shared political order. "Judicially enforced constitutionalism," emphasizes Issacharoff, offers an alternative model of nation building than "consociational" models that, such as Belgium, are built on power sharing among social groups.[59]

Also impressive are the ways that constitutional mechanisms are being adapted to the project of global governance. As I have argued elsewhere, participation in multilateral institutions can be seen as extensions of domestic constitutional strategies.

Mark Tushnet appears to regard global governance mechanisms as essentially antidemocratic. Perhaps partly because global institutions are so remote from direct electoral control. He quotes Professor Paul Stephen to the effect that: "international law in the new constitutional order 'engages three antidemocratic tendencies': it strengthens the president against Congress; it 'enhances the ability of concentrated interest groups to procure rules that benefit their own, rather than the general welfare'; and it 'bolsters the power of the bureaucracies of international institutions.'"

John Ferejohn has drawn a broad contrast between two different poles on a spectrum of ways of promoting democratic accountability.[60] At one end of the spectrum are mechanisms of direct accountability to publics: elections and other forms of direct authorization, such as referenda. At this populist or direct end of the spectrum, reason-giving requirements are often low. At the other end of the spectrum are institutions that are remote from direct accountability to the people: courts exercising the power of review, but also central banks, administrative agencies, and the like. A wide variety of mechanisms of the latter sort are employed by modern democracies, and for them, reason-giving requirements and evidentiary standards are typically very high. These institutions employ various mechanisms for discharging their reason-giving requirement: administrative agencies have elaborate procedures for hearings, publication of draft rules, notice and comment, and judicial review of ultimate decisions.[61] The Federal Reserve has been secretive, but its decision making is becoming more open in some respects, and its decisions are subject to intense scrutiny by experts, the media, and Congress. Supreme Court decisions are also subject to intense scrutiny by experts and the general public, and while its internal deliberations are secretive, the "inputs" (laws, briefs, evidence) and the outputs (decisions and supporting argument) are fully public. Indeed, dissenting opinions have proliferated, testifying to the robustness of argument and contestation within and around the court.

The important point here is that modern democracies employ complex mixes of institutions of different sorts: power is exercised on behalf of the people, and the people and their representatives are prepared to authorize institutions that are accountable to the people in different ways, often only indirectly. Such institutions are often only immediately accountable to other remote institutions along with attentive publics and experts. Accountability operates in many ways, including horizontally among experts and elites.[62]

Why prefer indirect rather than direct accountability? There are at least three categories of reasons: low salience, expertise, and impartiality.

Democratic publics often delegate relatively low salience issues to remote institutions that are only indirectly accountable to publics. The same issues that tend to be delegated within nation states to bureaucracies or courts that are remote from direct accountability are also often further delegated to, as it were, the next higher level: to a multilateral regional or global institution. As Andrew Moravcsik has argued in his influential studies of the European Union, these areas of public policy have low public salience (as compared with education or social welfare issues) and these are also areas in which expertise is required, or where a high premium is placed on impartiality. When it comes to such issues as currency regulation or minority rights protection delegation to specialized impartial agencies makes democratic sense. Publics often seem to recognize the need for expert or impartial decision. Criminal trials often capture the public's imagination but, even then, decisions are insulated from direct public accountability in the interests of justice (though some might like the idea of putting high-profile trials on a reality TV show, with decisions rendered by phone-in votes).[63] And when such matters are further delegated by national governments to multilateral institutions—such as the European Union—talk of a "democratic deficit" is typically hollow or exaggerated.[64]

Judicial review is one aspect of a much wider pattern of indirect accountability: arms-length governance on behalf of the people. Strikingly, such forms of governance are becoming ever more prevalent, not only in the newer constitutional systems but also with respect to multilateral institutions.

There are of course, populist critiques of these developments and scholars who call for visionary schemes of global mass elections and direct representation.[65] There are no serious prospects for the development of such institutions, and their creation would be fraught with difficulty (very many countries in the world are unable or unwilling to hold free and fair elections). A far more promising pathway to improved global governance is via strategies for indirect accountability that emphasizes transparency, contestation, and reason giving. Scholars are demonstrating the variety of forms of accountability other than the direct electoral variety that can help curb abuses of power and make remote institutions responsive to the interests of publics.[66]

Paradoxically, many forms of multilateral governance above the level of the nation states might properly be seen as democracy enhancing, at least if we view them from the standpoint of the constitutional conception of democracy. With Robert Keohane and Andrew Moravcsik, I have argued—against internationalist skeptics such as Jeremy Rabkin and Jed Rubinfeld—that international institutions can be seen as extensions of Madisonian constitutional strategies for improving democracy.[67] Global institutions can—but do not necessarily of course—help us better protect human rights, control domestic factions, and improve the deliberative or epistemic resources available to domestic publics. So, for example, learning from foreign and international courts and jurists can help us better understand which rights are fundamental, and how they should be protected. The World Trade Organization can help us better control domestic protectionist factions.[68] And finally, with respect to the deliberative or epistemic dimension of democracy, consider that foreign statesmen and international institutions frequently have a critical distance and perspective on our actions that might be missing in times of patriotic fervor in particular. International engagement can improve domestic deliberation, as when Colin Powell belatedly confronted the weakness of the evidence for weapons of mass destruction in Iraq when preparing his testimony for the United Nations Security Council. A less dogmatically inclined administration might have treated this as an opportunity for critical self-reexamination. Skeptics about global institutions, such as Professor Rabkin, doubt this, but consider Madison's remarks:

> An attention to the judgment of other nations is important to every government ... [I]n doubtful cases, particularly where the national councils may be warped by some strong passion or momentary interest, the presumed or known opinion of the impartial world may be the best guide that can be followed. What has not America lost by her want of character with foreign nations; and how many errors and follies would she not have avoided, if the justice and propriety of her measures had, in every instance, been previously tried by the light in which they would probably appear to the unbiased part of mankind? (*Federalist* No.63).

Is the American Constitution Ideal?

I have emphasized several points of difference with Mark Tushnet, so it is good to have the chance to register a point of agreement. I find interesting and plausible his claim that the peculiar features of US-style judicial review may not be optimal from the standpoint of democratic deliberation and interbranch dialogue. "Optimal" represents a high standard, of course, and it would be astonishing if the American Constitution—the first of the modern democratic constitutions—had gotten it exactly right!

Tushnet has defended "weak form" judicial review, according to which the executive or legislative branch can respond to and reject exercises of constitutional rulings by the judiciary, as long as they do so publicly. Under US "strong form" judicial review, it can be very difficult to reverse an erroneous Supreme Court decision. Citizens, public officials, and members of the bar can argue and protest. Congress can repass legislation in amended form. The damage can sometimes be limited by legislative or executive action, or by lower court resistance. Sitting justices do sometimes change their minds. Or resort can be had to the extremely onerous process of constitutional amendment. Nevertheless, because the justices have life tenure, and because presidents are nominating and Senates are approving young nominees who also often appear to be ideologically rigid, there is no question that the Supreme Court is hard to reverse (unless it decides itself to do so).

In the UK, Canada and elsewhere, there are institutional mechanisms that allow exercises of judicial review to be confronted and in turn overridden by legislative action. It is certainly possible that some of these models do a better job of promoting the democratic virtues of principled deliberation, rights protection, and pursuit of the public good. Even the most enthusiastic supporters of judicial review, such as Ronald Dworkin, allow that we might be better off if the justices had limited terms of service or at least a mandatory retirement age.

My argument here is not that US judicial review is perfect. It is rather that in principle it is fully compatible with democracy properly understood, indeed, it is designed to be democracy enhancing, and in practice, its record is flawed but overall defensible on balance.

Conclusion

So, considered against the background of democratic constitutionalism, the case for judicial review is: in principle good, as a matter of practice mixed (but defensible), as a matter of institutional design, it is possible to do better than the American arrangement but we Americans may do well to make the best of the institutions we have, second best though they may be. The costs of constitutional revision are very high. Political reform efforts to improve democracy should be focused within rather than upon the constitutional framework.

PART SEVEN

An Imperial
Presidency?

Chapter 12

The Imperial Presidency, or "Who Doesn't Belong and Why?": Lincoln, FDR, Bush 43 and Obama

Richard M. Pious

Is there an imperial presidency?[1] If so, is that problematic for American democracy and the national interest? And if problematic, what is to be done? These questions are at the core of the constitutional issues facing the nation, but answers to them turn out to be far more complex than simply applying separation of powers doctrine to determine if presidents have acted beyond a pre-determined constitutional boundary. Presidential power includes not only the powers of the office, but also the political influence emanating from the Oval Office. A powerful president is simultaneously the leader of a regime (defined as the party in government and its interest-group and electoral allies), the leader of an administration, and the commander-in-chief of the armed forces. The bounds that a president may overstep are not just the formal powers defined by the Constitution and statutory law, but also the customs and usages of the Washington community. A president may be not only imperial, but also imperious.

I

At the outset, I want to distinguish two separate criteria for the exercise of power. The first involves *legitimacy*: is power exercised by those who have the right to rule (either hereditary or elective)? Do rulers follow due process laid down by the Constitution and laws? We have been fortunate that issues regarding presidential electoral legitimacy (in 1800, 1824, 1876, and 2000) have been settled peacefully, albeit with ad hoc measures and expedient congressional and judicial decisions. As for the exercise of power, the federal courts have the power of judicial review, but their decisions dealing with presidential power are constrained by judicial procedures and norms: they involve procedural issues that often lead to dismissal without decision; they almost never provide advisory opinions or a full exposition of the powers at stake, preferring to rule on the narrowest grounds; they are dismissed through standing, political questions, justiciability, ripeness, remedial equity, and other doctrines, unless Congress has already taken a position opposed to a presidential exercise of power (which is rare). One may take the two hundred or so leading federal cases dealing with the powers of the presidency, summarize the results, and come away without anything resembling a statement of the powers of the presidency.

So legitimacy remains in the eyes of the beholder, based on doctrinal positions (Madisonian partial separation of powers, Hamiltonian energy in the executive, Whig congressional supremacy, Federalist Society unitary presidency). The judiciary does little to fill in the gaps in a document that was ambiguous, incomplete, or silent at key points: there is no mention in the document of concomitants of nationality and sovereign powers, nor of power to declare neutrality in conflicts, nor to acquire territory, nor to abrogate treaties, nor to remove officials from public office (save by impeachment) nor to declare martial rule or a state of emergency. Neither, for that matter, was there ever an explicit discussion of what "The Executive Power" meant or how it was to be exercised, either in the Constitutional convention, the state conventions or *The Federalist Papers*.[2] In spite of these silences and ambiguities, using the first criterion of legitimacy, an imperial president would be one who observers believed had attained office in an extra-constitutional manner and usurped another's right of place; or who transgressed constitutional limits, disregarded checks and balances and any clearly demarcated separation of powers, acted without sanction of law, or without due process of law or dispensed with the law, and did so on such a large scale that the nation was transformed from a constitutional republic into a de facto authoritarian regime. We have never had to endure such a regime.

The second criterion for characterizing a presidency as imperial comes from our history as an expansionist power: settling across the continent through Manifest Destiny in the nineteenth century, and then taking the role of a superpower in the aftermath of World War II and finally becoming the post-Cold War "hyperpower." In this sense, an imperial president is one who disregards the maxim that the prudent exercise of power requires leaving some in reserve. The nation becomes overextended in terms of diplomatic commitments and uses of force, and eventually cannot pay for its imperial excesses. Whether or not the president gains the advice and consent of the Senate for commitments, or the concurrence of Congress for the exercise of war powers, is of less significance than the decisions for imperial overrereach—decisions that call into question presidential authority (in the connotation of wisdom and judgment, as when we refer to "learned authorities" or talk about an authoritative statement). We expect our rulers not only to act with legitimacy, but also with authority, and when they take actions that fail or stall, and when they pursue policies that lead to an overshoot of capability and subsequent collapse, we lose confidence in them, irrespective of whether or not their actions were constitutional and legal. And worse, for those who exercise power, in many cases when confidence is lost, so too is legitimacy, and questions of policy become "constitutionalized" by their critics. We have gone through this experience many times in American history.

The arguments for vast presidential power and for increases in the powers of the office have always rested on pragmatic Hamiltonian principles: we are in perilous times, or we have a fleeting moment to exploit an opportunity and the executive must act unilaterally, or the president has the best "vantage point" from which to determine policy, and what he sees as the best policy for himself is also the best for the nation.[3] The Whig and neo-Whig counters have always been that the President has too much power, and that the system has become constitutionally unbalanced, and that the imbalances lead to the wrong policies.[4]

I would argue that Hamiltonians have often had the best of the argument—at least through the Second World War. The Framers believed that we needed a strong executive and vigorous administration: otherwise why convene to create the Constitution of 1787?

If the delegates to the Convention had preferred a weak national administration at Philadelphia, they needed to do nothing, since they already had such a system.[5] Consider an alternative American history had we functioned under a system of complete separation of powers and vigorous checks and balances, with presidents unwilling to go beyond a literal reading of the Constitution. Here are a few paragraphs from *that* history of the United States:

- Washington's refusal to declare neutrality in the midst of the Anglo-French wars of the early 1790s led to the naval hostilities with the British that proved catastrophic to the American economy.

- Jefferson's rejection of Napoleon's offer to sell Louisiana ended American expansion at the Mississippi River.

- Jackson's capitulation to South Carolina over the tariff led to the pernicious doctrine of concurrent majorities being accepted for national legislation.

- Lincoln's decision not to re-supply Fort Sumter paved the way for Seward's successful negotiations, postponing abolition of slavery until the 1890s and continuing southern domination of positions of political power in the Union, which in turn retarded industrialization due to the low tariffs passed by Congress.

- Roosevelt's unwillingness to go around Congress to aid the British at the outset of the European War led the United Kingdom to sue for peace, paving the way for the Reich's successful conquest of a vast Eurasian empire. Fortress America remained out of the grasp of the Nazis—but its isolationist policy left it at great risk.

Given this alternate history, who can be against a strong presidency? Absent the bold uses of executive power we would not have acquired much of the continent, or preserved the Union, or become a superpower.[6] All the Mount Rushmore presidents, and others whose portraits grace our stamps and our currency, have gone beyond the literal words of the Constitution, and exercised prerogative powers expansively, sovereign powers not explicitly mentioned in the document, and even on occasion Lockean emergency powers.[7]

Why then the disquiet over the assertion of presidential power? Is it merely the case that those who claim that either some presidents (LBJ and Nixon) or the office itself has evolved into an "imperial presidency" are being subjective, and that the motivation for their analysis involves policy disagreements rather than an institutional analysis? Is one person's imperial presidency another's democratic leader?[8] Or are there criteria, irrespective of policy disagreements and questions of authority, which may be used to describe such a presidency?

It may helpful to introduce a third criterion for the exercise of power: the *style of governance* adopted by a president: patterns of behavior that engender expectations about what the government will do, especially in dealing with its opponents. Governing style may be more significant to the maintenance of democratic norms than whether a particular "line" was crossed and a congressional prerogative usurped. If there is a conspiratorial atmosphere, in which opponents are considered "enemies," to be targeted by law enforcement and regulatory agencies, in which civil liberties are curtailed for the duration of the "emergency," in which internal security organs are corrupted for political purposes, in which people may be held indefinitely, mistreatment of detainees and prisoners occurs, trials may occur outside of lawfully constituted courts, and extra-judicial targeted assassinations by death squads becomes a tool of executive power, the result will be a "chilling effect" that corrupts American democracy. If there is pervasive secrecy and deception, so that no one knows what is true, and no one trusts the government to tell the truth, no checks and balances may be available for Congress or the judiciary to restrain executive power. That unchecked and unbalanced atmosphere is more important in determining whether a presidency has become "imperial" than any specific constitutional transgression.[9] It is the casual imperiousness of ex-President Richard Nixon in a television interview with David Frost: when confronted with evidence that he had approved the "Huston Plan" involving, as Frost described it, "the systematic use of wiretappings, burglaries, or so-called black bag jobs, mail openings and infiltration against antiwar groups and others" he responded "when the president does it that means it is not illegal" *by definition*.[10] It is that claim of unlimited power to rule irrespective of the limits placed on power by constitutional and international law, rather than isolated transgressions of the Constitution, that form the core of an imperial presidency.

II

Since original constitutional understandings are somewhat chimerical, public law scholars are engaged in a quasi-theological exercise, arguing over points of dogma with excerpts from sacred texts as to whether Congress or the president has the power to act. As Justice Jackson observed:

> Just what our forefathers did envision, or would have envisioned had they foreseen modern conditions, must be divined from materials almost as enigmatic as the dreams Joseph was called upon to interpret for Pharaoh. A century and a half of partisan debate and scholarly speculation yields no net result but only supplies more or less apt quotations from respected sources on each side of any question. They largely cancel each other.[11]

But this has never been the right question: it frames constitutional transgression as a zero-sum proposition involving boundary disputes. Courts usually avoid this trap: they have upheld the powers of a vigorous presidency, interpreting the office's powers expansively and preferring not to consider boundary disputes between president and Congress when these can be avoided.[12]

Lincoln's Constitutional Dictatorship

To understand the difference between presidents who transgress constitutional or legal limits, and those who promote an imperial presidency, consider Lincoln's exercise of executive power just prior to the start of the Civil War and in the 100 or so days thereafter. Although Lincoln reassured the South that he did not oppose continuation of slavery in the region, he did oppose its extension to the West, and therefore opposed various compromises floated by Seward, by ex-President Tyler's Peace Convention, and by some members of the House. He warned the secessionist states of the Lower South at his inauguration, "You have no oath registered in heaven to destroy the Government, while I shall have the most solemn one to preserve, protect and defend it."[13]

Although Lincoln was under pressure within his party to take a stronger stance, he had less support in Congress, which had not confirmed a new Collector of the Port of Charleston, which meant there was no federal official calling on the president to enforce the tariff. The lame-duck Democratic-controlled Congress in the Winter of 1861 had refused to pass a Force Bill that would have authorized enforcement of federal law in the South. It refused to pass a Militia Bill that would have authorized the call-up of troops to deal with the secession already under way. It passed no appropriations for military preparedness. Even Lincoln's decision to re-supply Fort Sumter involved sending supplies rather than manpower, and was a symbolic rather than substantive military maneuver, albeit one that the secessionist forces at the port could not accept.

Yet as soon as the news of the bombardment reached Washington, Lincoln instituted prerogative governance, unilaterally making and executing his policies, and not calling the new Congress into special session to exercise its war powers until July 4, 1861. (Until the 1930s, a Congress elected in an even-numbered election year did not convene until December of the following year, 14 months after the election, unless called, as it usually was, into special session). Lincoln issued a proclamation calling for 75,000 volunteers for ninety days of service to enforce the national laws.[14] This proclamation, and subsequent forays across the Potomac, led to the secession of states of the Upper South. In early May Lincoln accepted 42,034 volunteers from the militia for three years of service, later instituting a militia draft in 1862—although this was based on a statute, Lincoln stretched its provisions to meet the emergency. He later increased the regular army's strength by 22,000, violating ceilings in existing laws, and authorized the use of black troops without obtaining congressional authorization (of these 68,000 were killed or wounded during hostilities). Without obtaining congressional authorization Lincoln authorized the construction of nineteen warships and an increase in Navy personnel of 18,000 sailors, and used the enlarged Navy to blockade the ports of secessionist states (an act of war) also without seeking authorization from Congress. After Virginia seceded, Lincoln ordered $2 million transferred from the Treasury without appropriation, and delivered some of these funds to Union sympathizers in the western counties so they could be armed and form a new state.

A week after secessionist mobs in Baltimore attacked Union troops moving through the city to reinforce the Capital, Lincoln ordered the Union commander at Fort McHenry to institute martial rule and suspend the writ of habeas corpus along rail lines leading to the District of Columbia.[15] Then the following week Union troops arrested the chief and members of the Board of Police of Baltimore, charging them with conspiracy against the United States. Based on six proclamations to Union commanders, over the summer and for months thereafter Union troops rounded up, arrested, and held in military camps prominent citizens who sympathized with the secession throughout the border states and Midwest. In September 1862 Lincoln proclaimed a general cancellation of the writ.[16]

Lincoln justified these measures in the context of the national emergency: the capital was almost surrounded by Confederate sympathizers, and telegraph and rail lines were at risk of being cut. If Lincoln had not acted, Congress might not have been able to assemble at the Capitol. When Lincoln called Congress into special session on July 4, 1861, he posed the question: "Must a government, of necessity, be too strong for the liberties of its own people, or too weak to maintain its own existence?"[17] Lincoln thought there was a different way, through novel constitutional interpretation. He would fuse his powers with those of Congress (even in the absence of Congress): these war powers, Lincoln explained, did not go "beyond the Constitutional competency of Congress."[18] He explained that "these measures, whether strictly legal or not, were ventured upon, under what appeared to be popular demand and a public necessity, trusting ... that Congress would readily ratify them."[19] In the context of the emergency, Lincoln defended his prerogative to suspend the privilege of the writ of habeas corpus, even though the provision for suspension "in case of rebellion or invasion" appears in Article I, by observing, "... it cannot be believed the Framers of the instrument intended, that in every case, the danger should run its course, until Congress could be called together; the very assembling of which might be prevented, as was intended in this case, by the rebellion."[20] And even if what he had done had not been constitutional, he posed the question: "are all the laws, but one, to go unexecuted, and the Government itself go to pieces, lest that one be violated?"[21] Later Lincoln was to rest these powers on his obligation in his oath of office to preserve and protect and defend the Constitution, and on his power as commander in chief "to take any measure which may best subdue the enemy."[22] For Lincoln, context was everything: "certain proceedings are constitutional when in cases of rebellion or invasion, the public safety require them, which would not be constitutional when, in the absence of rebellion or invasion, the public safety does not require them."[23] In a letter to the newspaper publisher Albert Hodges in 1864, Lincoln returned to this idea: "I felt that measures, otherwise unconstitutional, might become lawful, by becoming indispensable to the preservation of the Constitution, through preservation of the nation."[24]

The congressional response was to support the president's policy by ratifying what Lincoln had done. In an Appropriations Act of August 6, 1861, Congress provided that all of Lincoln's "acts, proclamations and orders" after March 4, 1861 respecting the Army and Navy and militia and state volunteers, "are hereby approved and in all respects legalized and made valid, to the same as if they had been done under the previous express authority and direction of the Congress of the United States."[25] The following year Congress retroactively authorized Lincoln's seizure of telegraph lines, and the year after that Congress passed a draft law (in effect retroactively upheld Lincoln's prior draft) and a statute allowing the president to suspend the writ of habeas corpus.

The response of the judiciary was not as positive for the president. In the *Prize Cases* the Supreme Court, by a narrow 5–4 majority, upheld Lincoln's right to conduct the war without congressional authorization.[26] But in *Ex Parte Merryman*, Chief Justice Roger Taney initiated the first challenge to Lincoln's wartime prerogatives. Lieutenant John Merryman was part of a contingent of Maryland cavalry that escorted some Union troops out of the state, and then demolished a bridge to block further Union troop movements. After Lincoln ordered suspension of habeas corpus, Merryman was arrested and imprisoned at Fort McHenry. He petitioned for his release, and Chief Justice Taney, presiding over the appellate circuit, granted his petition in chambers. Lincoln ordered General Cadwallader, the commander at the fort, to ignore Taney's writ, and to refuse to appear before Taney to answer a citation for contempt of court. Taney thereupon wrote another opinion as chief of the circuit court of appeals, in which he tried to give Lincoln a graceful way out:

> I have exercised all the power which the constitution and laws confer upon me, but that power has been resisted by a force too strong for me to overcome. It is possible that the officer who has incurred this grave responsibility may have misunderstood his instructions, and exceeded the authority intended to be given him; I shall, therefore, order all the proceedings in this case, with my opinion, to be filed and recorded in the circuit court of the United States for the district of Maryland, and direct the clerk to transmit a copy, under seal, to the president of the United States. It will then remain for that high officer, in fulfillment of his constitutional obligation to "take care that the laws be faithfully executed," to determine what measures he will take to cause the civil process of the United States to be respected and enforced.[27]

Lincoln disregarded Taney's order. When Merryman appealed to the Supreme Court, it refused to take the case on procedural grounds.

The Supreme Court eventually exercised a check on presidential power. Lambdin Milligan, an Indiana Copperhead (Confederate sympathizer) was arrested by the military and tried in a military tribunal that Lincoln had established. He was convicted of conspiracy to organize an insurrection and sentenced to death in 1864. After his trial he petitioned in federal court for a writ of habeas corpus, claiming that the tribunal Lincoln had created on his own authority was not the proper venue for his trial. After delaying its opinion until the war was over, the Supreme Court in *Ex Parte Milligan* ruled that civilians could not be tried by military tribunals in a state of martial rule in any territory controlled by the Union where federal courts were open and functioning.[28] The following year in the *First Reconstruction Act of 1867* the Radical Republican majority in Congress provided for establishment of military tribunals throughout the South, even though federal courts were once again open, thus overturning *Milligan*. In the *Second Reconstruction Act of 1868* Congress took away jurisdiction from the Supreme Court to hear petitions for habeas corpus from those subject to trial by the tribunals.[29] When the constitutionality of this restriction on its jurisdiction was challenged in *Ex Parte McCardle* in 1868, the Supreme Court upheld the constitutionality of the statute.[30]

If one takes each of Lincoln's actions, or a complete listing of them, it would seem that Lincoln fits the definition of imperial president. But these acts must be seen in context. Although Lincoln waited several months to call Congress into special session, once he did so he reported on what he had done, and provided constitutional justifications. There was nothing to stop Congress at that point from checking and balancing, or indeed from impeaching and removing the President, had it so wished. Elections for Congress were held in 1862 and the opposition Democrats increased their seats in the House. The presidential election was held in 1864; Lincoln expected to lose and was fully prepared to turn over the White House to McClellan and the peace party, if that were the verdict of the voters. Though habeas corpus was suspended by presidential fiat, it was done under the circumstances provided for by the Constitution—invasion or rebellion. Lincoln did not proclaim a state of siege, did not suspend civil liberties guaranteed by the Constitution through a state of emergency, and exercised a light hand on many of those detained, most of whom soon were released or allowed to cross over to Confederate territory. Lincoln proclaimed a general and unconditional release of most prisoners in a military order of February 14, 1862.[31] In dealing with enemy combatants Lincoln requested the noted German jurist Francis Lieber to draft "Instructions for the Government of Armies of the United States in the Field." General Orders Number 100, Article 16, stated that "Military necessity does not admit of cruelty—that is, the infliction of suffering for the sake of suffering, or for revenge, nor of maiming or wounding except in fight, nor of torture to extort confessions."[32]

The power to approve or disapprove of Lincoln's prerogative style of governance rested ultimately in the electorate. Its verdict was to reject the Democratic platform of 1864, which resolved that the states "consider that the administrative usurpation of extraordinary and dangerous powers not granted by the Constitution—the subversion of the civil by military law in states not in insurrection; the arbitrary military arrest, imprisonment, trial and sentence of American citizens in states where civil law exists in full force" was calculated "to prevent a restoration of the Union and the perpetuation of a government deriving its just powers from the consent of the governed." Instead, it implicitly endorsed the Republican platform of 1864, which defended "as demanded by the emergency and essential to the preservation of the nation and as within the provisions of the Constitution, the measures and acts which he has adopted to defend the nation against its open and secret foes...."

Once the war was over, the wartime presidency using its prerogative to exercise the war powers of the United States was over as well. In its place was a system of Congressional government dominated by cabinet secretaries and the chairs of congressional committees. Constitutional jurisprudence for the next seventy years was dominated by public law jurists who distinguished between the almost unlimited powers exercised by the state (internal security against labor agitators, secessionists, and foreign intrigues) and the limited powers of the government to regulate interstate commerce and markets.[33]

The lessons of the Lincoln presidency are that we cannot determine if a president is "imperial" just by totting up the uses of power and marking their farthest advance across an imaginary demarcation line separating presidential from congressional and judicial powers. Lincoln could exercise imperial powers without being imperious: he looked always for a charitable reconciliation once the force needed to restore the constitutional order had been applied. He was, in Clinton Rossiter's terms, a "constitutional dictator" with an emphasis on *constitutional*.[34]

FDR's "Dr. Win the War" Prerogatives

Franklin D. Roosevelt was called "dictatorial" when he exercised unilateral prerogative powers (i.e. an executive agreement) in 1940 to transfer destroyers to the United Kingdom in exchange for a string of naval bases. Princeton constitutional law professor Edward Corwin claimed "no such dangerous opinion was ever before penned by an Attorney General of the United States" in discussing Attorney General Robert Jackson's opinion justifying the transfer.[35] Frank R. Kent, writing in his *Wall Street Journal* column "The Great Game of Politics," condemned "the ruthless sweeping aside of the constitution and dictatorial assumption of power."[36] The *Wall Street Journal* editorialized "By this road government in America approaches the political outskirts of Berlin."[37] Robert Shogun, writing in the aftermath of Watergate, the Vietnam War and the Iran-Contra affair, issued a sweeping condemnation:

> In the interests of his country's security and of his own political ambitions, the President would find it necessary to twist the law, flout the Constitution, hoodwink the public, and distort the political process. Roosevelt's handling of the destroyer deal with the British would set a pernicious precedent. His machinations would give impetus and legitimacy to the efforts of his successors to expand the reach of their powers, overriding constitutional guidelines and political principles, all in the name of national security.[38]

Shogun argued that the country had paid a "high price" for FDR's "undermining the rule of law." He not only thought the action raised the question of whether "they created circumstances in which attack became inevitable," but also that it paved the way for presidents to send US troops to Korea and Vietnam and elsewhere without congressional participation.[39]

Yet a close analysis of FDR's decisionmaking in the destroyer deal reveals that the prerogative power was not an imperious act, but a gambit to satisfy his own congressional party. On June 11, Churchill requested a six-month loan of 35 destroyers—with a right of recall if the US needed them. For almost two months he and Churchill squabbled over how the transaction was to be portrayed: FDR insisted that it be considered a "deal" and that the US would have to be seen to have gotten the better of it; Churchill wanted it to be considered a gift of bases on his part, and a gift of destroyers on the part of FDR. The prime minister finally acquiesced, and later wrote that FDR was "drawn to present the transaction to his fellow countrymen as a highly advantageous bargain," adding that it was "not exactly a convenient statement for me."[40]

The alliance question resolved, domestic politics became paramount. Was this to be done by a treaty, or an arrangement requiring congressional assent? Or should it be done by executive fiat? "That Destroyer arrangement seems to have worked out perfectly," FDR wrote to King George VI after his re-election in 1940, adding "There is virtually no criticism in this country except from legalists who think it should have been submitted to the Congress first. If I had done that, the subject would still be in the tender care of the Committees of the Congress."[41] Congressional inaction, bordering on paralysis, and its passage of various neutrality acts, form the backdrop to the decisions that Roosevelt took to implement the destroyer deal.[42]

Roosevelt initially assumed he would have to take the deal to Congress. On August 2, after a cabinet meeting discussed the transfer of ships, Roosevelt wrote up a memo of the meeting to himself, noting that all present agreed "legislation was necessary to accomplish any sale."[43] As late as August 14 Secretary of War Henry Stimson told British Ambassador Lord Lothian that an exchange would be "an attractive proposition for the President to make to the Congress."[44] And on August 17th Secretary of the Navy Knox declared that it was for Congress to decide.[45] But prospects for congressional approval were poor. On June 28, 1940 Congress had amended the Naval Appropriations Bill to require the Chief of Staff George Marshall or Chief of Naval Operations Harold Stark to certify that military equipment transferred to another nation was "not essential to" US defense. This would present a serious problem, since Admiral Stark had recently testified in Congress that the destroyers were not useless, after Congress complained that he was wasting money keeping the ships in mothballs.

The first task of the administration was to get around existing statutory prohibitions. On August 16 Attorney General Robert Jackson briefed the president. According to Jackson, the president had the power, as commander in chief, not only to *dispose* the Armed Forces, but also to *dispose of* them.[46] He referred to the "plenary powers of the President as Commander-in-Chief of the Army and Navy and as head of state in its relations with foreign countries." He then interpreted the prohibitions of the Neutrality Law of 1917 narrowly, claiming it referred only to the transfer of ships *built* for a belligerent power, even though a close reading of the intent of Congress when it drafted the law had been to prevent sending out of *any* warships, not just those constructed for them. Jackson also found a way around the Walsh Amendment of 1940 restricting the transfer of military materiel unless it was "not essential" to American defense. He noted a phrase that Congress had dropped, which was that the materiel could not be transferred unless it "cannot be used" for such defense. Walsh had agreed to drop that language so that warplanes and army supplies could be sent to the British—but he had no intention of allowing any ships to be sent, since the purpose of his amendment had been to prevent any reduction in the size of the Navy. "To exchange them for bases would give us far more than their equivalent in actual defense facilities," Jackson argued. "On this basis, it seemed to me, the Chief of Naval Operations could certify that the destroyers were 'not essential to the defense of the United States,' and thus the transaction would conform to the conditions of the Act of June 28, 1940."[47] Admiral Stark certified that "on balance" the exchange of destroyers for bases meant that they were not essential. And so FDR and Jackson evaded the clear intent of Walsh's amendment, exercising a dispensing power in all but name.

The deal ultimately became an exercise in prerogative power because Roosevelt had to protect himself in the presidential election. Roosevelt wanted Wendell Willkie, the Republican presidential nominee, to convince his party's congressional leaders to back the deal. Willkie wouldn't promise to support legislation that the administration had not yet introduced. FDR in turn would not introduce a bill until the Republicans made a commitment to back it. Roosevelt did not see any way to break out of the chicken and egg impasse. Moreover, he could not even obtain strong support from Democrats. When FDR had Senator Josh Lee (D. Oklahoma) sound out sentiment in the chamber in mid-August, Lee reported back that the mood of the Senate was hostile.[48] Senator Burton Wheeler (D. Montana), suggested canceling British war debts in return for bases, but indicated over the summer that he was concerned that the president might instead decide to transfer destroyers—a deal he opposed.[49] Senator Millard Tydings (D Maryland), a member of the Naval Affairs Committee that would have jurisdiction over any legislation that would be sent by the White House, indicated that sale of warships would be an act of war, and that if we wanted to send ships, we should send "the whole fleet, and we ought to declare war."[50] Without support from committee leaders, FDR decided to bypass Congress entirely.

The president announced the deal during the Labor Day weekend, summoning reporters at noon to the sitting room of the private car of his train, outside of South Charleston, West Virginia. Reporters asked Roosevelt if Congressional approval would be required. "It is all over. It is done," the president replied.[51] The president then sent a message to Congress—on a day when the Senate was not in session—stating that the text of the agreement was being transmitted "for the information of the Congress," not for its deliberations or approval. In late March 1941 he sent a copy of a subsequent 41-page contract implementing the deal that War, Navy and State had negotiated with the British, again for congressional information rather than approval.

Once Roosevelt announced the deal, Willkie tried to have it both ways: he attacked on the substance, claiming that the deal did not provide enough aid to the British. He also criticized the president the day after the deal was announced by condemning the fact that he "did not deem it necessary, in connection with this proposal, to secure the approval of Congress or permit public discussion prior to its adoption," warning that "we must be extremely careful in these times, when the struggle in the world is between democracy and totalitarianism, not to eliminate or destroy the democratic processes while seeking to preserve democracy."[52] During a conference with almost 100 editors of Midwestern farming community newspapers, he charged that the president's decision to bypass Congress was "the most dictatorial and arbitrary of any President in the history of the U.S."[53]

But FDR was hardly being dictatorial, imperial, or imperious. He had consulted widely within cabinet and Congress. He made the deal after bringing Republicans Henry Stimson and Frank Knox into his cabinet (to head War and Navy) and after consulting fully with them, as well as Secretary of State Cordell Hull, Attorney General Jackson, and the rest of the cabinet. Members of the cabinet were involved in defining the transaction as a deal rather than as a gift, loan, or sale. James Farley, the postmaster general and chairman of the Democratic Party insisted that Willkie's promise to back an exchange was essential.[54] Roosevelt also consulted congressional Republicans about bypassing Congress: the Senate minority leader McNairy (Willkie's candidate for vice president) told FDR that he would make no objection if the president came up with a method that would keep the Senate from having to vote. FDR consulted with Joe Martin, House minority leader, who also gave discrete support to the deal. Roosevelt also consulted with Democrats who controlled Congress as well: on Aug 22 he wrote to Senator David Walsh (D Mass.) chair of the Committee on Naval Affairs, asking him not to oppose the deal; by this point Roosevelt was seeking congressional acquiescence rather than authorization. This suited a majority of senators from both parties, who were pleased that FDR had let them off the hook.

FDR's wide consultation throughout the government paid off. The deal did not have many opponents, however vociferous the minority had been. Soon after the deal was announced Congress appropriated funds to build the bases on the islands and passed other enabling legislation, including a provision to assume military control over West Indies islands if necessary to protect the new bases and American warships based there—demonstrating what constitutional lawyers refer to as "joint concord" after the fact. It appropriated more than $66 million for construction of bases on the British islands; over the next two decades the US Congress appropriated more than $150 million for construction on the West Indies bases. Far from opposing what FDR had done, Congress facilitated the destroyer deal in every way possible.

III

If Lincoln and FDR were not imperial presidents, given the transgressions across the artificial separation of power boundaries, and the huge expansion of presidential power (including the relocation of the Japanese-Americans into concentration camps), what then constitutes an "imperial presidency"? I would submit that the Bush 43 presidency fits the imperial/imperious test: it involved an overreaching of geographical power when Bush ordered the invasion of Iraq and it involved the creation of parallel institutions to bypass Congress and the judiciary, centralizing power in the executive and attempting to legitimate it through unitary executive theory.[55]

Surveillance Authority

In the immediate aftermath of 9/11 President Bush authorized by a secret executive order the National Security Agency (NSA) to target calls made in or out of the US when one party was abroad and there might be a link to al Qaeda, and to do so without obtaining a judicial warrant from the Foreign Intelligence Surveillance Court, as the Foreign Intelligence Surveillance Act (FISA) required. The administration briefed selected congressional leaders more than a dozen times, but swore them to secrecy and refused to let them consult with outside counsel on the legality of the program. Under another program, Verizon, Bell South and AT&T allowed the NSA to conduct surveillance on domestic calls and e-mails without warrants. This program was in violation of sec. 222 of the Communications Act of 1934, which prohibits phone companies from giving out information about their customers' calls. Two years later Attorney General John Ashcroft and other senior officials threatened to resign, believing the way the program was administered by NSA was illegal. But President Bush reauthorized the program without Justice's concurrence.

Status of Enemy Combatants

President Bush applied the Geneva Conventions to Taliban prisoners captured in Afghanistan, but not to al Qaeda detainees (because al Qaeda is not a sovereign state and is not a party to the conventions), and ordered that neither group be granted prisoner-of-war status, both being considered "unlawful combatants." Under the *Geneva*

Conventions lawful combatants are granted significant due process guarantees, and they are entitled to defense by a qualified advocate or counsel of their own choice (Article 105), right of appeal of conviction to civilian courts (Article 106), and right to the same sentence as US personnel, which would limit the death penalty (Article 87).[56] But unlawful combatants are treated differently: their status is supposed to be determined, according to the *Geneva Conventions*, by a competent tribunal. President Bush made the determination unilaterally for the entire class of detainees, thus acting as the "competent tribunal" himself. Unlawful combatants are granted some due process rights, set forth in the First Additional Protocol to the Geneva Conventions.[57] But the US is not a signatory to that convention, and so the Afghan and Guantánamo Bay prisoners were granted no rights at all; their treatment depended completely on the sufferance of military authorities.

Indefinite Detention of American Citizens

American citizens judged to be unlawful combatants were placed in solitary confinement and indefinite detention in military facilities in the United States. In the past citizens had been subject to military detention and trial in military courts only when martial law had been proclaimed and when the military had occupied territory in secession or rebellion. They also had been subject to military justice if they had been enemy combatants during hostilities and had violated the laws of war. In *Ex Parte Quirin*, involving German saboteurs captured in the United States, the Supreme Court had taken up the question of whether one of those captured, who held American citizenship, could be subject to a presidential proclamation denying him access to civilian courts. The court held that "citizens who associate themselves with the military arm of the enemy government, and with its aid, guidance and direction enter this country bent on hostile acts, are enemy belligerents within the meaning of the Hague Convention and the law of war."[58] Therefore whether citizen or not, violations of the laws of war are enough to give the military jurisdiction.

Absent such violations of the laws of war, civilians had successfully challenged military detention and trials, as in *Ex Parte Milligan*. In *Duncan v. Kahanamoku*, the Supreme Court reaffirmed its reasoning in *Milligan*. The court held that since civilian courts remained open in Hawaii during World War II, martial law could not replace their jurisdiction over civilians.[59] On the other hand, *Hirabayashi v. US* and *Korematsu v. US* upheld the right of the government to place Japanese Americans on the West Coast under a curfew, and then to exclude them from the coast and intern them in concentration camps inland for the duration of the war. The Supreme Court, in upholding these actions, noted that they involved "joint concord" since Congress had acted as well as the President in developing the policy.[60] But there is more to the story than these two cases. The Supreme Court, as part of a package deal involving *Korematsu*, also decided *Ex Parte Endo*, a case in which it determined that without an *individual* determination that someone should be interned, there was no rational reason that could justify mass internments.[61] In all of these cases, the federal courts, not military authorities, had the final word on whether or not an action authorized by the president and carried out by military authorities was constitutional. And it had only ruled in favor of the government in the World War II cases because Congress had provided authorization.

So far as the Bush administration was concerned, anyone involved in the war on terror was not a civilian, but was an "enemy combatant" who might be held without charges, denied access to an attorney, and "softened up" by being kept in solitary confinement indefinitely. The government took the position that the president could order these actions on his own authority as commander in chief, and that courts could not thereafter review such indefinite detentions, that presidential prerogative superseded congressional prohibitions against indefinite detention that would otherwise apply to American citizens, and that when it comes to combating terrorism, Congress had implicitly authorized the president to detain unlawful combatants when after 9/11 it had passed the Authorization to Use Military Force against terrorists.

Interrogation of Unlawful Combatants

Under the Geneva Conventions governing treatment of POWs, *lawful* combatants do not have to provide information to their captors beyond "name, rank and serial number" or other basic identification, and may not be coerced or intimidated. But the Bush administration argued that these Geneva protections would not apply to unlawful combatants.[62] Under the Geneva Conventions even unlawful combatants have the right to humane treatment, and there are limits on interrogations. Common Article 3 of the Geneva Conventions provides that detained persons "shall in all circumstances be treated humanely," and that "[t]o this end," certain specified acts "are and shall remain prohibited at any time and in any place whatsoever." What are termed "grave breaches" of the conventions by captors mistreating "protected persons" in their custody are considered to be war crimes. These include the following: (1) willful killing of protected persons such as injured combatants, POWs, and civilians under their control; (2) murder, mutilations, torture, inhumane treatment, outrages upon personal dignity, humiliating or degrading treatment, or causing great suffering or bodily injury to protected persons. Article I of the Convention Against Torture prohibits torture and defines it as any act intentionally inflicting severe pain or suffering (physical or mental) to obtain information or a confession from that person or someone else (e.g. a close relative).

It had always been an American military tradition, dating from George Washington's generalship in the Revolutionary War and Lincoln's General Order Number 100, Article 16, that the armed forces were not to torture prisoners. Pursuant to the Convention Against Torture Congress passed a law making it a criminal offense for a US citizen or foreign national resident in the US to commit or attempt to commit torture under color of law outside the United States.[63] The law defines torture as an "act committed by a person acting under color of law specifically intended to inflict severe physical or mental pain...." Another prohibition against torture is the War Crimes Act of 1996 passed by Congress, which makes it a criminal offense for an American citizen or a member of the US armed forces (citizen or non-citizen) to commit in the US or abroad a grave breach of the Geneva Conventions.[64]

With the recommendation of the Department of Defense and over the objections of the State Department President Bush issued the following order: "the United States Armed Forces shall continue to treat detainees humanely and to the extent appropriate and consistent with military necessity, in a manner consistent with the principles of Geneva." This language invoked Geneva and pledged humane treatment, only to subvert that promise with the loophole of "military necessity." Department of Justice and Department of Defense civilian legal counsel then prepared legal memoranda justifying brutal interrogation methods: they argued that prisoners were unlawful combatants and not entitled to protection under the Geneva Conventions; if there were no violations of the Conventions then the Uniform Code of Military Justice prohibitions against war crimes would not be violated, because the Code requires that there be violation of the Conventions in establishing that a war crime has been committed.[65] Secretary of Defense Donald Rumsfeld prohibited only methods that would have *lasting* physical or mental effects akin to organ failure or *permanent* disability; those that inflicted *temporary* pain or suffering, or mental disorientation, would not be considered torture, no matter how painful. The first commander of coalition forces in Iraq, Lt. General Ricardo S. Sanchez, observed that the Bush administration set aside the legal prohibitions, training guidelines, and rules for interrogation that the military had used since 1949 under the Geneva Conventions, and that the Bush administration guidance set America on a path toward torture.[66] Eventually the use of torture was condemned by the top American commander in Iraq, General David Petraeus, who wrote a letter to his troops, explaining "Some may argue that we would be more effective if we sanctioned torture ... to obtain information from the enemy. They would be wrong. Beyond the basic fact that such actions are illegal, history shows that they are also frequently neither useful nor necessary."[67]

Military Tribunals

Evidence from these interrogations would be necessary to prosecute detainees, but it could not be admitted under the rules of military courts martial. The Bush administration decided that forums would be needed with different rules.[68] On November 13th, 2001, President Bush issued a military order based on his power as commander in chief.[69] It mandated the establishment of military tribunals (either inside or outside the territory of the U.S.), to be implemented subsequently through regulations developed by the Pentagon.[70] Those subject to the tribunals, at the discretion of the president, would be any non-citizen of the US (including a resident alien) who was a member of al Qaeda, involved in "acts of international terrorism," or had "knowingly harbored" others in the first two categories. US citizens would not be subject to their jurisdiction.

The president would appoint military judges to the tribunals. He would determine who would be tried by such commissions, and if defendants were found guilty, would determine the sentence. There were some elements of the due process model in the tribunal proceedings. Defendants would be presumed innocent, would be given notice of charges before trial, and would not have to testify against themselves, with no presumption being drawn from their refusal. They could choose their own counsel (if they could afford them) or military counsel would be provided for them. The burden of proof would remain with the government. Defendants could call witnesses in their defense. Two-thirds of the panel would have to vote to convict. According to DOD rules, the death penalty would be recommended only with a unanimous verdict. There was a right of appeal to an independent appeals board on which civilians might serve. Perhaps most important, illegally and unconstitutionally obtained evidence would be permissible if it had "probative value to a reasonable person." This stands in sharp contrast to courts-martial, in which strict rules of evidence similar to civilian courts apply. There would be no exclusionary rule for evidence illegally obtained, particularly by unreasonable search and seizure, or for illegally obtained confessions extracted by torture or maltreatment, or other statements made by an accused or by witnesses.

Rights of appeal were limited: the appeals board could only examine the evidence, and could not apply the Constitution or federal laws. There would be no right of appeal to the civilian courts: this stands in contrast to courts-martial cases, which may be reviewed by the Court of Criminal Appeals, then by the Court of Appeals for the Armed Forces, and then by the US Supreme Court. Finally, the Pentagon intimated that even a defendant acquitted by a tribunal might still be kept in custody if thought to be dangerous.[71]

The administration claimed the president had constitutional authority to establish such commissions by fusing his power as commander in chief with his oath of office to defend the Constitution. It pointed to what it considered to be past precedents under the Constitution, including the establishment of military courts in the Civil War, in the Second World War, and in the Korean War (though in the last instance they were never used). The government also cited the Authorization for the Use of Military Force (AUMF) in which Congress that had authorized the president "to use all necessary and appropriate force against those nations, organizations, or persons he determines planned, authorized, committed, or aided the terrorist attacks that occurred on September 11, 2001, or harbored such organizations or persons, in order to prevent any future acts of international terrorism against the United States by such nations, organizations or persons."[72] Using it for tribunals was a stretch since the resolution contemplated military action against Afghanistan, and was not passed in order to provide a framework for apprehending and trying terrorists. The administration also pointed out that the Uniform Code of Military Justice, established by Congress, refers to the establishment of military tribunals by the president.[73] But Congress had specifically provided in Section 36 of the law that such tribunals "may not be contrary to or inconsistent with the UCMJ."

As with the Civil War cases, the federal courts tended to give the executive the benefit of the doubt in many cases, but sometimes did strike down the more extreme claims made by the government. In *Rasul v. Bush*, involving the indefinite detention of three unlawful combatants (Shafiq Rasul, Asif Iqbal, and David Hicks) captured in Afghanistan and held at Guantánamo Bay, the Supreme Court, in a majority opinion, written by Justice Stevens, distinguished the status of the detainees from the German prisoners of war in the *Eisentrager* case, who had been held on German soil.[74] Rasul and others were not nationals of countries at war with the United States, they denied having plotted acts of aggression, they had not been afforded access to any tribunal or charged with any crime, and for more than two years they had been imprisoned in territory over which the United States exercised exclusive jurisdiction and control. Congress had provided for the right of habeas review on American territory. Stevens held that Guantánamo was such territory because the United States exercises plenary and exclusive jurisdiction, although not ultimate sovereignty, and so the petitioners had the right to habeas corpus review. He also held that in the absence of such a congressional statute the aliens would have had no constitutional right to such review. Shortly thereafter, British intelligence demonstrated to American authorities that the two English nationals (Rasul and Iqbal) had been in England at the time the video alleging their involvement with Bin Laden had been produced, and they were released and repatriated in 2005.

In *Hamdan v. Rumsfeld*, the Supreme Court in a 5–3 decision ruled that the president had authority granted by Congress to establish military commissions.[75] The court ruled that trials in civilian courts were not required for detainees, and none of the justices insisted on closure of Guantánamo or other military detention facilities. Justice Stevens, writing for the majority (himself a veteran of World War II) noted that ""Hamdan does not challenge, and we do not today address, the Government's power to detain him for the duration of active hostilities." The court's decision was not a complete victory for the government, since it then considered and rejected many of the procedures for the commissions established by the president. Stevens held that Congress had required that military commissions comply with the laws of war, and unless Congress otherwise provides, the president's conduct is subject to limitation by statutes and treaties, and must comply with the international laws of armed conflict. Congress had also provided that rules and regulations for such commissions be uniform so far as practicable with rules for courts-martial. But the military tribunals violated the UCMJ and the Geneva Conventions: a detainee could be excluded from the proceedings; the detainee or counsel could be denied the right to see evidence, and evidence obtained under duress could be admitted. The court ruled that only Congress had the authority to establish tribunals with such procedures; otherwise Common Article 3 of the Geneva Conventions applied to al Qaeda terrorists. They could only be tried and punished by a "regularly constituted court," which meant an "ordinary military cour[t]" that is "established and organized in accordance with the laws and procedures already in force in a country." A military commission is "regularly constituted" only if some practical need explains deviations from court-martial practice. The court found that no such need had yet been demonstrated by the administration. Four justices agreed with Stevens that the phrase "all the guarantees ... recognized as in-dispensable by civilized peoples" in Common Article 3 must be understood to incorporate at least some trial protections recognized by customary international law. Justice Breyer's concurring opinion invited Congress to clarify its intent about procedures for future trials of detainees.[76]

After the decision the Pentagon then accelerated its policy of transferring detainees back to their home countries: it released nearly one-third of the prisoners at Guantánamo because they posed no threat to US security, and Pentagon officials indicated that most of the remaining would eventually be sent to their home countries or released because they no longer had any intelligence value. Hamdan however was charged with conspiracy and providing support for terrorism (he was a driver and bodyguard for Osama bin Laden) and faced trial in 2007. The Pentagon intended to charge only 60 to 80 of the more than 600 detainees it had held.

Denial of Habeas Corpus and Counsel to American Citizens

A Saudi national, Yaser Esam Hamdi, was captured in Afghanistan, was sent to Guan-tánamo Bay, but then quickly transferred to the Navy brig in Norfolk Naval Station in Virginia, (where he was held in solitary confinement with only the Red Cross and interrogators having access) after it was learned that he had been born in the United States and was an American citizen. Hamdi was an "enemy combatant," ineligible for protections under the rules regarding prisoners of war, and the Justice Department argued that he could be held without trial indefinitely. It furthered argued that the executive, and not the courts, had the right to make the final determination on his status, and therefore Hamdi had no need for or right to counsel. This was the first time that the government had argued that an American citizen could be detained *indefinitely* without charges, without access to a lawyer, and without access to courts for habeas corpus review.

The Supreme Court decided in an 8–1 decision that even alleged "enemy combatants" have the right to a fair hearing to determine their status, and that federal courts retain habeas corpus review of the fairness of such procedures.[77] Justice O'Connor, writing the majority opinion, crafted a set of guidelines for the military to use in developing its hearing procedures. The government decided to end Hamdi's detention. He was deported to Saudi Arabia on condition that he renounce his American citizenship, which he did on October 11, 2004, shortly after he returned to Saudi Arabia, and agreed not to leave the Kingdom for five years, and never to travel to Afghanistan, Iraq, Israel, Pakistan, Syria, the West Bank, or the Gaza Strip.

IV

What distinguishes the Bush administration's use of prerogatives from that of Lincoln and FDR is not so much the context in which powers were exercised, since each faced an extraordinary threat to the security of the nation, but rather the *style of governance* that accompanied the claim of prerogative. Lincoln soon won congressional ratification for his actions; FDR consulted with Congress and acted with its acquiescence and encouragement, and then worked with Congress on implementing legislation creating "joint concord" for the destroyer deal. But Bush's "war" on terrorism was based on a system of parallel governance, in which the executive for an indefinite period of time was to exercise quasi-legislative and quasi-judicial powers and bypass Congress and courts.[78] When Congress did pass legislation dealing with the new procedures or courts Bush had created, they authorized much of what he had done, either explicitly or through legislative loopholes.

Partial Separation of Powers

James Madison in *Federalist* 47 observed, that the "accumulation of all powers legislative, executive and judiciary in the same hands, whether of one, a few or many, and whether hereditary, self appointed, or elective, may justly be pronounced the very definition of tyranny." He argued for a system of separation of powers, but pointed out that if a *complete* separation of power were achieved (so that Congress exercised all legislative power and only legislative power, the President exercised all executive power and only executive power, and the courts exercised all judicial powers and only judicial powers), the institution that was assigned all legislative power would be so powerful it would suck the other institutions into the "legislative vortex." Madison proposed *partial* separation of powers, in which some powers would overlap and some would blend, so one department could exercise powers considered to be a part of another department. And so, in spite of the fact that the Constitution assigned "the judicial power" to a Supreme Court, Congress has a power of subpoena, it may hold witnesses at hearings in contempt, and it conducts impeachments as a trial, and the president has a power to issue reprieves and pardons for offences against the United States. Similarly, Congress does not exercise all legislative powers: executive orders, executive agreements, military orders and proclamations all have the force of law, and Supreme Court "landmark" decisions are as broad as legislation passed by Congress.

Partial Separation and Parallel Governance

Partial separation doctrine allowed President Bush to cobble together a set of concurrent powers and institutional practices, first to set policies in the war on terror, then to implement them unilaterally, and finally to pass judgment, all the while claiming the power to avoid judicial review. He did so at a time when public opinion tended to be skeptical of the exercise of power yet insistent on strong measures for national security; when the judiciary acted at times to preserve its own jurisdiction but otherwise did not overturn presidential policies, and when Congress cared more about partisan solidarity than it did about insisting that framework laws it had passed to preserve civil liberties be faithfully executed by the president. Many of the political appointee lawyers in the Bush administration in the DOJ, White House Office of Legal Counsel, and in the Pentagon were adherents of the modern version of Hamilton's unity and "energy in the executive" exhortations in *Federalist* No. 70, which after two hundred years had congealed into "unitary executive" doctrine. Attorney General Edwin Meese framed it in a speech to the Heritage Foundation in 1986 as a renewal of the rightful role of the presidency after an unfortunate post-Watergate interlude in which Congress had intruded on executive power[79] when he said that the Reagan administration was "seeking to resuscitate the notion of an energetic and unitary executive."[80] This would involve challenges to congressional appointment powers to independent agencies, extension of congressional budget powers, limits on presidential removal powers, challenges to the legislative veto, and challenges to the independent counsel investigations. It also involved greater use of the "signing statement" to bypass congressional intent when the president wanted most, but not all, of the provisions of bills presented by Congress. But the most significant use of the doctrine involved foreign affairs, as the "sole organ of communication" doctrine of John Marshall was extended to an assertion that the president was the "sole organ" in making and executing foreign policy. Late in the Reagan presidency House Republicans (including Dick Cheney) defended the president's stewardship in foreign affairs in the Iran-Contra Minority Report of 1987, arguing that Congress should neither micro-manage nor conduct oversight in foreign affairs and national security. And they went further than Meese, defending presidential prerogative even though " ... the Chief Executive will on occasion feel duty bound to assert monarchical notions of prerogative that will permit him to exceed the law."[81] By the time George W. Bush assumed the presidency, those around him had shed traditional conservative ambivalence about executive power (conditioned during the New Deal and JFK-LBJ presidencies) and were ready to embrace unitary executive doctrine, which by this time included the full panoply of presidential prerogatives—those that had already been incorporated into the living constitution through precedent and congressional acquiescence, and those that had not.[82]

In the aftermath of the 9/11 attacks, the Bush administration relied on memos prepared primarily by lawyers at the Office of Legal Counsel in the Department of Justice (with other documentation from the Pentagon and Office of White House Counsel).[83] The first memo, prepared by John C. Yoo, claimed that "The centralization of authority in the President alone is particularly crucial in matters of national defense, war, and foreign policy, where a unitary executive can evaluate threats, consider policy choices, and mobilize national resources with a speed and energy that is far superior to any other branch."[84] Other memos provided a legal framework for use of American armed forces within the United States for anti-terrorism activities;[85] warrantless surveillance and broadened power for searches and seizures under FISA;[86] indefinite detention of Americans;[87] indefinite military detention of aliens seized on American territory as unlawful combatants;[88] the use of military tribunals not authorized by Congress under the Uniform Code of Military Justice;[89] and extraordinary renditions to other nations.[90] They also provided a rationale for the power to suspend the execution of domestic law barring torture and maltreatment of enemy combatants.[91]

Near the end of the Bush presidency, the Attorney General Alberto Gonzalez prepared the ground for distancing administration lawyers from the fruits of their labors. He characterized the memoranda he had prepared in 2002 as White House Counsel dealing with treatment of detainees merely as efforts "to explore the limits of the legal landscape as to what the Executive Branch can do within the law and the Constitution as an abstract matter...." The memoranda were mere "legal theory," which he contrasted with "the actual policy guidance that the President and his team directed." He claimed, "the policies ultimately adopted by the President are more narrowly tailored than advised by his lawyers, and are consistent with our treaty obligations, our Constitution and our laws." He referred to some of the theoretical conclusions as "irrelevant and unnecessary to support any action taken by the President." He characterized his own work as "Unnecessary, over-broad discussions in some of these memos that address abstract legal theories, or discussions subject to misinterpretation, but not relied upon by decision-makers." He observed that the memoranda circulated only among government lawyers, and that they never "made it into the hands" of soldiers in the field "nor to the President."[92] After congressional investigations of excesses involving interrogation of detainees, and with international condemnation of many of these excesses, the Office of Legal Counsel also attempted to backtrack. It indicated that it had "previously withdrawn or superseded a number of opinions" that depended on propositions of law in the earlier memos that it no longer could defend as valid constitutional law or statutory construction.[93]

V

The transition from George W. Bush to Barack Obama enables us to determine just how much the imperial presidency is institutionalized, irrespective of the ideology or partisan orientation of the incumbent.

Surveillance and Sovereign Immunity Claims. The Obama administration has defended Bush administration warrantless wiretapping practices in a case involving an Islamic charity that had been designated as an organization supporting terrorism, the Al-Haramain Islamic Foundation. The government had accidentally turned over information to the lawyers representing the foundation, which indicated that it had been placed under warrantless surveillance. A federal appeals court rejected the Justice Department's motion for an emergency stay of the case brought by the foundation challenging the surveillance practices, and ruled that the trial would proceed. Attorney General Eric Holder, who has argued that "policy differences" should not be criminalized, has indicated that he will not take legal action against administration officials who engaged in practices that violated law. Moreover, in *Jewel v. NSA*, the Obama administration demanded that a lawsuit against the government for its role in warrantless surveillance be dismissed on the grounds of "sovereign immunity": that the government had the right to conduct surveillance, and that only "willful disclosure" of the information to the public would be grounds for suit.[94]

State Secrets and Secrecy Systems. In the *Al-Haramain Islamic Foundation* case and in various others (such as 40 lawsuits by AT&T and other telecom customers claiming the NSA illegally intercepted their phone calls and records), the Obama administration has continued to rely on state secrets doctrine in urging federal courts to dismiss lawsuits, in spite of Attorney General Eric Holder's statement that the use of the doctrine was being reviewed. In that initial review of three cases, as of mid-April 2009, Holder indicated that the Bush invocation of the privilege "was correct."[95]

Indefinite detentions. The Obama administration no longer argues (as the Bush administration did) that the president has a prerogative power as commander-in-chief to indefinitely detain enemy combatants without charges, even if not captured on the battlefield. Instead, it claims that power based on its analysis of international laws of war, and on authority granted by Congress in the 2001 Authorization for the Use of Military Force (AUMF). "Law-of-war principles do not limit the United States' detention authority to this limited category of individuals" (i.e. POWs) it argued in a court filing involving several non-Afghan prisoners detained in other countries and then transferred to Bagram

Air Base in Afghanistan. The Obama administration also upheld the Bush administration's position that federal courts had no jurisdiction in such a case and cannot "second guess" the government because it involved military operations outside the United States.[96] Obama has accepted the Bush position that prisoners brought to Bagram have no rights of any kind—not even the rights granted by the Supreme Court to detainees held in Guantánamo involving status review (to determine if they could be tried as unlawful combatants). The Obama administration appealed a decision by US District Judge John Bates that the prisoners had a right to habeas corpus review that had cited a decision of the Supreme Court involving Guantánamo as applicable precedent for such proceedings.[97]

Renditions. President Obama issued an executive order ending the practice of using extraordinary rendition to send detainees to other nations for interrogation. Yet his administration has taken positions in federal court cases that have the effect of defending the prior actions of the Bush administration. In two cases, one involving Binyam Mohamed an Ethiopian who claimed torture at Guantánamo, and the other involving four other detainees incarcerated in Guantánamo suing a subsidiary of Boeing (Jeppesen Dataplan, Inc.) for arranging flights in the "extraordinary rendition" program, Obama administration lawyers made the same state secrets argument made by Bush administration lawyers several months before. "The change in administration has no bearing?" Judge Mary M. Schroeder inquired in the Mohamed case. "No, your honor" the Obama administration lawyer responded.[98] According to court papers filed by the plaintiff, he was "routinely beaten, suffering broken bones and, on occasion, loss of consciousness. His clothes were cut off with a scalpel and the same scalpel was then used to make incisions on his body, including his penis."[99] A panel of High Court judges in London had to close the case because American authorities threatened to end cooperation with Britain in counter-terrorism if British intelligence authorities provided the court with information about Mohamed's treatment. In the case of the renditions, the government argued that Jeppeson's role was a state secret, even though it had already been reported in the media and been a subject of discussion by Boeing shareholders.

Torture. President Obama issued a directive to officials indicating that they could not rely on any memoranda prepared during the Bush administration to justify interrogation methods. It also banned coercive interrogation. CIA director Leon Panetta stated that waterboarding is torture and has forbidden its use.[100] The Obama administration has created a task force to determine how interrogations should be conducted, and the CIA has indicated it will go back to traditional methods, i.e. "dialog style" that do not involve physical force. The CIA also has ended the practice of relying on contractors (such as ex-military psychologists) to handle the interrogations, In closing down CIA detention centers in foreign countries (some observers believe they existed in Afghanistan, Thailand, Poland, Romania, and Jordan) that had been used to torture prisoners, Panetta issued the following statement to CIA employees: "Officers who act on guidance from the Department of Justice—or acted on such guidance previously—should not be investigated, let alone punished. This is what fairness and wisdom require."[101] (Panetta's statement glossed over the fact that many of the interrogations occurred before the Department of Justice's John C.Yoo got around to justifying abusive tactics in his August 2002 memorandum). In court filings the CIA and the Justice Department indicated to a judge overseeing one of the torture cases that neither agency would produce any evidence of misconduct in interrogations prior to the issuance of the DOJ August 2002 opinion.

Military Tribunals. The Obama administration has moved by executive order to close down Guantánamo by the end of his first year in office and shift legal proceedings from the military tribunals there to federal courts on the mainland or military courts-martial. One of the first cases under the new policy involved Ali Saleh Kahlah al-Marri, suspected of being an al-Qaeda sleeper agent, and held in a military brig in South Carolina. He was expected to argue for dismissal on the grounds that any evidence obtained from him was due to his being subjected to stress positions and extreme sensory deprivation.

Defending Bush Administration Legal Counsel. The Obama Department of Justice is now defending Bush administration officials being sued by detainees for writing legal opinions that were used to justify unlawful imprisonment and mistreatment. Jose Padilla, arrested in Chicago, charged with plotting to blow up soft targets in the US, and imprisoned in a Navy brig in Charleston, South Carolina before being transferred in 2006 to civilian custody (where he was tried and eventually convicted), brought suit against John C. Yoo, claiming that Yoo's legal opinions encouraged his military jailors to subject him to unlawful interrogation threats and sensory deprivation. The Justice Department asked the federal judge handling the case to dismiss. It also asked a federal judge in another case brought by Padilla to dismiss charges against a dozen other Bush administration officials for unlawful detention.

President Obama has taken some steps to recede from the extreme claims of the Bush administration, but seems to be developing a variant of "soft prerogative," in which he keeps the option to act through prerogative power in reserve. In the court cases that have carried over from the Bush administration, he seems to be acting in accordance with the observation of Brad Berenson, a former counsel in the Bush White House, who pointed out that "The dirty little secret here is that the United States government has enduring institutional interests that carry over from administration to administration and almost always dictate the position the government takes."[102]

VI

What is to be done when presidents routinize programs that proceed outside the framework of constitutional and international law, and that bypass processes developed by Congress? The answer does not rest in changing the way the presidency attempts to function; it seems that an aggressive position about the legitimacy of prerogative, combined with White House hubris, are now institutionalized in the modern presidency. The answer lies with changing the way Congress and the courts function.

Congress and Interbranch Collaborative Frameworks

Congress should strengthen framework laws providing for interbranch policy co-determination to replace prerogative governance with collaborative governance. A legal framework has many advantages: the president must make his case before relevant congressional committees, which increases prior consultation at the staff or cabinet secretary level. Because decision making is slowed down, there is more of an opportunity on both sides of Pennsylvania Avenue for those counseling caution to make their case. Once the president has brought his party and congressional leaders along, he is better positioned over the long term to defend his policy. And Congress will have gone on record in support, which makes it more difficult for members to criticize his actions. A consultative presidential psychology replaces (with luck) the imperious psychology. Congress must then take these mechanisms seriously, and demand that the president comply with these laws.[103] At the very least this means that houses of Congress, acting as institutions, must if necessary pass resolutions that will grant them standing in federal courts so that difficulties in implementation or presidential nonfeasance and misfeasance can be litigated.[104] Congress can use these laws and judicial proceedings to dismantle systems of parallel governance. It could also consider seriously the State Secrets Protection Act (sponsored by Patrick Leahy D-Vt. and Jerrold Nadler, D-NY) to authorize judges to examine the evidence the Justice Department withholds in any state secrets claim.

When legal and constitutional abuses occur involving individuals who assert rights under the constitutional or international conventions (such as those involving detention, extraordinary rendition and torture), Congress also has a role to play. Its investigations so far have always been "bottom up," focusing on the lowest-level operatives and then moving up the chain of command. The buck stops well below the Oval Office, or even the top levels of the administration. It may be time for the congressional committees that undertake oversight in these matters or conduct special investigations to move to a "top down" model of inquiry—irrespective of the political costs that might be incurred to all concerned (such as Congress confronted in the Iran-Contra affair). Of course if congressional party and committee leaders have already been briefed on activities that violate the law, and have not objected, it will make it difficult for Congress to conduct vigorous oversight thereafter.[105]

Congress also needs to facilitate more effective prosecutorial inquiries. It could re-establish on a temporary basis an independent counsel to investigate and prosecute officials who have violated statutory law, such as the Anti-Torture Act, or who destroyed hundreds of hours of interrogation videotapes, or who might have given testimony that obstructed justice in various inquiries and criminal cases already conducted.[106] Sixteen of the twenty-three Democrats—but no Republican—on the House Judiciary Committee sent a letter to Attorney General Eric Holder recommending that he appoint a special prosecutor, but as of May 2009 the administration has refused to do so.[107] It could facilitate the lawsuits dealing with warrantless wiretaps by establishing a limited waiver of sovereign immunity for the government and preventing the defense of retroactive immunity for the carriers.

If legislators do not have the stomach for facilitating prosecutions, they at least could establish an independent "truth commission" with the clearance power to obtain access to information (and with appropriate power of subpoena), so that such a commission can publish the full record of executive transgressions.[108] One of its inquiries could focus on the process by which legal memoranda were prepared during the first few months after 9/11, and whether or not they were prepared in good faith or relied upon in good faith, which although not a defense against illegal conduct, could provide a mitigating factor for lower-level officials.[109] A separate national commission could be established to make recommendations for future antiterrorism policy.[110] The House Judiciary Committee could also consider the impeachment of federal judge Jay Bybee, author of the memo justifying waterboarding.[111]

Ending Judicial Evasion

Judicial abstention is another problem, especially with regard to presidential war powers. At times the Supreme Court refuses to grant certiorari to decide significant cases (such as presidential power to abrogate treaties, in *Goldwater v. Carter*), and this has occurred with the question of warrantless wiretapping in *ACLU v. NSA*.[112] Federal courts have utilized procedural dodges to avoid dealing with executive power. They find that most taxpayer suits lack standing;[113] that suits brought by individual members of Congress usually lack standing (based on the doctrine of equitable discretion which would require a suit backed by the entire chamber);[114] that on certain issues there is no case or controversy;[115] that the issue is not ripe for adjudication;[116] that the case is not justiciable, lacks manageable standards, or is not fit for adjudication;[117] or that it is a political question.[118] Even in the context of the war on terrorism, federal courts have evaded many of the issues much of the time, or else have limited the reach of their decisions. They do insist (contrary to administration arguments) that the courts have jurisdiction (and can issue writs of habeas corpus) in cases involving the power to detain non-Americans classified as combatants and arrested either in the United States or on foreign territory. In *Padilla v. Rumsfeld* the Court of Appeals for the Second Circuit rejected the presidential argument of inherent power as commander in chief to detain an American citizen on America soil indefinitely, especially since Congress had rejected giving the president such powers in the Non-Detention Act.[119] When the case first went to the Supreme Court, it sent it back on the grounds that the habeas petition had been filed against Rumsfeld rather than the brig custodian, thus avoiding a definitive ruling on the substantive issue. Moreover, when Padilla was transferred to civilian authorities, to block his further appeal about military detention to the Supreme Court, his petition was denied by the Supreme Court, effectively ending his challenge to his military detention.[120] In *Hamdi v. Rumsfeld*, the Supreme Court upheld the authority of the military to detain him as a prisoner of war, although it held that indefinite detention was not authorized by the AUMF, it was authorized by the laws of war to prevent him from returning to the battlefield. The main thrust of the decision was not to rule against indefinite detention, but rather to require the government to provide "meaningful opportunity to contest the factual basis for that detention before a neutral decisionmaker." The court then crafted limited due process protections in the military tribunal processes. The indefinite detention of noncitizens was reviewed by the Supreme Court in *Rasul v. Bush*, which reversed a lower court and held that since Guantánamo was under the control of the United States, it should be treated as if it were sovereign territory, and therefore statutory powers granted by Congress to federal courts involving the writ of habeas corpus should apply. In *Hamdan v. Rumsfeld*, the Supreme Court sidestepped the opportunity to strike down the military tribunals established by the president, though it did determine that Hamdan's tribunal would have to follow Geneva Convention Article III procedural safeguards, as well as courts martial procedures "insofar as practicable." Some federal district judges have also ruled against Bush administration claims that the president's constitutional authority trumped statutory law restricting the president to wiretapping by judicial warrant.[121] In the case that most directly deals with the issue of torture, a rendition case involving a lawsuit for damages brought by Maher Arer, Judge Trager dismissed the lawsuit on the grounds that entertaining the suit could embarrass Canada by exposing its involvement. In a footnote to the decision, Trager recognized the *Filatarga* precedent (the right of foreign torture victims to sue their torturers in American courts under the Alien Tort Statute), but dismissed the case on the grounds that the questions presented were exclusively the province of the president and Congress, and that it would be embarrassing to our government and its Canadian ally if the case went forward.[122]

The federal judiciary could end the practice of routinely ruling for the government when it raises the claim of state secrets, which is the claim that the government has a right to protect "secrets of the highest order," that it alone determine the necessity, and that the courts should defer to its judgment.[123] Originally it was asserted to prevent a defendant from seeing government evidence in a lawsuit; more recently the government asserts it to call for dismissal of the entire suit. Between 1954, when it was first raised in *U.S. v. Reynolds* and 1977 it was raised only four times, and then between 1977 and 2001 it was raised 50 times; between 9/11 and 2005 it was raised 23 times (perhaps more since some cases are under seal). It has been rejected only four times since 1953.[124] Courts provide much too much latitude, permitting claims that seem on their face not to involve state secrets (including the issues in *Reynolds*); they do not insist on examining evidence themselves *in camera*; and when they use a balancing test, they weigh government claims too heavily when issues of torture and maltreatment are at stake. Consider *El-Masri v. United States*, in which a German citizen of Lebanese descent alleged that while traveling in Macedonia he was detained by Macedonian law enforcement officials and then handed over to CIA operatives who flew him to an agency detention facility near Kabul, Afghanistan.[125] He claimed that he was held against his will, beaten, drugged, bound, and blindfolded during transport; confined in a small, unsanitary cell; interrogated several times; and prevented from communicating with anyone outside the detention facility, including his family or the German government. He was eventually released from custody in Albania. El-Masri alleged that his detention and interrogation were carried out pursuant to an unlawful policy devised and implemented by CIA director George Tenet. The government argued for dismissal on the grounds of state secrets. The court ruled in favor of the government motion, claiming that if the action proceeded, El-Masri might be able to produce "evidence that exposes how the CIA organizes, staffs and supervises its most sensitive intelligence operations...." El-Masri's lawyers had proposed that the court could receive anything the government thought was a state secret *in camera* and under seal, providing the plaintiff's lawyers with access to it on the basis of a non-disclosure agreement. But the court rejected this, based on the Supreme Court's ruling in *Reynolds* that judges should not see the evidence *in camera* if the government claims state secrets. At the very least, the courts should overturn this holding in the *Reynolds* case, and instead use the rule developed in *U.S. v. Nixon* in a case involving a claim of executive privilege, which required that the presiding judge in a trial be given the evidence *in camera* in order to judge the validity of the claim.[126]

In sum . . .

One should not expect any president to recede from full exploitation of contested prerogative powers. Indeed, presidents almost never admit that they have exceeded their powers under the Constitution; at most they will acknowledge that have used "war powers" of the nation without reference to which institution possesses them, but even that Lincolnesque claim is rarely invoked. Instead, presidents rely on concomitants of nationality, sovereign powers, and their version of inherent and implied powers in Article II. Thus they have reworked a "living Constitution" to be pliant enough to mold it into an instrument of unchecked and unbalanced executive power. Yet the blame for institutional imbalances does not rest solely with most of these presidents: Nixon excepted, it would be hard to find one who used these powers for partisan ends unrelated to the national interest. For the most part, the presidents who have made the boldest claims are those who have pursued policies that they believed were in this interest.[127] It is, instead, a Congress that rarely defends its own prerogatives and that usually subordinates its institutional powers to presidential initiatives that is primarily to blame for constitutional unbalances. And secondarily it is the courts that are to blame; they have ingeniously fashioned all sorts of procedural dodges by which to avoid judgment on what needs very much to be judged.

We need to understand a key insight of Hamilton, who observed in the New York ratifying convention that Rome was obliged to create dictators because Roman law in the

Republic was not powerful enough for emergencies. Yet at the same time, we need to appreciate the caution of Madison in *The Federalist Papers*, who noted that there would need to be "auxiliary precautions" of partial separation of powers and checks and balances, precisely because more power was being delegated by the people to a national government. If we are to have the strong state—and everything we know of the coming crises in the 21st century suggests we will need such a state—all the more reason to insure ourselves against the expediency of those would wield the power we are granting them. The Constitution does not need to be amended to avoid an imperial presidency: it needs to be preserved, protected and defended with the institutional powers currently possessed by Congress and the courts.

Chapter 13

Vindicating the Presidency in a Time of Terror

Marc Landy

Reviewing in 1792 the work of France's Constituent Assembly, Jacques Necker deplored that the ruling spirit in such recasting of institutions has been to present "Each successive defeat of the Executive power as a victory for liberty ... But wise men cannot fail to perceive that where the English have sought to restrain the abuses of the Executive while maintaining its activity, we clumsy legislators have struck out blindly and to prevent the abuses of the Administration have destroyed its power to serve."

Bertrand de Jouvenel[1]

Since Watergate a debate has raged about the "imperial presidency." Having coined the phrase, Arthur Schlesinger led the attack on the presidency as having usurped functions rightfully belonging to the other branches.[2] In response, defenders of the presidency echoed Necker's complaint that in the name of curbing abuses a clumsy Congress had established a "fettered presidency" hamstrung in its ability to perform its essential, constitutionally sanctioned, responsibilities. The debate over executive power reached a crescendo during the Bush administration. Critics charged that the conduct of the War on Terror and the War in Iraq were egregious examples of "imperialism." Defenders argued that the Constitution gave Bush ample authority to act as he did.[3]

This paper takes a complex and varied stance towards the charge of presidential "imperialism." On the one hand it concedes that presidents in modern times have acted imperially. But it maintains that the most serious offender was not Bush but Reagan. It also notes that the president violates the Constitution when he *fails* to make full use of his prerogative to protect the nation from external threat. As serious as Reagan's excessive unilateralism in the Iran Contra affair was Clinton's unwillingness to aggressively combat international terrorism. On the whole it defends the constitutional fidelity of Bush's conduct of the War on Terror and the War in Iraq but without accepting the theoretical basis for the defense offered by his most influential apologists. It does not accept the so-called unitary theory of the executive and it faults Bush both for failing to ask Congress for a declaration of war against Iraq and for waiting too long to ask Congress to establish a statutory basis for the detention of unlawful enemy combatants. Most importantly, it finds that the Supreme Court, eager to substitute its judgment for that of the president regarding critical matters of War on Terror tactics, has surpassed the presidency with regard to the imperial threat it poses. This welter of seemingly contradictory findings forms a coherent pattern of analysis only if one places the question of the proper extent and limits of executive power in a broader constitutional framework.

The president is part of a complex set of constitutionally mandated institutional arrangements. One cannot adequately consider the appropriateness of executive behavior apart from an understanding of what Congress and the court are doing and should be doing. The checking function which each branch exercises over the other was never intended to obviate the fact that each branch engages in a distinct *activity* for which it is uniquely suited. Judges judge. Legislators deliberate. Presidents execute. Therefore a decision by one branch, the judiciary for instance, to constrain or fail to constrain the activity of another branch cannot be made mechanically. It requires empathy. Neither Congress nor the court should overrule the president until they have first tried to see the world from his point of view. They cannot determine whether what the president is doing is unlawful or unconstitutional until they have themselves fully acknowledged the genuine problems facing him and the obligations those problems press upon him. Empathy is the thread that holds the following narrative together because a lack of empathy is the source of the most serious errors made by President Bush and by the Supreme Court regarding the Constitution and the War on Terror.

As theorists and statesmen from John Locke to Abraham Lincoln have recognized, chief executives have unstated but nonetheless real emergency powers. They can and must violate the Constitution in order to save it.[4] Only after coming to grips with this terrible but inescapable aspect of executive duty can either of the two other branches act to constrain him. The president also has a duty to be empathetic. Although invoking emergencies powers may not constitute a literal breach of the Constitution it places severe strain on constitutional order claiming to be composed of "laws not men." A system too frequently strained cracks. A president who invokes his prerogative indiscriminately has become too enraptured by the power at his disposal to empathize with the keen sense of responsibility that congressmen and judges have to make government as law abiding as possible. Therefore the same oath that provides the president with the power to act extra-constitutionally implies that he should do so as infrequently as possible.

President and Congress

President Bush's decision not to seek a declaration of war follows the well-worn path trod by presidents since Truman. Truman claimed that the U.S. was obligated by the UN Treaty to go to war with North Korea by virtue of the latter's refusal to abide by a UN Security Council Resolution requiring it to withdraw from its invasion of South Korea.[5] LBJ claimed that Congress's passage in August 1964 of the Gulf of Tonkin resolution authorizing the President to take all measures necessary to protect the armed forces was the functional equivalent of a declaration of war.[6] In January 1991, George H.W. Bush asked Congress for a joint resolution authorizing the use of military force against Iraq and Congress granted that request.[7]

Prior to Bush, no presidential administration promulgated a constitutional theory to defend this reticence. But the Bush administration did. Misleadingly dubbed "the unitary theory of the executive," it was vigorously asserted by several of Bush's key advisors most notably Vice President Richard Cheney, Cheney's chief legal advisor David Addington, and the prominent scholar of executive power John Yoo.[8] President Bush never formally or publicly subscribed to this view, but his repeated unwillingness to consult Congress regarding key antiterror initiatives and his failure to ask for a declaration of war are certainly consonant with the unitary theory point of view as his key subordinates and apologists expressed it.[9]

The unitary theory was given its clearest articulation by Yoo. Yoo states unequivocally that "The decision to deploy military force is executive in nature, the Framers understood it to be an attribute of the executive."[10] He bases this interpretation on a maximalist interpretation of the vesting clause in Article Two of the Constitution, which states, "The Executive Power shall be vested in a President of the United States." By contrast Article One limits Congress to only to those legislative powers "herein granted" meaning that Congressional authority is restricted to the specific powers that the Constitution enumerates. Because the executive power of the British monarch, and monarchs from time immemorial, encompassed all of foreign affairs the unitary executive proponents claim that this was the understanding of executive power intended by the Framers.

To hold this view one must somehow argue away the significance of the fact that Article Two of the Constitution gives *Congress*, not the president, the power to declare war. Yoo tries to deflate its importance by draining the word 'declaration' of its common sense meaning.

> The framers did not understand the phrase to "declare war" to amount to the power "make war" or "commence war" ... To use the eighteenth century understanding, they make public, show openly, and make known the state of international legal relations between the United States and another nation.[11]

Not only do declarations not mean what ordinary readers think they mean, but even if they did, the power they convey would be unnecessary. "Congress needs no check on the President through the Declaration of War Clause because it already possesses all the power it needs. Congress at any time may use its power of the purse to counter presidential war making."[12] In this view, the Framers meant to assign Congress the same foreign policy role accorded to the British Parliament, which was confined to revenue matters. If the Parliament disapproved of the monarch's actions it could withhold the monies needed to pay for them.

Yoo backs up his argument with references to Grotius and Vattel, to the ratification and even, improbably, to the Articles of Confederation, the very foundational straightjacket the framers were trying to escape from. But he pays no attention to the most obvious source for discerning the framers intent, their own debates at the Constitutional Convention. Had he done so he would have been forced to back off from his extreme claim of executive monopoly. The Convention debates clearly show that the framers were sufficiently fearful of executive domination that they had no intention of reducing Congress's declaration of war power to a mere formality. Such a fateful decision had to rest with the legislature. For example, when Pierce Butler offered the very argument made by Yoo, that only the president is equipped to determine when hostilities should begin, Madison agrees to strike the word 'make' and replace it with 'declare' war. But he gives a very specific reason for agreeing to this compromise. He wants to enable the president to "repel sudden attacks."[13] Thus Madison was making a distinction that escapes Yoo, the distinction between reacting to emergency threat and waging war. Yoo is intent on proving that only the president has the right to initiate hostilities. But not all hostilities are equal. Surely the president has the right, as Madison suggests, to repel attacks, to retaliate against attacks and even to take preemptive action to prevent attack. But this does not diminish the war power of Congress nor does it require a reinterpretation of what a declaration is.

A war is not an attack. It is a premeditated action that will, in all probability, last for an extended period of time. The framers granted the power to declare war to Congress because they recognized that, although there is no strict separation of powers between the branches, each one does have its unique functions and attributes. Declarations are firmer and more inflexible than policies. They are much more akin to the enduring, stable and broadly applicable elements characteristic of law. A war, unlike a retaliatory strike, is not merely a policy. It is an awesome and dreadful commitment. In a republic a commitment of that sort should only be undertaken by the legislature.

The power to declare war appears in Article One Section 8, which enumerates the powers of Congress. The section is divided into nineteen separate enumerations. Every other enumeration relates to a strong and substantive power of government—raising taxes, regulating commerce, and borrowing money. It would be strange indeed for Congress to place among these awesome powers one, and only one, that was meant to be purely a formality.

Nor is Congress's power of the purse a sufficient substitute for the power to declare war. Unlike eighteenth-century British monarchs, the American president has plenty of cash on hand to commence hostilities in advance of asking the Congress for money. As John Kerry learned to his sorrow, the American public will not tolerate withholding resources from American men and women who have already been put in harm's way.[14] Thus, in order to conduct a reasonably dispassionate deliberation, Congress must have the power to debate the wisdom of waging war before the president has faced it with a fait accompli.

The unitary executive recognizes the depth of the problem that foreign policy poses for constitutional government and particularly the weaknesses that any legislative body of any size confronts in coping with the delicacies and the exigencies that the relationships between states bring to bear. But its single-minded emphasis on these difficulties desensitizes it to the spirit of the great experiment in republican rule that the Framers engaged in. Hamilton aside, they did not want to recreate the British monarchy. They were searching for means to reconcile the exigencies of statecraft and war craft with constitutional rigor. The president was not intended to be a king and foreign policy was not intended to trump all republican cards. Somehow the conflicting demands of stealth and speed had to be made to coexist with the defense of liberty.[15]

The unitary theory did not cause the president to do anything literally unconstitutional. Bush *should* have asked for a declaration but the Constitution does not demand that he do so. The overtly unconstitutional failing was Congress's for not debating and voting on one. By granting an Authorization of the Use of Military Force (AUMF), Congress endorsed the president's proposed war making and therefore President Bush was within his constitutional rights to take the aggressive actions that he did. Bush's approach to Congress was not unconstitutional but it was highly imprudent. It made him much more vulnerable to attacks by war critics and undermined his credibility with the public with regard to his war leadership.

Although the AUMF was substantively similar to a declaration of war it lacked the same constitutional gravity. Both AUMFs made strong cases for war but the sheer fact that neither the president nor Congress viewed them as the full equivalent of a declaration of war diminished their significance. If Congressmen had exercised their due constitutional responsibilities they would have found it much more difficult to renounce their support as the tides of public opinion shifted. As the dreadful experiences of both the Vietnam and Iraq wars teach, binding the hands of future presidents might be an acceptable price to pay for striving harder to secure congressional and public support for wars whose very nature makes them grisly and hard to win.

A declaration of war is not only a constitutional requirement, it is also a great opportunity for the president to enrich public understanding and deepen public support. The gravity of the occasion rivets public and congressional attention enabling the president to educate Congress and the public about why war is necessary, why less dreadful alternatives are inadequate, and what are the gravest risks and exigencies to be faced. Such a full public airing would have greatly improved the quality of discussion and the level of public understanding about what was and what should be taking place. Obtaining a declaration also offers more narrowly political benefits to the president. It binds the Congress more tightly in its support of the war. It forces Congress to take on a greater level of responsibility for, and perhaps a level of thoughtfulness and sobriety about, the enterprise. This would have been very good for the country and for the capacity of President Bush to operate as commander in chief. It would have deprived his critics of crucial arguments which although facile found great traction with an undereducated public. And it would have made it much more difficult for the judicial aggrandizers on the Supreme Court to undermine his power.

Adhering to the unitary theory had a similarly politically damaging impact on Bush administration policy for detaining enemy combatants. Rather than obtaining a statutory underpinning for these policies from Congress, the administration chose to forge detainee policy entirely on its own, and only resorted to Congress when ordered to do so by the Supreme Court. Jack Goldsmith reports that on numerous occasions during his tenure as a Defense Department lawyer and as head of the Justice Department's Office of Legal Counsel (OLC) his suggestions that the administration obtain congressional backing for various aspects of its detainee program were rebuffed. Opposition to Goldsmith's views was led by David Addington who argued that the administration already had the constitutional power to take the actions necessary and therefore it was counterproductive to seek support from Congress. Addington's reasoning was the same as that of those presidents who refrained from asking Congress for a declaration of war. Even if Congress was certain to support the administration position, or, at worst make only marginal changes, it was wrong to go to Congress because that would set the precedent that the administration *ought* to seek congressional approval. It would therefore constrain the administration, and future administrations, from acting unilaterally on occasions when congressional approval might not be forthcoming.

> Addington would always ask two simple questions whenever someone proposed that the White House work with Congress to clear away a legal restriction or to the legislature on board: "Do we have the legal power to do it ourselves?" (meaning on the president's sole authority), and "Might Congress limit our options in ways that jeopardize American lives?"[16]

The Bush administration's response to the *Hamdi* case illustrates the problems inherent in Addington's approach. After the Supreme Court announced that it would review the case of Yaser Hamdi, a Guantanamo detainee, Attorney General Gonzales called a meeting of lawyers to review the government's position. Goldsmith suggested that the position could be strengthened by asking Congress to approve of the detainee program. He was supported by the representatives of the Solicitor General, the State Department and the Defense Department present at the meeting, but they were opposed by Addington and therefore the suggestion was not acted on.[17] "Addington's hard-line nonaccommodation stance always prevailed when the lawyers met to discuss legal policy issues in Alberto Gonzales' office."[18]

The Supreme Court overruled the government's refusal to grant habeas corpus to Hamdi and later ruled against its overall detainee program in *Hamdan.* In both cases the Court rested its decision not on constitutional grounds but on the lack of statutory underpinning for the program. After these decisions the executive did indeed obtain congressional approval for the detainee program but only after the *Hamdi* and *Hamdan* rulings had significantly undermined political support for it. Had Congress been involved from the beginning in the program's design, the Supreme Court would have faced a much less propitious environment in which to declare the heart of the program, the denial of habeas corpus to unlawful enemy combatants, unconstitutional. Instead of doings so, as it did in *Boumedienne,* in the wake of two setbacks for the administration based on its failure to gain a statutory underpinning for the detainee program from Congress, the court would have had to assert its constitutional interpretation *against* the united front of the two other sap-laden branches.

Judicial Supremacy

The Supreme Court's aggrandizement of judicial power with regard to the War on Terror is grounded in the recognition of the gravity of the threat to liberty this peculiar form of war poses. Terrorists are not soldiers; they are not automatically accorded the protection that enemy combatants normally receive. Since it is so difficult to tell a real terrorist from an innocent civilian, many ordinary law-abiding people are likely to be treated harshly by mistake. But the court did not accord the president the same laudable empathy it extended to the subjects of detention and interrogation. In the series of cases that concern the detainment of unlawful combatants, several of which have been mentioned already, the majority opinions reveal a consistent inability to apprehend and appreciate the cruel necessities of executive leadership.

Hamdan v. Rumsfeld demonstrates this lack of empathy and understanding on the majority's part.[19] The case involved the administration's establishment of military tribunals to try unlawful enemy combatants. Salim Hamdan, who had worked for Osama Bin Laden for five years as a driver and auto mechanic, was captured in Afghanistan in November of 2001 and was the first enemy combatant to be brought before a military tribunal. He was alleged to have committed four "overt acts" sometime between 1996 and November 2001 in furtherance of the terror conspiracy:

(1) He acted as Osama bin Laden's "bodyguard and personal driver," "believe[ing]" all the while that bin Laden "and his associates were involved in" terrorist acts prior to and including the attacks of September 11, 2001;

(2) He arranged for transportation of, and actually transported, weapons used by al Qaeda members and by bin Laden's bodyguards (Hamdan among them);

(3) He "drove or accompanied Osama bin Laden to various al Qaida-sponsored training camps, press conferences, or lectures," at which bin Laden encouraged attacks against Americans;

(4) He received weapons training at al Qaeda-sponsored camps.[20]

The rules for the tribunals were written by the Defense Department with no prior approval or review by Congress. Hamdan's counsel filed a writ of habeas corpus in federal district court claiming that the military tribunal had no right to try him because its procedures were unlawful and that the charge of conspiracy leveled against him did not violate the laws of war. The judge who heard the case sided with Hamdan but the Appeals Court sided with the government and so Hamdan appealed to the Supreme Court, which took the case in 2005.

Solicitor General Paul Clements defended the government. He argued that civilian courts were not appropriate for trying such people because unlawful enemy combatants were not criminal defendants in the conventional meaning of the term. According them the full panoply of protections provided by civilian courts would hinder the war effort and place innocent lives in danger. In a civilian trial, prosecutors could be faced with a situation where in order to avoid exposing classified information, they would have to either allow defendants to go free, or accept a lighter sentence, a dangerous practice the case of hardened Taliban or al Qaeda terrorists.[21]

Military tribunals would allow the use of classified information without endangering sources and methods. To produce a witness in open trial might well be to give that person a death sentence. The procedures also permitted more inclusive rules of evidence. In a war, especially one with no clearly defined battlefields waged against a homeless enemy that obeys no rules, the conventional rules of authentification and admissibility of evidence are simply too stringent to apply under all circumstances. Civilian courts reject testimony obtained through coercive methods and yet how else can such testimony be obtained from terrorists? Clements argued that critical evidence that could protect the American people from dangerous terrorists should not be excluded simply because it was obtained under these trying conditions.[22]

As discussed earlier, in *Hamdan* the court did not declare military tribunals unconstitutional but rather insisted that Congress put them on a sound statutory basis. It is not the decision itself but rather Justice Stevens' majority opinion that is of concern. Stevens displayed a remarkable disregard of the nature of the war being fought and hence of the president's responsibilities for commanding such a war effort. He ignores the critical differences between conventional war and war conducted by terrorists. He finds the military tribunals in violation of the Geneva Convention and the Uniform Code of Military Justice without recognizing that neither of those applies.

> The commission's procedures set forth in Commission Order No. 1, provide, among other things, that an accused and his civilian counsel may be excluded from, and precluded from ever learning what evidence was presented during any part of the proceeding the official who appointed the commission or the presiding officer decides on. Grounds for closure include the protection of classified information, the physical safety of participants and witnesses, the protection of intelligence and law enforcement sources, methods, or activities, and "other national security interests." Appointed military defense counsel must be privy to these closed sessions, but may, at the presiding officer's discretion, be forbidden to reveal to the client what took place therein. Another striking feature is that the rules governing Hamdan's commission permit the admission of any evidence that, in the presiding officer's opinion, would have probative value to a reasonable person. Moreover, the accused and his civilian counsel may be denied access to classified and other "protected information," so long as the presiding officer concludes that the evidence is "probative" and that its admission without the accused's knowledge would not result in the denial of a full and fair trial.[23]

Stevens acknowledges that Hamdan's military counsel would have access to all the evidence against him but he makes no effort to consider why allowing the accused or his civilian counsel to examine the evidence presented against him is potentially highly damaging to national security and to the lives of those providing the information.

Stevens admits that nonconformity with the Geneva Convention and the UCMF is sometimes permissible but only when exigency dictates it.[24] But it is not evident to him why "the dangers posed by international terrorism, considerable though they may be, should require, in the case of Hamdan's trial, any variance from the courts-martial rules." He claims that there is not "any showing of impracticality" that could warrant deviation from the strict evidentiary rules of the courts-martial. This despite his knowledge that Hamdan only came into U.S custody because a bounty was paid to the warlords who captured him and that anyone who could personally testify about the precise nature of his services to al Queda would be exposing himself and his family to terrorist reprisal.

In addition, Stevens found that Hamdan could not be considered a war criminal because the bulk of the time he spent as a member of al Queda occurred before the war took place. He defined the beginning of the war as September 11, 2001 and September 18, 2001 date of passage of Congress' AUMF. But a conspiracy always predates the event that it is organized to produce. As Justice Thomas points out in his dissent, there is no logical reason to require that a conspiracy to commit an act of war occur *after* the war has started.[25]

The dangerous potential inherent the faulty majority reasoning in *Hamdan* was fully realized in *Boumediene v. Bush*. Despite Congress's enactment of a law specifically designed to give the detainee program the statutory underpinning the court demanded, the court still found the program to be unconstitutional.

Boumediene was captured in Bosnia in 2001 on suspicion of conspiring to bomb the American Embassy there. After being taken to Guantanamo he filed a writ of habeas corpus in U.S. federal court that was denied because he was not a US citizen nor was he being held on US soil. In 2004 the Supreme Court ruled in *Rasul v. Bush* that Guantanamo detainees could bring challenge in federal court.[26] In response the Bush administration created the Combatant Status Review Tribunal (CSRT) to provide the detainees with an opportunity to challenge their detention.

Boumedienne's CSRT confirmed the validity of his detention. Boumedienne again filed a habeas corpus petition claiming that the CSRT was not a full substitute for the habeas corpus action in federal court that the Constitution entitled him to. To blunt this and similar challenges the Bush administration convinced Congress to pass the Detainee Treatment Act (DTA) of 2005 which gave exclusive power to review habeas corpus requests by Guantanamo detainees to the US Court of Appeals for the District of Columbia and established restrictive procedures to govern those reviews. In *Hamdan* the Supreme Court found that this new act did not apply to cases like *Boumediene* where the habeas corpus writs were filed before the DTA was enacted. Congress sought to undercut this decision by passing the Military Commissions Act of 2006, which made clear its intent to subject *all* detainees, including Boumediene, to the DTA process.[27]

The Supreme Court ruled in favor of Boumediene finding that the procedures outlined in the DTA did not amount to full habeas corpus and that despite the fact that he was an alien being held outside the territorial bounds of the United States he did enjoy a full right to habeas corpus in US courts. The Justice Kennedy's majority opinion goes to elaborate lengths to demonstrate the centrality of habeas corpus for safeguarding liberties but it makes no attempt to demonstrate either that the Constitution intended to include aliens with regard to this right or that it applies outside US territory. Much of its argumentation is devoted simply to showing that such an expansion of constitutional protections is not *excluded* by the language of the Constitution or by previous court rulings. "It is true that before today the Court has never held that non-citizens detained by our Government in territory over which another country maintains de jure sovereignty have any rights under our Constitution." But it finds that this lack of precedent to be "no barrier" to its holding because the cases under consideration are unprecedented.[28]

In a concurring opinion Justice Souter, writing on behalf of Justices Ginsburg and Breyer as well, claims that the question of whether aliens are entitled to habeas corpus protection need not be rehashed because the majority in a previous case, *Rasul*, concluded that it was applicable.[29] But he neglects to mention that the conclusion in *Rasul* likewise offered no positive evidence that prior court decisions or the language of the Constitution required or permitted aliens to enjoy habeas corpus, only that a careful reading of the prior cases did not exclude such a possibility.[30]

Not being able to rely either on constitutional language or precedent, the majority's argument in favor of the plaintiffs rests on a certain reading of the overall design of the Constitution and on the novel character of the War on Terror. The framers saw the separation of powers scheme enshrined in the Constitution as not only a means for making government accountable but also for protecting liberty. The writ of habeas corpus was a vital instrument for protecting liberty and an essential part of the separation of powers scheme. It is this sheer integrality that, despite the lack of precedent, requires the court to extend the reach of habeas corpus as far as it can reasonably go, surely as far as to include noncitizens and far enough to reach the shores of Cuba.

> It is true that before today the Court has never held that noncitizens detained by our Government in territory over which another country maintains de jure sovereignty have any rights under our Constitution. They [the cases] involve individuals detained by executive order for the duration of a conflict that, if measured from September 11, 2001, to the present, is already among the longest wars in American history. See Oxford Companion to American Military History 849 (1999). The detainees, moreover, are held in a territory that, while technically not part of the United States, is under the complete and total control of our Government. Under these circumstances the lack of a precedent on point is no barrier to our holding.[31]

Although Kennedy agrees, in principle, that there could be extenuating circumstances that makes such an extension of the reach of habeas corpus imprudent, he finds no such circumstances in this case. Despite the pleas from the Solictor General about the national security risks that could arise from the court's siding with Boumediene, Kennedy substitutes his own quasi-executive judgment to find that "The Government presents no credible arguments that the military mission at Guantanamo would be compromised if habeas corpus courts had jurisdiction to hear the detainees' claims."[32]

The minority opinions, issued by Chief Justice Roberts and Justice Antonin Scalia were most scathing in their condemnation of the majority's judicial supremacism. Roberts noted that the immediate practical impact of the decision would be minimal because the exigencies of the situation would force the federal courts to embed habeas corpus in a set of special procedures that would end up looking a lot like those prescribed by the DTA. The damage caused by the decision was not to the justice system per se but to the constitutional order itself, taking power away from democratically accountable executives and legislatures and giving it to nonaccountable judges.

> This decision is not really about the detainees at all, but about control of federal policy regarding enemy combatants ... All that today's opinion has done is shift responsibility for those sensitive foreign policy and national security decisions from the elected branches to the Federal Judiciary.[33]

Scalia's dissent sums up the case against judicial aggrandizement.

> The Court today decrees that no good reason to accept the judgment of the other two branches is "apparent." "The Government," it declares, "presents no credible arguments that the military mission at Guantanamo would be compromised if habeas corpus courts had jurisdiction to hear the detainees' claims." What competence does the Court have to second-guess the judgment of Congress and the President on such a point?[34]

Partisanship and Foreign Policy

The excessive dogmatism inherent in both the unitary executive and the judicial supremacy doctrines is not simply the result of abstract reasoning. It is rooted in the intensifying foreign policy partisanship that took hold during the Vietnam War, intensified during the 1970s and 1980s and has had a powerful resurgence sparked by the Iraq War. The seemingly technical and legalistic arguments about executive power discussed above are undergirded by powerful partisan differences about the *substance* of American foreign policy. Thus the "imperial president" accusation should be understood to have a dual meaning. He is imperial not only because he usurps power properly left to the other branches but because he is an imperialist, promoting the American empire. It is no coincidence that the two presidents, Reagan and George W. Bush, who, post-Nixon, have been accused of imperialism, are both Republicans who take an aggressive approach to foreign policy that does not preclude the use of force and the toppling of hostile regimes.

The Democrats' criticisms of specific presidential aggrandizements dovetails with their understanding of themselves as anti-imperialists. On the whole, they are far more pacific, more sympathetic to left wing insurgency, opposed to preemptive military actions, concerned about world opinion and more convinced of both the necessity and the desirability of participating in and abiding by the decisions of international organizations. A Brookings Institution study reveals the polarity of public opinion that has arisen over foreign policy.[35] It is also clearly evident in the Congress where Republicans consistently supported Bush's antiterror initiatives while the leadership of the Democrats in both House and Senate indulged in strident denunciations. Only one member of the Senate Democratic caucus, Joseph Lieberman, was a consistent champion of President Bush's approach and he lost his party renomination bid in 2006 winning re-election not as a Democrat but as an Independent.

From the late 1960s to the early twenty-first century American government was dominated by divided government. One party controlled *the presidency as well as* both houses of Congress for only 6 years during the 34-year period from1968 until 2002. From 1968 until 1992 the prevailing pattern was Republican control of the executive and Democratic control of Congress. Therefore the only device open to Democratic opponents of aggressive Republican foreign policy was to constrain presidential discretion. Starting in the early 1970s Congress enacted a plethora of restrictions on presidential foreign policy authority. Peter Rodman compiled the following list of legislative restraints enacted during the 1970s and 1980s:

- The War Powers Act, passed over Nixon's veto in November 1973.
- Prohibitions on US military action in support of allies in Indochina, and reductions in security assistance to them, from 1970 to 1975.
- An embargo on US military aid to Turkey after the Cyprus crisis in 1974

- Prohibition of a US covert program of military assistance to forces opposing the Cuban-Soviet military intervention in Angola.

- Expanded oversight and control over intelligence activities, resulting from the investigations into alleged intelligence abuses.

- Freedom of Information Act amendments, enacted over Ford's veto in 1974, removing the executive branch's exclusive power to determine what information can be kept classified on national security grounds.

- Limitations on numbers of US military personnel deployed abroad, such as the ceilings on the number of US Marines in Lebanon in 1983–1984 and on US military trainers in El Salvador in the 1980s.

- A variety of legislated restrictions based on human rights considerations, which limit or attach conditions on economic and security assistance to friendly countries (e.g., El Salvador and Indonesia).

- A regime of nonproliferation controls and sanctions restricting various forms of bilateral cooperation with countries that have failed to comply with international safeguards or have violated unilaterally set US criteria (e.g., at various times, India, Pakistan, Brazil, Argentina, China, and Egypt).

- Limits on the president's power to impose economic sanctions or controls for foreign policy purposes (or, in some cases, conversely, mandating such sanctions without allowing presidential discretion).

- Elaborate new procedures of congressional oversight over US arms transfers to friendly countries.

- Much tightened requirements for reprogramming of funds, by which congressional committees can deny presidents the flexibility they used to have in the use of authorized or appropriated funds to respond to rapidly changing conditions.

- Growing use of earmarking of aid funds to compel the expenditure of designated amounts for countries favored by Congress, which usually has the effect of squeezing out funds for other friendly countries under the fixed ceiling of the assistance budget.[36]

Some of these restrictions, most notably the War Powers Act, have been ignored by presidents. Nonetheless, taken as a whole, they represent a set of considerable, and in several instances arguably unconstitutional, restrictions on the president's freedom of action in foreign and military policy. More troubling than any one in particular (the War Powers Act excepted) is the sheer quantity of restrictions and the welter of procedural hurdles they erect. As *The Federalist Papers* persuasively argue, the Constitution creates an energetic executive. In an emergency, an energetic president must also be nimble, and flexible. He can hardly be expected to award scarce time, energy and staff resources to ensuring compliance with such a complex and exacting set of restrictions. Therefore, these congressional constraints violates the spirit of the Constitution. Unfortunately the Reagan Administration's response to them in the Iran-Contra affair violated not only the spirit of the Constitution but the letter as well.

Iran Contra

The aggressively anticommunist tone and substance of Ronald Reagan served to greatly increase friction with Congress over foreign policy culminating in the Iran-Contra scandal that broke out in 1986. Prior to the War on Terror, this scandal represented the high point in tension between Congress and the president with regard to foreign policy post-Nixon.

Central America has long been a focal point for American policy controversy. The left has tended to view Central America as a long-suffering victim of American political and economic oppression symbolized by the nickname "banana republic."[37] The right sees it as a hotbed of communist-inspired unrest instigated and aided by Cuba and the Soviet Union.[38] Hence the acrimony when the Reagan administration embarked on an ambitious program of aid to the insurgents fighting against the left wing Sandinista regime.

To hamstring Reagan's efforts Congress passed a series of amendments designed to reign in Reagan's aid to the Contras. The version of the amendment that stood at the center of the subsequent controversy said:

> During fiscal year 1985, no funds available to the Central Intelligence Agency, Department of Defense, or any other agency or entity of the United States involved in intelligence activities may be obligated or expended for the purpose or which would have the effect of supporting, directly or indirectly, military or paramilitary operations in Nicaragua by any nation, group, organization, movement or individual.[39]

The Reagan administration did indeed eliminate arms aid to the Contras from the CIA and other intelligence agencies. Instead the National Security Council (NSC) embarked upon a covert scheme of selling arms to Iran and using the proceeds to buy arms for the Contras. The arms sales to Iran were linked to an effort to obtain the release of US citizens held hostage in Lebanon by terrorists associated with the Iranian regime.[40] When the scheme was exposed it set off a roar of protest in Congress and the media and an equally vociferous defense by friends of the Reagan Administration. This dispute is especially important for our consideration because it revolved at least as much about the constitutional relationship between the executive and the legislature as it did about the merits of the Reagan initiatives.

The case against the Reagan Administration is well illustrated by the majority portion of the report issued by the Select Committees appointed by each house to investigate the affair.[41] It charged the administration with conducting a distinct secret foreign policy at odds with its public one. The public version opposed concessions for release of hostages; banned arms shipments to Iran, punished terrorists, abided by the "letter and spirit" of the Boland Amendment, promised to consult with congressional committees regarding covert operations, and conducted such operations solely through the CIA.[42] The secret policy violated each of those prescriptions.

The congressional report contains three different lines of criticism of the administration. Because it organized and conducted the arms sales to Iran and the aid program to the Contras in secret it deprived the American people of what they most expect from government, accountability. Congress, as the branch of government most responsible for maintaining public accountability, could not do so with regards to executive actions that it did not even know were taking place.[43] Because its officials withheld information from and lied to the Congress about what they were doing, the executive branch was also guilty of evading its responsibility to work cooperatively with Congress and to accord Congress an appropriate measure of respect.[44] Finally, the report charged the administration with specific breaches of laws passed by Congress, the most important of which was its violation of the "letter and spirit" of the Boland Amendment which cut off funding for the Contras.[45]

The minority report admits to mistakes in judgment by the administration but exonerates it of all the other charges made by the majority.[46] But it does not remain on the defensive.

It seeks to lay the constitutional and precedential basis for unfettering the presidency of what it takes to be excessive congressional interference and constraint. It devotes three chapters of its report to analyzing the framer's intent, the historical record and the relevant court cases that bear on the president's foreign policy powers.[47]

The chapter on the Framers' intent rehearses the arguments for a strong executive made by Hamilton and others. It asserts that the primary concern that the Framers had for creating Congress was to create a body that was both representative and deliberative. Whereas the Framers' intent for the executive was to enable "energetic government" such energy being especially important to deal with internal and foreign threat.[48] It goes into great detail regarding historical precedents for the president's unilateral resort to force, withholding information from Congress and instigation of covert operations without Congressional approval.[49] It relies heavily on the *Curtiss Wright* decision and Justice Jackson's famed concurring opinion in *Steel Seizures* to support the idea that

> There are some foreign policy matters over which the president is the "sole organ" of government and Congress may not impinge on them ... That is, the president and his agents are the country's eyes and ears in negotiations, intelligence sharing and other forms of communication with the rest of the world.[50]

Based on this interpretation of the concept of "sole organ," the minority concludes that "it is beyond question that Congress did not have the power to prohibit the president from sharing information, asking other governments to contribute to the Nicaraguan resistance, or enter into secret negotiations with factions inside Iran."[51]

Thus the minority dismisses all of the majority's charges relating to the president's power to conduct the whole raft of secret negotiations and dealings that comprised Iran-Contra. By implication these arguments also dispose of the majority's criticism that administration officials withheld information from Congress and lied under oath. Officials cannot withhold or mislead about matters that Congress has no right to know about in the first place.

Not only does the minority refute the claim that the administration violated congressional statute, but it turns the tables on Congress, accusing the legislative branch of being the one undermining democratic accountability.

> When Congress is narrowly divided over highly emotional issues, it frequently ends up passing intentionally ambiguous laws or amendments that postpone the day of decision. In foreign policy, those decisions often take the form of restrictive amendments of money bills that are open to being amended again *every year,* with new and equally ambiguous language replacing the old.[52]

The claim that the Boland Amendment is ambiguous is not credible. Congress used a power that it unquestionably possessed, the power of the purse, to send a direct policy message to the president. It was unfortunate that Congress limited the purview of the amendment to "intelligence agency." But it can hardly be faulted for failing to anticipate the Byzantine and nefarious effort of an entity, the NSC, with only advisory responsibilities to transform itself into an action agency and sell arms to a sworn enemy of the United States in order to spend the proceeds to evade congressional intent. The claim of ambiguity is further undermined by the fact that when, in the wake of Iran-Contra, Congress passed a more explicit version of the Boland Amendment, Reagan made clear that the president was not bound by it. This 1989 version did not limit its ban on military aid to Nicaragua only to intelligence agencies but extended it to "any agency or entity of the United States." Reagan signed the bill but his accompanying signing statement declared that the bill did not apply to initiatives undertaken by the president.

I have signed the Act with the understanding that the extension of the restriction to all entities of the United States Government is not intended to, and does not, apply in a manner and to an extent that would conflict with my constitutional authority and duty to conduct the foreign relations of the United States.

Why not? How can the president possibly justify a refusal to abide by an explicit command of Congress based on powers the Congress unambiguously possesses? The only plausible justification would be a national emergency so dire that the president could not afford to wait to ask Congress to rescind its proscription. But the Nicaragua situation did not by any stretch of the imagination constitute such an emergency and therefore the spending proscription did not in fact interfere with the president's emergency powers. The most that one could say is that it was a foreign policy matter. Only if the president's foreign policy powers are unlimited is he empowered to ignore such an explicit Congressional spending prohibition. This is the only unmitigated invocation of the foreign policy unitary theory on record. Nothing that the Bush Administration did, as opposed to what some apologist might have claimed, approached this level of unilateralism. The failure of the politically attentive public to grasp the full import of Reagan's statement was due to the "false peace" that descended during the 1990s temporarily diffusing the foreign policy tensions between president and Congress that suffused the Reagan years.

The False Peace

The heated differences fueled by the Iran-Contra affair cooled down during the 1990s because of the domestic political dynamics surrounding the 1991 War in the Persian Gulf and NAFTA. Although a large majority of Democrats voted against the Senate resolution endorsing the Gulf War, ten Democrats did support it. The speed with which the war was won greatly enhanced its popularity and legitimacy and discouraged Democrats from turning it into a partisan issue. President Clinton sided with the Republicans on the most important and controversial foreign policy initiative of his two terms, the North American Free Trade Agreement (NAFTA). With the full support of the Republicans in Congress, Clinton was able to win over a sufficient minority of Democrats to obtain congressional approval. In the House, 156 Democrats opposed NAFTA and only 102 supported it. Republicans supported NAFTA by more than three to one, 132 to 43. In the Senate, 28 Democrats opposed NAFTA and 27 supported it. Republicans supported it by a margin almost identical to that of their House colleagues, 34 in favor and 10 opposed.[53] Thus the 1990s represented something of a thaw in partisan conflict over foreign policy. However the fact that majorities of congressional Democrats opposed both the Gulf War and NAFTA did not auger well for a continuance of that thaw, especially in the face of the far grimmer foreign policy challenges that arouse in September of 2001.

9/11, the War Metaphor and the Rebirth of Foreign Policy Partisanship

The reassertion of foreign policy partisanship and therefore of conflict over executive power did not take place immediately after 9/11. The subsequent U S attack on Afghanistan was viewed by most mainstream Democrats as retaliatory and therefore legitimate. Opposition grew however as the full outline of Bush's antiterror strategy became clear. That strategy was premised on the principle that the nation was at war. At the prayer service held for the victims of 9/11 at the National Cathedral on 9/14, Bush asserted that 9/11 was indeed the equivalent of Pearl Harbor and Fort Sumter. "War has been waged against us by stealth and deceit and murder." Because it was war, the objective was to win. "This conflict was begun on the timing and terms of others. It will end in a way, and at an hour, of our choosing."[54] Winning the war would not be subordinated to other goals, however laudable, such as respecting the authority of international institutions or placating the sensibilities of friends and allies.

Adoption of the war metaphor was the critical step that divided supporters of a strong assertion of executive power in the name of fighting terror from those seeking to contain the terror effort within a conventional legal and judicial framework. Wars are irreducibly lawless. Although there do exist international laws of war and international institutions that try to enforce them, war is not *governed* the way crime is governed because it does not take place within a constitutional context. Even so-called civilized war is hardly that. Consider the saturation bombing of Kosovo, which utterly reversed the traditional norms of war by causing the deaths of *no* American soldiers but 500 civilian casualties.[55] A War on Terror was by its very nature impelled in an even more barbaric and lawless direction by an enemy that wore no uniforms, killed randomly, used civilians as human shields, and deployed women and children as suicide bombers.

A second critical consequence of declaring war on such an unconventional enemy concerns the manner in which enemy combatants would be treated. Unlike criminal suspects, enemy soldiers are not presumed innocent nor do they enjoy the full panoply of procedural rights that criminal suspects enjoy. On the other hand, if they have acted honorably, they are accorded respect not given to criminals. The key question posed with regard to a noncriminal enemy combatant regards the future risk the person poses. When honor governed war a captured officer might obtain his release simply by offering his *parole*, French for "word," that he would not return to combat. No such dignified treatment is likely to be accorded a combatant who has posed as a civilian, killed indiscriminately and scoffed at the ordinary rules of civilized conduct. And, indeed many of the Guantanamo detainees who have been released have resumed their former terrorist careers.[56] Wherever one comes down on the specific disputes regarding the treatment of unlawful enemy combatants one has to admit that their mode of conduct places enormous strain on the capacity of the judicial system to cope with them.

But the War on Terror could not be meaningfully defined solely according to conventional notions of war. Terrorists have no state of their own. Therefore a war on terror has no obvious spatial dimension. Bush adopted an expansive view of enemy terrain as including the territory of all those nations that give terrorists safe harbor.

> Every government that supports them … every nation in every region, has a decision to make. Either you are with us, or you are with the terrorists. From this day forward any nation that continues to harbor or support terrorism will be regarded by the United States as a hostile regime.[57]

The United States has traditionally adhered to the doctrine of "imminent threat." It abstains from bellicose action until the enemy gives clear signs that it is making preparations to attack. The manner in which terrorist's plan and carry out their attacks means that they do not mass soldiers in advance nor give other evidence that offensive preparations are underway. They rely on stealth and target innocent civilians. It is impossible to predict when and where they will strike. By rejecting prevailing norms of warfare—concentration on military targets, providing warning of attack, putting one's forces in uniform—the enemy has rendered the concept of imminence meaningless and therefore the United States is justified in abandoning it as a condition for preemptive attack.

The Bush Administration abandoned the principle of imminent threat in exchange for a far more aggressive approach called the preemption doctrine. The Defense Department's 2002 National Strategy Document rejects the principle that the United States should not initiate hostilities unless it is imminent danger of being attacked. The document calls for a modification of this reliance on imminence based on the novel dangers that rogue states and terrorists pose.[58]

Virtually every partisan conflict over executive power and the War on Terror stems from the invocation of the war metaphor and the subsidiary concepts of safe harbors and preemption. These include: the decision to go into Iraq, the detention of unlawful enemy combatants in general and at Guantanamo, the use of military tribunals, and coercive interrogation. My defense of the constitutionality, and in most cases the wisdom, of the Bush Administration regarding these various contentious matters rests on the essential soundness of the war metaphor itself and its safe harbor and pre-emption corollaries.

The War on Terror

It was President Clinton not President Bush who misunderstood the responsibilities of the presidency for combating terror. Clinton had ample justification for declaring a war on terror, but he refrained from doing so. The first attack on the World Trade Center in 1993 as well as the 2000 bombing of the USS Cole, the 1998 bombing of American embassies in Kenya and Tanzania, the 1996 bombing of US military barracks in Saudi Arabia, were clear indications that a well armed and financed international terror network was in existence and that it posed a grave threat to American national security.

The Clinton Administration's failure to respond to that threat is understandable yet regrettable. Clinton's highest foreign policy priority, expanding free trade, required the maintenance of close relations with our traditional allies and improving relations with former foes like China and Russia. It would have been very difficult to maintain a clear focus on economic matters and to avoid serious conflicts with allies and former enemies alike had a war on terror been declared. Nonetheless, the price of limiting US retaliation to lobbing some missiles at a few sites in Sudan and Afghanistan was to embolden the terrorists. Such a feckless response demonstrated that indeed the United States was not prepared to take serious, sustained action against them. One cannot say with certainty that prosecuting such a war before 9/11 would have prevented the devastating attacks on that day, but the failure to do so was highly imprudent. Such prudence is the sine qua non of good statesmanship because statesmanship always involved choosing among valuable ends. By placing other concerns above the imperative to preserve and protect the safety of Americans, Clinton inappropriately elevated a desirable goal, freer word trade, above his paramount responsibility, keeping the nation secure.

Prior to 9/11 Bush also failed to take an aggressive approach against terror but his failure is more excusable since, unlike Clinton, he was not faced by any overt act of terrorism to which to respond. Once 9/11 occurred, Bush acted appropriately. Since it was impossible to accurately assess the strength of the world terror network in the immediate aftermath of 9/11 he accepted the risk of *overestimating* the danger, and all the serious economic and diplomatic consequences that such an overestimation would cause, rather than emulate Clinton's error of underestimation. This statesmanlike outlook had specific and unsettling consequences. Minimizing the likelihood of further attack on US soil required the United States to go on the offensive and attack terrorists on their home ground. Since terrorists claim no home territory, this meant attacking them wherever they were being given safe harbor even if the harboring state claimed to be a nonbelligerent. Otherwise the stateless enemy could plan future attacks and avoid reprisal for past attacks with impunity.

Preemption is a similarly disturbing but ineluctable consequence of prosecuting a war on terror. If the enemy does not make it possible to know when an attack is imminent than imminence is an impossible principle upon which to base a war strategy. Indeed critics of preemption do not apply war reasoning at all but resort to the criminal analogy of "innocent until proven guilty." An attack is unjustified unless one is certain beyond a reasonable doubt that the enemy is planning to attack. Such standards are laudable in criminal circumstance but when the goal is not justice for an individual but protecting the safety of entire populations it is not relevant. Nor does it require that attacks occur wantonly. If the United States warns that it will make a preemptive attack it is well within the ability of the object of that threat to demonstrate its innocence in an unambiguous fashion. This option was available to Saddam Hussein until hours before the US attack.

Perhaps Saddam chose not to save his country from attack because he considered the price of relinquishing any hope of leading an alliance of rogue states and terrorists against the West was too high. He seems to have preferred to take the enormous risk that France, Germany and the other states that opposed the invasion would succeed in deterring the United States from launching the attack.[59] Such a risk estimation was not only foolish in the extreme but reflected the depth of his unconcern regarding the wellbeing of his countrymen. As the Duelfur Report documents, even Saddam's senior military officials thought that Iraq had WMDs.[60] Given the limited intelligence that Bush had, which did point towards Saddam having WMDs, and the certain knowledge that Saddam had had them in the past, it would have been the height of imprudence for Bush to assume that despite the fact that Saddam had banished weapons inspectors and sent a key aide to Niger (a key source of yellow cake) that Iraq did not indeed pose a serious WMD threat.[61] Critics condemn the U.S. for its failure to prove that Saddam had WMDs. They do not ask the more relevant question of why Saddam refused to make a strenuous effort to show that he did not have WMDs even when faced with likely attack and, in that event, certain defeat.[62] In war it is perfectly appropriate to adopt a standard of guilty until proven innocent particularly when the accused has it within his power to offer clear-cut evidence of "innocence."

Acquitting Bush

Bush's actual conduct of the War on Terror for the most part acquits him of the charge of being an "imperial" president. He passed the most essential test of presidential responsibility to the Constitution, he protected the American people. Post 9/11, not a single American life was lost to terror attack on American soil. Correlation is not causation. Perhaps it is simply a coincidence that terror on American soil subsided in the wake of the aggressive initiatives taken by the president. Perhaps 9/11, as some have argued, was an anomaly and the terror threat has been drastically over-rated.[63] But statesmen cannot live by social science strictures. Nor can they responsibly make their decisions based on the most optimistic assumptions. Unlike the bankers who chose to take inordinate risks because they made plausible but highly optimistic assumptions about the continued buoyancy of the American economy, Bush recognized that his responsibilities as president required him to lean toward the pessimistic end of the terror risk continuum. He understood that statesmanship demanded taking the terrorists at their word that 9/11 was just the beginning of a jihad against the West and he acted accordingly.

This paper has faulted Bush for his failure to ask for a declaration of war but this by itself does not rise to the level of imperialism since it has been the norm since 1948 and has been perpetrated by such decidedly non-imperial presidents as Truman and George H.W. Bush. With regard to his other dealings with Congress regarding the War on Terror, Bush did not allow the unitary theory to prevent a series of important instances of interbranch cooperation. Although the Bush administration's first instinct was to ignore Congress in its creation of detainee policies, it changed its attitude after the *Hamdi* decision at which time it did seek to obtain congressional support for its policies. In both the Military Commissions Act of 2006 and the Detainee Treatment Act of 2005 Congress acted to provide a statutory underpinning for the administration's policies.[64]

In 2006 Congress also renewed the Patriot Act as the president had requested.[65] In December of 2005 the *New York Times* published a front page article revealing that the administration was engaged in very aggressive electronic surveillance.[66] These revelations resulted in a firestorm of criticism of Bush substantially fueling the imperialism charge. And yet, in 2008 the Congress, which was now composed of Democratic majorities in both houses, passed a revision of the Foreign Intelligence Surveillance Act that gave Bush substantially what he asked for in terms of a statutory foundation for his surveillance programs. Even as intense a critic of the Bush Administration as Barack Obama voted for the statute.[67] Bush's impressive ability to obtain cooperation and support from majority Republican and majority Democratic Congresses constitutes an impressive rebuke to the view of Bush as an imperial usurper of congressional authority.

The inability of war critics to acknowledge either the success of the War on Terror or the statesman's imperative to adopt pessimistic assumptions is not entirely explicable. But it seems to stem in part from the intense and personalized hatred of Bush, often expressed in vulgar terms even by otherwise intelligent and sober political intellectuals and politicians.[68] As *New York Times* columnist Nicholas Kristof observed,

> Bookshops are filled with titles about Mr. Bush like "Lies and the Lying Liars Who Tell Them," "Big Lies," "Thieves in High Places" and "The Lies of George W. Bush." A consensus is emerging on the left that Mr. Bush is fundamentally dishonest, perhaps even evil—a nut, yes, but mostly a liar and a schemer.[69]

Because Bush was a war criminal a religious zealot and a swaggering bully he could not be responsible for an accomplishment that, in the wake of 9/11, no thoughtful prognosticator thought possible.[70]

A related source of the underestimation of Bush's accomplishment is the contempt held not just for his persona but also for his religiously derived moral absolutism. The demonization of terrorists as unmitigated villains and of the rogue states that support them as belonging to an "axis of evil" is philosophically and politically unacceptable to "sophisticated" analysts whose own unquestioned tenet is that all moral and political questions must be portrayed in varying shades of gray. The simplistic "good guys vs. bad guys" Bush approach simply could not work.[71] Hence the remarkable reluctance to overtly express what all but the most hardened critics now seem ready to acknowledge, the surge worked, the situation in Iraq verges on being stable and the prospects for the future are modestly good.[72]

Not only did Bush's strategy succeed, but, compared to previous wartime presidencies, it did so with relatively mild curbs on civil liberties. We have already commented on the relative modesty of his war powers claims as compared to Reagan. He also did nothing to compare with Lincoln's suspension of habeas corpus, Woodrow Wilson's Red Scare or FDR's internment of Japanese Americans, only the first of which had any plausible national security justification.[73] Opposition to the war was unrepressed to the point that it became *the* fashionable point of view. Despite claims that their patriotism was being challenged, Democrats were able to win back both houses of Congress in 2006.[74] The initial mass detainments of large numbers of Arabs and Arab Americans created considerable inconvenience but the numbers were quickly whittled down.[75] Egregious examples of military misconduct, most notably the treatment of prisoners at Abu Ghraib, were investigated and, when sufficient evidence was produced, the perpetrators were punished.[76]

Coercive Interrogation

As the War in Iraq began to succeed, criticism of the Bush Administration shifted from the conduct of the war itself to the tactics used for interrogating unlawful enemy combatants. The administration was accused of torturing its captives. But just like the Supreme Court's critique of Bush's approach to detention of unlawful enemy combatants, this critique made no effort to empathize with the difficulties this issue created for the executive and what sort of approach would best reconcile national security needs, in this case the need for intelligence, with a humane consideration for the wellbeing of the detainee. The rhetorical power of the word "torture" substituted for any serious consideration of what means were appropriate for extracting valuable information from recalcitrant subjects.

Serious public debate about coercive interrogation has been hampered both by a lack of an agreed upon definition of what constitutes torture and by credible evidence about how well different forms of interrogation work. The United States is a signatory to the 1984 United Nations Convention Against Torture and Other Cruel, Inhuman, or Degrading Treatment or Punishment (CAT).[77] But the definition of torture is hopelessly vague.

> For the purposes of this Convention, torture means any act by which severe pain or suffering, whether physical or mental, is intentionally inflicted on a person for such purposes as obtaining from him or a third person information or a confession, punishing him for an act he or a third person has committed or is suspected of having committed, or intimidating or coercing him or a third person.[78]

By this definition routine actions taken by US correctional institutions, such as lock downs and solitary confinement, indeed any form of long term confinement, could be called torture because they no doubt inflict severe mental suffering on at least some of those who are subject to them. In a memo to White House Counsel Alberto Gonzales, lawyers for the OLC provided a far more specific definition of what constituted torture under existing federal law.

We conclude that for an act to constitute torture as defined in Section 2340, it must inflict pain that is difficult to endure. Physical pain amounting to torture must be equivalent in intensity to the pain accompanying serious physical injury such as organ failure, impairment to bodily function or even death. For purely mental pain or suffering to amount to torture under Section 2340, it must result in significant psychological harm of significant duration, e.g., lasting for months or even years. We conclude that the mental harm also must result from one of the predicate acts listed in the statue, namely: threats of imminent death; threats of infliction of the kind of pain that would amount to physical torture; infliction of such physical pain as a means of psychological torture; use of drugs or other procedures designed to deeply disrupt the sense or fundamentally alter an individual's personality; or threatening to do any of these things to a third party.[79]

Although this definition shocked the conscious of much of the legal and journalistic community, although not the public at large, nowhere in the reams of articles and editorials condemning this definition does one find the presentation of an *alternative* that is demonstrably capable of fulfilling the twin goals of eliciting the information and protecting the person of the subject. Instead of empathy with the deep ethical and practical dilemma that coercive interrogation poses the reader is greeted with screeds of shock and indignation.

Both the proponents and the critics of the coercive interrogation methods used on unlawful enemy combatants claim that they have evidence demonstrating, respectively, that it is or it is not effective in eliciting useful intelligence information but all they present are anecdotes. Each side is able to find former intelligence officers who will attest to either the success or failure of these methods. Admittedly, conducting a reliable empirical study of these matters is both ethically and practically challenging, but in its absence the dispassionate observer lacks grounds for arriving at an independent judgment. The situation is worsened by the selective manner in which classified material related to coercive interrogation has been dealt with by the Obama Administration. It released the memos pertaining to OLC guidelines for coercive interrogation, but, as of this writing, its has refused former Vice President Cheney's requests that it release information that, he claims, would demonstrate the critical contribution of coercive interrogations to the success of the War on Terror.

One might argue that the lack of definitional and evidentiary clarity is grounds for executive deference. It is necessary to gather intelligence from captives. Executives must do what is necessary. In the absence of dispositive proof that the methods under consideration do *not* work and given that reasonable people can disagree about whether they cross the line from harsh to torturous, determining the best means to achieve the necessary end is quintessentially an executive decision. But deferring to the executive has not indeed been the approach adopted by leading opinion makers. The *New York Times* is often referred to as the "newspaper of record." Its handling of the coercive interrogation issue provides a powerful illustration of how leading organs of opinion debased and cheapened the discussion of this sensitive and morally complex issue.

On April 16, 2009 the Obama Administration released four OLC memos, one written in 2002 and three in 2005 that provided guidelines to the CIA regarding the conduct of coercive interrogation. The *New York Times* headline for its article on the memos read, "Memos Spell Out Brutal CIA Mode of Interrogation."[80] By comparison, the *Los Angeles Times* entitled its story "Memos Reveal Harsh CIA Interrogation Methods."[81] The difference between "brutal" and "harsh" is indeed the question that serious people have to wrestle with and yet the oddest aspect of the account in the *Times* is its lack of interest in distinguishing between the forms of coercive interrogation that might be considered brutal, and those that are more akin to fraternity hazing. On the latter score, the *Times* includes in its list of "brutal" methods taking a subject who is afraid of insects and putting him into a confined space with an insect. The subject is told it is a stinging insect but it is not. He is also told that the insect will not kill him or even produce severe pain.[82]

The account in the *Times* also exaggerates the level of harshness because its selective excerpts from the memos do not include the full range of mitigations taken by the interrogators to prevent injury and pain. For example when describing "walling," pushing the subject against a wall, the *Times* concedes that the subjects head and neck are protected to prevent whiplash and that the sound created by the push is far greater than the injury. But it fails to mention *how* the sound is magnified. It is because the wall is not rigid or solid. It is made of special flexible materials designed to magnify the sound of impact and also to enable the subject to cushion physical impact and to enable the subject to bounce off.[83]

Likewise, the *Times* does explain that the facial slap permitted by the memos is done with fingers spread, but then fails to add that the slap is only administered to the fleshy part of the face, the cheek. The *Times* describes "water dousing" as water poured on the detainee "from a container or from a hose without a nozzle." It concedes that the memos require that the water be potable and that interrogators must ensure that water does not enter the detainee's nose, mouth or eyes. But it fails to point out the other critical safeguards specified in the memos that require the ambient air temperature to be no less than 64 degrees and limit the amount of time the dousing will continue depending on the temperature of the water. Dousing is limited to 20 minutes at 41 degrees, 40 minutes at 50 degrees and 60 minutes at 59 degrees. Medical personnel are present and engage in continual monitoring for hypothermia.[84]

The technique described in the memos that is indisputably harsh and therefore worthy of the most considered and probing scrutiny is "waterboarding." The intent of waterboarding is to produce the perception of drowning.

> The detainee is placed on a gurney that is inclined at an angle of ten to fifteen degrees with the detainee on his back … A cloth is placed over the detainee's face and cold water is poured on the cloth from a height of approximately 6 to 18 inches. The wet cloth creates a barrier through which it is difficult — or in some cases not possible — to breathe. A single application of water may not last for more than forty seconds.[85]

The technique inflicts no pain but it does induce dreadful fear. The technique is only to be employed if: 1. The CIA has credible intelligence that a terrorist attack is imminent; 2. There are substantial and credible indicators the subject has actionable intelligence that can prevent, disrupt or delay this attack; and 3. other interrogation methods have failed or are unlikely to yield actionable intelligence in time to prevent the attack.[86]

But as it did with regards to the other lesser forms of coercion, the Times ignores information contained in the memo that describes the various safeguards employed to protect the subject and other vital information that might lead a reasonable person to conclude that waterboarding, harsh as it is, is not torture. Three days prior to waterboarding, detainees are placed on a liquid diet to reduce the risk of vomit-induced suffocation. A physician and a psychiatrist are present at all times. Sessions are limited to two per day.[87] None of these specific mitigations is discussed in the article.

In the same vein, the *Times* reveals that after World War II "the United States prosecuted some Japanese interrogators for waterboarding,"[88] but it fails to mention that waterboarding is a routine aspect of US Air Force Survival, Evasion, Resistance, Escape (SERE) training, and by the Navy as well. Between 1992–2001 it was inflicted upon 26,829 Air Force personnel and at least one thousand Navy personnel. No adverse mental health effects were reported among those who had to endure it.[89] It is safe to say that no military in human history has ever tortured its own soldiers as a training exercise. And yet none of this evidence deterred the *Times* for titling its editorial about the memos "The Torturer's Manifesto" and comparing the authors of the memo's to "dungeon masters throughout history" by whom they presumably mean Spanish Inquisitors and Nazi death camp operators whose brutalities and murderers they blithely liken to techniques that do not maim or kill nor even cause severe pain.[90]

Conclusion

The Constitution is not at all obsolete with regard to the president's role in the War on Terror. Rather, it has been subject to misinterpretation, especially by the Supreme Court and parts of the media, but also by the Congress and by the president himself. Despite what apologists for the Reagan and Bush administrations claim, the president does not enjoy unfettered power regarding war making. The unitary theory properly understood is a way of interpreting the extent of the president's capacity to control the operations of the executive branch, it is not a theory about war making. The irony of the Bush administration is that most of what the administration actually did to execute the War on Terror and the War in Iraq was fully constitutional even according to a much less grandiose theory of executive power, one that pays great deference to the president's need for flexibility and discretion in emergency circumstances but stops well short of exonerating him from his appropriate obligations to Congress and the court. Bush did violate the spirit of the Constitution by not asking Congress for a declaration of war in Iraq but the seriousness of that failure was mitigated by Congress's passage of meaningful if not totally adequate substitute in the form of an AUMF.

Article One grants Congress the sole power to declare war. Admittedly it is not always clear whether a particular engagement of hostilities rises to the level of true warfare. But the power to declare war must include the power to determine what is and is not a war. Otherwise Congress would not be able to tell when it is proper to engage in a deliberation about whether or not to issue a declaration. Thus the declaration process has two steps. First Congress determines whether indeed the initiation of hostilities at hand should be considered a war. If not, it need not act at all or it can content itself with issuing an AUMF. But if the engagement being contemplated is serious enough to merit the designation of war it is the clear constitutional obligation of Congress to declare either for it or against it.

A decision by Congress to consider a declaration of war in Iraq would not have been without risk. It would surely have involved a more extended congressional deliberation, thus allowing Saddam to stir up even more world opposition to the war. But much would have been gained. Congress would have had the opportunity to engage the issue fully. The administration would have had to provide a fuller explanation of its war aims and a more textured discussion of both the risks and the opportunities posed by defeating Iraq.

Because the Republicans controlled Congress at the time it is very probable that Congress would indeed have declared war. But such a momentous step would have been taken only after serious reflection and strenuous efforts at public engagement. This is what the Framers intended and the unhappy consequences of failing to engage in such a deliberation demonstrate their wisdom and foresightedness. The decision to go to war was not sufficiently vetted. The public had only a dim and excessively narrow understanding of the war aims. Therefore public backing could only be counted upon as long as things went smoothly which, after the initial military triumph, they did not.

In its haste, the Bush Administration did not adequately anticipate the terrible difficulties to be faced *after* military victory. A declaration of war deliberation might not have fully overcome these defects but it would have created the appropriate setting for trying to do so. And, it would have been *constitutional*. It would have restored the common sense meaning of a crucial clause of the Constitution a half century after that meaning was first evaded by Harry Truman.

Presidents have no power to obstruct Congress from deliberating about and voting on a declaration of war. Its failure to do so in Korea and Viet Nam, and Kuwait as well as in Iraq is a reflection of its preference for keeping its options open. Congress is keenly aware that most military actions are popular at first but become highly unpopular if victory is not quickly achieved. Therefore it has often chosen to allow the president to begin a war without giving him the full endorsement that a declaration would constitute. This sort of bet hedging is what the unequivocal placement of the war power with Congress was intended to preclude. By its nature, Congress cannot compete with the president for primacy in foreign policy or in military matters. It is not there to tinker with presidential initiatives. Its role is limited but decisive. In the 1970s and 1980s Congress tried to act expansively but indecisively. It constricted presidential discretion without being willing to assert its declaration power. So far it has not repeated this mistake during the War on Terror. When required to do so by the court, it provided an adequate statutory basis for the president's detention policies a fact that, unfortunately, the court failed to acknowledge.

In its rulings regarding Bush's detention policies, the Supreme Court has demonstrated a willingness to second guess and overrule the president's conduct of the war to a degree unprecedented in prior wars. This aggrandizement reveals less about presidential misdeeds than it does about shifts in judicial philosophy. After reading the various Supreme Court opinions that reprove the administration for operating with insufficient statutory authority or in violation of the Constitution, the overall impression is that the writers of those opinions simply do not accept the war metaphor. Even though they are not all Democrats, their opinions are saturated with the antipathy to aggressive foreign policy associated with that party. But contesting the direction of American foreign policy is *not* a judicial prerogative. Nonetheless, the court improperly pressed the Bush administration to abide by standards of criminal prosecution that were inappropriate to the war taking place. The court showed that it simply does not understand what a war on terror entails and therefore could not empathize with the problems and the obligations involved in executing it.

Unlike the three branches of government, the Constitution places no positive obligations on the press. Its freedom verges on being absolute. And yet one can only lament the damage done to the constitutional order when its greatest journalistic outlets become afflicted by a lack of empathy for the executive greater even than that shown by the Supreme Court. Even the Constitution does not offer sufficient protection of the nation's liberty and security to enable those values to survive in the face of a poorly educated public. The distortions imparted by much of the establishment media, and by the *New York Times* in particular, threaten the viability of the constitutional order no less than the usurpations of power by the Supreme Court. The presidency is currently occupied by a man whom the establishment media vastly prefer to Bush. This has served to greatly enhance its empathetic sensibilities. One can only hope that this heightened awareness and approval of the need for presidential energy and discretion represents a genuine growth in political understanding that will extend itself even to those future presidents who might prove to be less to the media's liking.

PART EIGHT

SUMMARY

Chapter 14

Conclusions and Further Questions

Akhil Reed Amar

When Professor Main initially asked me if I would like to participate in a conversation about whether the Constitution was obsolete, I said "Yes!" When he then asked me whether I was a strong critic or a staunch defender of the Constitution, I said "Yes!" (Meaning, of course, "both!"—depending on the specific issue.) Then he said that what he really wanted to know is: Did I have thoughts about particular topics such as slavery or the Electoral College or judicial review or the executive/legislative separation of powers? Again, I said, "Yes!" (Meaning, of course, all of the above.) At that point, he asked me if I would be interested in offering concluding remarks that would try to pull together the themes of all the previous, more focused, panels. Again, I said, "Yes!" So here we are.

I have read with great interest all the papers for this conference. I have learned a great deal from each of them—and I have some thoughts about each one. I'll try to organize those thoughts around four large admonitions for us all.

We the People

The first admonition is that we should remember the people.

"We the people of the United States ... do ordain and establish this Constitution." This phrase is performative. It is not merely a text; it is actually a deed, a doing. What is being described is an act of ordainment and establishment of truly epic proportions. Up and down an entire continent, ordinary people are actually getting to decide how they and their posterity will be governed.

Such a thing had never happened in the history of the world up to that point. From a democratic point of view, this is the most momentous event in world chronology—it is the hinge of history. Before this moment democracies had existed in very few places. Today democracy reigns over half the globe.

It is useful to remind ourselves about the epic democratic deed that occurred in 1787–88. It gives the lie to the view made popular by the most important book of the last century—Charles Beard's *Economic Interpretation of the Constitution*. It also gives the lie to the view of Beard's predecessor, J. Allen Smith, who is quoted quite appropriately by Professor Main in the opening paper to this conference. Let's remember what Smith claimed: "The evidence is overwhelming that the men who sat in that convention had no faith in the wisdom or political capacity of the people." Well, then why did they put the thing to a vote up and down a continent, a vote that they did not control? Why did they allow the freest speech in opposition? Why did they allow and superintend a process that lowered or eliminated the ordinary property qualifications that applied to ordinary elections in 8 of the 13 states? These are facts that Beard knew but didn't tell you, and they contradict his view and Smith's view that the essence of the Constitution is anti-populist. Au contraire. Remember the people.

So the good news for Daniel Lazare is that he can actually claim the Framers on his side to a very important degree. The Framers did believe in popular sovereignty. Indeed, their very founding act—the "We do" deed—embodied popular sovereignty. It is sometimes more fun to write a polemic against the powers that be than to side with them, but as a matter of political strategy, it is typically more effective to wrap oneself in the flag than to burn it. Whether or not they are aware of it, Mr. Lazare and his fellow populists have a lot of the flag on their side.

The extraordinary nature of the democratic act behind the text also helps explain why there is such veneration of the Constitution, veneration that Professor Rabkin nicely highlights. There are reasons for this veneration. It is not mere idolatry or ancestor worship.

Of course, one key question is: Does preamble-style popular sovereignty continue to be an ongoing principle in the American republic? To answer this question, we will need to talk about the amendment process and I shall do so momentarily.

But before I do, here are a few more thoughts on this extraordinary preamble phraseology, "We the people of the United States." First, we must note that the people of different states are coming together. The Preamble is not just the most democratic deed in world history. It is also effects the largest corporate merger in world history. Thirteen previously separate regimes are coalescing into one genuine nation—no longer a mere alliance or a confederation or a treaty, but a new more perfect union much stronger than its predecessor.

President Lincoln was right about the indivisibility of this more perfect union, which was consciously modeled on and publicly analogized to the 1707 union of Scotland and England, which was likewise indivisible. America's new union was created for geostrategic purposes. What was being proposed at the Founding was nothing less than a kind of world government for the New World—a continental government of extraordinary proportions. It would be as if someone today were proposing serious world government. That was what was really on the table in 1787: We the people of the United States.

Why is this important for our deliberations today? In the initial debate at this conference—a conversation between Mr. Lazare and Professor Rabkin—here is what Professor Rabkin said: "Under this Constitution, the United States has risen to the status of the world's largest economy and greatest military power, and held these distinctions for many decades. The people of the United States have been the richest and arguably the freest in the world for well over a century." And Mr. Lazare admitted in his paper that this notable fact is something to be reckoned with. He explicitly noted, albeit in passing, the argument that "since America is the world's number-one superpower, there most be something to its system, some hidden spark of genius,that the more prosaic minded cannot grasp." I think that there is a lot to this passing point. It deserves our attention. This more perfect union was created largely for geostrategic national security purposes, and it largely succeeded (apart from the Civil War—about which more anon).

This conversation between Lazare and Rabkin and the Constitution's connection to geostrategy should frame our understanding of executive power. Which brings me to the discussion between Professors Landy and Pious. We cannot understand the presidency if we do not understand that its original purpose was largely to serve as a national security institution, a foreign-policy institution. At the Founding, the key concern was not — with apologies to James Carvel (and Charles Beard) — "the economy, stupid." Rather, it was actually national security.

Thus, every one of the elected presidents up to Lincoln, with a single exception, was either a general or the secretary of state (if you count John Adams — one of America's key early diplomats, along with Jay, Franklin, and Jefferson — as a proto-secretary of state under the Articles of Confederation). With this interesting factoid, we see once again the unusualness of President Lincoln — a point highlighted by both Professor Finkelman and Professor Graber. Lincoln did not fit the standard presidential model; he was neither a general nor a diplomat at the time of his election — which tells us that something really interesting and unusual was going on in the 1860 election.

If this emphasis on geostrategy helps us see Abraham Lincoln in a clearer light, so too with James Madison. More than half of our contributors have talked about Madison — but none has made the following key point: Madison is not on Mount Rushmore. He was an unsuccessful President because the nation's capital was burned on his watch — a fact that is quite relevant to the themes of the preceding panel on the presidency. James Madison might have been a great thinker, but he did not understand executive power so well. Nor did he understand the rest of the world and European balance of power in an exceptionally sophisticated way. Academics love him because he is like us. He is an intellectual. And he is also a doer as well as a thinker. But he is not a Rushmore president.

A couple of final points about this extraordinary phrase, "We the people of the United States." We need to understand that the Constitution was not designed for the benefit of people other than the people of the United States. Indeed, maybe the Constitution was designed for their detriment. In important respects, the Constitution was a war machine. It was all about kicking out the British and eventually the French and the Spanish and being hegemons in our hemisphere.

Does that original vision make sense today? This is a question that Professor Rabkin mentioned in his presentation. It was not a central theme of his chapter, but it raises a huge question for reflective Americans today. Does this idea of a New World separate from all the problems of the Old World continue to make sense today? After all, we are now at a moment when we have One-World challenges and opportunities — from pandemic viruses to global terrorism — and when half the world is democratic, as it most emphatically was not when the Founders were thinking and doing.

Reflective Americans would be talking about world government if we had reason to believe that the Martians were coming. The question is whether nuclear proliferation and pandemic viruses are like Martians.

The phrase, "We the people of the United States" has a glorious side but I also want us to see its darker flip side — that many persons in the world are not part of this people and might even be threatened by this people. Which leads me to the final point about this Preamble phrase: Slaves were not part of the people. Remember the people — and remember who were excluded from the people: Not just the British and the French and the Spanish but the Native Americans and the slaves. Some free blacks were indeed part of the people. But unfree blacks — slaves — were not part of the people. The document was not designed for the benefit of the slaves. The slaves' interests were compromised, as were the interests of the British, the French, the Spanish, and the Native Americans.

On the slavery issue, we are powerfully reminded how different our Constitution is from the Founders' Constitution. Epic changes were wrought by the Civil War and its ensuing amendments, but these amendments have not been fully integrated into many contemporary constitutional conversations.

Consider, for example, the Electoral College. Two genuine experts on the Electoral College, Professors Edwards and Sabato, have just squared off—but neither of those experts highlighted the fact that the origins of the Electoral College were tightly bound up with the politics of slavery and the perceived need to protect the political power of slaveholders. We heard about slavery from Professor Graber and from Professor Finkelman. But we did not hear about slavery in the focused conversation about the Electoral College. And if slavery was indeed tightly bound up with the American Electoral College (especially its reincarnation in the Twelfth Amendment), doesn't this fact mean that we today have special reasons to view this peculiar electoral institution with skepticism?

Here, too, I invite us all to rethink our worship of Madison. Not only was he a mediocre president, but he was also a slaveholder who never freed his slaves. (George Washington, by contrast, did at his death provide for his slaves' freedom.) James Madison co-founded a political party that was up to its elbows, if not its eyeballs, in its complicity with slavery. Later in life, Madison actually even expressed doubts about the free-soil provisions of the Missouri Compromise. Disgraceful!

So much for my first admonition: Remember the people. As we ponder our Constitution's virtues and vices, we must remember both who was included and also who was excluded.

Remember the States

My second admonition is that we should remember the states. Critics of the Constitution often that say we have the regime we do because we are in effect stuck with it. The document is hard to amend. Its basic contours are obdurate; they are incorrigible; they cannot be fixed—and that is why we have them. This theme is very prominent in Daniel Lazare's paper, for example, and in much of the recent work of Sandy Levinson.

But if we remember the states, here is one thing that snaps into focus: All 50 state constitutions look like the federal Constitution in many ways. And that is not because these state constitutions are obdurate to change. Rather, it is because the American people have actually opted for a certain model. Academic critics or ideologues might not like this basic model, but with minor variations virtually all the states have opted for it. This model features a written constitution and a separate bill of rights, a bicameral legislature, and a separately elected chief executive who serves a four-year term and wields a veto pen. The basic model also features a regime of judicial review—a power and duty enjoyed by every ordinary court and not just one specially designated constitution court. The model includes a legislative election system based on single-member districts, with two parties—the same two parties across the continent—vying in each district and each election to be first past the post.

The very existence of this basic American model in virtually all the states calls into question the claim that we have this system because we are stuck with it rather than because Americans actually seem to embrace this system. Maybe Americans are wrong to believe and act as they do. But most critics of the federal Constitution pay insufficient heed to state constitutional practice. The only paper in this collection that seriously grapples with the state experience is Professor Melnick's, which tries to discuss how state and federal policies and structures intermesh in various ways. I would encourage others in this discussion — and outside this discussion! — to pay more attention to states when doing their analysis.

For example, earlier we heard a lot about the Electoral College. Most of the arguments made in favor of the Electoral College proved too much because if they were truly good arguments, then in fact the states are picking their governors the wrong way. "Oh my God," says Larry Sabato, "how are we going to deal with a presidential recount?" Well, you know, we deal with recounts in California. You know what we do in California? Everyone votes for governor and we count the votes equally and if it is really close, we count them again carefully. That is how we do it in Texas, and that is how we do it in Pennsylvania, and in New York and in virtually every other state.

So most of the arguments against direct election of the president really don't wash because their logic applies equally to governors, and yet Americans have embraced direct elections, one person one vote, for governors everywhere. The only arguments for the Electoral College that really work are arguments about inertia or about federalism — arguments about how changing the existing presidential election rules will have unintended and disastrous consequences, or arguments about how presidents are distinctly different than governors for foreign policy or other reasons. Many of the arguments that we heard earlier are deeply unpersuasive if we take the 50 states as data points.

Here is another example of unfortunate inattention to the state constitutional experience. On the very first page of his intriguing essay, Professor Levinson asserts that the current federal separation-of-powers gridlock exists simply because Article V of the federal Constitution makes the document nearly impervious to structural constitution change, howsoever sensible. I disagree. If Article V were the only explanation, why do states have this same basic separation of powers model (with its attendant risk of gridlock)?

Professor Levinson apparently dislikes the presidential veto, but every state governor has a veto pen. Now the states don't all have the same two-thirds rule for veto overrides. Some of them have three-fifths rules. Some of them have two-majority rules. But quite a lot of them have two-thirds rules — and not because these states were born that way. At the time of the Constitution, 8 of the 13 states did not have independently elected chief executives. They had chief executives picked in the modern prime ministerial way, by legislative majorities. Over the ensuing decades, they changed from that. In 1787, only one state governor had a strong personal veto pen. Since then, the states one by one have chosen to sculpt their governors in the image of the president. Maybe the states have been mistaken in doing so, but serious political science needs to engage and analyze this state data, not ignore it with a grand theoretical sweep of the hand.

Let's talk about judicial review. We can make theoretical arguments for it or against it. But one key fact to keep in view is that all the states have state court judicial review of state legislatures under state constitutions. Again, we can talk about interesting differences among the states. None of them, except Rhode Island, has the pure life tenure model. But all have versions of judicial review. This key fact was not even mentioned by Professor Macedo or Professor Tushnet in their otherwise thoughtful discussion of judicial review. Both of them were more inclined to make international comparisons than to focus on the 50 states. Indeed, Professor Tushnet has a great casebook on comparative constitutions using international comparisons. But the state constitutional comparisons are also worthy of our attention.

On the last page of his essay, Professor Tushnet says that "perhaps popular acceptance of judicial review is more a sign of resignation to the fact that democratic majorities have been unable to eliminate a practice favored by political elites than a positive support for the practice." Perhaps, but is there elite domination in every one of the states? Many states have a process of initiative and referendum, but they haven't gotten rid of judicial review. Now, state court judicial review might exist in a weaker form precisely because state constitutions are easier to amend, but all this needs to be brought into the analysis.

One last point about the states. The state constitutions provide road-tested exemplars of constitutional reform and therefore define a sensible American reform agenda. This is a Brandeisian point. Reforms get road tested by individual states and then they can be copied by other states and eventually federalized.

Professor Rabkin is particularly anxious about what he terms "entirely novel and untried designs." For much of American history, the state constitutional experience has defined the parameters of what are plausible federal reforms. In general—albeit with some notable exceptions—stuff that the states have done is a plausible basis for a proposed federal constitutional reform, and stuff that the states have not done is not. So instead of each academic coming up with an individual list of his favorite constitutional reforms, a la Levinson or Sabato, I suggest that serious reformers should remember the people, remember the states, and be real political scientists—data-driven scholars who look at the actual state experience.

To be more specific: Westminister-style parliamentary government is un-American. Maybe it should be American, but it ain't. So that particular theoretical reform bandwagon is not going anywhere. Or take the idea of a single, nonrenewable six-year presidential term. This proposed federal reform looks weird because we don't elect governors that way. Another example: If we are going to have direct election of the president, I personally might prefer a system of single transferable voting—a.k.a. an instant runoff system. But the states don't do things that way, so that is not going to be the version that is the most plausible federal reform proposal. If we do move away from the current Electoral College system, I suggest that we will move towards picking presidents just like we pick the state governors. How about the recent reform suggestion of super-senators? No, Professor Sabato. No, Professor Levinson. Labor leaders ex officio or ex-presidents ex officio are not going to be part of the US Senate, because upper houses of state legislatures do not look like this. If this proposed reform is truly a good idea, get it road tested. Get Cambridge, Massachusetts to adopt it first and then maybe New Hampshire and then several other states, and only then should we seriously put it on the possible federal reform agenda.

Independent counsels are mentioned in passing by Professor Pious. The reason that that independent counsels embody a plausible image of federal reform is that we have state attorneys general who are independent of governors. In my view, having federal judges appoint federal independent counsels violates various provisions of our existing federal constitution, but a system of independent counsels would be a perfectly plausible federal constitutional amendment to propose because it would fit with actual the American practice at the state level.

Remember the Amendments

My third admonition is to remember the amendments. We have an extraordinary array of federal constitutional amendments. They create an amazing tradition and trajectory.

Daniel Lazare quotes a piece from *Newsweek* as follows: "[T]he founders did provide an amendment process and it's served us rather well over time. Not perfectly, God knows, but it's enabled us to muddle along for well over two centuries, always expanding not contracting individual liberty under law." Lazare says that this comforting line from *Newsweek* is not true as a description of actual American practice. American liberty over the centuries, says Lazare, has in fact ebbed and flowed. But as a description of our constitutional amendments, the *Newsweek* line is pretty accurate, and the amendment pattern it describes is quite remarkable.

As a younger man, I was quite critical of the federal Constitution's Article V. I thought it set the amendment bar too high. But upon further reflection, here is one strong argument in favor of Article V: America has had many good amendments that have expanded liberty and equality, but very few bad amendments. This fact should be duly weighed when we ponder the balance of risk that Professor Levinson identified in his remarks.

When many Americans today speak of the appeal of greater democracy, that intuition is not just purely subjective. The intuition is also rooted in an interpretation (sometimes implicit) of the entirety of our constitutional tradition, a tradition with an extraordinary pro-democratic arc. This arc gives liberals a conservative argument of a certain sort: "Here is what proper amendments are—amendments that that actually expand liberty and equality in keeping with what our tradition has in fact been."

I find Professor Rabkin's chapter quite musical. But there was one clunky note, when he talked about the Nineteenth Amendment in a rather dismissive way. From a democratic point of view this Women's Suffrage Amendment is an extraordinary achievement. It doubles the eligible franchise. None of the contributors did justice to this amendment, and most do not fully integrate all the amendments into their thinking about their respective topics.

Professor Graber's chapter is an exception. He explained that we all must think about how different aspects of the Constitution connect up—for example, how slavery might have been connected to various other constitutional issues that do not on their surface seem to be directly concerned with slavery. In the same spirit, let me return to the Nineteenth Amendment, which is not mentioned in the Edwards-Sabato Electoral College debate. The amendment should have been mentioned because it is hugely relevant both to what the problems with the current Electoral College are (the Edwards position) and also to what the problems of Electoral College reform would be (the Sabato position).

Suppose that the Constitution had provided for a directly elected President and then, much later, a women's suffrage movement emerged, and became the focus of debate and reform. In this world, some states would begin to enfranchise their women and others would not—but then these resisting states would pay a political price, as I shall explain momentarily.

As history actually unfolded, with the real-life Electoral College, a given state got the same number of electoral votes whether or not it let women vote. So the actual Electoral College did little to spur reform. It rewarded states even if they made it hard for people to vote and had a very limited franchise. But in a direct presidential world, any state that let women vote would have dramatically increased—in most cases, doubled—its electoral clout. Direct election would have created a very different political dynamic, a real spur to suffrage expansion. In the absence of direct election, what we in fact experienced was a certain dampening force, a dog that didn't bark, a spur that did not exist. As Professors Graber and Finkelman and other slavery scholars understand, the Founders' (and especially the Twelfth Amendment framers') Electoral College was not designed to expand suffrage but to prop up slavery.

Now, what does all this mean for Electoral College reform today? It suggests that under a future direct election system, states might have some incentives to increase turnout. Up to a certain point good, this would be good. It would be federalism in action: Some states would likely facilitate absentee balloting; others would opt for same-day registration; still others would make Election Day a paid holiday; and so on. But if California says "we are going to let 17-year-olds vote" and Texas says "well, then we are going to let 16-year-olds vote" and then Arkansas says "well, then we are going to let dogs vote," that arms race might well raise some issues requiring federal oversight.

We do not have quite the same issues within each state election for state governor, because suffrage eligibility rules tend to be more uniform within each state. But not across the several states—so federalism here does make a difference, and presidential races in this respect are different from gubernatorial races. Under a direct election system, we would, for the very first time in American history, have votes from different states (with different franchise rules) put in the same bin. I myself favor a direct election system, but I do see that this new system would raise some very serious issues requiring more federal oversight.

Alas, we do not find any detailed discussion of these key issues in the Edwards-Sabato debate over the Electoral College. But I think we would have heard more about these issues had the debaters, for example, paid more attention to the Nineteenth Amendment experience, and how the women's suffrage issue would have played out differently in an alternative, direct-election universe.

One final point about the amendments: the amendments also illustrate the power of informal adaptation as a precursor to formalization. Before we adopted a formal two-term amendment for the presidency, we had an informal two-term tradition. Before we formally had direct election of senators, via the Seventeenth Amendment, we had a series of informal improvisations moving towards direct election. For example, we had the Lincoln-Douglas debates in which each party told the electorate whom it would back for the US Senate even before the general election of state legislators had taken place, thereby enabling that state election to become a proxy vote for senator. Later, some states began to hold senatorial primaries, which approximated direct election of senators whenever one party in effect dominated the state. We also began to develop the "Oregon plan" whereby legislators promised that they would vote for the person picked in a statewide senatorial beauty contest election. These are examples of what Professor Melnick referred to (quoting Weaver and Rockman) as "countervailing mechanisms." They are informal adaptations working around the formal rules in various ways. And such informal adaptations laid the groundwork for many of the formal constitutional amendments that followed. When we begin to think about reforms for the future, it is very helpful to remember how past reforms were actually achieved.

Imagine

My final admonition, with apologies to John Lennon, is that we must imagine.

Let me draw your attention to a fascinating line that appears in Professor Levinson's essay: "It is only with regard to the United States Constitution, drafted 220 years ago, that what I'm sometimes temped to call a cult of stasis stifles our imaginative faculties." Freud would have had so much fun with that claim that "our imaginative faculties" were being stifled. Does Professor Levinson mean that our mental processes—our cognitive faculties—are being constrained? Or does he mean that our imaginative tenured and untenured colleagues in the academy—our university faculties—were being repressed? Maybe he means both. But my claim in conclusion is that if we are sufficiently imaginative, we would need to rethink many of the things that are said in the preceding essays about how we cannot change certain things in our existing system.

Take the Senate. (Please.) Many critics of the Constitution say that they do not love the Senate's malapportioned structure, but that Americans are stuck with equality of representation in the Senate because unless every state agrees, America cannot get rid of this terrible malapportionment. That is what Melnick, Levinson, and Lazare all say. Well, I say: Imagine!

An ordinary Article V amendment could say the following: "The Senate shall continue to be apportioned as it always has been—two Senators for each state—but all powers heretofore vested in the Senate, except the power to confirm the nominations of assistant postmasters, shall hereinafter be vested in a new body, which shall be known as the Fenate." That's an ordinary Article V amendment. It would as a practical matter require the support of two-thirds of the House, two-thirds of the Senate, and three-quarters of the states, but it would not require state unanimity.

At this point, we need to confront a second issue: What should be the formula for apportionment in our imagined Fenate? Professor Rabkin rightly says that credible reformers need to offer an actual alternative to the status quo. My preferred alternative would be that each state shall be entitled to a number of senators equal to the state's percentage of the national population, rounded to the nearest whole number—provided that each state would have at least one senator. What that would mean, just to work out the math, is that each state that has less than 1.5 percent of the total population would get one senator. That would be about half the states today. California would get about a dozen Senators. When you add everything up it turns out that the Senate on this formula would be somewhere around 108 members if we use the figures from the most recent census. And our imagined Fenate would look like the House of Representatives. It would not be too weird or outlandish. It would not look oddly European.

But of course, Wyoming would probably not embrace my imagined Fenate Amendment; nor would other small states. Even under the ordinary rules of Article V, a small number of small states could realistically block this proposed constitutional reform.

So here's another imaginative point: Our imaginary amendment need not go into effect immediately. Rather, we should support an amendment that would not go into effect today or tomorrow or even for the next 50 years. Let's have a national conversation about what fair rules should be for the future. We today can be founders, too—founders for the nonimmediate but vastly expansive future. It is hard for any generation to generate fair procedural rules for itself from scratch. Any set of procedural rules would have to bootstrap itself into existence; would be plagued by infinite regress problems—how do we decide how we decide how we decide?—and would be prey to all sorts of extortionist threats created by current distributions of power that may themselves be unfair. Instead, I am proposing that Americans today begin a Rawlsian conversation behind a veil of ignorance about what the fair rules would be for our nonimmediate posterity.

Current residents of Wyoming may be biased toward Wyoming for reasons of self-interest; but they may also understand that their children and grandchildren may well not be Wyoming residents. Their posterity may well be more likely to be Californians and New Yorkers. Now, if today's residents of Wyoming are fully persuaded that the Senate's apportionment structure is the proper one in principle for all time, fine. But if they are not fully persuaded of this, but only favor the status quo because it works to their immediate advantage, then a time-delayed amendment proposal can help them put aside immediate considerations of self-interest and think instead about long-term principle.

Let's call these proposed time-delayed measures sunrise amendments, as distinct from sunset laws. Sunrise clauses are hardly something novel. The Constitution's 1808 clause concerning the international slave trade is a sunrise provision. The Eighteenth Amendment also contains a sunrise/time-lag clause.

Consider also the infamous three-fifths clause. Could the Framers have done any better than this? I think so. Here is what the framers should have said: Three-fifths—heck, four-fifths!—now, but in 1810 two-fifths, and in 1840 and thereafter, zero-fifths. This sliding scale/sunrise clause would have put the Constitution's extra credit for extra slaves on a path of ultimate extinction. If the framers agreed that slavery was essential to their existing economy but also agreed that it was wrong in principle to get extra clout for extra slaves, a sensible approach would have been a sliding scale sunrise clause for apportionment.

A few final, imaginative reactions to various proposed constitutional reforms that are often claimed to be desirable but impossible to achieve. The debate over the Electoral College often seems to say that America could not achieve a direct national vote system without a constitutional amendment. But wait! Imagine. Not only is there a current movement underway to achieve direct national vote via coordinated state action—the so-called national popular vote initiative—but I have argued elsewhere that America could also achieve direct national vote, de facto, via an agreement between the two major-party candidates. If both presidential candidates believe that in fact things should be governed by a direct popular vote, they both could publicly commit in advance to abide by national majority-rule election and they could even come up with a detailed set of procedures about how they will actualize and implement that national majority-rule ideal. They could for example have rules about who will arbitrate disputes; they could devise an elaborate regime of private ordering. These things can happen. Most elections are not decided by courts. Rather, they are decided by the loser who concedes—by a certain regime of private ordering between the candidates, if you will. So there are ways to do things if we are imaginative. And then an informal constitutional tradition can emerge, and lay the foundation for a later formal amendment on the two-term model.

How about the issue of life tenure for Supreme Court justices? Are we stuck with life tenure, absent a formal amendment? Not at all. First of all, we could probably have a statute that says that a newly appointed Supreme Court Justice may serve in the Article III judiciary for life, but on the Supreme Court for only, say, 18 years; after that, the justice must sit on circuit courts and only sit on the Supreme Court when the court is understaffed because of recusals or vacancies. Alternatively, the Senate could from now on ask every nominee to make a certain kind of promise at the confirmation hearings. Not a promise that the nominee, once confirmed, will rule a certain way on a certain legal issue—abortion or school prayer. Rather, a promise that the nominee will step down at, say, age 75 or after, say, 18 years of service. The British do things like that. They have informal conventions, understandings. So do Americans. Not everything requires a formal constitutional amendment.

How about the lame duck problem? Professor Levinson is particularly worried about the time window when the electorate has clearly repudiated an incumbent president but the incoming president with the fresh mandate cannot yet begin his formal constitutional term. Professor Pious notes that one of the worst times in American history was the lame duck period right before Lincoln grasped the reins of power. If we are imaginative, this problem is easy enough to solve without a constitutional amendment. We need only change the date of the election, and/or use the Twenty-fifth Amendment in creative ways to have presidents step down when their mandates have expired.

Continuity in government? Again, there are things you can do short of Article V amendment that will solve most of the obvious problems.

Where am I coming up with some of these imaginative solutions? From American history. Before we had the Seventeenth Amendment, we had "countervailing mechanisms" of an informal sort—the Oregon Plan and so on. In 1916 Woodrow Wilson laid plans to step down early if he lost his bid for reelection. Had Charles Evans Hughes won the election in 1916, Woodrow Wilson was going appoint Hughes to be secretary of state, and then Wilson and his Vice President would step down, leaving Hughes as the acting President under the presidential succession law then in operation. Had this transition occurred, we would not have had a long lame duck period. Hughes would have been in power British-style right after the election. And the Twenty-fifth Amendment currently allows for something similar to occur. So I am not getting these proposed solutions only from my own imagination; rather, I am getting them by heeding the admonitions I gave you before to look at actually state practice, to look at past amendments, to take seriously the teachings of history.

In sum, to those of you who think the current situation is deeply dysfunctional, here is the good news: the Constitution, the framers, your forbears—all these are not the insuperable obstacles to reform than you thought they were. The current regime is far more corrigible than you have acknowledged.

Now all you have to do is persuade your fellow citizens in the here and now that you genuinely have a better mousetrap. Good luck.

Notes

Chapter 1

1. Jeremy Rabkin, "Constitutional Unease," *The American Spectator*, May 2008, pp. 64–66.

2. John R. Vile, *Rewriting the Unites States Constitution: An Examination of Proposals from Reconstruction to the Present* (New York: Praeger, 1991), 155.

3. John F. Manley and Kenneth M. Dolbeare, *The Case Against the Constitution: From the Antifederalists to the Present* (Armonk, NY: M.E. Sharpe, 1987), ix.

4. Quoted in, Clyde W. Barrow, "Charles A. Beard's Social Democracy: A Critique of the Populist-Progressive Style in American Political Thought," *Polity*, Vol. 21, No. 2, (Winter 1988), 254.

5. Howard E. Dean, "J. Allen Smith: Jeffersonian Critic of the Federalist State," *American Political Science Review*, Vol. 50, No. 4 (Dec., 1956), 1094.

6. J. Allen Smith, *The Spirit of American Government* (Cambridge, MA: Harvard University Press, 1965), pp. 31–32, p. 298.

7. Ibid, 305.

8. Ibid, 296.

9. Ibid, 293.

10. Dean, "J. Allen Smith: Jeffersonian Critic of the Federalist State," 1096.

11. Daniel Lazare, *The Frozen Republic: How the Constitution is Paralyzing Democracy* (New York: Harcourt Brace & Company, 1996), 45.

12. Woodrow Wilson, *Congressional Government: A Study in American Government* (New York: Meridian Books, 1956), 27.

13. Quoted in Daniel D. Stid, *The President as Statesman: Woodrow Wilson and the Constitution* (Lawrence, Kansas: University Press of Kansas, 1998), 11.

14. Wilson, *Congressional Government*, 48.

15. Stid, *The President as Statesman*, 12.

16. Charles A. Beard, *An Economic Interpretation of the Constitution of the United States* (New York: Macmillan Company, 1941), 324.

17. Pope McCorkle, "Charles Beard and the Constitution Reconsidered," *The American Journal of Legal History*, Vol. 8, No 4 (Oct. 1984), 316.

18. Cecelia M. Kenyon, "Men of Little Faith: the Anti-Federalists on the Nature of Representative Government," *The William and Mary Quarterly*, third Series, Vol. 12, No. 1 (Jan. 1955), 4.

19. Ibid, 23.

20. Ibid, 25.

21. "Brutus," Essay 1, October 18, 1778, in *The Anti-Federalist Papers and the Constitutional Convention Debates*, edited By Ralph Ketcham, (New York: Signet Classic, 2003), 275.

22. "Agrippa," Letter XVIII, February 5, 1788, in *The Antifederalists*, edited by Cecelia M. Kenyon (Boston: Northeastern University Press, 1985), 154.

23. "John De Witt," Letter III, November 5, 1787, in *The Antifederalists*, edited by Kenyon, 105.

24. Robert A. Dahl, *How Democratic is the American Constitution?* (New Haven: Yale University Press, 2001), 15

25. Robin L. Einhorn, "Patrick Henry's Case against the Constitution: The Structural Problem with Slavery," *Journal of the Early Republic*, Vol. 22, No. 4, (Winter, 2002), 549–550.

26. Wendell Phillips, editor, *The Constitution a Pro-Slavery Compact or Extracts from the Madison Papers, Etc.*, Third Edition, Enlarged, (New York: American Anti-Slavery Society, 1856), 9.

27. James H. Hutson, "The Creation of the Constitution: Scholarship at a Standstill," *Reviews in American History*, Vol. 12, No. 4 (Dec, 1984), 465, 466.

28. Phillips, *The Constitution a Pro-Slavery Compact*, 8.

29. Ibid, 9.

30. Frederick Douglass, "The Constitution of the United States: Is It Pro-Slavery or Anti-Slavery?" Retrieved from TeachingAmericanHistory.org.

31. Smith, *The Spirit of American Government*, 27–28.

Chapter 2

1. Simon Schama, *Citizens: A Chronicle of the French Revolution* (New York: Knopf, 1992), 57–9.

2. Quoted in G.D.H. Cole and Raymond Postgate, *The Common People 1746–1946* (London: Methuen, 1971), 91.

3. According to the US Census, the thirteen least populous states (Wyoming, Vermont, North Dakota, Alaska, South Dakota, Delaware, Montana, Rhode Island, Hawaii, New Hampshire, Maine, Idaho, and Nebraska) have an estimated combined population of 13.4 million as of July 1, 2008, versus 304 million for the nation as a whole. Wyoming's population, meanwhile, was just 532,668. See http://www.census.gov/popest/states/NST-ann-est.html.

4. Delaware's population was 59,000 as of 1790 while Virginia's was 692,000. See US Bureau of the Census, *Historical Statistics of the United States, Colonial Times to 1970* (Washington, D.C.: US Government Printing Office, 1975), Series A 195–209.

5. Edmund Burke, *Reflections on the Revolution in France* (Stanford: Stanford University Press, 2001), 170.

6. "[W]ith the possible exception of Descartes, no theologian or philosopher has seriously maintained that God can bring it about that contradictories are true together." Anthony Kenny, *The God of the Philosophers* (Oxford: Clarendon Press, 1979), 93.

7. The ten smallest states according to the most recent estimates are: Wyoming, Vermont, North Dakota, Alaska, South Dakota, Delaware, Montana, Hawaii, New Hampshire, and Maine, with a total population of just over nine million. If Senate seats were accorded on the basis of population, they would have three in all. Instead, they have thirty.

8. Frances E. Lee and Bruce I. Oppenheimer, *Sizing Up the Senate: The Unequal Consequences of Equal Representation* (Chicago: University of Chicago Press, 1999), 10–11.

9. Colin Randall, "Anger in France as politician under suspicion wins an election—and immunity from criminal charges," *Daily Telegraph*, Sept. 30, 2004, p. 18; Julian Nundy, "Senate, after threatening to block legislation, bows to wish of country's most powerful men," *Globe and Mail*, March 5, 1999.

10. For the state-by-state distribution of electoral votes, see http://www.archives.gov/federal-register/electoral-college/2008/allocation.html.

11. For a state-by-state racial breakdown, see U.S. Census table SC-EST2007-05, available at:

http://www.census.gov/popest/states/asrh/SC-EST2007-04.html.

12. Cole and Postgate, *The Common People*, 155; Clinton Rossiter, ed., *The Federalist Papers* (New York: Mentor, 1961), vii.

13. Richard Brookhiser, *What Would the Founders Do? Our Questions, Their Answers* (New York: Basic Books, 2007), 1.

14. Carl Hulse, "Filibuster Fight Nears Showdown," *New York Times*, May 8, 2005.

15. Jon Meacham, "America remains a center-right nation—a fact that a President Obama would forget at his peril," *Newsweek*, October 27, 2008, 32.

16. Out of 219,259,405 Americans aged twenty and above, some 2,299,116, or 1.05 per cent, are currently in jail or prison. See: http://www.sentencingproject.org/Admin/Documents/publications/inc_factsaboutprisons.pdf and http://www.census.gov/popest/national/asrh/NC-EST2007-sa.html.

17. David R. Sands and S.A. Miller, "Obama to sign $410 billion catchall with 9,000 earmarks," *Washington Times*, March 11, 2009.

18. Sheryl Gay Stolberg, "What's Wrong With a Healthy Helping of Pork?," *New York Times*, May 28, 2006.

19. Sidney George Fisher, *The Trial of the Constitution* (New York: Negro University Press, 1969), 38–9, 57.

20. Michael Kammen, *A Machine That Would Go of Itself: The Constitution in American Culture* (New York: Knopf, 1986), 186.

21. "President on President: Bill Clinton's Take on Things," *ABC News Transcript*, February 20, 2009.

22. As Reagan said in declaring "Small Business Week" in 1983: "Our Founding Fathers envisioned a nation whose strength and vitality would emerge from the ingenuity of its people and their commitment to individual liberty. They understood that a nation's prosperity is dependent on the freedom of its citizens to pursue their hopes, dreams, and creative ambitions. American entrepreneurs and small business owners enthusiastically embraced the challenges of freedom and through the miracle of the marketplace set in motion the forces of economic growth that made our nation uniquely productive. This pattern of economic development has inspired people throughout the world to look to America for a better life." 19 Weekly Comp. Pres. Doc. 361, *Public Papers of the Presidents*, Mar. 7, 1983.

23. Charles Duhigg, "Pressured to Take More Risk, Fannie Reached Tipping Point, *New York Times*, February 8, 2009.

Chapter 3

1. Daniel Lazare, *The Frozen Republic, How the Constitution Is Paralyzing Democracy* (New York: Harcourt Brace, 1996); Sanford Levinson, *Our Undemocratic Constitution: Where the Constitution Goes Wrong and How We the People Can Correct It* (Oxford: Oxford University Press, 2006); Larry J. Sabato, *A More Perfect Constitution. 23 Proposals to Revitalize Our Constitution and Make America A Fairer Country* (New York: Walker, 2007).

2. *Federalist* No. 39 (attributed to James Madison) in Alexander Hamilton, James Madison, and John Jay, *The Federalist Papers* ed. Charles Kesler and Clinton Rossiter (Signet Classic, 2003), 236.

3. Sabato, *More Perfect Constitution*, 182–83.

4. Arthur C. Brooks, *Gross National Happiness* (Basic, 2008) reports results from a 2002 international survey at 221–22: Asked whether they were "happy" or "completely happy" 56 percent of American respondents answered yes, compared with 48 percent of respondents in Britain, 35 percent in France, 31 percent in Germany, 22 percent in Poland.

5. "Views of a Changing World, June 2003," Report from Pew Global Attitudes Project (available

at http: pewglobal.org/reports/pdf/185.pdf), reporting only 32 percent of Americans agree that "success is determined by forces outside our control" (63 percent disagree), while 68 percent agree in Germany (31 percent disagree), 54 percent agree in France (44 percent disagree), 48 percent agree in Britain (48 percent disagree), 63 percent agree in Poland (29 percent disagree).

6. Daniel Lazare, *The Velvet Coup: The Constitution, the Supreme Court and the Decline of American Democracy* (London: Verso, 2001).

7. For useful overview of the Australian debate — complaining that constitutional change is easier in Canada, because not subject to direct referendum — see Glenn Patmore, "Choosing the Republic: The Legal and Constitutional Steps in Australia and Canada," *Queen's Law Journal*, Vol. 31, 2006.

8. For background on the early stages of this "crisis," see H. Peter Russell, *Constitutional Odyssey, Can Canadians Become A Sovereign People?* (Toronto: University of Toronto Press, 1992).

9. Grant Huscroft, "A Constitutional 'Work in Progress'?" *Supreme Court Law Review* (Canada), Vol. 23, No. 2, (2004) on difficulties with the activist jurisprudence of the Canadian Supreme Court.

10. *Federalist* No. 49, 378.

11. For a useful overview of the system, see the initial essay ("Reception of the ECHR in National Legal Orders") in Helen Keller and Alec Stone Sweet, eds., *A Europe of Rights, The Impact of the ECHR on National Legal Systems* (Oxford: Oxford University Press, 2008), explaining the "constitutionalizing" force of the Human Rights Court's jurisprudence, though it is not directly binding on national judges. An account of British experience in this volume (Samantha Besson, "The Reception Process in Ireland and the United Kingdom") concludes that in Britain, with its traditions of parliamentary supremacy, national judges have given "quasi-constitutional status" to the European Convention, whereas Irish judges, working with "a vibrant tradition of constitutional rights and creative judicial review" (under Ireland's national constitution) have treated the ECHR as little more than a "legal irritant" (97).

12. *Notes of Debates in the Federal Convention of 1787, Reported by James Madison* (Norton, 1987), 410 (Aug. 8).

13. *Federalist* No. 63, 378.

14. Sabato, *More Perfect Constitution*, 97–101.

15. *Federalist* No. 41, 253.

16. Levinson, *Undemocratic Constitution*, 6, 173.

17. Lazare, *Velvet Coup*, 10.

18. Sabato, *More Perfect Constitution*, 4.

19. Levinson, *Undemocratic Constitution*, 12.

Chapter 4

1. This originates from Isaiah, 28:18: "And your covenant with death shall be disannulled, and your agreement with hell shall not stand; when the overflowing scourge shall pass through, then ye shall be trodden down by it." (King James Trans.) An earlier version of this chapter appears in Paul Finkelman, *Slavery and the Founders: Race and Liberty in the Age of Jefferson*, 2nd ed. (Armonk, NY: M.E. Shape, 2001), 3–36.

2. William Lloyd Garrison to Rev. Samuel J. May, July 17, 1845, in Walter M. Merrill, ed. *The Letters of William Lloyd Garrison* (Cambridge, MA: Harvard University Press, 1973) 3:303. *The Liberator*, May 6, 1842. See also William M. Wiecek, *The Sources of Antislavery Constitutionalism in America, 1760–1848* (Ithaca, NY: Cornell University Press, 1977), Chapter 10; and James Brewer Stewart, *Holy Warriors: The Abolitionists and American Slavery* (New York: Hill and Wang, 1976), 98–99, 158–159.

3. Wendell Phillips, *Can Abolitionists Vote or Take Office Under the United States Constitution?*

(New York: American Anti-Slavery Society, 1845), 3.

4. Justice Joseph Story, a native of Massachusetts, took this position in *Prigg v. Pennsylvania*, 41 U.S. (16 Pet.) 339 (1842). See also, Paul Finkelman, "Story Telling on the Supreme Court: *Prigg v. Pennsylvania* and Justice Joseph Story's Judicial Nationalism," *Supreme Court Review* (1994) 247–94.

5. James Henry Hammond, "Speech on the Admission of Kansas under the Lecompton Constitution," March 4, 1858, in Paul Finkelman, *Defending Slavery: Proslavery in the Old South* (Boston: Bedford Books, 2003) 85.

6. Samuel J. May, *Some Recollections of Our Antislavery Conflict* (Boston: Fields and Osgood, 1869) 143–44. May offered this confession after the Civil War was over, when he could "rejoice, therefore, with joy unspeakable that the question is at length practically settled...."

7. Wendell Phillips, *The Constitution A Pro-Slavery Compact; or, Selections from the Madison Papers*, 2d ed. (New York: American Anti-Slavery Society, 1845), v–vi.

8. Eric Foner, *Free Soil, Free Labor, Free Men: The Ideology of the Republican Party before the Civil War* (New York: Oxford University Press, 1970), chap. 3; Salmon P. Chase, *Reclamation of Fugitive from Service* (Cincinnati, Ohio: R.P. Donough, and Co., 1847). This was Chase's written brief in *Jones v. Van Zandt*, 46 U.S. (5 How.) 215 (1847). Here Chase was unsuccessful in his attempt to persuade the Supreme Court to overturn the verdict against Van Zandt for helping a group of fugitive slaves claimed by Jones. William M. Wiecek, "Slavery and Abolition before the United States Supreme Court, 1820–1860," *Journal of American History*, 65 (1978–1979), 34–59. Chase's only success before the Supreme Court was in *Norris v. Cocker*, 54 U.S. (13 How.) 429 (1851) which turned on a technical aspect of a statute. For a discussion of that case, see Paul Finkelman, "Fugitive Slaves, Midwestern Racial Tolerance, and the Value of Justice Delayed," *Iowa Law Review*, 78 (1992) 89, 105–07. The only other antislavery success before the Supreme Court was in *United States v. The Amistad*, 40 U.S. (15 Pet.) 518 (1841), which involved the illegal African slave trade and issues of international law. George Bradburn to Gerrit Smith, December 15, 1846, Gerrit Smith Papers, box 4, Syracuse University, Syracuse, New York. The Garrisonian analysis was not, of course, designed to give aid and comfort to defenders of slavery. The Garrisonians merely read the Constitution and the debates of the Convention and analyzed what they found. Similarly, an acceptance of the Garrisonian view of the Constitution — that it was a document which explicitly protected the institution of slavery — is not an endorsement of the Garrisonian cure: a rejection of political activity and disunion.

9. Max Farrand, ed., *The Records of the Federal Convention of 1787*, rev. ed. (New Haven CT: Yale University Press, 1966), 1:561; 2:415; Jonathan Elliot ed., *The Debates in the Several State Conventions on the Adoption of the Federal Constitution*, 5 vols. (New York: Burt Franklin, 1987, reprint of 1888 edition) 4:176. See also Staughton Lynd, "The Abolitionist Critique of the Constitution," in *Class Conflict, Slavery, and the United States Constitution: Ten Essays* (Indianapolis: Bobbs-Merrill, 1967), 159–160.

10. Curiously, Don Fehrenbacher finds that "only three [clauses of the Constitution] were directly and primarily concerned with the institution of slavery." Fehrenbacher acknowledges only that other clauses "impinged upon slavery." Fehrenbacher also asserts that "the Constitution had some bias toward freedom but was essentially open-ended with respect to slavery" Fehrenbacher fails, however, to explain what part of the Constitution was profreedom, while at the same time ignoring many proslavery aspects of the Constitution. Don E. Fehrenbacher, *The Federal Government and Slavery* (Claremont, Calif.: Claremont Institute, 1984), 3, 6. In his last book Fehrenbacher argued that the Fugitive Clause was the only "unambiguously proslavery provision of the Constitution." Don E. Fehrenbacher, *The Slaveholding Republic: An Account of the United States Government's Relations to Slavery* (New York: Oxford University Press, 2001), 44. For an analysis of the Constitution closer to the one presented here, see Wiecek, *Sources of Antislavery Constitutionalism*, 62–63. Wiecek lists 11 separate clauses in the Constitution that "directly or indirectly accommodated the peculiar institution," but makes no distinction between direct and indirect protections of slavery.

11. Wendell Phillips considered this clause, and the one of Article IV, Section 4, to be among the five key proslavery provisions of the Constitution (*The Constitution A Pro-Slavery Compact*, vi).

12. Although no slave state would have levied such a tax, a free state like New York, Massachusetts, or Pennsylvania might conceivably have taxed products produced in other states but exported through the harbors of New York, Boston, or Philadelphia.

13. Had all 15 slave states remained in the Union, they would to this day be able to prevent an

amendment on any subject. In a fifty-state union, it takes only 13 states to block any amendment.

14. William W. Freehling, "The Founding Fathers and Slavery," *American Historical Review*, 77 (1972), 81, quote at 82.

15. The proslavery implications of this clause did not become fully apparent until the Supreme Court issued its opinion in *Dred Scott v. Sandford*, 60 U.S. (19 How.) 393 (1857). There the Court held that ever free blacks could not sue in diversity in federal courts.

16. *Dred Scott v. Sandford*, 60 U.S. (19 How.) 393 (1857). Throughout the antebellum period the slave states refused to grant privileges and immunities to free blacks from other states or countries. Most of the slave states prohibited free blacks from even entering their jurisdictions. In *Elkison v. Deliesseline*, 8 F. Cas. 493 (1823) Supreme Court Justice William Johnson refused to strike down such a law in South Carolina, although he believed it to be unconstitutional. For more on this problem see Paul Finkelman, *An Imperfect Union: Slavery, Federalism, and Comity* (Chapel Hill, N.C.: University of North Carolina Press, 1981) 109n; Paul Finkelman, *Slavery in the Courtroom* (Washington, D.C.: Government Printing Office, 1985) 256–63 and my articles "States Rights North and South in Antebellum America," in Kermit Hall and James W. Ely, Jr., eds., *An Uncertain Tradition: Constitutionalism and the History of the South* (Athens, GA.: University of Georgia Press, 1989) 125–158 and "The Protection of Black Rights in Seward's New York," *Civil War History*, 34 (1988) 211–234.

17. In *Dred Scott v. Sandford* Chief Justice Taney held unconstitutional the Missouri Compromise, which banned slavery in most of the western territories.

18. Under various clauses of the Constitution the Congress might have protected, limited, or prohibited the interstate slave trade (Article I, Section 8, Paragraph 3), slavery in the District of Columbia or on military bases (Article I, Section 8, Paragraph 17), or slavery in the territories (Article IV, Section 3, Paragraph 2). None of these clauses permitted Congress to touch slavery in the states. Some radical abolitionists argued that under the guarantee clause, Article IV, Section 4, Congress had the right to end slavery in the states. See Wiecek, *Sources of Antislavery Constitutionalism*, 269–271. The delegates in Philadelphia did not debate these clauses with slavery in mind, although, as will be shown later in this essay, the commerce clause was accepted as part of a bargain over the African slave trade.

19. Pinckney quoted in Elliot, ed., *Debates*, 4:286. Patrick Henry, using any argument he could find to oppose the Constitution, feared that, "among ten thousand implied powers which they may assume, they may, if we be engaged in war, liberate every one of your slaves if they please." Elliot, ed., *Debates*, 3:589. Ironically, the implied war powers of the president would be used to end slavery, but only after the South had renounced the Union.

20. Fehrenbacher, *Federal Government and Slavery*, 6 n. 2; Earl Maltz, "Slavery, Federalism, and the Structure of the Constitution," *The American Journal of Legal History* 36 (1992) 468. Maltz argues that because of its respect for federalism the Constitution did not affect slavery as it existed in the states. However, the Constitution interfered with the power of the states in other areas, such as denying them the right to abridge contracts, coin money, set up their own foreign policy, or tax exports or imports. Surely it would not have been beyond the scope of the Constitution to allow Congress to regulate slavery in the states in a number of ways.

21. Elliot, ed., *Debates*, 3:598–99 (Randolph) (emphasis in the original), 4:286 (Pinckney).

22. It is perhaps an exaggeration to assert, as Staughton Lynd has, that the "sectional conflict between North and South was the major tension in the Convention," simply because there were so many other "major" tensions; it is clear, however, that sectional conflicts and the role of slavery in the new nation caused as much tension as any other individual issue ("The Abolitionist Critique," in Lynd, *Class Conflict, Slavery, and the United States Constitution*, 160).

23. Farrand, ed., *Records*, 1:18.

24. In the First Congress the North had 35 representatives and the South had 30. However, after the first federal census the original northern states had 55 members of Congress, the southern states had only 44. Had slaves not been counted for congressional representation, the South's members of the House after 1790 would have been only about 34. In this article I consider the North to be those states which ended slavery before the beginning of the Civil War and the South to include those states which retained slavery until the war. Thus, I consider Delaware to be a southern state, but not New Jersey or New York, although neither had taken steps to end slavery before the Convention. New York

passed its gradual emancipation act in 1799, New Jersey in 1804.

25. Farrand, ed., *Records*, 1:20. In 1790 Virginia had a free population of 454,983. The next largest free populations were Pennsylvania, 430,630; Massachusetts, 378,693; and New York, 318,824. Virginia also had 292,627 slaves, whereas the entire North had only 40,089 slaves.

26. Farrand, ed., *Records*, 1:36–38. It seems likely that the Delaware delegation exaggerated the constraints on their commission in a shrewd attempt to avoid a potentially catastrophic debate over slavery and representation. When the Convention did in fact adopt representation based on population, the Delaware delegates remained and did not threaten to leave.

27. Approval by the Convention did not mean permanent adoption, for until June 20 the Convention debated the proposed Constitution as a Committee of the Whole, which allowed for full discussion without binding the delegates to any final resolution of an issue. Anything approved by the Convention as a Committee of the Whole would have to be voted on again when the Convention was in regular session. Furthermore, under the standing rules of the Convention, delegates were free to ask for a reconsideration of decisions on one day's notice. Finally, all clauses of the new Constitution were eventually sent to two drafting committees, the Committee of Detail and the Committee of Style. The reports of these committees were also subject to full debate and amendment by the entire Convention.

28. Historians presenting the traditional view include Francis Newton Thorpe, *The Story of the Constitution of the United States* (New York: Chautauqua Press, 1891), 131; Max Farrand, *The Framing of the Constitution of the United States* (New Haven, CT: Yale University Press, 1913), 108; Charles Warren, *The Making of the Constitution* (Boston: Little, Brown, 1928), 290–291, 584–586; Clinton Rossiter, *1787: The Grand Convention* (New York: Macmillan, 1966), 173, 188–189.

29. Farrand, ed., *Records*, I, 196. This motion by Sherman somewhat undermines the traditional notion of a split between the "small" and "large" state over representation. Sherman, from the small state of Connecticut, was willing to accept population as a basis for representation in the lower house of the legislature, as long as slaves were not counted, and provided that there was equality in the upper house. A week earlier George Mason of Virginia had suggested the importance of sectionalism in a long speech arguing for an executive "vested in three persons, one chosen from the Northern, one from the Middle, and one from the Southern States" (112–113).

30. For a more complete discussion of Wilson's position on slavery, see Paul Finkelman, "Slavery, the Pennsylvania Delegation, and the Constitutional Convention: The Two Faces of the Keystone State," *Pennsylvania Magazine of History and Biography*, 112 (1988) 49–72.

31. Gerry's arguments must be pieced together from the various notes taken by Madison, Yates, Paterson, Butler and Lansing found in ibid., 201, 205–206, 208, and James H. Hutson, ed., *Supplement to Max Farrand's The Records of the Federal Convention of 1787* (New Haven CT: Yale University Press, 1987), 69–70. (Hereinafter cited as Hutson, *Supplement*).

32. The debate over the three-fifths ratio in the Congress is in Worthington Chauncey Ford et al., eds., *Journals of the Continental Congress, 1774–1789* (Washington, D.C.: Library of Congress, 1904–1937), 25:948–952 (debates of Mar. 28 to Apr. 1, 1783); 24:214–216, 223–224.

33. Rossiter, *The Grand Convention*, 173; Donald L. Robinson, *Slavery in the Structure of American Politics, 1765–1820* (New York: Harcourt, Brace, Jovanovich, 1971), 156–158. Max Farrand adopted a similar analysis in *The Framing of the Constitution*, arguing that "one finds references in contemporary writings to the 'Federal ratio,' as if it were well understood what was meant by that term" (108). It is probably true that many of the delegates at the Convention accepted the ratio of three to five as a proper one for determining the value of slaves in society, but this does not mean that they agreed the ratio ought to be applied to representation.

34. Farrand, ed., *Records*, 1:227. The final draft of the Constitution would omit the word "white," thus leading the antislavery radical Lysander Spooner to argue that the "other persons" referred to resident aliens. Spooner's argument seems more polemical than serious. Lysander Spooner, *The Unconstitutionality of Slavery* (Boston: Bela Marsh, 1845), 94. Whatever strength it had lay in the ambiguity of the wording of the Constitution, which avoided such terms as "slave," "white," and "black."

35. Staughton Lynd makes this argument in "The Compromise of 1787," in *Class Conflict, Slavery, and the United States Constitution*. Gunning Bedford of Delaware observed in the debates of June 30 that Georgia, "though a small State at present," was "actuated by present interest and future prospects."

and North Carolina had "the same motives of present and future interest." Farrand, ed., *Records*, 1:491.

36. Farrand, ed., *Records*, 1:486–87. The day before, June 29, Alexander Hamilton had made a similar observation. Hamilton, not surprisingly perhaps, saw the issue solely in economic terms. "The only considerable distinction of interests, lay between the carrying and non-carrying States, which divide instead of uniting the largest States" (466).

37. As if to directly refute Madison's sectional arguments, Delaware's Gunning Bedford argued that his state had little in common with "South Carolina, puffed up with the possession of her wealth and negroes," or Georgia and North Carolina. All three states had "an eye" on "future wealth and greatness," which was predicated on slavery, and thus they were "united with the great states" against the smaller states like Delaware (ibid., 500 [Yates's notes]). Nevertheless, Delaware would remain a slave state until the adoption of the Thirteenth Amendment. New Jersey, which also opposed representation based on population, might also be considered a slave state. At this time New Jersey had taken no steps to end slavery. New Jersey would be the last northern state to pass a gradual emancipation statute, not doing so until 1804. See, generally, Arthur Zilversmit, *The First Emancipation: The Abolition of Slavery in the North* (Chicago: Univ. of Chicago Press, 1967). In the Virginia ratifying convention James Madison asserted that New York and New Jersey would "probably oppose any attempts to annihilate this species of property" (Elliot, ed., *Debates*, III, 459). However, as William Paterson's subsequent antislavery statements suggest, the New Jersey delegates were even more offended by counting slaves for purposes of representation than they were fearful of population-based representation.

38. Farrand, ed., *Records*, I, 516 (from Yates's notes), 510 (from Madison' notes).

39. Ibid., 526.

40. Ibid., 542.

41. Ibid., 560–561. Paterson's animosity towards counting slaves is indicated in an analysis of state population reprinted ibid., 572. Paterson tried to estimate the population of each state and the numbers of slaves that would augment representation. For the Deep South he noted, "In the lower States the acc[oun]ts are not to be depended on." Paterson was of course correct about the allocation of representation in the slave states. No slave state at this time based representation solely on population. In Virginia, for example, each county had two representatives in the lower house of the state legislature. In South Carolina the representatives per parish varied, but the allocations were not based on slave population. In 1808, when South Carolina did go to a population-based system, the representatives were allocated according to "the whole number of white inhabitants in the State." Ironically, Paterson came from northern slaveholding state, New Jersey, and he personally owned a few slaves.

42. Ibid., 562.

43. Ibid., 1:563; U.S. Constitution, Article I, Section 2, Paragraph 3.

44. Ibid., 1:566.

45. Ibid., 566–567.

46. Ibid., 567.

47. Ibid., 568–570.

48. Ibid., 580–581.

49. Ibid., 1:586–88. South Carolina apparently opposed the three-fifths clause because the state was holding out for full representation for slaves. Maryland opposed the clause because of its current wording. Thus, even though the three-fifths clause had been defeated, it seemed that a majority in favor of it could be found. Delaware, also a slave state, voted no, but this was because that state consistently opposed any representation scheme based on population.

50. Ibid., 594.

51. Ibid., 593.

52. Ibid, 593.

53. Ibid., 597. The two divided delegations were Massachusetts and South Carolina. In the former delegation some members apparently opposed this concession to the South. In the latter, some members apparently were holding out for full representation for slaves. In this debate Pierce Butler had argued

for full representation for blacks (ibid., 592). The two negative votes came from Delaware and New Jersey, states which had consistently opposed population-based representation.

54. Ibid., 1:592.

55. Farrand, ed., *Records*, I, 601–602. Gouverneur Morris would later argue that the application of the three-fifths clause to direct taxes was inserted "as a bridge to assist" the Convention "over a certain gulph" caused by slavery. Once the Convention had passed this point, Morris was ready to abandon direct taxation based on the three-fifths clause (ibid., II, 106).

56. Ibid., I, 602–603.

57. Ibid., 603–604.

58. Ibid., 605.

59. Ibid., II, 9–10.

60. Ibid., II, 13, 15. The negative votes were from Virginia, South Carolina, Georgia, and Pennsylvania.

61. Ibid., 17. The recommittal vote ended in a tie (and thus lost). The only northern state to vote for it was Connecticut, which almost always voted with the Deep South on issues concerning slavery. The only Deep South state to oppose the recommittal was North Carolina.

62. Ibid., I, 500; II, 27.

63. Ibid., 30–32. Roger Sherman, who virtually always voted with the South on important matters, also opposed direct election of the president.

64. Ralph Ketcham, *James Madison: A Biography* (New York: Macmillan, 1971), 181, 186–89. Madison did not have unlimited faith in the people, as his essay "Vices of the Political System of the United States" indicates and indeed, he had some sympathies for the indirect election of officials because such a system limited the power of the people. However, this is not the position he took in the Convention, where he argued for the theoretical value of direct election, but in the end opposed it, at least in part because of slavery.

65. Farrand, ed., *Records*, II, 56–57. The acceptance of the Electoral College based on the House of Representatives took place on July 20, the day after Madison's speech (64). On July 25 the Convention reconsidered this vote. Once again Madison argued that the North would have an advantage in a popular election, although here Madison did not specifically mention slavery (111). For a more extensive discussion of this issue see Paul Finkelman, "The Proslavery Origins of the Electoral College," *Cardozo Law Review,* 23 (2002): 1145–1157.

66. Ironically, this antidemocratic system which Madison ultimately supported subsequently had a major impact on his career. Thomas Jefferson's victory in the election of 1800, and Madison's elevation to the position of secretary of state and heir apparent, would be possible only because of the electoral votes the southern states gained on account of their slaves. This point is made by Lynd in "The Abolitionist Critique," in *Class Conflict, Slavery, and the United States Constitution,* 178; and Robinson, *Slavery in the Structure of American Politics,* 405. Many northerners believed the outcome of the 1812 election would have been different if it were not for the three-fifths clause, although this is probably not the case. However, without the three-fifths clause John Quincy Adams might have had more electoral votes than Andrew Jackson and might have been elected outright in 1824.

67. Farrand, ed., *Records*, II, 95.

68. Ibid., 177–189. All references to numbered sections are to those of the printed report, as reproduced in ibid. That report goes up to Article XXII because there are two articles numbered VI.

69. Ibid., 220.

70. Ibid., 220–223.

71. Ibid., 223.

72. For example, North Carolina's Richard Spaight expressed fear that the capital would always remain in New York City, "especially if the President should be a Northern Man" (*ibid.*, 261). In debates over qualifications for office holding, clear sectional differences emerged. Southerners usually favored property qualifications and strict residency, or even nativity qualifications. Northerners did not. Ellsworth of Connecticut argued that a meaningful property qualification in the South would

preclude almost all northerners from holding office, and a fair qualification in the North would be meaningless in the South, where the delegates presumed there was more wealth (ibid., 248–249, 267–272).

73. Ibid., 305–308.

74. Ibid., 306.

75. Ibid., 360, 363–364.

76. Ibid., 363–365.

77. Ibid., 2:369–370. During the ratification process proponents of the Constitution would similarly confuse the power to end "the slave trade" after 1808, which Congress had, with congressional power to end the slavery itself, which Congress clearly did not have. James Wilson, for example, told the Pennsylvania ratifying convention that after "the lapse of a few years ... Congress will have power to exterminate slavery from within our borders" (Elliot, ed., *Debates*, 2:484). Since Wilson attended all the debates over this clause, it is impossible to accept this statement as his understanding of the slave trade clause. More likely, he simply made this argument to win support for the Constitution. In New Hampshire a supporter of the Constitution also argued that the slave trade clause gave Congress the power to end slavery. He was quickly disabused of this notion by Joshua Atherton (ibid., 2:207).

78. Ibid., 369–370. On scholarly and popular misunderstandings of Mason's views on slavery, see Peter Wallenstein, "Flawed Keepers of the Flame: The Interpreters of George Mason," *Virginia Magazine of History and Biography,* 102 (April, 1994) 229–260, quoted at 253.

79. Farrand, ed., *Records*, II, 378 (McHenry's notes).

80. Ibid., 370–371.

81. Ibid., 371–375.

82. Ibid.

83. Ibid.

84. Ibid., 372–373. Wilson's position here must be contrasted with the position he took in the state ratifying convention (see above, n. 74). Nathaniel Gorham of Massachusetts also registered his opposition to the slave trade, but only after the issue was recommitted.

85. Ibid., 374. McHenry's notes on this debate are quite revealing. Although not attributing remarks to any particular delegate, McHenry's notes make clear that part of the conflict between Virginia and the Deep South on the issue was economic. Virginia had surplus slaves to sell south, and the value of those slaves would be undermined by the African trade.

86. Ibid., 414–415.

87. Ibid., 415–416. The Convention then changed the wording of the tax provision of the clause, limiting the tax on slaves to ten dollars. Walter Berns in "The Constitution and the Migration of Slaves," *Yale Law Journal*, 78 (1968–1969), 198, argues that the term "migration" in the slave trade clause referred to the interstate slave trade, and that the term "importation" referred to the African slave trade. If this analysis were correct, then it would appear that the delegates from the Deep South were willing to allow Congress to prohibit the domestic slave trade as well as the African slave trade after 1808. This analysis defies all understanding of the Convention. Berns, moreover, provides no evidence that anyone at the Constitutional Convention or in any of the state ratifying conventions believed this. As William Wiecek more accurately argues in *Sources of Antislavery Constitutionalism*, 75, the term "migration" was "potentially a weapon in the hands of moderate abolitionists" of the mid-nineteenth century. But certainly no one in the Convention saw it that way. More importantly, in the nineteenth century only a few radical opponents of slavery thought the clause could be used this way. At no time before 1861 did any president, leader of Congress, or a majority in either house of Congress accept this analysis.

88. Farrand, ed., *Records*, 2:443. This problem is examined in Finkelman, *An Imperfect Union*.

89. Ibid. James Hutson has found a draft of the fugitive slave clause in the Pierce Butler papers that is not in Butler's handwriting and concluded that this unknown "author would seem to challenge Butler for the dubious honor of being the father of the fugitive slave clause" ("Pierce Butler's Records of the Federal Constitutional Convention," *Quarterly Journal of the Library of Congress*, 37 (1980),

64, quote at 68). The draft of the bill is reprinted in Hutson, *Supplement*, 246. Butler was not one of the great minds of the Convention, and it is certainly likely that he collaborated in drafting the provision with someone else, especially Charles Pinckney. It seems clear, however, that Butler was the delegate who actually introduced, and pushed for, the fugitive slave provision at the Convention. In any event, the idea for the fugitive slave clause probably came from the Northwest Ordinance, which the Congress, sitting in New York, had passed in July. The Ordinance contained the first national fugitive slave provision.

90. Farrand, ed., *Records*, II, 449.

91. Ibid., 2:449–452. Luther Martin, *The Genuine Information Delivered to the Legislature of the State of Maryland Relative to the Proceedings of the General Convention Lately Held at Philadelphia*, in Herbert J. Storing, ed., *The Complete Anti-Federalist* (Chicago: Univ. of Chicago Press, 1981), 2:60–61. Martin, who later opposed the Constitution, made this point in his letter to the Maryland ratifying convention. He had been on the committee that drafted the compromise over commerce and the slave trade.

92. Farrand, ed., *Records*, II, 451–453. Other scholars have noted this compromise as well, but most have done so approvingly. Charles Warren believed that slavery was relatively insignificant in the making of the Constitution. Arguing that the morality of the slave trade was unimportant, he wrote that "historians have underestimated the importance of the concession made on commerce by the South." He approvingly quoted George Ticknor Curtis: "The just and candid voice of History has also to thank the Southern statement who consented to this arrangement for having clothed a majority of the two Houses with a full commercial power." *The Making of the Constitution*, 585, 585n, quoting Curtis, *History of the Origin, Formation, and Adoption of the Constitution of the United States* (New York: Harper Bros., 1854–1858), II, 306–307. Curtis was a northern ally of the South—a doughface in the language of antebellum America—and his history clearly reflected his political biases. Warren's analysis follows Max Farrand, "Compromises of the Constitution," in *Annual Report of the American Historical Association for the Year 1903* (Washington, D.C., 1904), I, 73–84. The historiography of this issue is discussed in Lynd, "The Abolitionist Critique," in Lynd, *Class Conflict, Slavery, and the United States Constitution*.

93. Farrand, ed., *Records*, II, 453–454.

94. William W. Freehling, "The Founding Fathers and Slavery," *American Historical Review*, 77 (1972), 81, quote at 84.

95. Freehling has recently reiterated his position, calling mine "cynical." Freehling writes that "I believe Carolinians meant their ultimatum—and that a majority of the delegates so believed." William W. Freehling, *The Road to Disunion: Secessionists at Bay, 1776–1854* (New York: Oxford University Press, 1990), 584, n.30. However, Freehling seems to hedge a little, by also noting that Jefferson was "not present to cave in when South Carolina threatened not to join the Union if the Constitutional Convention of 1787 empowered Congress to end the African slave trade immediately." Ibid., 135. It strikes me that "cave in" is much more on the mark, and implies that there might have been greater room for tough negotiation or actually opposition to this position.

96. Maltz, "Slavery, Federalism, and the Structure of the Constitution," 469.

97. Ibid.

98. Many South Carolinians expected to be able maintain the trade after 1808. They expected that the new western states would favor the trade, at least in part because the states of the Southwest—what became Kentucky, Tennessee, Mississippi, and Alabama—would want imports because that would lower the price of slaves for them. Some leaders in the Deep South also expected New Englanders to support the trade. During ratification struggle David Ramsey, one of the leading intellectuals and politicians in South Carolina, argued that this same sort of economic self-interest would prevail after 1808. He argued in favor of ratification, noting: "Though Congress may forbid the importation of negroes after 21 years, it does not follow that they will. On the other hand, it is probably that they will not. The more rice we make, the more business will be for their shipping: their interest will therefore coincide with our's." Civis [David Ramsey], "To the Citizens of South Carolina," *Charleston Columbian Herald*, Feb. 4, 1788, reprinted in Merrill Jensen, ed., *Documentary History of the Ratification of the Constitution*, 16:25 (Madison, Wis.: Wisconsin Historical Society, 197).

99. Farrand, ed., *Records*, II, 371, 373,; Freehling, "The Founding Fathers," 84.
100. Farrand, ed., *Records*, II, 466–467. The vote on the Dickinson motion was three to eight. The

three yes votes came from the middle states, New Jersey, Pennsylvania, and Delaware. Delaware was also a slave state, and would remain one until the adoption of the Thirteenth Amendment in 1865. But, by this time in the Convention, it was clear that Delaware did not think of itself as a slave state.

101. For example, in a vote to limit the president's treaty power, Maryland, South Carolina, and Georgia voted yes, and the other states present voted no (ibid., II, 541).

102. Ibid., 537–538, 541–542, 543. On August 31 he had declared "that he would sooner chop off his right hand than put it to the Constitution" (ibid., 479). Ultimately, he refused to sign the Constitution. On Sept. 12 Mason would use sectional arguments in an attempt to create a stronger prohibition on states levying an export tax (ibid., 588–589, 631).

103. Ibid., 559–561.

104. Ibid., 623–627.

105. Ibid., 601–602, 628 (angle brackets in Farrand); there is no indication who requested this change. A similar change of wording was made in the three-fifths clause at the suggestion of Edmund Randolph, changing the word "servitude" to "service" for describing indentured whites. Randolph argued that the original term "being thought to express the condition of slaves" would be inappropriate, while the new term described "the obligations of free persons" (ibid., 607). There was also a little more discussion about the amendment clause as it affected the slave trade, but nothing resulted from this (ibid., 629).

106. Ibid., 443.

107. Elliot, ed., *Debates*, IV, 286.

108. Farrand, ed., *Records*, II, 633, 640.

109. Letters from a Countryman from Dutchess County (letter of Jan. 22, 1788), in Storing, ed., *The Complete Anti-Federalist*, VI, 62; Elliot, ed., *Debates*, II, 203. Essays by Republicus (essay of Mar. 12, 1788), in Storing, ed., *Complete Anti-Federalist*, V., 169.

110. Consider Arms, Malichi Maynard, and Samuel Field, "Reasons for Dissent," in Storing, ed., *Complete Anti-Federalist*, 4:262–263.

Chapter 5

1. Abraham Lincoln, *The Collected Works of Abraham Lincoln* ed. Roy P. Basler (New Brunswick, NJ: Rutgers University Press, 1953), 3: 117.

2. *Congressional Globe*, 31st Cong., 1st Sess., 451.

3. Max Farrand, ed., *The Records of the Federal Convention of 1787* (New Haven CT: Yale University Press, 1937), 2: 417.

4. *Prigg v. Pennsylvania*, 41 U.S. 539, 540 (1842).

5. *See* "North Carolina Ratification Debates," in *A Necessary Evil?: Slavery and the Debate Over the Constitution* ed. John Kaminski (Madison, WI : Madison House, 1995), 200.

6. *See* Mark A. Graber, *Dred Scott and the Problem of Constitutional Evil* (New York: Cambridge University Press, 2006), 101–06; Paul Finkelman, "Slavery and the Constitutional Convention: Making a Covenant With Death," in *Beyond Confederation: Origins of the Constitution and American National Identity* ed. Richard Beeman, Stephen Botein, and Edward C. Carter II (Chapel Hill: University of North Carolina Press, 1987).

7. *Annals of Congress*, 1st Cong., 1st Sess., 451.

8. The post-Civil War amendments did alter the balance of power between the federal and state governments. The extent of that alteration has been the subject of ongoing debates in American constitutional politics.

9. *See* Graber, *Dred Scott*, 1.

10. Wendell Phillips, *The Constitution a Pro-Slavery Compact or, Extracts From the Madison Papers, Etc.* (New York: American Anti-Slavery Society: 1856).

11. Paul Finkelman, "Slavery and the Constitutional Convention: Making a Covenant With Death."

12. William E. Gienapp, "The Republican Party and the Slave Power," in *New Perspectives on Race and Slavery in America: Essays in Honor of Kenneth Stampp* ed. by Robert H. Abzug and Stephen E. Maizish (Lexington: University Press of Kentucky, 1986), 57.

13. Graber, *Dred Scott*, 127–28.

14. Farrand, *Records*, 1: 20–22.

15. Graber, *Dred Scott*, 101–06.

16. Ibid., 126–28.

17. See Cong. Globe, 36th Cong., 2d Sess., pp. 78 (speech of John W. Noell), 82–83 (speech of Andrew Johnson), 329 (speech of Robert Hunter).

18. Robert M. Weir, "South Carolina: Slavery and the Structure of the Union," in *Ratifying the Constitution*, ed. Michael Allen Gillespie and Michael Lienesch, (Lawrence: University Press of Kansas, 1989), 208.

19. Farrand, *Records*, 2: 10.

20. Farrand, *Records*, 1: 144.

21. Ibid., 605.

22. Ibid., 567.

23. Farrand, *Records*, 2: 57.

24. Ibid., 32.

25. Ibid., 81.

26. Farrand, *Records*, 1:164. *See* Farrand, *Records*, 1: 131.

27. *See* Joseph M. Lynch, *Negotiating the Constitution: The Earliest Debates over Original Intent* (Ithaca: Cornell University Press, 1999), 15.

28. *Federalist* No. 42, Alexander Hamilton, James Madison, and John Jay, *The Federalist Papers* (New York: New American Library, 1961), 266.

29. Ibid., 339.

30. *Federalist* No. 68, 380.

31. *See* Graber, *Dred Scott*, 112.

32. *See* Herbert Storing, *What the Anti-Federalists Were For* (Chicago: University of Chicago Press, 1981), 48–52.

33. "Essays of Brutus," Herbert Storing ed., *The Complete Anti-Federalist* (Chicago: University of Chicago Press, 1981), 2: 420

34. William Rotch, Sr., to Moses Brown, November 8, 1787 in *A Necessary Evil?*, 74.

35. *Salem Mercury*, January 8, 1788 in *A Necessary Evil?*, ed. Kaminski, 79.

36. *Annals of Congress*, 4th Cong., 1st Sess., 776.

37. One particularly important problem, emphasized by Jack Rakove, is that the members of the ratifying conventions were asked to ratify the Constitution as a whole, not approve particular provisions. *See* Jack N. Rakove, *Original Meanings: Politics and Ideas in the Making of the Constitution* (New York: Alfred A. Knopf, 1996), 11. Hence, all that can be established from ratification is that majorities at free-state constitutional conventions perceived the Constitution as a whole to be superior to any practical alternative. We cannot discern from the vote to ratify any clear consensus on the meaning of a particular provision, the principles that best justify particular constitutional arrangements, or the principles that best justify the Constitution as a whole.

38. David Ramsay (Civis), Charleston *Columbian Herald*, February 4, 1788, *A Necessary Evil?*, 178.
39. Farrand, *Records*, 3: 334.

40. Jonathan Elliot, ed., *The Debates in the Several State Conventions on the Adoption of the Federal Constitution As Recommended by the General Convention at Philadelphia in 1787,* vol. IV (Philadelphia: J.B. Lippincott Company, 1836), 268.

41. John P. Kaminski and Gaspare Saladino, eds., *The Documentary History of the Ratification of the Constitution by the States: Ratification of the Constitution by the States: Virginia [3]* (Vol. X) (Madison: State Historical Society of Wisconsin,1993), 1483.

42. Farrand, 3: 334.

43. John P. Kaminski and Gaspare Saladino, eds., *The Documentary History of the Ratification of the Constitution by the States: Ratification of the Constitution by the States: Virginia [2]* (Vol. IX) (State Historical Society of Wisconsin: Madison, 1990), 1002–03.

44. Jonathan Elliot, ed., *The Debates in the Several State Conventions on the Adoption of the Federal Constitution As Recommended by the General Convention at Philadelphia in 1787* vol. IV (Philadelphia: J.B. Lippincott Company, 1836), 276–77.

45. For a more general and excellent meditation on constitutional failure, see Mark E. Brandon, *Free in the World: American Slavery and Constitutional Failure* (Princeton NJ: Princeton University Press, 1998).

46. Alexander Hamilton, James Madison, and John Jay, *The Federalist Papers* (New American Library: New York, 1961), 83.

47. *See* Gordon S. Wood, *The Radicalism of the American Revolution* (Alfred A. Knopf: New York, 1992).

48. *See* Stephen M. Feldman, *Free Expression and Democracy in America: A History* (University of Chicago Press: Chicago, 2008); Stephen M. Feldman, *Please Don't Wish Me a Merry Christmas: A Critical History of the Separation of Church and State* (New York University Press: New York, 1996).

49. This paragraph summarizes Graber, *Dred Scott,* 126–28.

50. *See Annals of Congress,* 16th Cong., 1st Sess., 1091.

51. *See* Graber, *Dred Scott,* 135–53.

52. *Congressional Globe,* 31st Congress, 1st Session, 451.

53. Eric Foner, *Free Soil, Free Labor, Free Men: The Ideology of the Republican Party before the Civil War* (London: Oxford University Press, 1970), 58, 222, 236.

54. Abraham Lincoln, *The Collected Works of Abraham Lincoln* (Vol. IV) (edited by Roy P. Basler) (Rutgers University Press: New Brunswick, New Jersey, 1953), 268.

55. See, i.e., Sanford Levinson, *Our Undemocratic Constitution: Where the Constitution Goes Wrong (And How We the People Can Correct it)* (Oxford University Press: New York, 2006).

56. See *Congressional Globe,* 27th Cong., 2nd Session, 894.

57. See *Congressional Globe,* 37th Cong., 2nd Sess., 26.

58. *The Federalist Papers,* 352.

59. Ibid, 314.

60. See David Adamany, "The Supreme Court's Role in Critical Elections," *Realignment in American Politics: Toward a Theory* (edited by Bruce A. Campbell & Richard J. Trilling) (University of Texas Press: Austin, TX, 1980), 246.

61. See Damon Wells, *Stephen Douglas: The Last Years, 1857–1861* (University of Texas Press: Austin, Texas, 1971), 282–88.

62. Abraham Lincoln, *The Collected Works of Abraham Lincoln* (Vol. II) (edited by Roy P. Basler) (Rutgers University Press: New Brunswick, New Jersey, 1953), 246.

63. Abraham Lincoln, *The Collected Works of Abraham Lincoln* (Vol. V) (edited by Roy P. Basler) (Rutgers University Press: New Brunswick, New Jersey, 1953), 410.

64. See Douglas C. North and Barry R. Weingast, "Constitutions and Commitment: The Evolution of Institutions Governing Public Choice in Seventeenth-Century England," 49 *Journal of Economic History* 803 (1989).

Chapter 6

1. Robert A. Dahl, *On Democracy* (New Haven, CT: Yale University Press, 2000), 37. See also Robert A. Dahl, *Democracy and Its Critics* (New Haven, CT: Yale University Press, 1989), 110.

2. See George C. Edwards III, *Why the Electoral College Is Bad for America* (New Haven, CT: Yale University Press, 2004), chap. 2.

3. Darshan J. Goux and David A. Hopkins, "The Empirical Implications of Electoral College Reform," *American Politics Research* 36 (November 2008): 860–864.

4. See Edwards, *Why the Electoral College Is Bad for America*, 48–51, for a discussion of the 1960 election.

5. See, for example, Samantha Luks, Joanne M. Miller, and Lawrence R. Jacobs, "Who Wins? Campaigns and the Third Party Vote," *Presidential Studies Quarterly* 33 (March 2003): 9–30.

6. See, for example, Barry C. Burden, "Did Ralph Nader Elect George W. Bush? An Analysis of Minor Parties in the 2000 Presidential Election" (paper delivered at the annual meeting of the American Political Science Association, San Francisco), 2001.

7. These figures are from the Clerk of the House of Representatives, Jeff Trandahl, *Statistics of the Presidential and Congressional Election of November 7, 2000*, US House of Representatives, 2001.

8. See, for example, Tara Ross, *Enlightened Democracy: The Case for the Electoral College* (Los Angeles, CA: World Ahead, 2004).

9. Raymond Tatalovich, "Electoral Votes and Presidential Campaign Trails, 1932–1976," *American Politics Quarterly* 7 (October 1979): 489–497; Scott C. James and Brian L. Lawson, "The Political Economy of Voting Rights Enforcement in America's Gilded Age: Electoral College Competition, Partisan Commitment, and the Federal Election Law," *American Political Science Review* 93 (March 1999): 115–131; Daron R. Shaw, "The Methods behind the Madness: Presidential Electoral College Strategies, 1988–1996," *Journal of Politics* 61 (November 1999): 893–913, Daron R. Shaw, *The Race to 270* (Chicago, IL: University of Chicago Press, 2007).

10. Jack Rakove, "The Accidental Electors," *New York Times,* December 19, 2000.

11. James Madison to George Hay, August 23, 1823. Gaillard Hunt, ed., *The Writings of James Madison,* vol. 9 (New York: G. P. Putnam's Sons, 1900–1910), 47–55.

12. Max Farrand, ed., *The Records of the Federal Convention of 1787,* rev. ed., vol. II (New Haven, CT: Yale University Press, 1966), 111.

13. Judith A. Best, *The Choice of the People? Debating the Electoral College* (Lanham, MD: Rowman and Littlefield, 1996), 37.

14. Best, *Choice of the People?,* p. 35.

15. See Robert A. Dahl, *How Democratic Is the American Constitution?* (New Haven, CT: Yale University Press, 2001), 50–53, 84.

16. Farrand, *Records* vol. I, 483.

17. Ibid., vol. I, 447–449.

18. Ibid., vol. II, 403.

19. Ibid., vol. I, 447–449.

20. I have omitted Washington, DC, from this analysis because it is limited to the number of electoral votes of the least populous state and is not overrepresented in the Electoral College.

21. U.S. Department of Agriculture, 2007 *Census of Agriculture,* Vol. 1, (Washington, DC: National Agricultural Statistics Service, 2009), Table 2, 294–302.

22. Ross, *Enlightened Democracy*, 41, 87; Michael M. Uhlman, "Creating Constitutional Majorities: The Electoral College after 2000," in Gary L. Gregg, ed., *Securing Democracy: Why We Have an Electoral College* (Wilmington, Del.: ISI Books, 2001), p. 106; Paul A. Rahe, "Moderating the Political Impulse," in Gregg, ed., *Securing Democracy*, p. 63.

23. Edwards, *Why the Electoral College Is Bad for America*, pp. 101–102.

24. The speeches are provided by the *Annenberg/Pew Archive of Presidential Campaign Discourse* (CD-ROM), 2000. The results are reported in Edwards, *Why the Electoral College Is Bad for America*, pp. 102–103.

25. The author collected the data for 2000, 2004, and 2008. The data for 2000 are reported in Edwards, *Electoral College*, 103–109.

26. Larry J. Sabato, *A More Perfect Constitution: 23 Proposals to Revitalize Our Constitution and Make America a Fairer Country* (New York: Walker & Co., 2007), 139.

27. Stanley Kelley, Jr., "The Presidential Campaign," in Paul T. David, ed., *The Presidential Election and Transition 1960–1961* (Washington, DC: Brookings Institution, 1961), 70–72; Daron R. Shaw, "The Effect of TV Ads and Candidate Appearances on Statewide Presidential Votes, 1988–96," *American Political Science Review* 93 (June 1999): 359–360; Edwards, *Why the Electoral College Is Bad for America*, pp. 103–109. See also Larry M. Bartels, "Resource Allocation in a Presidential Campaign," *Journal of Politics* 47 (August 1985): 928–936; Steven J. Brams and Morton D. Davis, "The 3/2's Rule in Presidential Campaigning," *American Political Science Review* 68 (March 1974): 113–134; Claude S. Colantoni, Terrence J. Levasque, and Peter C. Ordeshook, "Campaign Resource Allocation under the Electoral College," *American Political Science Review* 69 (March 1975): 141–154; Steven J. Brams and Morton D. Davis, "Comment on 'Campaign Resource Allocations under the Electoral College,'" *American Political Science Review* 69 (March 1975): 155–156.

28. Edwards, *Why the Electoral College Is Bad for America*, pp. 109–114.

29. "Testimony of Hon. Hubert H. Humphrey, U.S. Senator from the State of Minnesota, "*The Electoral College and Direct Election: Hearings before the Committee on the Judiciary, United States Senate,* January 27, February 1, 2, 7, and 10, 1977, 95th Congress, 1st session, 25, 35; "Testimony of Douglas Bailey," *The Electoral College and Direct Election: Hearings before the Subcommittee on the Constitution of the Committee on the Judiciary, Supplement, United States Senate,* July 20, 22, 28, and August 2, 1977, 95th Congress, 1st session, pp. 267, 258–273; as well as the testimony at the same hearings by Sen. Robert Dole, "Testimony of Hon. Robert Dole, U.S. Senator from the State of Kansas," *The Electoral College and Direct Election: Hearings before the Subcommittee on the Constitution of the Committee on the Judiciary, Supplement,* p. 30, who also stressed the campaign distortions created by the Electoral College. See also Bartels, "Resource Allocation in a Presidential Campaign"; Shaw, "The Effect of TV Ads and Candidate Appearances on Statewide Presidential Votes, 1988–96"; Shaw, *The Race to 270,* chap. 4.

30. Martin Diamond, *The Electoral College and the American Idea of Democracy* (Washington, DC: American Enterprise Institute, 1977), 20; Michael Barone, "The Electoral College and the Future of American Political Parties," in Gregg, ed., *Securing Democracy,* 82–83, 85; Arthur M. Schlesinger, Jr., *The Cycles of American History* (Boston, : Houghton Mifflin, 1986), 319–320; Rahe, "Moderating the Political Impulse," 68–69;Walllace S. Sayre and Judith H. Parris, *Voting for President: The Electoral College and the American Political System* (Washington, DC: Brookings Institution, 1970), 73–82, 85, 146–147; Judith A. Best, *The Choice of the People?,* 56, 58; Arthur M. Schlesinger, Jr., "Not the People's Choice," *The American Prospect,* March 25, 2002, 275; Uhlman, "Creating Constitutional Majorities," 111–112. An exception is Sabato, *A More Perfect Constitution,* 138–139, 142, who makes a broader assertion.

31. CBS/*New York Times* poll, May 9–12, 2003.

32. See, for example, Arend Lijphart, *Patterns of Democracy: Government Forms and Performance in Thirty-Six Countries* (New Haven, CT: Yale University Press, 1999), 168–170; Gary W. Cox, *Making Votes Count: Strategic Coordination in the World's Electoral Systems* (New York: Cambridge University Press, 1997), chap. 10, 190. See also Peter Ordeshook and Olga Shvetsova, "Ethnic Heterogeneity, District Magnitude, and the Number of Parties," *American Journal of Political Science* 38 (February 1994): 100–123.

33. See, for example, Frank J. Sorauf, *Party Politics in America* (Boston: Little, Brown, 1968), 35–37.

34. Maurice Duverger, *Political Parties* (New York: Wiley, 1954), 217–218, 239. See also Maurice Duverger, "Duverger's Law: Thirty Years Later," in Arend Lijphart and Bernard Grofman, eds., *Choosing an Electoral System: Issues and Alternatives* (New York: Praeger, 1986).

35. See, for example, G. Bingham Powell, *Contemporary Democracies: Participation, Stability, and Violence* (Cambridge, MA: Harvard University Press, 1982), 205; William H. Riker, "The Two-Party

System and Duverger's Law: An Essay on the History of Political Science," *American Political Science Review* 76 (December 1982): 753–766; Giovanni Sartori, *Comparative Constitutional Engineering* (New York: New York University Press, 1994); Rein Taagepera and Matthew Soberg Shugart, *Seats and Votes: The Effects and Determinants of Electoral Systems* (New Haven, CT: Yale University Press, 1989); Douglas W. Rae, *The Political Consequences of Electoral Laws* (New Haven, CT: Yale University Press, 1967), 67–129; Lijphart, *Patterns of Democracy*, 226.

36. An exception is an assertion written more than 50 years ago by Alexander Heard in *a Two-Party South?* (Chapel Hill, NC: University of North Carolina Press, 1952), 169.

37. Cox, *Making Votes Count*, esp. p. 96.

38. Clinton Rossiter, *Parties and Politics in America* (Ithaca, NY: Cornell University Press, 1962), 8.

39. V. O. Key, Jr., *Politics, Parties, and Pressure Groups*, 5th ed. (New York: Crowell, 1964), 209.

40. James MacGregor Burns, "A New Course for the Electoral College," *New York Times Magazine*, December 18, 1960.

41. John F. Bibby and L. Sandy Maisel, *Two Parties — or More?* (Boulder, CO: Westview, 1998), 56–64.

42. Leon D. Epstein, *Political Parties in the American Mold* (Madison, WI: University of Wisconsin Press, 1986), 173.

43. Allan Cigler, Joel Paddock, Gary Reich, and Eric Uslaner, "Changing the Electoral College: The Impact on Parties and Organized Interests," in Paul D. Schumaker and Burdett A. Loomis, *Choosing a President* (New York: Chatham House, 2002), 87.

44. V.O. Key, Jr., *Southern Politics* (New York: Vintage, 1949), 300, 420.

45. Sabato, *A More Perfect Constitution*, 143–144.

46. See Edwards, *Why the Electoral College Is Bad for America*, pp. 139–141.

47. Sabato, *A More Perfect Constitution*, 139; Ross, *Enlightened Democracy*, 53; Best, *The Choice of the People?*, 55; William C. Kimberling, "The Electoral College," on the Federal Election Commission website (www.fec.gov/pdf/eleccoll.pdf); James R. Stoner, Jr., "Federalism, the States, and the Electoral College," in Gregg, ed., *Securing Democracy*, 51–52.

48. Diamond, *The Electoral College and the American Idea of Democracy*, 4.

49. Twentieth Century Fund, *Winner Take All* (New York: Holmes and Meier, 1978), chap. 6.

50. See Richard G. Niemi and Paul S. Herrnson, "Beyond the Butterfly: The Complexity of U.S. Ballots," *Perspectives on Politics* 1 (June 2003): 317–326.

51. Caltech/MIT Voting Technology Project, *Voting: What Is, What Could Be* (2001).

52. Remarks of President George W. Bush at signing ceremony for the Help America Vote Act of 2002, The White House, October 29, 2002.

53. Ross, *Enlightened Democracy*, 41, 87, 109, 142, 182, 187, 170, 188; Uhlman, "Creating Constitutional Majorities," in Gregg, *Securing Democracy*, 109–110; Rahe, "Moderating the Political Impulse," in Gregg, *Securing Democracy*, 63, 72–73; Best, *The Choice of the People?*, 14, 21, 23–24, 27, 36–37.

54. Voter News Service Exit Polls; Gallup News Service, "Candidate Support by Subgroup," News Release, November 6, 2000 (*Based on 6-Day Average, October 31–November 5, 2000*).

55. Sabato, *A More Perfect Constitution*, 142.

56. See Eric R. A. N. Smithy and Peverill Squire, "Direct Election of the President and the Power of the States," *Western Political Quarterly* 40 (March 1987): 29–44.

57. "Prepared Statement of Senator Bob Dole," *The Electoral College and Direct Election: Hearings before the Subcommittee on the Constitution of the Committee on the Judiciary, Supplement,* 40.

58. Goux and Hopkins, "The Empirical Implications of Electoral College Reform."

59. Michael Hagen, Richard Johnston, and Kathleen Hall Jamieson, "Effects of the 2000 Presidential Campaign" (paper delivered at the Annual Meeting of the American Political Science Association, August 29–September 1, 2002), 3.

60. Quoted in U.S. Congress, Senate, Committee on the Judiciary, *Report on Direct Popular Election of the President and Vice President of the United States*, 95th Congress, 1st session, 1967, 124.

61. "Prepared Statement of Senator Bob Dole," *The Electoral College and Direct Election*, 39.

62. See Edwards, *Why the Electoral College Is Bad for America*, chap. 1.

Chapter 7

1. Prior to 1804, the candidate for president with the second-highest number of electoral votes was to become the vice president. In 1800 Jefferson and Burr attempted to run on a ticket, and the electors split their votes evenly among the two men, causing an unexpected tie. The House of Representatives was called upon to decide the winner, resulting in a week of deadlock that finally ended with a win for Jefferson. In 1804 the Twelfth Amendment established separate electoral ballots for president and vice president. For more on the 1800 election, see Dumas Malone, *Jefferson and His Time* (Charlottesville, VA: University of Virginia Press, 1962), vol. 3, chap. 30, as well as John Ferling, *Adams vs. Jefferson: The Tumultuous Election of 1800* (New York: Oxford University Press, 2004).

2. In 1824 the college took center stage again, as four candidates received electoral votes, but none with a majority. The 1824 election was the only election since the passage of the Twelfth Amendment where a presidential election had to be resolved by a vote in the House of Representatives. After the Federalist Party dissolved, only the Democratic-Republican Party remained to field candidates, resulting in a four-way presidential election between Andrew Jackson (99 votes), John Quincy Adams (84 votes),William Harris Crawford (41 votes), and Henry Clay (37 votes). This led to the infamous backroom bargaining that sent John Quincy Adams, who had received fewer popular and electoral votes than Andrew Jackson, to the presidency. For more on the 1824 election, see Robert V. Remini, *John Quincy Adams* (New York: Times Books, 2002).

3. In 1876 neither New York governor Samuel Tilden nor Ohio governor Rutherford B. Hayes managed to secure the necessary number of electors, because the results in four states remained contested. Tilden's total stood at 184 undisputed votes, just one shy of the total needed at that time, and Hayes had 165. To resolve the dispute, the fifteen-member Electoral Commission (five members from the Republican Senate, five members from the Democratic House, and five from the Supreme Court) was convened. The Electoral Commission voted 8 to 7, along party lines, to give the electoral votes in each of the four disputed elections to the Republican Hayes, granting him the necessary 185 votes. See also William H. Rehnquist, *The Centennial Crisis: The Disputed Election of 1876* (New York: Knopf, 2004).

4. Only twelve years after the tumultuous 1876 election, a candidate for president would again win the popular vote and lose the electoral vote. Incumbent president Grover Cleveland earned 100,000 more votes than challenger Benjamin Harrison, but Harrison won the election by a landslide plurality of 65 electoral votes.

5. For more on the 1968 election, see Lewis L. Gould, *1968: The Election That Changed America* (Chicago: Ivan R. Dee, 1993).

6. Later in his career as governor of Alabama, Wallace recanted his segregationist past, and he even received the backing of a large share of African American Alabamans. Still, his role in the racial cauldron that was the 1960s was disgraceful, and he will always be remembered for "standing in the schoolhouse door" to try to prevent the admission of black students to his state's universities in 1963. See Lloyd Rohler, *George Wallace: Conservative Populist* (Westport, CT: Praeger, 2004) and Jody Carlson, *George C. Wallace and the Politics of Powerlessness: The Wallace Campaigns for the Presidency, 1964–1976* (New Brunswick, NJ: Transaction Books, 1981).

7. The first Deep South presidential candidate since 1848, Carter won all southern states except Virginia, most by wide margins, and this produced his popular vote lead, which was not matched in the state-by-state-based Electoral College. See also Patrick Anderson, *Electing Jimmy Carter: The Campaign of 1976* (Baton Rouge: Louisiana State University Press, 1994). In-depth statistics from the 1976 election can be found on the web site of the Office of the Clerk of the House of Representatives at http://clerk.house.gov/members/electionInfo/.

8. Due to a faithless elector in Minnesota, Kerry's official tally was 251 electoral votes.

9. Larry J. Sabato, ed., *Divided States of America* (New York: Pearson/Longman, 2005), 58–59.

10. See George C. Edwards III, *Why the Electoral College Is Bad for America* (New Haven, CT: Yale University Press, 2004), as well as Lawrence D. Longley and Neal R. Pierce, *The Electoral College Primer, 2000* (New Haven, CT: Yale University Press, 1999).

11. Frederic D. Schwarz, "The Electoral College: How It Got That Way and Why We're Stuck With It," *American Heritage Magazine* 52.1 (Feb.–Mar. 2001), online at http://www.american heritage.com/magazine/.

12. Two constitutional amendments (the Twelfth and Twenty-third) affect the Electoral College directly, and three amendments (the Fourteenth, Seventeenth, and Twenty-fourth) affect the qualifications and selection of electors. The Twelfth Amendment established two distinct ballots for president and vice president, a departure from the arrangement set forth in Article II whereby the runner-up in the electoral vote would be awarded the vice presidency. The Fourteenth Amendment dispensed with the three-fifths clause of Article I, declaring all persons regardless of color to be equally counted for the purposes of electoral apportionment. The Seventeenth Amendment mandated that electors in any given state must, at a minimum, meet the same qualifications as members of that state's largest house of legislature. The Twenty-third Amendment granted D.C. three electoral votes. The Twenty-fourth Amendment forbade poll taxes from being imposed on citizens when voting for electors.

13. The Federal Registrar provides instructions for state officials who oversee the selection of electors (http://www.archives.gov/federal-register/electoral-college/state_responsibilities.html). Those instructions state: "Under the Constitution, State legislatures have broad powers to direct the process for selecting electors, with one exception regarding the qualifications of electors. Article II, section 1, clause 2 provides that 'no Senator, Representative, or Person holding an Office of Trust or Profit under the United States' may be appointed as an elector. It is not settled as to whether this restriction extends to all Federal officials regardless of their level of authority or the capacity in which they serve, but we advise the States that the restriction could disqualify any person who holds a federal government job from serving as an elector. While this remains an open question at the federal level, many states have had to determine the meaning of the phrase *office of trust or profit* with respect to their own, internal operations. For example, in April of 2005 the attorney general of Tennessee concluded that the phrase only encompassed those individuals required to take an oath of office in support of the Tennessee state constitution (Opp. Tenn. Attorney General 05-064, 27. April 2005)."

14. Actually, an elector could vote for unqualified or even fictitious persons, but these votes could not elect a constitutionally qualified president or vice president in any event.

15. No constitutional provision or federal statute requires electors to vote for the popular vote winner in their states. In many states, electors are bound either by party pledges or by state law to vote for the popular vote winner. In *Ray v. Blair*, 343 U.S. 214 (1952), the Supreme Court ruled that such party pledges are constitutional—though the constitutionality of state laws binding electors has never been tested in the courts, nor has any potential enforcement mechanism for such provisions. At least one observer concluded that "the preponderance of legal opinion seems to be that statues binding electors, or pledges that they may give, are unenforceable." See Longley and Pierce, *The Electoral College Primer*, 109–16. According to the Federal Registrar (http://www.archives.gov/federal-register/electoral-college/laws.html), the following states bind electors either through pledges or by statute: Alabama, Alaska, California, Colorado, Connecticut, the District of Columbia, Florida, Hawaii, Maine, Maryland, Massachusetts, Michigan, Mississippi, Montana, Nebraska, Nevada, New Mexico, North Carolina, Ohio, Oklahoma, Oregon, South Carolina, Vermont, Virginia, Washington, Wisconsin, and Wyoming.

16. A faithless Republican election in the 1972 elector, Roger MacBride of Virginia, voted for John Hospers, the Libertarian nominee for president, instead of Republican Richard M. Nixon. Four years later, MacBride became the Libertarian nominee for president. Thus, faithlessness produced a political career, but it could not be termed successful. McBride secured only 172,000 votes, or 0.21 percent of the 1976 national vote.

17. The Twelfth Amendment lays out the tie-breaking procedures in greater detail. In breaking an electoral tie for president, the House of Representatives shall only vote among the top three electoral vote recipients. A quorum will consist of "a member or members from two-thirds of the states," and a

"majority of all the states shall be necessary to a choice" (meaning, in theory, a quorum of thirty-four representatives and a majority of twenty-six representatives could select a president—emphasizing even further the need for a continuity of government amendment). In breaking an electoral tie for vice president, the Senate selects between the two highest electoral vote recipients. A quorum consists of "two-thirds of the whole number of Senators, and a majority of the whole shall be necessary to a choice." It is unclear from the language of the Twelfth Amendment if the "whole number of Senators" means the whole number of Senate seats (100) or the whole number of Senators serving—something else a continuity of government amendment could clarify. For more information, see *Provisions of the Constitution and United States Code Pertaining to Presidential Elections*, Office of the Federal Registrar, National Archives and Records Administration (July 20, 2000); Alexandra Kura, ed., *Electoral College and Presidential Elections* (Huntington, NY: Nova Science, 2001); Robert M. Hardaway, *The Electoral College and the Constitution: The Case for Preserving Federalism* (Westport, CT: Praeger, 1994).

18. Maine and Nebraska law provides for the allocation of one elector to the winner of each congressional district, and the two bonus senatorial electors go to the winner of the statewide vote. The Maine system was established in 1972 and the Nebraska version in 1996. See Richard E. Berg-Andersson's *The Green Papers*, online at http://www.thegreenpapers.com. Interestingly, until 2008, when Barack Obama carried Nebraska's second congressional district, every presidential winner in these two states had managed to capture all the state's electoral votes since the starting dates, preventing any split electoral tally.

19. The Republicans became the main opposition party, replacing the Whigs, in 1856, when the Democrat James Buchanan defeated the Republican John C. Fremont.

20. For more information on American political party development, see: Sidney M. Milkis, *Political Parties and Constitutional Government: Remaking American Democracy* (Baltimore: Johns Hopkins University Press, 1999); Wilfred E. Binkley, *American Political Parties: Their Natural History* (New York: Knopf, 1962); John Gerring, *Party Ideologies in America, 1828–1996* (Cambridge UK: Cambridge University Press, 1998); Joel H. Sibley, *The Partisan Imperative: The Dynamics of American Politics Before the Civil War* (Oxford: Oxford University Press, 1987); Gerald M. Pomper, *Party Renewal in America: Theory and Practice* (New York: Praeger, 1980); William Nisbet Chambers and Walter Dean Burnham, *The American Party Systems: Stages of Political Development* (Oxford: Oxford University Press, 1967).

21. According to a Gallup Poll conducted October 11–14, 2004 (telephone interview with a random sample of 1,012 adults, error of plus or minus 3 percent), 61 percent of Americans favor abolishing the Electoral College in favor of electing the president on the basis of the popular vote. The poll asked: "Thinking for a moment about the way in which the president is elected in this country, which would you prefer—to amend the Constitution so the candidate who receives the most total votes nationwide wins the election, or to keep the current system, in which the candidate who wins the most votes in the Electoral College wins the election?" Sixty-one percent responded that they would favor an amendment, 35 percent said they would keep the current system, and 4 percent had no opinion. Poll results available online at http://www.fairvote.org/electoral_college/Gallup_Polls.pdf.

22. In all, nine faithless electors have defected since the inception of the Electoral College. For information on each incident, visit Richard E. Berg-Andersson's *The Green Papers*, specifically http://www.thegreenpapers.com/Hx/FaithlessElectors.html.

23. Bills proposing constitutional amendments to abolish the Electoral College in favor of direct election of the president and vice president have never been in short supply. Since 1999, sponsors of such bills have included Representative Barney Frank (D-MA), Senator Richard Durbin (D-IL), Senator Dianne Feinstein (D-CA), Representative Jesse Jackson Jr. (D-IL), Representative Ray LaHood (R-IL), Representative Jim Leach (R-IA), Representative Zoe Lofgren (D-CA), Representative Jim McDermott (D-WA), Representative Jose Serrano (D-NY), Representative Fortney Stark (D-CA), Representative Robert Wise Jr. (D-WV), and Representative Lynn Woolsey (D-CA). The direct-vote method is just one of many proposals that have been considered for ending the Electoral College. For more information, see *The Report of the National Symposium on Presidential Selection* (Charlottesville, VA: University of Virginia Center for Governmental Studies, 2001), 43–46.

24. In "Gallup Poll Analyses" on January 5, 2001, Frank Newport discussed the public's view of the Electoral College. "One of the earliest times in which the public was asked about the Electoral College system was June 1944, just before Franklin Roosevelt's reelection to his fourth term. A Gallup

Poll question asked, 'It has been suggested that the electoral vote system be discontinued and presidents of the U.S. be elected by total popular vote alone. Do you favor or oppose this proposal?' The answer: 65% of Americans said they favored the proposal, with 23% saying they opposed it, and another 13% saying they had no opinion." For more information, see "American Support to Eliminate Electoral College System," January 5, 2001, http://gallup.com/poll/releases/pr010105.asp.

25. See Chris Mooney, "Why Does Louisiana Have Such an Odd Election System?" *Slate.com*, November 13, 2002, http://www.slate.com/?id=2073912.

26. See "Louisiana's Nonpartisan Primary: Model or Travesty of Reform?" published by *FairVote: The Center for Voting and Democracy*, February 2004, online at http://www.fairvote.org/?page=1495.

27. See Donald O. Dewey, "Madison's Views on Electoral Reform," *Western Political Quarterly* 15.1 (Mar. 1962): 140–45 (available online at http://links.jstor.org/sici?sici=00434078%28196203%2915%3A1%3C140%3AMV OER%3E2.0.CO%3B2-K). At the time of publication, Dewey was the assistant editor of the Papers of James Madison, University of Virginia. Madison's reforms included the abolition of the system of winner-take-all "bloc" electoral voting—with the candidate receiving a plurality of the vote in a state sweeping all the state's electors. Madison thought that one elector should be assigned to each congressional district, with the winner of that district receiving the elector. Actually, Madison insisted that the one-elector-per-district allocation was the intention of the framers, even though it had not been spelled out in the text of the Constitution. Bloc voting had come about in part because of partisan conflict in the 1800 presidential election. Supporters of President Adams sought to deny challenger Thomas Jefferson key electors in states where Adams's forces held sway, and the Jefferson backers did precisely the same thing in states they controlled. By the way, each state had and has the right to choose for itself either the winner-take-all system or the district allocation system. The Constitution does not mandate any method of elector allocation.

28. Ibid. Madison had much company in his preference for district allocation, by the way. Quite a number of the founders favored the reform by the 1820s, but the partisan maneuvering that accompanied the controversial election of 1824 between John Quincy Adams and Andrew Jackson, and Jackson's unrelenting comeback campaign for 1828, took center stage in the nation. Suspicions about who might gain or lose under a new system of electoral allocation may well have prevented the reform from progressing further.

29. Proponents of voting by electoral district began their campaign before the passage of the Twelfth Amendment and continued it for many years in the Senate. Chief Justice Melville Fuller summarized the history of this debate in *McPherson v. Blacker*, 146 U.S. 1, 33–34 (1892).

30. Rhodes Cook, "This Just In: Nixon Beats Kennedy," *The Rhodes Cook Letter*, May 2001.

31. Rhodes Cook discusses the results of historically close elections in "Electoral Reform: If the Electoral Vote was by Congressional District?" in the March 2001 issue of *The Rhodes Cook Letter*. He writes: "The election that would have been reversed was the razor-tight contest in 1960 between Democrat John F. Kennedy and Republican Richard M. Nixon. Kennedy's 118,574-vote edge in the popular vote was magnified into a comfortable 303–219 triumph in the Electoral College. But employing the district plan—which gives two electoral votes in each state to the statewide winner and one electoral vote for each congressional district carried—Nixon would have won 280 to 252."

32. Arthur Schlesinger Jr., "Fixing the Electoral College," *Washington Post*, December 19, 2000, p. A39.

33. See Larry J. Sabato and Glenn R. Simpson, *Dirty Little Secrets: The Persistence of Corruption in American Politics* (New York: Times Books, 1996), 274–301. Also see Bruce K. Felknor, *Political Mischief: Smear, Sabotage, and Reform in U.S. Elections* (New York: Praeger, 1992) as well as Louise Overacker, *Money in Elections* (New York: Macmillan, 1932).

34. For more on the election of 1800, see note 20 above. For more on Burr, see Roger G. Kennedy, *Burr, Hamilton, and Jefferson: A Study in Character* (New York: Oxford University Press, 2000) and Joseph Wheelen, *Jefferson's Vendetta: The Pursuit of Aaron Burr and the Judiciary* (New York: Carroll and Graf, 2005).

35. See also note 20 above.

36. In other cases, an illness may take away the deciding vote, leaving a state delegation tied. Or some representatives may choose to cast a ballot for the winner of their district, or of their state,

against their own party affiliation, taking untied delegations and tying them. One can easily conjure up other confusing scenarios that would utterly perplex the general public and fill the news media with critical speculation.

37. Since the District of Columbia has electoral votes, the delegate from D.C. should certainly be permitted to cast a ballot alongside the other 435 members. The delegates from territories without electoral votes would not have a presidential ballot.

38. By the way, if the Senate is expanded in the manner we have proposed, the possible selection of a vice president by the Senate would also be more democratic and representative of the broad body of the public, since the larger Senate would be more reflective of the heavily populated states. Of course, the vice president is only chosen by the Senate when no candidate receives a majority of the Electoral College vote.

39. Dewey, "Madison's Views on Electoral Reform," p. 144. See also James Madison's letter to George Hay, written from Madison's Virginia home, Montpelier, August 23, 1823, Library of Congress, Papers of James Madison (available online at http://presspubs.uchicago.edu/founders/documents/a2_1_2-3s10.html). My proposal here differs from Madison's 1823 suggestion only in that Madison wanted the whole House and Senate, voting together in a joint ballot, to choose the president whenever the Electoral College had deadlocked. Madison saw the inclusion of the Senate to be a useful concession to the smaller states—since their Senate representation was equal to that of the larger states. I would argue that this dilution of the democratic principle is unwarranted today, given the values of twenty-first-century America.

40. Larry J. Sabato, *A More Perfect Constitution: Why the Constitution Must Be Revised: Ideas to Inspire a New Generation* (New York: Walker and Company, 2007), 23–26.

41. Article V of the Constitution reads, in part that, "no State, without its Consent, shall be deprived of its equal Suffrage in the Senate."

42. Florida is still counted in Bush's column, obviously.

43. Certainly, the court would still have had to rule on Florida, and it presumably would have made the same decision, but no unelected judicial body would have had the final word on the identity of the next president. The elected House would have done so. While it is impossible to say for certain, it is very likely that George W. Bush would still have become president, since the Republicans controlled a total of twenty-six House delegations in the Congress that convened in early January 2001, when the selection would have taken place.

Chapter 8

1. See Donald Lutz, "Toward a Theory of Constitutional Amendment," in Sanford Levinson, ed., *Responding to Imperfection: The Theory and Practice of Constitutional Amendment* (Princeton, NJ: Princeton University Press, 1995), 237–274.

2. See, e.g., Jose Antonnio Cheibub, *Presidentialism, Parliamentarism and Democracy* (Cambridge, UK: Cambridge University Press, 2007).

3. *McCulloch v. Maryland*, 17 U.S. (4 Wheat.) 316, 415 (1819) (emphasis omitted).

4. See generally, Thomas Mann and Norman Ornstein, *The Broken Branch: How Congress is Failing America and How to Get It Back on Track* (New York :Oxford University Press 2006).

5. David Mayhew, *Divided We Govern*, 2nd ed. (New Haven, CT: Yale University Press, 2002). See also David Mayhew, "Is Congress 'The Broken Branch'?" *Boston University Law Review* 89 (2009): 357–369. Not surprisingly, the answer is "no."

6. See, e.g., the important article by Darryl Levinson and Richard Pildes, "Separation of Parties, Not Powers," 119 *Harvard Law Review* (2006): 2311.

7. Medicare Prescription Drug, Improvement, and Modernization Act, Pub. L. No. 108-173, 117 Stat. 2066 (2003).

8. A classic article, extremely influential in the debates of the 1960s, and not irrelevant today, is Peter Bachrach and Morton S. Baratz, "Two Faces of Power," *American Political Science Review* 56 (1962): 947, discussing the opposing ideological perspectives of "[s]ociologically oriented researchers" and political scientists.

9. See Fowler V. Harper and Edwin D. Etherington, "What the Supreme Court Did Not Do during the 1950 Term," 100 *University of Pennsylvania Law Review* 354 (1951); Fowler V. Harper and Arnold Leibowitz, "What the Supreme Court Did Not Do during the 1952 Term," 102 *University of Pennsylvania Law Review* 427 (1954).

10. H. W. Perry, *Deciding to Decide: Agenda Setting in the United States Supreme Court* (Cambridge, MA:Harvard University Press, 1990).

11. See Alexander Bickel, *The Least Dangerous Branch* (Indianapolis: Bobbs-Merrill, 1962), 111ff.

12. Ibid., 112.

13. See Barbara Sinclair, "Question: What's Wrong with Congress? Answer: It's a Democratic Legislature," *Boston University Law Review* 89 (2009): 387–397.

14. Ibid., 392–92, where she notes that "there were 36 filibusters in the 109th Congress ... and 52 in the current one." Interestingly enough, the *New York Times* on March 1, 2009, published (at least electronically) two pieces on the dysfunctionality of the contemporary filibuster. See David E. RePass, "Make My Filibuster," *New York Times*, March 1, 2009, A23, calling on Majority Leader Harry Reid to force Republicans to engage in a "real" filibuster by having to keep the floor during all night sessions and the like.

15. Jean Edward Smith, "Filibusters: The Senate's Self-Inflicted Wound," *New York Times*, March 1, 2009, http://100days.blogs.nytimes.com/2009/03/01/filibusters-the-senates-self-inflicted-wound/. ontaining a good history of the development of the modern "trivialized" filibuster that has become an almost perfunctory method of delaying or preventing legislation desired by the majority.

16. See Ben Eidelson, "How Undemocratic Is the Filibuster in Practice," available at http://leftsideoftheroad.wordpress.com/2009/02/18/how-undemocratic-is-the-filibuster-in-practice/.

17. Norman Ornstein, "Our Broken Senate," *The American: The Journal of the American Enterprise Institute*, March/April 2008, 74–76 available at http://www.american.com/archive/2008/march-april-magazine-contents/our-broken-senate.

18. See Carl Hulse, "Senate Republicans Block No. 2 Interior Nominee," available at http://the caucus.blogs.nytimes.com/2009/05/13/senate-republicans-block-no-2-interior-nominee/?hp.

19. See Paul C. Light, "Nominate and Wait," *New York Times,* March 23, 2009, available at http://www.nytimes.com/2009/03/24/opinion/24light.html?scp=4&sq=Paul%20Light%20op-ed&st=cse.

20. See, e.g., Michael J. Gerhardt, "Non-Judicial Precedent," *Vanderbilt Law Review*. 61 (2008) 713, 729. Explaining how Republicans claimed that the cloture requirement for overcoming filibusters was unconstitutional.

21. US Constitution, Article 1, Section 5.

22. See, e.g., George Tsebelis and Jeannette Money, *Bicameralism* (Cambridge, UK: Cambridge University Press, 1997), 44–70, tbls. 2.2A, 2.2B. Describing the institutional features of the world's senate bodies, including who has "final decision" power. Samuel C. Patterson and Anthony Mughan, "Senates and the Theory of Bicameralism," in *Senates: Bicameralism in the Contemporary World* 1, eds. Samuel C. Patterson and Anthony Mughan (Columbus: Ohio State University Press, 1999) 24–26, tbl.1.3. Comparing the powers of the senates of nine different nations.

23. Tsebelis and Money, *Bicameralism,* tbls. 2.2A, 2.2B.

24. Where I disagree with him is his seeming love for a two-party system and his apparent lack of support for a system of popular election that would guarantee, either because of a runoff procedure or an alternative transferrable vote, that the winner would have a more plausible claim to representing majority preferences than is the case with the classic first-past-the-post system.

25. See, e.g., Elena Kagan, "Presidential Administration," *Harvard Law Review* 114 (2001): 2245, 2383–84. Describing the emergence of a far more presidentially-controlled executive bureaucracy.

26. Sinclair, "Question: What's Wrong with Congress?," 389.

27. See Sanford Levinson, *Our Undemocratic Constitution: Where the Constitution Goes Wrong (and How We the People Can Correct It)* (New York: Oxford University Press, 2006), 20.

28. See Jack Rakove, *Original Meanings: Politics and Ideas in the Making of the Constitution* (New York: Knopf, 1996): 75–81. Detailing the debate at the Philadelphia Convention on allocation of voting power in the Senate. See also Levinson, *Our Undemocratic Constitution*, 62. Discussing the Connecticut Compromise of 1787, which forced Madison and others to approve the equality of voting power in the Senate because "small states would simply refuse to agree to any constitution that did not include equal voting power in the Senate."

29. *Federalist* No. 62 (James Madison) Jacob E. Cooke ed., 1961.

30. See U.S. Constitution Article 5: "[N]o State, without its Consent, shall be deprived of its equal Suffrage in the Senate."

31. Sinclair, "Question: What's Wrong with Congress?," 396.

32. Larry Sabato, *A More Perfect Constitution: 23 Proposals to Revitalize Our Constitution and Make America a Fairer Country* (New York: Walker Publishing Company, 2007), 26. Proposing to enlarge the Senate to 135 members by apportioning additional Senators to the largest states.

33. Ibid.

34. US Census Bureau, *Historical National Population Estimates 1* (2003), *available at* http://www.census.gov/statab/hist/HS-01.pdf. Estimating that the United States population was 177,830,000 people on July 1, 1959; Press Release, US Census Bureau, *Census Bureau Projects Population of 305.5 Million on New Year's Day* (Dec. 29, 2008), http://www.census.gov/Press-Release/www/releases/archives/population/013127.html (estimating that the US population would be 305,000,000 on January 1, 2009).

35. See Federal-Aid Highway Act of 1956, Pub. L. No. 84-627, 70 Stat. 374 (1956). Codified as amended at 23 U.S.C. §§ 101–166 (2006).

36. See Perry Bacon Jr., "Would-Be Senators From Minn. Describe Life in Election Limbo; Democrat Leans About Capital; Republican Goes to Court," *Washington Post*, February 15, 2009, A8.

37. Sabato, *More Perfect Constitution,* 23–32.

38. US Constitution Article. 1, Section 3.

39. Ibid., Section 4, clause. 2. Amended by US Constitution, Amendment.20, Section 1.

40. See Clinton Rossiter, *Constitutional Dictatorship* (New Brunswick, NJ: Transaction Press, 2002) 224.

41. See Paul Brest et al., *Processes of Constitutional Decisionmaking*, 5th ed. (New York: Aspen Publishers, 2006) 273–74 (5th ed. 2006). Questioning whether a president committed to democratic governance would have put off the new session as long as Lincoln did.

42. Jim Hoagland, "Obama's 77-Day Spring," *Washington Post*, December 7, 2008, B7.

43. Ibid.

44. I note that Senator Russell Feingold, responding to the fiasco in Illinois regarding now-impeached Illinois Governor Rod Blagojevich's appointment of Senator Roland Burris to succeed Barack Obama, *has* introduced a proposed amendment to strip governors of their power, authorized by the Seventeenth Amendment, to make such appointments. *See* Bernie Becker, *A Call for Elections to Vacant Senate Seats*, N.Y. TIMES, Jan. 28, 2009, http://thecaucus.blogs.nytimes.com/2009/01/28/a-call-for-elections-to-vacant-senate-seats/. Though one might easily sympathize with Senator Feingold's views with regard to what might be termed "retail" vacancies (i.e., one or two empty Senate seats, where it may well be worth the time it would take to hold a special election and thus gain the added legitimacy that comes through choice by the electorate), his proposal is out-and-out dangerous should the Senate be faced with "wholesale" vacancies as the result, say, of a catastrophic attack on Washington that kills or even disables many senators. For further discussion of this, see Levinson, *Our Undemocratic Constitution*, 69–75 (discussing the desirability of assured continuity in government following catastrophic attack).

45. Sinclair, "Question: What's Wrong with Congress?," 396.

Chapter 9

1. Sanford Levinson, *Our Undemocratic Constitution: Where the Constitution Goes Wrong (and How We the People Can Correct It)* (New York: Oxford University Press, 2006), 38.

2. Ibid., p. 26.

3. James MacGregor Burns, *The Deadlock of Democracy* (Englewoods Cliffs, NH: Prentice-Hall, 1963); Lloyd Cutler, "To Form a Government, *Foreign Affairs* (Fall, 1980); James Sunquist, *Constitutional Reform and Effective Government* (Washington DC: Brookings Institution Press, 1992); Robert Dahl, *How Democratic is the American Constitution?* (New Haven CT: Yale University Press, 2002).

4. *Federalist* No. 63. The Democratic Party's constant tinkering with its delegate selection rules provides a vivid example of the hazards of rapid rule changes. The party has made major changes in its rules nearly every four years since 1968. Often the campaign organization that is clever enough to understand the implications of the new rules wins the nomination. In 1972 the candidate who best grasped the opportunities created by the delegate selection system established by the McGovern Commission was — surprise, surprise — George McGovern. In 1976 Jimmy Carter figured out how to use the new Iowa caucuses as a springboard toward winning the New Hampshire primary. In 1992 Bill Clinton saw how to take advantage of the growing number and clumping of southern primaries. Every four years presidential aspirants try to rig the rules for the next primary season to increase their influence and their prospects for success.

5. *Federalist* No. 48.

6. Myers v. United States, 272 U.S. 293 (1926).

7. Paul Pierson *Dismantling the Welfare State? Reagan, Thatcher, and the Politics of Retrenchment* (Cambridge, UK: Cambridge University Press, 1994), 18.

8. In their comparative study of pension reform, Paul Pierson and Kent Weaver write, "What the pension cases reveal most clearly, however, is that loss imposition is a difficult task for any government that can be held accountable by its populace." "Imposing Losses in Pension Policy," in Kent Weaver and Bert Rockman, eds, *Do Institutions Matter? Government Capabilities in the United States and Abroad*(Washington DC:Brookings Institution Press, 1993).

9. Hugh Heclo, "One Executive Branch or Many?" in Anthony King, ed., *Both Ends of the Avenue* (Washington DC: AEI Press, 1983).

10. Barbara Sinclair, *Party Wars: Polarization and the Politics of National Policy Making* (Norman, OK: University of Oklahoma Press, 2006), esp. ch. 4; and Thomas Mann and Norman Ornstein, *The Broken Branch: How Congress is Failing America and How to Get it Back on Track* (New York: Oxford University Press, 2006).

11. Mann and Ornstein, *The Broken Branch*, 123.

12. *CQ Weekly*, December 7, 2002, 3176.

13. Levinson, *Our Undemocratic Constitution*, 108.

14. *CQ Weekly*, June 28, 2010, 1572.

15. Barry Rabe, *Statehouse and Greenhouse: The Emerging Politics of American Climate Change Policy* (Washington DC: Brookings Institution Press, 2004), xii.

16. Quoted in Deborah Schoch and Janet Wilson, "Governor, Blair Reach Environmental Accord," *Los Angeles Times*, August 1, 2006.

17. *Massachusetts v. EPA* 549 U.S. 497 (2007).

18. The reporter quotes a coal-state Democrat as saying, "Most people would rather have Congress act. We can be more balanced; we can take into account the effects on the economy. But if we don't undertake this, E.P. A. certainly will." John M. Broder, "Obama, Who Vowed Rapid Action on Climate Change, Turns More Cautious," *New York Times*, April 11, 2009, A10.

19. R. Shep Melnick, *Regulation and the Courts: The Case of the Clean Air Act* (Washington DC: Brookings Institution Press, 1983), ch. 4.

20. I present this case study and develop this argument at greater length in "Separation of Powers and the Strategy of Rights: The Expansion of Special Education," in Landy and Levin, eds., *The New Politics of Public Policy* (Baltimore: Johns Hopkins University Press, 1995) and in "Entrepreneurial Litigation: Advocacy Coalitions and Strategies in the Fragmented American Welfare State," in Joe Soss, Jacob Hacker, and Susanne Mettler, eds.*Remaking America: Democracy and Public Policy in an Age of Inequality* (New York: Russell Sage Foundation, 2007).

21. Hugh Davis Graham, *The Civil Rights Era: Origins and Development of National Policy* (New York: Oxford University Press, 1990): John Skrentny, *The Ironies of Affirmative Action* (University of Chicago Press, 1996).

22. Steven Teles, *Whose Welfare? AFDC and Elite Politics* (Lawrence, KS: University of Kansas Press, 1996), Kent Weaver, *Ending Welfare as We Know It* (Washington DC: Brookings Institution Press, 2000), and Lawrence Mead, *Government Matters: Welfare Reform in Wisconsin* (Princeton University Press, 2004).

23. Lawrence Brown and Michael Sparer, "Poor Program's Progress: The Unanticipated Politics of Medicaid Policy," *Health Affairs* (2003), 31–49. Others have reached the same conclusion: Aaron Wildavsky, *New Politics of the Budgetary Process* (Glenview, IL: Scott, Foresman and Company, 1988), 303–308; and Michael Greve, "Washington and the States," *AEI Federalism Outlook*, no.13 (May, 2003).

24. Nathan, "Federalism and Health Policy," *Health Affairs*, November 2005, 1.

25. David Mayhew, *Divided We Govern: Party Control, Lawmaking, and Investigations, 1946–1990* (New Haven CT: Yale University Press, 1991).

26. Timothy Conlan et al, *Taxing Choices* (Washington, DC: CQ Press, 1989).

27. Martha Derthick, *Up in Smoke* (Washington, DC: CQ Press, 2002), ch. 9

28. Wyeth v. Levine, 555 U.S. — (2009)

29. Quoted in Brown and Sparer, "Poor Program's Progress."

30. Christopher Howard, *The Welfare State Nobody Knows: Debunking Myths About U.S. Social Policy* (Princeton University Press, 2007).

31. Those who promote parliamentary government as a cure for gridlock should consider the implications of a 2009 *New York Times* article by Ethan Bronner and Isabel Kershner entitled, "In Israeli Vote, With Two Parties Nearly Tied, the Winner Is Gridlock." It begins as follows: "Israelis awoke Wednesday to find that their parliamentary elections had yielded not a new government but political gridlock instead, along with the prospect of weeks of wrangling and deal making before the country's direction becomes clear." *New York Times*, February 11, 2009.

32. Anthony King, "Running Scared," *Atlantic Monthly*, January, 1997.

33. Kent Weaver and Bert Rockman, *Do Institutions Matter? Government Capabilities in the United States and Abroad* (Washington DC: Brookings Institution Press, 1993).

34. Ibid., 445.

35. Ibid., 450.

36. Ibid., 455.

37. Ibid., 452.

38. Ibid., 445–46, 449.

39. David Mayhew, *Parties and Policies: How the American Government Works* (New Haven CT: Yale University Press, 2008), ch. 11.

40. *CQ Weekly*, January 31, 2011, 260–61. Interestingly, only a handful of Democrats favored elimination of the filibuster rule.

41. Weaver and Rockman, *Do Institutions Matter?*, 452.

42. Lawrence Becker, *Doing the Right Thing: Collective Action and Procedural Choice in the New Legislative Process* (Columbus, OH: The Ohio State University Press, 2005), ch. 2.

43. Douglas Arnold, *The Logic of Congressional Action* (New Haven CT: Yale University Press, 1990), ch. 5.

Chapter 10

1. I put aside here the complications arising from federalism. For the United States, my view, admittedly idiosyncratic, is that the scope of congressional power is so wide, especially through Congress's power to enforce the Reconstruction amendments properly construed, that judicial invalidations of state and local legislation should be understood as the exercise of a power delegated to the courts by Congress and revocable by it. For a brief discussion, not cast in the terms offered here and outdated in terms of precedent, see Mark Tushnet, *Red, White, and Blue: A Critical Analysis of Constitutional Law* (Cambirdge, MA: Harvard University Press, 1981), p. 86.

2. I note some possible objections to particularly aggressive *ultra vires* review in my discussion of the positive component of the argument against judicial review.

3. Even if the legislature cannot retroactively repair the judicial action in the particular case, such an inability does not, I think, raise large questions about *ultra vires* review.

4. For my discussion of weak-form judicial review, see Mark Tushnet, *Weak Courts, Strong Rights: Judicial Review and Social Welfare Rights in Comparative Constitutional Law* (Princeton: Princeton University Press, 2007).

5. For purposes of this chapter I put aside the question of judicial review in systems where judges are elected. The details of selection and retention processes, as well as the length of tenure, and the ease of constitutional amendment all would affect the application of the analysis developed here to such systems. My (tentative) view is that judicial review in such systems is problematic only to the extent that displacing the judges' choices in such systems is more difficult for the people than is displacing the choices made by the people's legislators — that is, that the only issues in such systems relate to the difficulty of the process of constitutional amendment and to the back-end controls in the retention process.

6. This formulation allows for some degree of inertia associated with the status quo, whether that be "no relevant policy" or "a policy that many people, perhaps even a majority, believe bad." What matters, I think, is that the status quo inertia be no larger for novel policies than it is for policy revision.

7. I emphasize that my argument does not rely on simple majoritarianism as the people's decision rule for ordinary legislation, but rather on the proposition that whatever that decision rule is, judicial review is problematic when the courts' results can be displaced only by processes using decision rules requiring (significantly) more political agreement than the decision rule for ordinary legislation.

8. If the amendment process is relatively easy in the sense defined in the text, the objection to judicial review would disappear.

9. The reasons go to the desirability of judicial independence in "ordinary" cases, meaning those that raise no constitutional questions.

10. Related but somewhat different is the difficulty of ensuring that new judges will in fact overturn the objectionable decision. There is no guarantee that newly elected representatives will similarly displace undesired policies, but at least such representatives can pledge in their campaigns that they will do so, and can be held to account if they do not, whereas judges typically do not campaign in the same way — and in most constitutional systems pledges with respect to particular outcomes would be regarded as improper.

11. See, e.g., Terri Peretti, *In Defense of a Political Court* (Princeton: Princeton University Press, 1999).

12. This is the view taken by Jeremy Waldron, "The Core of the Case Against Judicial Review," *Yale Law Journal* 115 (2006) 1346–406.

13. Robert Bork, "Neutral Principles and Some First Amendment Problems," 47 *Indiana Law Journal* 47 (1971) 1–35.

14. See Samuel Issacharoff, "Fragile Democracies," *Harvard Law Review* 120 (2007) 1405–67.

15. Learned Hand, *The Spirit of Liberty* (New York: Knopf, 1953), 190, speech at an I Am an American Day ceremony, Central Park, New York City, May 21, 1944 ("Liberty lies in the hearts of men and women; when it dies there, no constitution, no law, no court can save it.").

16. But note the provisions of the Swedish and Finnish constitutions that authorize the courts to set aside legislation on the ground of "evident" inconsistency with the constitution. ("Evident" is one possible translation of the terms used in those constitutions.) Notably, the courts in those nations have not exercised this power in any interesting manner.

17. See section on "Democracy-Related Justifications."

18. The drafters of South Africa's post-apartheid constitution attempted to finesse this problem by creating a new institution, the Constitutional Court, that was given authority to determine whether the proposed constitution confirmed to a number of agreed-upon principles.

19. As far as I know, no such grounds are available in the geographical case, and democrats either ignore the problem or believe that, unlike all other questions of policy choice, it can be resolved on the basis of historical, cultural, or like grounds.

20. See section on "Justice-Related Justifications."

21. And that the incremental improvement in public policy—including of course compliance with the constitution—is offset by unjustifiable interferences with other public policies because of the kind of judicial overreaching identified by the second answer. Consider, for example, the defense of judicial review that it provides a venue for the development of reasons accessible to all reasonable people for and against the proposition that some statute violates fundamental rights. The opponent of judicial review asks whether judicial review's *incremental* contribution to the development of such reasons is justifiable in light of either the operation of a well-designed legislature which might have, for example, an institution like an Office of Constitutional Issues to inform its deliberations, as discussed in Adrian Vermeule, *Mechanisms of Democracy Institutional Design Writ Small* (New York: Oxford University Press, 2007), at pp. 234–44, or the operation of legislatures as they actually are now, taking into account the risk of mistaken judicial decisions interfering with the implementation of policies that do not violate fundamental rights.

22. Judicial errors are not in themselves enough to undermine the case for judicial review, because all institutions, including legislatures, make mistakes (and evaluating the relative importance and comparative numbers of errors by courts and legislatures is for all practical purposes impossible). For additional discussion, see section on "Redundancy Justifications."

23. I do not discuss originalist "justifications" for judicial review because, as the scare-quotes indicate, the argument that judicial review is justified simply because a constitution's designers and ratifiers placed the practice in the constitution (if they did) is not a justification in an interesting sense. The observation about the designers' and ratifiers' understandings does no more than invite the question, why should today's polity respect those understandings? Answers to that question do provide justifications for judicial review—and are typically either justice-related or democracy-related.

24. The literature here is large and I do not pretend to address the details of particular arguments made by proponents of judicial review on justice-related grounds. For important contributions, see Ronald Dworkin, *A Matter of Principle* (Cambridge: Harvard University Press, 1985); Lawrence Sager, *Justice in Plain Clothes: A Theory of American Constitutional Practice* (New Have: Yale University Press, 2004).

25. Here the argument relies on the Rawlsian characterization of the circumstances of justice, in which there are ineradicable reasonable disagreements about the good. Those circumstances mean that, for a wide range of important issues, people can offer reasons for the policies they prefer, cast in terms that other reasonable people *could* but need not accept.

26. I discuss other examples of purportedly unjust legislation below.

27. This is the reason why the unelaborated invocation of judicial review as a technique for defending minority rights is unavailing. The problem lies in distinguishing between minorities who are unfairly treated and mere losers in a political contest over what reasonable public policy should be. The distinction will inevitably be justice-related, but the argument sketched in this section shows why drawing the distinction will probably not justify judicial review in its current form.

28. For an explanation of why legislators have electoral incentives to take the interests of enfranchised minority groups into account, see Tushnet, *Weak Courts*, note 4 above, at pp. 94–99. (I use this citation to show that the point has been known for a long time, not to establish any particular priority or insight for myself.)

29. The argument in the text is developed with respect to the particularly dramatic *DeShaney* case, *DeShaney v. Winnebago County Dep't of Social Services*, 489 U.S. 189 (1989), in Louis Michael and Mark Tushnet, *Remnants of Belief: Contemporary Constitutional Issues* (New York: Oxford University Press, 1996).

30. For a development of this argument, see Frederick Schauer, "Do Cases Make Bad Law?," *University of Chicago Law Review* 73 (2006) 883–918.

31. For a more qualified version of the "as applied" argument, see section on "Redundancy Justifications."

32. John Hart Ely, *Democracy and Distrust: A Theory of Judicial Review* (Cambridge: Harvard University Press, 1980).

33. *Reynolds v. Sims*, 377 U.S. 533, 562 (1964).

34. Or, perhaps even more dramatically because it addresses precisely the issue Warren raised (though obviously fancifully), suppose a legislature influenced by ideas about animal rights decided that cows deserved representation, and allocated seats in the legislature treating farmers as the cows' virtual representatives.

35. This was one of the earliest criticisms of Ely's work. See, e.g., Laurence Tribe, "The Puzzling Persistence of Process-Based Constitutional Theories," *Yale Law Journal* 89 (1980) 1063–80.

36. That is, in a world where politics is necessary.

37. One might argue that human autonomy is the first-order value, promoted by the second-order value of democracy and implemented by a "third order" institution, judicial review, and that the second- and third-order value and institution operate by screening human autonomy out of direct consideration, in the way that rules screen from direct consideration the reasons justifying them. For myself, the argument about rules and their justifications is itself problematic, but independent of that, I am not sure what reasons there might be for screening the first-order value out of consideration in the setting of judicial review. My sense is that the argument for doing so rests on an essentially and clearly contestable empirical judgment, that courts can do a decent job of protecting human autonomy if they think only about democracy but will do a worse job if they think about autonomy directly.

38. A proponent of judicial review who relied on a democracy-related justification might resist the extension described in this paragraph by invoking institutional capacity, that is, by arguing that courts have the capacity to identify and enforce restrictions on the democratic process but lack the capacity to do the same for restrictions on autonomy generally. I confess that I do not know what dimensions of judicial capacity would come into play here, unlike the questions of judicial capacity that arise in connection with judicial enforcement of justice's requirements with respect to material well-being.

39. This basis is only seemingly narrower because it invites the question, why should preferences be respected? To which the answer will inevitably invoke ideas about autonomy.

40. For a recent discussion, see Neil M. Richards, "Intellectual Privacy," *Texas Law Review*, 87 (2008) 387–445.

41. I believe that something along these lines is the best way to understand the otherwise puzzling discussion of reliance in *Planned Parenthood of Southern Pennsylvania v. Casey*, 505 U.S. 833 (1992).

42. For a judicial recognition that common-law property rules can cause material deprivation in a legally significant sense, see *West Coast Hotel v. Parrish*, 300 U.S. 379, 399 (1937) (Hughes, C.J.) ("The community is not bound to provide what is, in effect, a subsidy for unconscionable employers.").

43. The constitutional systems of Japan, Sweden, and Finland use such committees, but backstop them with courts empowered to set aside legislation as unconstitutional. Perhaps unsurprisingly, courts in those nations rarely (or never) find statutes unconstitutional. The Parliamentary Joint Committee on Human Rights in Great Britain performs a similar, though more advisory, role.

44. The most important recent version of a redundancy justification is Richard H. Fallon, "The Core of an Uneasy Case For Judicial Review," *Harvard Law Review*, 121, (2008) 1693–736.

45. I note that a great deal is concealed by the phrase "objectively unconstitutional," but it is unnecessary to expand on that point here. As suggested by my earlier discussion, the only defensible definition of "objectively unconstitutional" is something like "unconstitutional according to any reasonable interpretation of the relevant constitutional provisions."

46. See Sager, *Justice in Plain Clothes*.

47. C. Neal Tate and Torbjorn Vallinder, *The Global Expansion of Judicial Power* (New York: New York University Press, 1995).

48. There are pressures to repeal or limit significantly the operation of the British Human Rights Act, but its ultimate fate remains unclear.

49. A political scientist might observe that political systems are always dominated by elites, and that the more interesting questions revolve around identifying which elites dominate and are harmed or benefited by which institutions. It might be that, from a democrat's point of view, a system with judicial review is better overall than one without it because the elites who dominate the institution of judicial review are different from and might offset the influence of elites who dominate other institutions. I thank Mark Graber for provoking this observation.

Chapter 11

1. Both Waldron and Tushnet distinguish between "strong" and "weak" forms of judicial review, with the former including the power of courts to invalidate acts of legislation, and the latter involving only the judicial power to require or facilitate legislative reconsideration of legislation, see Tushnet, this volume, and Jeremy Waldron, "The Core of the Case Against Judicial Review," *Yale Law Journal* 115 (2006): 1346.

2. Ronald Dworkin, among the warmest defenders of judicial review, for example, advocates term limits for US Supreme Court justices, see *Justice for Hedgehogs*, (Cambridge, Mass.: Harvard University Press, 2011), 399.

3. See for example Sanford Levinson's *Our Undemocratic Constitution: Where the Constitution Goes Wrong (and How We the People Can Correct It)* (New York: Oxford University Press, 2006); to which I have written a partial reply "Our Imperfect Democratic Constitution: The Critics Examined," *Boston University Law* 609 (2009): 89; part of the symposium issue: Toward a More Democratic Congress?

4. Samuel Issacharoff, "Constitutionalizing Democracy in Fractured Societies," *Texas Law Review* 82 (2004): 1861.

5. Corey Brettschneider, *Democratic Rights* (Princeton: Princeton University Press, 2007).

6. As Mark Tushnet says, this volume.

7. The view I defend is similar to Dworkin's "partnership conception," see *Is Democracy Possible Here?* (Princeton: Princeton University Press, 2007).

8. The real difference between ancient democracies and modern republics lies, according to Madison, in "the *total exclusion of the people in their collective capacity* from any share in the" direct exercise of administration, *Federalist*, No.63.

9. For an excellent account of the ways in which rule of law devices can function as "veil mechanisms" to promote impartiality, see Adrian Vermeule, *Mechanisms of Democracy: Institutional Design Writ Small* (New York: Oxford University Press, 2007).

10. See the helpful discussion in Philip Pettit, "Democracy: Electoral and Contestatory," in Ian Shapiro and Stephen Macedo, *Designing Democratic Institutions: NOMOS XLII* (New York: New York University Press, 2000).

11. This sentence and the previous paragraph are drawn from "Democracy-Enhancing Multilateralism," Robert O. Keohane, Stephen Macedo and Andrew Moravcsik, *International Organizations*, v. 63, no. 1 (Winter 2009) 1–31.

12. Jeremy Waldron, "The Constitutional Conception of Democracy," in *Democracy*, David Estlund, ed. (Oxford: Blackwell, 2002) 68. Democracy is founded on the premise of political equality: individuals are equally rights holders, and that includes an equal right to participate in making majority decisions (the right to participate is, he says, the "right of rights").

13. These paragraphs draw on a draft paper co-authored with Christopher L. Karpowitz and Evan Oxman, "Two Conceptions of Democracy," Unpublished ms. on file with author.

14. Waldron, "Constitutional Conception," 66.

15. Ibid., 64.

16. Ibid., 68. As with utilitarianism, another aggregative standard for decision: everyone counts for one, nobody counts for more than one.

17. In Dworkin, *Justice for Hedgehogs*.

18. Add a third alternative and the possibility of intransitive preferences and the familiar Arrow-type cycling problems (varying the order in which several pair-wise alternatives come up for a vote) make it impossible to say that any particular results are preferred by a majority.

19. E. E. Schattschneider, *Party Government* (New York: Holt, Rinehart, and Winston, 1942), 52.

20. Normal adult individuals who satisfy residency or other such requirements.

21. See Jane J. Mansbridge, *Beyond Adversary Democracy* (Chicago: University of Chicago, 1983).

22. See Mathias Risse, "Arguing for Majority Rule"*Journal of Political Philosophy* (2004) *12 (1):41–64.;* and see Beitz, *Political Equality*. Waldron—in "The Core of the Case Against Judicial Review"—cites May, Kenneth O., "A Set of Independent Necessary and Sufficient Conditions for Simple Majority Decision," *Econometrica* 20:4 (1952), 680–684 Under a stringent set of conditions, majority rule does indeed have some uniquely equality-preserving properties (including features designated as "neutrality" and "anonymity"). However, the specified conditions (which include strictly pair-wise alternatives, strictly individualistic preferences (no factions or coalitions), no linkages across decisions, no accounting for intensity of preferences, no asymmetry of gains and losses (no preference for avoiding bads over achieving goods) do not hold under real world conditions, particularly in the presence of known majority and minority factions, see Douglas W. Rae, 1969. "Decision-Rules and Individual Values in Constitutional Choice", *American Political Science Review* vol. 63, no. 1: 40. If we depart from these conditions (by allowing for the existence of factions, by including non-individualistic preferences, etc.), majority rule loses its appeal.

23. Though, oddly, he argues that New Zealand's unicameral parliamentary system exacerbates various legislative pathologies that might be better dealt with in bicameral (and therefore, super-majority) systems, including adequate attention to minority interests, see, Jeremy Waldron, "Compared to What? Judicial Activism and the New Zealand Parliament," 1 *New Zealand Law Journal* 441 (2005); and James Allan & Andrew Geddis, "Waldron and Opposing Judicial Review—except, sort of, in New Zealand," 2 *New Zealand Law Journal* 94 (2006).

24. See Beitz, *Political Equality*, Rae "Decision Rules."

25. *Carolene Products Co. v. United States* (1944) 323 US 18, Footnote 4; and see the discussion in John Hart Ely, *Democracy and Distrust: A Theory of Judicial Review*. Cambridge MA: Harvard, 1980). Note here that the objection to a simple aggregation approach refers to the underlying strategy of justification.

26. See the recent account in Charles R. Beitz, *The Idea of Human Rights* (Princeton: Princeton University Press 2009).

27. Of course, the majoritarian democrat might not deny this, but could say that democratic values are not enough for political legitimacy: democracy must be limited for the sake of protecting basic rights. But then the disagreement collapses. No interesting substantive argument is going to be settled on the basis of definitions. I am operating here on the assumption—as I believe are those I have criticized, such as Waldron—that "democracy" names a legitimate and morally attractive system of collective self-rule. It is open for others to stipulate that for a political system to be morally legitimate and attractive it must be a "constitutional democracy," combining "democratic" values and institutions with "liberal" protections for individual and minority rights. For reasons I have suggested, this seems to me cumbersome and confusing. This is not, moreover, what Waldron and Tushnet argue.

28. See Ronald Dworkin, *Freedom's Law: The Moral Reading of the American Constitution* (Cambridge, Mass.: Harvard University Press, 1997), ch. 1, "The Moral Reading and the Majoritarian Premise"; and Beitz, *Political Equality*.

29. John Stuart Mill, *Representative Government*, online: http://philosophy.eserver.org/mill-representative-govt.txt, Chapter 7, section 1.

30. See Aristotle, *Politics*, online: http://classics.mit.edu/Aristotle/politics.html, Book III; in the correct regimes one part of the city rules—the one, the few, or the many—but they rule on behalf of the common good.

31. Christopher L. Eisgruber, *Constitutional Self-Government* (Cambridge, Mass.: Harvard University press, 2001), p. 19.

32. *Federalist* No. 10, online: http://www.constitution.org/fed/federa10.htm.

33. They may do so procedurally and substantively, by insuring that channels for political discussion and change remain open (see Ely's *Democracy and Distrust*), but also by insuring that particular substantive individual interests are protected against encroachment. The process/substance distinction is superficial, because substantive values underlie fair process, and because "substantive" rights often correct for process-based flaws, including "nosey preferences" and prejudices: they protect individuals and minorities against preferences that ought not to operate in an egalitarian political system (preferences at odds with the premise of political equality on which democracy is based).

34. "It is of great importance in a republic not only to guard the society against the oppression of its rulers, but to guard one part of the society against the injustice of the other part. Different interests necessarily exist in different classes of citizens. If a majority be united by a common interest, the rights of the minority will be insecure. There are but two methods of providing against this evil: the one by creating a will in the community independent of the majority—that is, of the society itself; the other, by comprehending in the society so many separate descriptions of citizens as will render an unjust combination of a majority of the whole very improbable, if not impracticable." *Federalist* No. 51, online: http://www.constitution.org/fed/federa51.htm.

35. "In republican government, the legislative authority necessarily predominates. The remedy for this inconveniency is to divide the legislature into different branches; and to render them, by different modes of election and different principles of action, as little connected with each other as the nature of their common functions and their common dependence on the society will admit."

36. We might require approval in successive referenda with a period for debate and discussion in between.

37. These are not exhaustive—responsiveness and decisiveness would be other principles or values that we would want a political system to answer to, and there are others.

38. It rules out Mill's proposals for extra votes for the better educated (plural voting). Beitz holds that the "foundational requirement" of egalitarianism is that "fair terms of participation should be reasonably acceptable to everyone," *Political Equality*, p. 24.

39. Ronald Dworkin, Charles Beitz, David Miller, and others, draw an important distinction between democratic institutions and practices, on the one hand, and regulative democratic principles, rightly insisting that there is no simple relationship between these, see Dworkin, *Freedom's Law*; Beitz, *Political Equality*; David Miller "Deliberative Democracy and Social Choice," in Estlund, *Democracy*, 289–307. Elections and majority decision rules are among the devices that may often contribute to the well-working of democracy, but which institutions and practices best realize democratic values is often an open question.

40. See Waldron, "The Core of the Case."

41. See Angus Campbell, Philip E. Converse, Warren E. Miller, Donald E. Stokes, *The American Voter* (New York: John Wiley and Sons, 1960); and more recently, Larry Bartels, "Homer Gets a Tax Cut: Inequality and Public Policy in the American Mind." *Perspectives on Politics* 3:1 (March 2005), 15–31.

42. Bernard Grofman, Robert Griffin and Amihai Glazer, "Is the Senate More Liberal than the House? Another Look," *Legislative Studies Quarterly*, vol. 16, no. 2 (May 1991), 281–95.

43. Dworkin, "Introduction: The Moral Reading and the Majoritarian Premise," *Freedom's Law*; Christopher L. Eisgruber, *Constitutional Self-Government*.

44. See Ely, *Democracy and Distrust*.

45. See James E. Fleming, *Securing Constitutional Democracy: The Case of Autonomy* (Chicago: University of Chicago Press, 2006); Brettschneider, *Democratic Rights*.

46. See for example Waldron, "The Core of the Case."

47. A point well made in Fleming, *Securing Constitutional Democracy*.

48. See Ronald Dworkin, "The Forum of Principle," in *A Matter of Principle*(Cambridge, Mass.: Harvard University Press, 1986).

49. Adrian Vermeule, *Mechanisms of Democracy*.

50. See Rawls, *Justice as Fairness: A Restatement* (Cambridge, Massachusetts: Belknap Press, 2001).

51. See Michael J. Klarman, *Brown V. Board of Education and the Civil Rights Movement* (New York: Oxford University Press, 2007).

52. *Political Foundations of Judicial Supremacy: The Presidency, the Supreme Court, and Constitutional Leadership in U.S. History* (Princeton: Princeton University press, 2009), 122.

53. Stephen Ansolobehere and Jack Snyder, *The End of Inequality: One Person, One Vote and the Transformation of American Politics* (New York: Norton, 2008).

54. See David Fontana, who compares the US Supreme Court and the more active—on these issues—Canadian Constitutional Court, see "The Supreme Court: Missing in Action," *Dissent*, spring 2008, 68–74.

55. See, for example, Eisgruber, *Constitutional Self-Government*, and Dworkin, *Freedom's Law*.

56. See Benjamin Wittes, "The Supreme Court's Looming Legitimacy Crisis" Brookings online: http://www.brookings.edu/opinions/2007/0625governance_wittes.aspx.

57. See Morris P. Fiorina, et al., *Culture War? The Myth of a Polarized America* (White Plains, NY: Longman, 2005).

58. Issacharoff, "Fractured Societies," 1863.

59. Ibid., 1865.

60. "Accountability In a Global Context," October 2006, from the NYU Global Administrative Law web site: http://www1.law.nyu.edu/kingsburyb/fall06/globalization/speakers_papers.html.

61. See Benedict Kingsbury, Nico Krisch, and Richard B. Stewart, "The Emergence of Global Administrative Law," 68 *Law and Contemporary Problems* 15 (2005), 15–61.

62. See Ruth W. Grant and Robert O. Keohane, ""Accountability and Abuses of Power in World Politics," *American Political Science Review*, vol. 99, no. 1 (2005), 29–43.

63. In many ways, the criminal justice system in the US could use a stronger dose of insulation from direct accountability. The public's frequently punitive instincts ill serve the cause of criminal justice.

64. See Andrew Moravcsik, "In Defense of the 'Democratic Deficit': Reassessing Legitimacy in the European Union" *Journal of Common Market Studies* 40:4 (November 2002), 603–624.

65. Notable work has been done by Richard Falk, David Held, and Danielle Archibugi, among others.

66. See Grant and Keohane, "Accountability and Abuses of Power"; Kingsbury, Krisch, and Stewart, "Emergence of Global Administrative Law."

67. See Keohane, Macedo, and Moravcsik, "Democracy Enhancing Multilateralism."

68. In advancing this argument, we draw on John O. McGinnis and Mark Movsesian, "The World Trade Constitution," *Harvard Law Review*, 2000, 114:2, 511–605.

Chapter 12

1. The literature on the subject includes the following indispensable works: Arthur M. Schlesinger, Jr., *The Imperial Presidency* (Boston: Houghton Mifflin, 1973); Athan Theoharis, *The Truman Presidency:*

The Origins of the Imperial Presidency and the National Security State (1979); David Adler and George, L., eds., *The Constitution and the Conduct of American Foreign Policy* (Lawrence: University of Kansas Press 1998); David Adler and Genovese, M., eds. *The Presidency and the Law: The Clinton Legacy* (Lawrence: University Press of Kansas 2002); Andrew Rudalevige, *The New Imperial Presidency: Renewing Presidential Power after Watergate* (Ann Arbor: University of Michigan Press, 2006); Jack Goldsmith, *The Terror Presidency: Law and Judgment Inside the Bush Administration* (2007); Charlie Savage, *Takeover: The Return of the Imperial Presidency and the Subversion of American Democracy* (Boston: Bay Back Books, 2008); Peter Irons, *War Powers: How the Imperial Presidency Hijacked the Constitution* (Metropolitan Books, 2005); F.A.O. Schwarz, Jr., and Huq, A., *Unchecked and Unbalanced.* (New York: New Press., 2007); James R. Silken and Shulman M. eds., *The Imperial Presidency and the Consequences of 9/11: Lawyers React to the Global War on Terrorism* (Boulder: Praeger Security International, 2007); James Pfiffner, *Power Play: The Bush Presidency and the Constitution* (Washington, D.C.: Brookings Institution Press, 2008); Eric Lichtblau, *Bush's Law: The Remaking of American Justice,* (New York: Pantheon, 2008); Bruce P. Montgomery, *Richard B. Cheney and the Rise of the Imperial Vice Presidency* (Boulder: Praeger Publishers, 2009).

2. For a discussion of executive power in the Constitution and its judicial interpretations, see Richard M. Pious, "Inherent War and Executive Powers and Prerogative Politics," *Presidential Studies Quarterly,* Spring 2007, 66–84.

3. On the vantage point argument see Richard E. Neustadt, *Presidential Power* (New York: John Wiley, 1960), 183–185.

4. Some trenchant critiques of presidential pretensions are found in the following articles: Edward S. Corwin, "The Presidency in Perspective," *Journal of Politics,* vol. 11, no. 1, February 1949, 7–13; Arthur S. Miller, "Implications of Watergate: Some Proposals for Cutting the Presidency Down to Size," *Hastings Constitutional Law Quarterly,* vol. 2, Winter 1975, 33–74; Theodore Sorensen, "Making the President More Accountable to the People," *Human Rights,* vol. 5, Fall 1975, 47–61; Archibald Cox, "Watergate and the U.S. Constitution," *British Journal of Law and Society,*" vol. 2, Summer 1975, 1–13; Theodore Lowi, "Presidential Power: Restoring the Balance" *Political Science Quarterly,* vol. 100, no. 2, Summer 1985, 185–213; James W. Ceasar, "In Defense of the Separation of Powers," in *Separation of Powers—Does It Still Work?* eds. Robert A. Goldwin, Art Kaufman, American Enterprise Institute, 1986. Also see Abel Upshur, *A Brief Inquiry Into the Nature and Character of Our Federal Government* (New York: Da Capo Press, 1971); Henry Lockwood *The Abolition of the Presidency*(New York: R. Worthington, 1884); Amaury de Riencourt, *The Coming Caesars* (New York: Coward McCann, 1957); Gene Healey, *The Cult of the Presidency* (Washington D.C.: The Heritage Foundation, 2008).

5. Louis Fisher, "The Efficiency Side of Separation of Powers," *Journal of American Studies,* vol. 5, no. 2, August 1971, 113–131.

6. On the successes of the presidency see Marc Landy and Milkis, S., *Presidential Greatness,* (Lawrence: University Press of Kansas, 2001).

7. On different kinds of prerogative power and the politics accompanying their use, see Richard M. Pious "Prerogative Power and Presidential Politics," in George Edwards, ed., *The Oxford Handbook of the American Presidency* (New York: Oxford University Press, 2009); Larry Arnhart, "'The God-Like Prince': John Locke, Executive Prerogative, and the American Presidency," *Presidential Studies Quarterly,* vol. 9, Spring 1979, 121–130; Thomas Langston and Michael Lind, "John Locke and the Limits of Presidential Prerogative," *Polity,* vol. 24, no. 1, Fall 1991, 49–68; Leonard R. Sorenson, "The Federalist Papers on the Constitutionality of Executive Prerogative," *Presidential Studies Quarterly,* vol. 18, Spring 1988, 267–283; Robert Scigliano, "The President's 'Prerogative Power,'" in Thomas E. Cronin, ed., *Inventing the American Presidency,* (Lawrence: University Press of Kansas, 1989), 236–256; Joseph Bessette and Jeffrey Tulis, "The Constitution, Politics and the Presidency," in *The Presidency in the Constitutional Order,* (Baton Rouge: Louisiana State University Press, 1981), 3–30; Harvey Mansfield, Jr., "The Modern Doctrine of Executive Power," *Presidential Studies Quarterly,* vol. 17, no. 2, Spring 1987, 237–252; James R. Hurtgen, "The Case for Presidential Prerogative," *Toledo Law Review,* vol. 7, no. 1, Fall 1975, 59–87.

8. Richard Rose, *The Postmodern President* (Chatham, N.J.: Chatham House, 1991) p. 39 and Fig. 3.3 p. 56.

9. One can distinguish between "hard" prerogative, based on a confrontational style, which usually accompanies divided government, such as Nixon's confrontations over war powers,

impoundments, the item veto, and the dispensing power, or Clinton's use of war powers in the Balkans, with a "soft" prerogative, in which a president seems to be cooperating with Congress but keeps the prerogative to act in reserve (examples include Reagan's signing of the Beirut Resolution to keep marines in Lebanon, and Bush 41 in the Persian Gulf War). A second issue involves transparency; although Bush 43 acted in Iraq based on an authorization granted by Congress, it may well have involved deliberate deception or exaggeration of the threat of Iraqi WMD. See Richard M. Pious, *Why Presidents Fail* (Lanham, MD: Rowman and Littlefield, 2008): 217–244.

10. David Frost interview with Richard Nixon, *New York Times*, May 20 1977 p. B-10; also accessed at http://www.landmarkcases.org/nixon/nixonview.html. Similarly consider the defense of interrogation policy in the war on terrorism by former Secretary of State Condoleezza Rice, at Stanford University after leaving office: "… by definition, if it was authorized by the President, it did not violate our obligations under the Convention Against Torture."

11. *Youngstown v. Sawyer* 343 U.S. 579 (1952).

12. See Frankfurter's concurring opinion in *Youngstown Sheet and Tube v. Sawyer* 343 U.S. 579 (1952) discussing the "gloss" on the Constitution; Jackson's concurring opinion in the same case observing that "practice will integrate the dispersed powers into a workable government"; *Orlando v. Laird* 443 F. 2d 1039 (1971) "mutual and joint action" test to uphold military operations in Southeast Asia; *Massachusetts v. Laird* 451 F2d 26 (1971) and *Mitchell v. Laird* 488 F.2d 611 (1973) test of "joint concord," *Da Costa v. Laird* test of "mutual participation" 471 F 2d 1146 (1973); and *Doe v. Bush* 323 F.3d 133 (2003) recognition of a "war power" not subject to analysis by the courts applying separation of power doctrine.

13. *The Inaugural Addresses of Presidents of the United States*, (Washington D.C.: Government Printing Office, 1965), 126.

14. Abraham Lincoln, Complete *Works*, eds. John G. Nicolay and John Hay, (New York: The Century Co., 1894) VOl. 6: 246–48.

15. James D. Richardson, *Messages and Papers of the Presidents*, (Washington, D.C. 1897), 18.

16. Richardson, *op. cit.*, Vol. VI, pp. 98–99; also see S.G. Fisher, "The Suspension of the Writ of Habeas Corpus During the War of the Rebellion," *Political Science Quarterly*, Vol. 3, No. 4, 1888.

17. James D. Richardson, *Messages and Papers of the Presidents* (Washington, D.C.: Bureau of National Literature and Art, 1900) Vol. 7, pp. 3215–3219.

18. Ibid.

19. Ibid.

20. Ibid.

21. Ibid.

22. Nicolay and Hay, *Abraham Lincoln, A History*, (New York: 1890), VI, 155–156.

23. Abraham Lincoln, *Complete Works*, Vol. VI, 303.

24. Abraham Lincoln, *Complete Works*, Vol. VII, p. 281.

25. 12 U.S. Stat. 326

26. *The Prize Cases* 2 Black 635 (1863).

27. *Ex Parte Merryman* 17 F. Cas. 144 (1861).

28. *Ex Parte Milligan* 4 Wall. (71 U.S.) 2 (1866).

29. Act of March 27, 1868, 15 Stat. at Large, 44.

30. *Ex Parte McCardle*, 74 U.S. 506 (1868), In contrast, state courts often stood up to Congress and the president, even during the height of hostilities. In 1863 Congress passed a statute providing that presidential orders would be a valid defense in any habeas corpus court proceedings involving military actions taken against civilians. In *Griffin v. Wilcox* (21 Indiana Reports 370), a state court ruled that any military order must be valid under the Constitution or the common law, and if not, no act of Congress could make it legal. When the question of whether a statute could define the legality of presidential war powers came before the Supreme Court in *Beckwith v. Bean* (98 U.S. Reports 266), the court evaded the issue.

31. Richardson, *op. cit.*, Vol. VI, pp. 102–104.

32. Official Records, *War of the Rebellion*, Series III, Volume 3.

33. Classics of post-Civil War jurisprudence dealing with these issues include Simeon Baldwin *The American Judiciary* (New York: The Century Co., 1905); John Burgess *Political Science and Comparative Constitutional Law*(Boston, Ginn and Co., 1890); Christopher Tiedemann *The Unwritten Constitution of the United States* (New York: G.P. Putnam's Sons 1890); Woodrow Wilson *The State* (London: D.C. Heath, 1888); W.W. Willoughby, *The Nature of the State* (New York: MacMillan, 1896).

34. Clinton Rossiter, *Constitutional Dictatorship* (New York: Harcourt Brace and World, 1948).

35. Edward S. Corwin, "Executive Authority Held Exceeded in Destroyer Deal" *New York Times*, October 13, 1940, p. E6, Col. 5.

36. Frank R. Kent, "Effect of the Deal" *Wall Street Journal*, September 11, 1940, p. 6.

37. Editorial, *Wall Street Journal*, September 5, 1940. p. 20.

38. Robert Shogun, *Hard Bargain* (New York: Basic Books, 1999) 17.

39. Ibid.

40. Jon Meacham, *Franklin and Winston: An Intimate Portrait of an Epic Friendship* (New York: Random House, 2003) p. 71.

41. Shogun, *Hard Bargain*,. 259.

42. The litany of congressional irresponsibility prior to the destroyer deal includes the Neutrality Act of 1935, instructing the president to declare at his discretion an embargo against all belligerents; a 1936 arms embargo against all third parties entering hostilities and bar against loans to belligerents (including private loans), and entry of U.S. ships into war zones which then was triggered by joint resolution during the Spanish Civil War, which applied to the aggressors and the victims of aggression alike. In 1937 Roosevelt called for quarantine against aggressors but Congress did not act. In 1938 he called for a huge naval construction program and creation of a large air force but Congress refused his request. After the Germans annexed Czechoslovakia in 1939, Roosevelt asked Congress to repeal the Neutrality Act of 1935, and this time Congress did act; its November 1939 revisions allowed arms purchases by belligerents, but required the purchaser to take possession of the goods in the US ports, and then to ship them so that no American ships would ply belligerent waters — so-called "cash and carry." In March 1940 FDR proposed a program of lend-lease assistance to the allies — a way around the fact that as a belligerent the British could not be extended loans under Neutrality Act of 1939, and under the Johnson Act of 1934, as a defaulting debtor from WWI Britain it was not eligible for new loans — but Congress took no immediate action.

43. Robert H. Jackson, *That Man*, (New York: Oxford University Press, 2004), 88.

44. Ibid., 92.

45. Ibid.

46. Robert Jackson, "Exchange of Destroyers for Bases, United States — United Kingdom" in *Opinions of the Attorneys General* 39 *Op.A.G.* 484 (27 August 1940).

47. Ibid., 97.

48. "Senate Hostile to New Deal's Destroyer Plan," *Chicago Daily Tribune*, August 15, 1940, 3.

49. "Wheeler for Deal to Get Navy Bases of Great Britain," *New York Times*, August 18, 1940, 1.

50. Ibid.

51. Doris Kearns Goodwin, *No Ordinary Time*. (New York: Simon and Schuster, 1994), 147.

52. Percy Wood, "Willkie Assails Secrecy Behind Destroyer Deal," *Chicago Daily Tribune*, September 4, 1940, 6.

53. Percy Wood, "Willkie Brands Destroyer Deal A Dictator's Act," *Chicago Daily Tribune*, September 7, 1940, 8.

54. Jackson, *That Man*, 87.

55. In what was perhaps the most unintentionally hilarious description of Bush's decision making, the former president, giving a talk in Calgary, Canada, promised that when he publishes

his memoirs (about the twelve toughest decisions he made), "I'm going to put people in my place, so when the history of this administration is written at least there's an authoritarian voice saying exactly what happened." Rob Gillies, "Bush Declines to Criticize Obama in Canada Speech," *Associated Press*, March 18, 2009. For a discussion of Bush's decisions to bypass Congress and the courts, see Nancy Kassop, "The Bush White House: Governing Without Congress or the Courts," *Law and Courts Newsletter*, Vol. 15, No. 1, Winter 2005, pp. 21–26, available at http://www.law.nyu.edu/law courts/pubs/newsletter/index.html.

56. POWs are those who have engaged in open, announced combat in accordance with the customs of war. According to the Third Geneva Convention, they are members of armed forces or militia, or organized resistance groups against the established government if they are under a chain of command and have a fixed recognition sign or uniform and carry arms openly, and conduct operations according to the laws and customs of war.

57. Unlawful combatants under Article 75 of the Geneva Convention are supposed to have trial by impartial and regularly conducted court, necessary rights and means of defense, presumption of innocence, the right to examine witnesses and right not to testify.

58. *Ex Parte Quirin*, 317 U.S. 1 at 38.

59. *Duncan v. Kahanamoku, Sheriff*, 327 U.S. 304 (1946).

60. *Hirabayashi v. U.S.* 320 U.S. 81 (1943); *Korematsu v. US* 323 U.S. 214 (1944).

61. *Ex Parte Endo*, 323 U.S. 283 (1944).

62. On the Bush Administration policies involving interrogation of detainees, see Richard M. Pious, "Torture of Detainees and Presidential Prerogative Power" in George Edwards, ed. *The Polarized Presidency of George W. Bush* (New York: Oxford University Press 2007).

63. 18. U.S.C. sec.2340A.

64. War Crimes Act 18 U.S.C. sec. 2441 (1996).

65. On the role of the Department of Justice see "Justice Departments Office of Legal Counsel," Hearing before the Subcommittee on the Constitution, Civil Rights and Civil Liberties, Committee on the Judiciary, House of Representatives, 110th Cong. 2d Sess., February 14, 2008, Serial No. 110-129.

66. Lt. Gen. Ricardo S. Sanchez, *Wiser in Battle* (New York: HarperCollins 2008).

67. David H. Petreaus, General, United States Army Commanding, "Soldiers, Sailors, Airmen, Marines and Coast Guardsmen Serving in Multi-National Force—Iraq," May 10, 2007, accessed at http://andrewsullivan.theatlantic.com.

68. On the Bush administration use of military tribunals see Richard M. Pious. "Military Tribunals, Prerogative Power, and the War on Terrorism" in Joseph Bessette and Jeffrey Tulis, eds., *The Constitutional Presidency* (Baltimore, Md: Johns Hopkins Press, 2009).

69. "Military Order on Detention, Treatment and Trial of Certain Non-Citizens in the War Against Terrorism," 66 Fed. Reg. 57831 (2001).

70. *Procedures for Trials by Military Commissions of Certain Non-United States Citizens in the War Against Terrorism*, Department of Defense Military Commission Order No. 1, March 21, 2002. The rules promulgated by the Pentagon are available at: www.defenselink.mil/news/Mar2002/d20020321 ord.pdf.

71. According to Pentagon official William J. Hayes, II, in Katharine Q. Seelye, "Pentagon Says Acquittals May Not Free Detainees," *New York Times*, March 22, p. 13.

72. P.L. 107-40 Sec. 2(a) (2001).

73. The use of commissions has been recognized by Congress in the Articles of War in 1920, the Uniform Code of Military Justice in 1950, and the War Crimes Act of 1996.

74. *Rasul v. Bush* 542 U.S. 466 (2004).

75. *Hamdan v. Rumsfeld* 126 S. Ct. 2749 (2006).

76. Jeremy Rabkin, "Not As Bad As You Think: The Court Hasn't Crippled the War on Terror," *Weekly Standard*, July 17, 2006, Volume 11, Issue 41.

77. *Hamdi v. Rumsfeld*, 542 U.S. 507 (2004).

78. On parallel governance see Richard M. Pious, *Why Presidents Fail* (Lanham, MD: Rowman and Littlefield, 2008), 217–244; also generally Richard M. Pious, *The War on Terrorism and the Rule of Law* (New York: Oxford University Press, 2006).

79. On the increased role of Congress in the aftermath of Watergate see Daniel P. Moynihan, "Imperial Government," *Commentary*, vol. 65, no. 6, June 1978, 25–32; Thomas E. Cronin, "A Resurgent Congress and the Imperial Presidency," *Political Science Quarterly*, vol. 95, no. 2, Summer 1980, 209–237; Louis W. Koenig, "Reassessing the 'Imperial Presidency'" in Richard M. Pious, ed., *The Power to Govern*, Academy of Political Science, New York, 1981, 31–44.

80. Edwin S. Meese, III, *Major Policy Statements of the Attorney General Edwin Meese III, 1985–88.* (Washington D.C. Government Printing Office, 1989) pp. 188–189.

81. U.S. Congress. *Report of the Congressional Committees Investigating the Iran-Contra Affair with Supplemental, Minority, and Additional Views.* 100th Cong., 1st sess., 1987. H. Rept. No. 100-433, S. Rept. No. 100-216. p. 465.

82. Terry Eastland, *Energy in the Executive: The Case for the Strong Presidency.* (New York: Free Press 1992); John C. Yoo, "The Continuation of Politics by Other Means: the Original Understanding of War Powers," 84 *California Law Review* No. 167 (1996): 196–241; John C. Yoo *The Power of War and Peace: The Constitution and Foreign Affairs After 9/11* (Chicago: University of Chicago Press, 2006); Steven Calabrese *The Unitary Executive: Presidential Power from Washington to Bush*, (New Haven CT: Yale University Press, 2008).

83. One of these lawyers, John C. Yoo, had relatives in the Korean War. His first academic work at Harvard College and Yale Law School included a defense of President Harry Truman's military actions in Korea, which were undertaken without a declaration of war or specific congressional authorization. Yoo himself has speculated about his work on unitary executive theory in foreign affairs "Maybe some of it is from being Korean." John C. Yoo interview, *Korea Times*, April 21, 2001, quoted in Charlie Savage, *Takeover* (New York: Little, Brown), 80. Most other proponents of unitary executive theory have had different experiences, including service during the Vietnam War and/or the Iran-Contra Affair.

84. John C. Yoo, U.S. Department of Justice, Office of Legal Counsel, "The President's Constitutional Authority to Conduct Military Operations Against Terrorists and Nations Supporting Them." September 25, 2001.

85. John C. Yoo, U.S. Department of Justice, Office of Legal Counsel, "Authority for the Use of Military Force to Combat Terrorist Activities *Within the United States*," October 23, 2001.

86. John C. Yoo, U.S. Department of Justice, Office of Legal Counsel, "Constitutionality of Amending Foreign Intelligence Surveillance Act to Change the 'Purpose' Standard for Searches" September 25, 2001.

87. John C. Yoo, U.S. Department of Justice, Office of Legal Counsel, "Memorandum for Daniel J. Bryant," June 27, 2002.

88. Jay S. Bybee, U.S. Department of Justice, Office of Legal Counsel, "Determination of Enemy Belligerency and Military Detention" June 8, 2002.

89. Patrick Philbin, U.S. Department of Justice, Office of Legal Counsel, "Re: Swift Justice Opinion," April 8, 2002.

90. Jay S. Bybee, U.S. Department of Justice, Office of Legal Counsel, "Memorandum: Re: The President's Power as Commander in Chief to Transfer Captured Terrorists to the Control and Custody of Foreign Nations," March 13, 2002.

91. John C. Yoo, "Re: Military Interrogation of Unlawful Enemy Combatants Held Outside the United States," March 14, 2003.

92. "Press Briefing," June 22, 2004.

93. U.S. Department of Justice, Office of Legal Counsel, "Re: Status of Certain OLC Opinions Issued in the Aftermath of the Terrorist Attacks of September 11, 2001."

94. *Jewel v. Obama*, "Government Defendant's Notice of Motion and Motion to Dismiss and for Summary Judgment," Case 3:08-cv-044373-VRW, Document 18, filed April 3, 2009.

95. Katie Couric interview with Attorney General Eric Holder, *CBS News*, April 9, 2009.

96. *Fadi al Maqaleh v. Robert Gates*, "Motion for Certification of This Court's April 2, 2009 Order

for Interlocutory Appeal Pursuant to 28 U.S.C. Sec. 1292(b) and for a Stay of Proceedings Pending Appeal," Case 1:06-cv-01669-JDB, April 10, 2009.

97. *"Fadi al Maqaleh, et al. v. Robert Gates"* Memorandum Opinion, United States District Court for the District of Columbia, Civil Action No. 06-1669, April 2, 2009.

98. John Schwartz, "Administration Invokes State Secret Argument," *New York Times*, February 9, 2009. Some members of the House and Senate responded to these arguments with a proposed "State Secret Protection Act" requiring judicial review of claims of torture, by limiting government claims of state secrets.

99. Scott Horton, "Secret Crimes" posted in "No Comment," *Harpers Magazine*, February 10, 2009.

100. On the history of waterboarding and court decisions banning the practice by police departments see Evan Wallach, "Drop by Drop: Forgetting the History of Water Torture in U.S. Courts," *The Columbia Journal of Transnational Law*, 2007, pp. 468–506.

101. Scott Shane, "C.I.A. to Close Secret Overseas Prisons for Terrorism Suspects," *New York Times*, April 10, 2009, p. A9.

102. Josh Gerstein, "Obama Lawyers Set to Defend Yoo" *Associated Press*, January 28, 2009.

103. For an extended discussion on this point see Louis Fisher, *Congressional Abdication on War and Spending* (College Station: Texas A&M University Press, 2000). See also Michael J. Glennon, "The War Powers Resolution: Sad Record, Dismal Promise," *Loyola of Los Angeles Law Review*, vol. 17, 1984, 657–670; John Hart Ely, "Suppose Congress Wanted a War Powers Act That Worked?" *Columbia Law Review*, Vol. 88, November 1988, 1379–1431.

104. Federal district courts in the District of Columbia Circuit have developed a threshold inquiry as to the propriety of an equitable remedy, resulting in a doctrine of equitable discretion counseling restraint with regard to congressional challenges. See *Lowry v. Reagan* (676 F. Supp. 333 (1987); *Ange v. Bush* 752 F. Supp. 509 (1990).

105. Intelligence sources in 2009 leaked information to the media claiming that House Speaker Nancy Pelosi knew of NSA warrantless surveillance activities, and the interrogation methods described in 2002 White House memos. See Paul Kane, "Memo Says Pelosi Knew About use of Harsh Tactics," *Washington Post*, May 8, 2009; Glenn Thrush "Pelosi Playing Defense on Torture," *Associated Press*, April 27, 2009.

106. 18 U.S.C. sec. 2340, contains a provision which makes torture a felony. President Obama went on record ruling out prosecutions of those who conducted the interrogations, then backtracked slightly to claim that the determination would be made by the Attorney General. Keith Perine and Seth Stern, "Obama Says No Prosecutions, No 'Laying Blame' for Interrogation Techniques" *CQ Today Online News*, April 126, 2009. Major General Antonio Taquba, who led an investigation into abuses at Abu Ghraib prison, accused Bush administration officials of "war crimes" and called for them to be "held to account." Warren Strobel, "General Who Probed Abu Ghraib Says Bush Officials Committed War Crimes," *McClatchy Newspapers*, April 23, 2009. This might include Secretary of Defense Rumsfeld (who authorized interrogations), and National Security Adviser Condoleezza Rice, who verbally approved the CIA's request to use waterboarding on Abu Zubaydah in July 2002. Pamela Hess, "Rice OK'd CIA Waterboard Request as Bush Adviser," *Associated Press*, April 23, 2009. See Office of the Attorney General, "Release of Declassified Narrative Describing the Department of Justice Office of Legal Counsel's Opinions on the CIA's Detention and Interrogation Program," April 22, 2009. Columbia University Law Professor Scott Horton, in analyzing the narrative, points to the significant role of top officials in the National Security Council staff, and in the Department of State, and says the narrative "also makes clear that Vice President Cheney and President Bush were fully informed...." See Scott Horton, "Straight to the Top,", *No Comment*, Harper's, April 24, 2009.

107. In this refusal it seems to be following public opinion. In a February 1. 2009 *USA Today/Gallup Poll*, 38 percent of the respondents backed a criminal investigation of interrogation policies, 24 percent backed an independent panel, and 34 percent did not back either approach.

108. The Senate Judiciary Committee held hearings in March 2009 on the possibility of creating such a commission, but as of May 2009 President Barack Obama was on record in opposition, and Senate Majority Leader Harry Reid was backing the president. Speaker Pelosi backed Leahy.

109. This could continue the work of H. Marshall Jarrett, head of the Office of Professional Responsibility, Department of Justice, whose 2009 report found "misconduct" in the advice given the

government by Office of Legal Counsel attorneys John Yoo and Jay Bybee. See Department of Justice, Office of Professional Responsibility, "Report: Investigation into the Office of Legal Counsel's Memoranda Concerning Issues Relating to the Central Intelligence Agency's Use of 'Enhanced Interrogation Techniques' on Suspected Terrorists, July 29, 2009" 5.

110. The difficulty in setting up a commission of inquiry is a problem of traffic control: if it had the power to grant immunity to witnesses, it could interfere with the future prosecutions of former officials. The publicity involved, even without grants of immunity, could be taken by federal judges as evidence that fair trials could not be conducted. This was one of the lessons of the committee inquiries into the Iran-Contra Affair.

111. Impeachment of Bybee has been called for by, among others, newspapers such as *The New York Times,* Jerry Nadler of the House Judiciary Committee, and Yale Law Professor Bruce Ackerman.

112. *ACLU v. NSA,* 438 F. Supp. 2d 754 (2006), dismissed on appeal, 493 F.3d 644 (6th Cir. 2007). The Supreme Court declined to hear the ACLU's appeal, *ACLU v. NSA.* 128 S. Ct. 1334 (2008). For a discussion of this case and the possibility of requiring review by the Supreme Court see Arlen Specter, "The Need to Roll Back Presidential Power Grabs" *New York Review of Books,* Vol. 56, No. 8, May 14, 2009.

113. *Velvel v. Nixon,* 415 F. 2d 236 (10th Cir. 1969).

114. *Lowry v. Reagan,* 676 F. Supp. 333 (D.D.C. 1987); *Campbell v. Clinton,* 203 F. 3d. 19 (D.C. Cir. 2000).

115. *Doe v. Bush,* 323 F. 3d.133 (1st Cir. 2003).

116. *Dellums v. Bush,* 752 F. Supp. 1141 D.D.C. 1990); *Ange v. Bush,* 752 F. Supp. 509 (D.D.C. 1990)*; Doe v. Bush,* 323 F. 3d 133 (1st Cir. 2003).

117. *Da Costa v. Laird II,* 471 F. 2d 1146 (2d Cir. 1973).

118. *Orlando v. Laird,* 443 F. 2d 1039 (2d Cir. 1971), *Mitchell v. Laird,* 488 F. 2d 611 (D.C. Cir. 1973); *Holtzman v. Schlesinger,* 484 F 2d 1307 (2d Cir. 1973).

119. (18 U.S.C. Sec. 4001(a).

120. *Padilla v. Hanft* 126 S.Ct. 1649.

121. *Al-Haramain Islamic Foundation v. Bush,* No. 06-36083 D.C. (November 16, 2007); Eric Lichtblau, "Judge Rejects Bush's View on Wiretaps" *New York Times,* July 3, 2008.

122. *Maher v. Ashcroft,* 414 F. Supp. 2d 250 (2006).

123. *Hepting v. ATT* 439 F. Supp. 2nd 974 (2006). See generally Louis Fisher, *In the Name of National Security: Unchecked Power and the Reynolds Case* (Lawrence: University of Kansas Press, 2006).

124. *United States v. Reynolds* 345 U.S. 1 (1953).

125. *El-Masri v. United States* 479 F.3d 296 (2007).

126. *United States v. Nixon,* 418 U.S. 683 (1974). Some federal courts are now applying scrutiny to government claims; see *Binyam Mohamed et al. v. Jeppeson Dataplan, Inc.*, No. 08-15693, D.C. No. 5:07-CV-02798-JW, April 28, 2009.

127. For an insightful and sympathetic reading of presidential claims of prerogative see Jeffrey K. Tulis, "On Constitutional Statesmanship" in Stephen Macedo and Tulis, eds., *The Limits of Constitutional Democracy* (Princeton: Princeton University Press, 2010), pp. 112–123.

Chapter 13

1. Bertrand de Jouvenel, "The Principate," Dennis Hale and Marc Landy, eds, *The Nature of Politics: Selected Essays of Bertrand de Jouvenel,* (New Brunswick NJ, Transaction Publishers, 1992), 231. The quote is from Necker, *Executif dans les Grands Etats, 1792* (no publisher listed).

2. Arthur Schlesinger Jr., *The Imperial Presidency* (Boston: Houghton Mifflin Company, 1973).

3. An encyclopedic account of the arguments and evidence regarding Bush's imperial presidency can be found in *Reining in the Imperial Presidency: Lessons and Recommendations Relating to the Presidency of George W. Bush*. House Committee on the Judiciary Majority Staff Report to John Conyers Jr., January 13, 2009, U.S. House of Representatives. An impressive defense of Bush's handling of the War on Terror and the War in Iraq is contained in Douglas Feith, *War and Decision: Inside the Pentagon at the Dawn of the War on Terrorism*, (New York: Harper, 2008). www.house.gov/delahunt/imperialpresidency.pdf.

4. The magisterial treatment of this question is by Harvey Mansfield in his *Taming of the Prince* (Baltimore: Johns Hopkins U. Press, 1989).

5. Statement, dated June 27, 1950, by President Harry S. Truman, announcing his order to send U.S. air and naval forces to help defend South Korea and explaining the rationale for his decision, Papers of George M. Elsey, Harry S. Truman Library and Museum, http://www.trumanlibrary.org/whistlestop/study_collections/korea/large/week1/kw_27_1.htm.

6. "Lyndon Baines Johnson: Foreign Affairs—Vietnam," American President An Online Reference Resource, Miller Center of Public Affairs, University of Virginia http://millercenter.org/academic/americanpresident/lbjohnson/essays/biography/5.

7. Authority for Use of Military Force Against Iraq, Public Law 102-1, http://www.milnet.com/public-law-102-1.html.

8. This foreign policy oriented use of the term "unitary theory" is a misnomer. Previously the term was used primarily with respect to the president's removal power as reflected in the difference of opinion between Madison and Hamilton as to whether that power resides solely with the president or must and should be shared with the Senate.

9. In various signing statements, Bush does use the term "unitary executive branch" but in context it is clear that he is referring not to the foreign policy oriented "unitary theory," which I have characterized as a misleading use of the term, but to the view first articulated by Madison about the president's right and obligation to control the actions of his subordinates. See for example Statement on Signing the Intelligence Authorization Act for Fiscal Year 2005, December 23, 2004, *The American Presidency Project*, http://www.presidency.ucsb.edu/ws/index.php?pid=62642, and Statement on Signing the National Defense Authorization Act for Fiscal Year 2006, January 6, 2006, *American Presidency Project* http://www.presidency.ucsb.edu/ws/index.php?pid=65172.

10. John C. Yoo, "War and the Constitutional Text," *The University of Chicago Law Review* Vol. 69, No. 4 (Autumn, 2002), 1678.

11. Ibid., 1669, 1672.

12. Ibid., 1674.

13. Madison's notes Friday August 17 http://www.constitution.org/dfc/dfc-0817.txt.

14. "Battle lines drawn for first presidential debate on Iraq," *Sydney Morning Herald*, October 1, 2004, http://www.smh.com.au/articles/2004/09/30/1096527871614.html.

15. For example, John Pinckney favored a strong executive but feared that the executive would usurp "the powers of war and peace." then held by the Congress. John Rutledge was for a single executive but was not for giving him the power of war and peace. Madison's Notes on the Constitutional Convention, June 1, The Avalon Project, http://avalon.law.yale.edu/18th_century/debates_601.asp.

16. Jack Goldsmith, *The Terror Presidency: Law and Judgment Inside the Bush Administration*(W.W. Norton: New York, 2007) 124.

17. Ibid., 123–124.

18. Ibid., 128.

19. Hamdan v. Rumsfeld, Secretary of Defense, et al. (No. 05-184) 415 F. 3d, 33.

20. Ibid., 4.

21. Brief for Respondents Donald H. Rumsfeld, Secretary of Defense, et al. on Writ of Certiorari to the United States Court of Appeals for the District of Columbia Circuit Paul D. Clement Solicitor General Counsel of Record.

22. Ibid.

23. Ibid., Syllabus 4.

24. Ibid., Syllabus 5.

25. Thomas, J., dissenting Supreme Court of the United States Alim Ahmed Hamed, Petitioner v. Donald Rumsfeld, Secretary of Defense, et al. tttp://www.law.cornell.edu/supct/html/05-184.ZD1.html.

26. *Rasul v. Bush* (03-334) 542 U.S. 466 (2004) 321 F.3d 1134, http://www.law.cornell.edu/supct/html/03-334.ZO.html.

27. This complex set of Court-Congress interactions is carefully laid out by Richard Ellis in his edited volume, *Judging Executive Power* (Lanham MD, Rowman and Littlefield, 2009), 180–182.

28. *Lakhdar Boumediene, et al., Petitioners 06-1195 v. George Bush, President of the United States, et al. Khaled A.F. Al Odah* next friend of *Fawzi Khalid Abdullah Fahad Al; Odah et al., Petitioners 06-1196 v. United States et al.*on writs of certiorari to the United States Court of Appeals for the District of Columbia circuit [June 12, 2008].Justice Kennedy delivered the opinion of the Court. VC http://caselaw.lp.findlaw.com/scripts/getcase.pl?court=US&vol=000&invol=06-1195#opinion1.

29. Souter, Concurring Opinion, *Boumediene v. Bush.*

30. Justice Stevens, Majority Opinion, *Rasul v. Bush*

31. *Boumediene v. Bush, Kennedy Opinion, op. cit. 41.*

32. Ibid., 39.

33. Ibid., Roberts dissent http://caselaw.lp.findlaw.com/scripts/getcase.pl?court=US&vol=000&invol=06-1195#dissent1.

34. Ibid., Scalia Dissent, http://caselaw.lp.findlaw.com/scripts/getcase.pl?court=US&vol=000&invol=06-1195#dissent2.

35. Peter Beinart, "When Politics No Long Stops at the Water's Edge: Partisan Polarization and Foreign Policy" in Pietro S. Nivola and David W. Brady, eds., *Red and Blue Nation? Volume II: Consequences and Correction of America's Polarized Politics* (Washington D.C: Brookings Institution Press and Hoover Institution, 2008), 151–167. See also Bartels, B. L. and Christopher, P. "Partisan Polarization in Public Opinion Toward Executive Power: Comparing the Mass Public with Executive and Legislative Elites" Paper presented at the annual meeting of the Midwest Political Science Association 67th Annual National Conference, The Palmer House Hilton, Chicago, IL.

36. Peter W. Rodman, *Presidential Command* (New York: Knopf, 2009), 113–114.

37. For an encyclopedic treatment of the left critique of American foreign policy, especially as it involves the overthrow of regimes see Stephen Kinzer *Overthrow: America's Century of Regime Change from Hawaii to Iraq* (New York: Macmillan, 2007). For a typical invocation of the term "Banana Republic" see Mark Moberg, "Crown Colony as Banana Republic: The United Fruit Company in British Honduras, 1900–1920,"*Journal of Latin American Studies*, Vol. 28, No. 2 (May, 1996): 357–381.

38. The most influential and articulate defender of this point of view was Ronald Reagan himself. See especially his speech on Central America delivered to a joint session of Congress, April 27, 1983, Ronald Reagan Presidential Library, Archives, www.reagan.utexas.edu/archives/speeches/1983/42783d.htm Central America—Ronald Reagan's radio address—transcript, US Department of State Bulletin, May, 1984 http://findarticles.com/p/articles/mi_m1079/is_v84/ai_3243638/.

39. Department of Defense Appropriations Act for Fiscal Year 1985, Pub. L. No. 98-473, § 8066(a), 98 Stat. 1837, 1935 (1984). The act further provided that the prohibition could be avoided after February 28, 1985, upon the satisfaction of certain conditions. Id. § 8066(b), 98 Stat. at 1935–36. Earlier versions of the limitation were contained in: Joint Resolution of Oct. 3, 1984, Pub. L. No. 98-441, § 106(c), 98 Stat. 1699, 1700–01; Intelligence Authorization Act for Fiscal Year 1984, Pub. L. No. 98-215, § 108, 97 Stat. 1473, 1475 (1983); Department of Defense Appropriation Act, 1983, Pub. L. No. 97-377, § 793, 96 Stat. 1833, 1865 (1982). See generally United States: Legislation Relating to Nicaragua, 26 I.L.M. 433 (1987) (outlining all legislative restrictions on Nicaragua funding from 1980 to 1987, with reprints of relevant texts).

40. Excerpts from the Tower Commission's Report, The American Presidency Project, http://

www.presidency.ucsb.edu/PS157/assignment%20files%20public/TOWER%20EXCERPTS.htm.

41. Report of the Congressional Committees Investigating the Iran Contra Affair With Supplemental Minority and Additional Views, Union Calendar no. 277, 100th Congress, 1st Session, H. Rept No. 100-433, S. Rept No 100-216.

42. Ibid., 12.

43. Ibid., 16–17.

44. Ibid., 19–20.

45. Ibid., 18.

46. Ibid., 437.

47. Ibid., 457–479.

48. Ibid., 459.

49. Ibid., 463–469.

50. Ibid., 472–3.

51. Ibid., 473.

52. Ibid., 449.

53. North American Free Trade Agreement (NAFTA) implementation, 1993–1994 legislative chronology. (1997). In *Congress and the Nation, 1993–1996* vol. 9. (Washington DC: CQ Press) Retrieved April 5, 2009, from CQ Press Electronic Library, CQ Congress Collection, http://library.cqpress.com/congress/catn93-0000141149. Document ID: catn93-0000141149.

54. http://www.whitehouse.gov/news/releases/2001/09/20010914-2.html.

55. "Civilian Deaths in the NATO Air Campaign, Human Rights Watch.org http://www.hrw.org/legacy/reports/2000/nato/index.htm.

56. Bumiller, Elizabeth, "One in seven freed from Guantanamo reportedly return to terrorism," *New York Times* 05/20/2009 09:04:40 PM PDT, Updated: 05/20/2009 09:39:43 PM PDT, San Jose Mercury News, http://www.mercurynews.com/ci_12416410?nclick_check=1.

57. George W. Bush, Address to a Joint Session of the United States Congress, September 20, 2001 http://www.whitehouse.gov/news/releases/2001/09/20010920-8.html.

58. The National Security Strategy of the United States of America, September 2002, The White House, Washington D.C., http://www.globalsecurity.org/military/library/policy/national/nss-020920.pdf.

59. Charles Duelfur, *Comprehensive Report of the Special Advisor to the DCI on Iraq's WMD*, 34, 49, Iraq Study Group, University of Michigan Library Documents Center, http://www.lib.umich.edu/govdocs/duelfer.html.

60. *Duelfur Report* 34, 59, 62, 65.

61. Christopher Hitchens, *Case Closed, Slate, The truth about the Iraqi-Niger "yellowcake" nexus*, Slate, Posted Tuesday, July 25, 2006, http://www.slate.com/id/2146475/.

62. These questions are very well addressed in the *Duelfur Report* (see endnote 60) The findings of this the second report of the Iraq Study Group were largely ignored by the press even though the first report, written by David Kaye, was widely cited and quoted. Nor did the Bush Administration choose to accord it the publicity and prominence it deserved.

63. John Mueller, "Is There Still a Terrorist Threat?: The Myth of the Omnipresent Enemy" *Foreign Affairs*, (September/October 2006) 2–8, Glenn L. Carle, "Overstating Our Fears,"*Washington Post*, July 13, 2008; Page B07.

64. Public Law 109-366—Oct. 17, 2006, Military Commissions Act of 2006 120 STAT. 2600 Public Law109-366—OCT. 17, 2006, 109th Congress. Pub.L. 109-148, div. A, tit. X, §§ 1001–1006, 119 Stat. 2680, 2739–44 (2005). Congress also enacted a nearly identical version of the DTA as a component of the National Defense Authorization Act for Fiscal Year 2006.

65. Joel Roberts, "Bush Signs Patriot Act Renewal: Renewal Comes A Day Before Expiration; Ends Months Of Debate," *CBS News*, March 9, 2006, http://www.cbsnews.com/stories/2006/03/09/

politics/main1387710.shtml.

66. James Risen and Eric Lichtblau, "Bush Lets U.S. Spy on Callers Without Courts," *New York Times*, December 16, 2005, A1. http://www.nytimes.com/2005/12/16/politics/16program.html?pagewanted=all.

67. Tim Starks, "Bush Signs FISA Rewrite Into Law," *CQ Weekly Online* (July 14, 2008): 1900–1902. http://library.cqpress.com/cqweekly/weeklyreport110-00000291604.

68. Timothy Noah, "Can Bush Be Both Ignorant *and* a Liar? Yes. There's no reason for Bush-bashers to choose between the two" slate.com, June 23, 2003.

69. Nicholas Kristof, "Calling Bush A Liar," *New York Times*, July 30, 2004, New York Times.com, http://www.nytimes.com/2004/06/30/opinion/calling-bush-a-liar.html.

70. Charles Krauthammer coined the term "Bush Derangement Syndrome." He defines it as "*the acute onset of paranoia in otherwise normal people in reaction to the policies, the presidency — nay — the very existence of George W. Bush.*" Among the acute sufferers he cites Howard Dean who stated that "the most interesting" theory as to why the president is "suppressing" the 9/11 report is that Bush knew about 9/11 in advance. Other celebrated sufferers include "Bill Moyers, ranting about a 'right-wing wrecking crew' engaged in 'a deliberate, intentional destruction of the United States way of governing" and *New York Times* columnist Paul Krugman, whose recent book attacks the president so virulently that Krugman's British publisher saw fit to adorn the cover with images of Dick Cheney in a Hitler-like mustache and Bush stitched-up like Frankenstein."

71. Sonya Ross, "Religion Takes Spotlight in Terror War" *Atlanta Journal-Constitution*, October 27, 2004, 13A; Paul Krugman, "A Willful Ignorance", *New York Times*, October 28, 2003, Section A, 25; E.J. Dionne Jr. "George Bush's Legacy: The many lessons of a failed presidency," *The Oregonian*, January 19, 2009, A13; E.J. Dionne Jr. "'Staying the course' means disaster," *Charleston Gazette*, August 27, 2005, 4A; E.J. Dionne Jr, "How Are We Safer?: Penetrating the Haze of Rhetoric and Ideology on Iraq," *Pittsburgh Post-Gazette*, July 12, 2005, B-7.

72. Dennis Blair, Obama's intelligence chief gave perhaps the most telling backhanded compliment to the success of Bush's Iraq policy. In defending the Obama Administration's controversial decision to release Bush era Office of Legal Counsel memos condoning certain coercive interrogation techniques. Blair defended those decisions on the grounds that immediately after 9/11 we did not have a clear understanding of the enemy we were dealing with, and our every effort was focused on preventing further attacks that would kill more Americans. It was during these months that the CIA was struggling to obtain critical information from captured al Qaida leaders, and requested permission to use harsher interrogation methods. The OLC memos make clear that senior legal officials judged the harsher methods to be legal.

However,

> "Those methods, read on a bright, sunny, safe day in April 2009, appear graphic and disturbing. As the President has made clear, and as both CIA Director Panetta and I have stated, we will not use those techniques in the future. But we will absolutely defend those who relied on these memos and those guidelines."

Thus for all the scorn heaped on Bush by his critics, including the current president, he did in fact bring about a "bright sunny safe day" for his people.

Quotes are from Statement by the Director of National Intelligence Dennis C. Blair upon the release of the Office of Legal Counsel memos, April 16, 2009. *New York Times.com*. http://www.nytimes.com/2009/04/16/us/politics/16text-blair.html.

73. Richard A. Posner, *Not A Suicide Pact*, (New York: Oxford University Press, 2006), 51.

74. The war and issues of executive power played a less clear cut role in 2008 largely because of the success of the surge. In the primaries, before the surge's success was fully evident, Obama criticized Hillary Clinton for her support of the war. But during the general election Obama very much soft pedaled the war issue because he rightly discerned that McCain's staunch support for the war was not a great source of vulnerability and that the choice of Sarah Palin and McCain's inept response to the financial crisis provided far more inviting targets.

75. Posner, *Not A Suicide Pact*, 45.

76. Mark Follman and Tracy Clark-Flor, "Prosecutions and Convictions: A Look at Accountability to Date for Abuses at Abu Ghraib and in the Broader 'War on Terror,'" Salon.com, Mar 14, 2006, http://www.salon.com/news/abu_ghraib/2006/03/14/prosecutions_convictions/print.html.

77. Convention Against Torture and Other Cruel, Inhuman or Degrading Treatment or Punishment, G.A. Res. 39/46, Annex, 39 U.N. GAOR Supp. No. 51, U.N. Doc. A/39/51 (1984) [hereinafter "CAT"].

78. Ibid. Article One Section 1.

79. U.S Department of Legal Counsel, Office of the Assistant Attorney General, Memorandum for Alberto Gonzales Counsel to the President Re: Standards of Conduct for Interrogation und 18 U.S.C 2340-2340A, August 1 2002. 1.

80. Mark Mazzetti and Scott Shane, "Memos Spell Out Brutal CIA Mode of Interrogation," *New York Times*, April 17, 2009, A1.

81. Greg Miller and Josh Meyer "Memos Reveal Harsh CIA Interrogation Methods." *Los Angeles Times*, April 17, 2009, LA Times.com, http://www.latimes.com/news/politics/la-na-interrogation17-2009apr17,0,7758699.story?track=rss.

82. New York Times Ibid.

83. Justice Department Memo on Interrogation Techniques, August 1, 2002. 2. Reprinted at *New York Times*.com, http://documents.nytimes.com/justice-department-memos-on-interrogation-techniques#p=2.

84. Justice Department Memo on Interrogation Techniques, May 10, 2005, 11. New York Times.com, http://documents.nytimes.com/justice-department-memos-on-interrogation-techniques#p=47.

85. Justice Department Memo on Interrogation Techniques May 10, 2005, 15. New York Times.com, http://documents.nytimes.com/justice-department-memos-on-interrogation-techniques#p=51.

86. Justice Department Memo on Interrogation Techniques, May 10, 2005, 57. New York Times.com, http://documents.nytimes.com/justice-department-memos-on-interrogation-techniques#p=26. The *New York Times* printed a follow up article the next day which sights unnamed former interrogators as asserting that Abu Zubaydah, the first victim of waterboarding did not in fact have any additional valuable information to relate. It mentions a footnote in one of the memos that describes a difference of opinion between Zubaydah's interrogators and CIA headquarters about whether the use of the "brutal treatment"(Times's choice of words) was necessary. Scott Shane, "Divisions Arose on Rough Tactics for Qaeda Figure," *New York Times*, April 18, 2009, A1. Michael Hayden, Director of the CIA for the last two years of the Bush Administration defended the account in the memos that Zubaydah did in fact respond to harsh interrogation by revealing information that led to the capture of terror suspect Ramzi Binailshibh. Scott Shane, "Memo Says Prisoner Got Waterboard 183 Times," *New York Times*, April 20, 2009, A10.

87. Justice Department Memo on Interrogation Techniques, May 10, 2005, 7. 40. New York Times.com, http://documents.nytimes.com/justice-department-memos-on-interrogation-techniques#p=43.

88. Mark Mazzetti and Scott Shane, "Memos Spell Out Brutal CIA Mode of Interrogation," *New York Times*, April 17, 2009, A1.

89. Justice Department Memo on Interrogation Techniques, August 1, 2002. 5–6. Reprinted at New York Times.com, http://documents.nytimes.com/justice-department-memos-on-interrogation-techniques#p=5.

90. Editorial, *New York Times*, April 19,2009, Week in Review, 9.

About the Authors

Akhil Reed Amar is the Sterling Professor of Law and Political Science at Yale, where he teaches constitutional law in both Yale College and Yale Law School. After graduating in 1980 from Yale College and in 1984 from Yale Law School, he clerked on the First Circuit for Judge Stephen Breyer in 1984-85 and then joined the Yale faculty in 1985. In 1994 he received the Paul Bator award from the Federalist Society; in 1998 his work on the Bill of Rights earned the ABA Certificate of Merit and the Yale University Press Governors Award; and his most recent book earned the ABA Silver Gavel Award of 2006. He is a member of the American Academy of Arts and Sciences and in 2008 he received the DeVane Medal--Yale's highest award for teaching excellence. He is also the author of several books, including *America's Constitution: A Biography* (Random House 2005).

George C. Edwards III is Distinguished Professor of Political Science at Texas A&M University and holds the Jordan Chair in Presidential Studies. He has written or edited 23 books on American politics and is also editor of *Presidential Studies Quarterly* and consulting editor of the *Oxford Handbook of American Politics* series. Professor Edwards has served as president of the Presidency Research Section of the APSA, which has named its annual Dissertation Prize in his honor and awarded him its Career Service Award.

Paul Finkelman is the President William McKinley Distinguished Professor of Law and Public Policy and Senior Fellow in the Government Law Center at Albany Law School.. He received his B.A. in American Studies from Syracuse University (1971) and his M.A. and Ph.D. in U.S. history from Chicago (1972, 1976) and was a fellow in law and humanities at Harvard Law School (1982-83). He is the author, co-author, or editor of more than twenty-five books and more than one hundred and fifty scholarly articles. His books include: *Slavery and the Founders: Race and Liberty in the Age of Jefferson* (M.E. Sharpe, 2001); *The Political Lincoln* (CQ Press, 2009); and *Dred Scott v. Sandford: A Brief History* (Bedford, 1995).

Mark A. Graber is a professor of Law and Government at the University of Maryland School of Law and the University of Maryland, College Park. He is the author of three books and many articles on American constitutional law, development, theory and politics.

Marc Landy is Professor of Political Science at Boston College. He and Sidney Milkis wrote *Presidential Greatness and American Government: Balancing Liberty and Democracy*. He is an author of *The Environmental Protection Agency From Nixon to Clinton: Asking the Wrong Questions*. He is an editor of *Creating Competitive Markets: The Politics of Regulatory Reform* (2007), *Seeking the Center: Politics and Policymaking at the New Century* (2001) and *The New Politics of Public Policy* (1995).

Daniel Lazare has written several books about the Constitution and other topics, among them *The Frozen Republic: How the Constitution Is Paralyzing Democracy* (Harcourt Brace, 1996) and *The Velvet Coup: The Constitution, the Supreme Court, and the Decline of American Democracy* (Verso, 2001). His work has also appeared in *The Nation, New Left Review, Le Monde Diplomatique, Harper's,* and numerous other publications.

Sanford Levinson is the W. St. John Garwood and W. St. John Garwood Jr. Centennial Chair in Law at the University of Texas Law School, as well as a Professor of Government at the University of Texas at Austin. He is a co-editor of a widely used constitutional casebook, *Processes of Constitutional Decisionmaking,* and the author of *Our Undemocratic Constitution: Where the Constitution Goes Wrong (and How We the People Can Correct It)* (2006), and *Framed: America's 51 Constitutions and the Crisis of Governance* (2012). He was elected in 2001 to the American Academy of Arts and Sciences.

Stephen Macedo is Laurance S. Rockefeller Professor of Politics and the University Center for Human Values at Princeton University. He is author of *The New Right vs. The Constitution, Liberal Virtues: Citizenship, Virtue, and Community in Liberal Constitutionalism* and many other works.

Thomas J. Main is Associate Professor at the School of Public Affairs at Baruch College, City University of New York. He holds a Ph.D. in politics from Princeton University and an MPA from the Kennedy School of Government at Harvard University. Besides the American Constitution, his research interests include welfare and social policy, urban politics, and homelessness. He has published articles in the *Public Interest, Commentary,* the *City Journal,* the *Journal of Urban Affairs, Public Affairs Quarterly, Perspectives on Political Science,* and *Review of Policy Research.*

R. Shep Melnick is the Thomas P. O'Neill, Jr. Professor of American Politics at Boston College and co-chair of the Harvard Program on Constitutional Government. His books include *Regulation and the Courts: The Case of the Clean Air Act* (1983) and *Between the Lines: Interpreting Welfare Rights* (1994). He has also taught at Harvard and Brandeis, and served on the research staff of the Brookings Institution. He received both his BA and Ph.D. from Harvard.

Richard M. Pious is Adolph and Effie Ochs Professor at Barnard College and professor at the Graduate School of Arts and Sciences at Columbia University. His books include *The American Presidency* (1979), *The President, Congress and the Constitution* (1984), *The War on Terrorism and the Rule of Law* (2006) and *Why Presidents Fail* (2008).

Jeremy Rabkin is professor of law at George Mason University where he teaches, among other things, a course called "The Founders' Constitution." He serves on the Board of Directors of the Center for Individual Rights (a public interest law firm) and of the US Institute of Peace (a U.S. government agency). He holds a PhD in political science from Harvard University.

Larry J. Sabato is University Professor of Politics at the University of Virginia. Dr. Sabato is the author of over 20 books and many essays on politics. He has received every major teaching award at the University of Virginia, and in 2001 he was named the Thomas Jefferson Award winner, U.Va's highest honor that has been given to one person each year since the 1950s. He is author of *A More Perfect Constitution* (2007), and *The Year of Obama: How Barack Obama Won the White House* (2009).

Mark Tushnet is William Nelson Cromwell Professor of Law, Harvard Law School. He is the co-author of several casebooks, including the most widely used casebook on constitutional law, has written more than fifteen books, including a two-volume work on the life of Justice Thurgood Marshall, and has edited ten others. He was President of the Association of American Law Schools in 2003. In 2002 he was elected a fellow of the American Academy of Arts and Sciences.

Index

Entries marked with an *n.* are references to notes

103rd Congress, 126
1960s, 106, 124, 126, 137, 138, 173, 216, 262*n*.6, 267*n*.8
1970s, 22, 26, 94, 110, 137, 216, 229
1980s, 31, 137, 138, 141, 144, 216, 217, 229
2000 presidential election, 21, 29, 35, 87, 88, 92, 93, 94, 95, 96, 98, 100, 101, 105, 109, 111, 112, 113, 114, 115, 139, 181, 259*n*.6, 259*n*.22, 260*n*.25, 261*n*.59
21st century, 122, 133, 205
9/11, 29, 34, 35, 140, 191, 193, 198, 202, 204, 220, 221, 222, 223, 224, 278*n*.1, 282*n*.82, 288*n*.70, 288*n*.72

A

abolitionists, 10, 11, 12,44,45,248*n*.2, 248*n*.3,250*n*.18, 254*n*.87
abortion, 122, 159
Abu Ghraib, 289
ACLU v. NSA, 202, 284*n*.112
Adams, John, 105, 106, 235
Adams, John Quincy, 105, 114, 253*n*.66, 262*n*.2, 265*n*.28
Afghanistan, 191, 195, 196, 204
Africa, 58
African Americans, 87, 100
Agrippa, 9, 246*n*.22
Air Force Survival, Evasion, Resistance, Escape, 228
al Qaeda, 191, 194, 196
Al-Haramain Islamic Foundation, 199
al-Marri, Ali Saleh Kahlah, 200

Alabama, 95, 115, 116, 263
Alaska, 116, 127, 246, 263
Alien Tort Statute, 203
Amar, Akhil Reed, 132, 233, 291
ambition, 123
amendments, 70, 72, 74, 76, 77, 81, 83, 125, 238
American Revolution, 38, 258*n*.47
Ancien régime, 15, 22
Anti-Torture Act, 202
Antifederalists, 2, 6, 8, 9, 10, 11, 12, 48, 67, 72, 75, 76, 78, 245*n*.3, 246*n*.22
Ansolobehere, Stephen, 173, 277*n*.53
Appropriations Act, 186
Arer, Maher, 203
Argentina, 217
Aristotle, 276
Arizona, 116
Arkansas, 93, 95, 116
Army, 185, 189
Articles of Confederation, 22, 45, 49, 50, 51, 64, 209, 235
Ashcroft, John, 191
Asian-Americans, 100
AT&T, 123, 124, 126, 191, 193, 199
Australia, 146
Australian Parliament, 31
Authorization to Use Military Force, 193, 199

B

Baltimore, 94, 185, 264, 270, 281, 285
Bates, John, 200

Beard, Charles A., 6, 8, 233, 235, 245n.4, 245n.16, 245n.17
Beitz, Charles R., 168, 275n.26
Bell South, 191
Berenson, Brad, 201
Berlin, 188
Best, Judith, 89
bicameralism, 128, 132, 135, 267
Bickel, Alexander, 125
Bill of Rights, 25, 28, 33, 236
Binailshibh, Ramzi, 289n.86
bin Laden, Osama, 196, 212
Blacks, 45, 90
Blackstone, 16
Boeing, 200
Boland Amendment, 218, 219
Bork, Robert, 153, 271n.13
Boumedienne v. Bush, 214
Brandeis, 125, 292
British North America Act, 31
Brookhiser, Richard, 20, 247n.13
Brown, Robert E., 8
Brown v. Board of Education, 172, 173, 277n.51
Browne, Harry, 88
Brutus, 9,76, 245n.21, 257n.33
Buchanan, Pat, 88
Bundesrat, 18
Bundestag, 18
Burke, Edmund, 17, 246n.5
Bush, George H.W., 36, 209, 224
Bush, George W., 20, 21, 28, 29, 36, 87, 88, 92, 93, 95, 96, 100, 105, 107, 111, 115, 138, 139, 198, 199, 216, 224, 259n.6, 261n.52, 266n.43, 281n.62, 285n.3, 287n.57, 288n.70,
Bush (George W.) Administration, 34, 36,139, 140, 141, 143, 192, 193, 194, 197, 198, 199–201, 207, 208, 211, 214, 220, 222, 224, 225, 228, 229, 278n.1, 281n.62, 281n.68, 283n.106, 285n.16, 287n.62, 289n.86
Butler, Pierce, 73
Bybee, Jay, 202
Byrd, Robert, 126

C

Calhoun, John C., 69, 80
California, 17, 80, 89, 109, 116, 130, 263

Canada, 15, 31, 38, 146, 154, 177, 203, 248n.7, 248n.9 280n.55, 281n.55
Canadian Supreme Court, 31, 248n.9
Capitol Hill, 21, 135, 138, 145
Carolene Products Co. v. United States, 275n.25
Carvel, James, 235
Case Against the Constitution: From the Antifederalists to the Present, The, 6, 245n.3
Catholic church, 15
Catholics, 100
Central America, 38, 140, 218, 286n.38
certiorari, 124
Charlotte, 94
Chase, Salmon P., 45
checks and balances, 182, 183
Cheney, Richard (Dick), 93, 198, 208, 288n.70
Chicago, 201, 246, 252, 255, 257–259, 262, 275, 276, 282, 286
Chief Executive, 57, 109, 114, 198, 208, 236, 237
China, 217
Churchill, Winston, 188
CIA, 200, 204
Civil War, 16, 21, 37, 39, 67, 69, 70, 72, 74, 75, 76, 77, 79, 81–83, 185, 195, 236, 249n.6, 249n.8, 250n.16, 250n.24 258n.53,
Clean Air Act, 292
Cleveland, Grover, 21, 105, 262n.4
Clinton Administration, 126
Clinton, Bill, 20, 21, 92, 247n.21, 269n.4
Cochran, Thad, 20
Cold War, 37, 39
Colorado, 93, 116, 263
combatants, 187, 191–193, 195, 198, 199, 203, 225
Commander-in-Chief, 181, 189, 199
Common Article 3, 193, 196
Communications Act of 1934, 191
Compromise of 1850, 79
Compromise of 1877, 21
concentration camps, 191
Congress, 36, 45, 57, 70, 73–75, 77, 80, 83, 90, 123–133, 135, 137, 181–187, 189–193, 195, 197, 199, 201–205, 208, 218, 262, 271, 282, 287, 292

Congressional government, 123, 129

Congressional Government: A Study in American Government, 8, 245*n*.12

Connecticut Compromise, 99, 268*n*.28

consensus, 73, 80, 82, 96

conservatism, 20, 25, 37–39

conservative, 25, 26, 89, 122

conservatives, 81, 129

Constitution, 1, 5, 6, 9–11, 13, 15, 25, 41, 43, 44, 56, 69–84, 121–123, 125, 127, 128, 130, 131, 133–135, 176, 181–184, 186–188, 194, 195, 198, 205, 233, 236, 249, 252, 257, 268, 276, 278, 285, 291–293

  abolitionist critique, 10

  antifederalist critique, 9

  Article I, 46, 47, 126, 128, 132, 185, 193

  Article II, 47, 83, 204

  Article IV, 46–48

  Article V, 46–48, 83, 121, 122, 125, 128, 131–134

  Article VI, 32

  preamble, 130

  progressive critique, 6

  war powers, 182, 185, 197, 202

Constitution a Pro-Slavery Compact, The, 10, 44, 246*n*.26, 246*n*.28, 249*n*.7, 249*n*.11, 257*n*.10

constitutional conceptions of democracy, 164

Constitutional Convention, 72, 73, 130, 182

constitutional democracy, 79, 164, 165, 170

constitutional dictatorship, 184-188, 268*n*.40, 280*n*.34

constitutional obsolescence, 70–72, 74, 77–79, 81, 83, 123

Contras, 218

Convention Against Torture, 193

Corwin, Edward S., 278

countervailing mechanisms, 148, 240, 243

Court of Appeals for the Armed Forces, 194

Court of Criminal Appeals, 194

Cox, Archibald, 278

Curtiss Wright decision, 219

D

Dahl, Robert, 5, 10, 87, 135, 136, 147, 246*n*.24, 259*n*.15, 269*n*.3

Dakotas, 17

Dallas/Ft. Worth, 94

de Gaulle, Charles, 18

de Jouvenel, Bertrand, 207, 284*n*.1

de Tocqueville, Alexis, 122

De Witt, John, 9, 246*n*.23

Declaration of Independence, 11, 39

Deep South, 44, 45, 48, 53, 56, 58, 59, 60, 61, 62, 64, 65, 87, 94, 105, 252*n*.41, 253*n*.61, 254*n*.85, 254*n*.87, 255*n*.98, 262*n*.7

Delaware, 44, 81, 116, 130, 246, 252

deliberation, 75, 129

Democracy-Related Justifications, 157-159, 272*n*.17

Democracy, 6, 11, 15, 16, 26, 29, 37–39, 79, 122, 149, 154, 158, 163–165, 170, 181, 183, 190, 248, 274–276, 284, 291, 292

Democratic Deficit, 28, 175, 277*n*.64

Denver, 94

Department of Defense, 193

Department of Justice, 126, 196, 200

DeShaney v. Winnebago County Dep't of Social Services, 273*n*.29

dictatorship, 153

direct election, 87, 101

direct tax, 46

dirty compromise, 57, 59, 62, 63

District of Columbia, 94, 106, 109, 110, 115, 116, 185, 214, 250*n*.18, 265*n*.15, 266*n*.37, 283*n*.10

divided government, 74, 123, 124, 128

Do Institutions Matter? Government Capabilities in the United States and Abroad, 146

Dolbeare, Kenneth M., 6, 245*n*.3

Dole, Robert, 92, 101, 102, 260*n*.29

Douglas, Stephen, 69, 71, 82, 259*n*.61

Douglass, Frederick, 11, 246*n*.30

Dred Scott v. Sandford, 47, 48, 80, 172, 173, 250*n*.15, 250*n*.16, 250*n*.17, 256*n*.6, 256*n*.9, 257*n*.13, 257*n*.15, 257*n*.31, 258*n*.49, 258*n*.51

Duncan v. Kahanamoku, 192

Dworkin, Ronald, 167, 177, 272*n*.24, 274*n*.2, 275*n*.28, 276*n*.39, 277*n*.48

E

Eighteenth Amendment, 224
eighteenth century, 18, 22, 38, 27, 47, 81, 99,127,209, 210,
Eisenhower Administration, 131
Eisgruber, Christopher L., 276*n*.31, 276*n*.43
El-Masri v.United States, 204, 284*n*.125
electoral college, 69, 74–76, 79, 80, 83, 85, 98, 105, 107–110, 113, 116, 128, 264
electoral votes, 19, 30, 80, 87, 88, 89, 90, 91, 92, 93, 98, 99, 105, 106, 107, 108, 111, 112, 113, 114, 115, 239, 246*n*.10, 253*n*.66, 259*n*.9, 259*n*.20, 262*n*.1, 262*n*.2, 262*n*.3, 262*n*.4, 263*n*.8, 263*n*.12, 264*n*.18, 265*n*.31, 266*n*.37
Eleventh Amendment, 25
emancipation, 69, 72–78
enemy combatants, 187, 192, 198, 199
energy in the executive, 182, 198
energy policy, 131, 137
Equal Rights Amendment, 26
equality, 27, 37, 39, 70, 75, 81, 130, 167, 168
Estlund, David, 274*n*.12
Europe, 7, 18, 28, 34, 38, 39, 139, 248*n*.11
European Convention on Human Rights (ECHR), 28, 34
European Union, 28, 175, 277*n*.64
Ex Parte Endo, 192, 281*n*.61
Ex Parte McCardle, 187, 279*n*.30
Ex Parte Merryman, 186
Ex Parte Quirin, 192, 281*n*.58

F

Farley, James, 190
federal budget, 138
Federal Drug Administration, 122
Federal Intelligence Surveillance Act, 140
Federal Reserve Board, 132
federalism, 79, 82, 83, 98, 99, 144, 250, 255, 261
Federalist No. 10, 276*n*.32
Federalist No. 39, 247*n*.2
Federalist No. 42, 75, 257*n*.28
Federalist No. 51, 123
Federalist No. 54, 75

Federalist No. 62, 130, 268*n*.29
Federalist No. 63, 176, 274
Federalist No. 70, 198
Federalist No.63, 176, 274
Federalist Papers, The, 72, 75–77, 82, 205
Federalist Society, 291
Federalists, 70, 72, 75, 76, 78
Fehrenbacher, Don, 48, 249*n*.10
Fifteenth Amendment, 70, 72, 77
Fifth Amendment, 22, 243
Filatarga, 203
filibuster, 18, 20, 90, 125, 126, 127, 128, 142, 147, 148, 169, 247*n*.14, 267*n*.14, 267*n*.15, 267*n*.16, 267*n*.20, 270*n*.40
Finkelman, Paul, 10, 70,248*n*.1, 249*n*.4, 249*n*.5, 249*n*.8, 250*n*.16, 251*n*.30, 253*n*.65,256*n*.6, 257*n*.11, 291
First Additional Protocol to the Geneva Conventions, 192
First Amendment, 33, 34, 79, 153, 271*n*.13
First Reconstruction Act of 1867, 187
Fleming, James E., 171, 276*n*.45
Florida, 18, 91, 109, 116, 263
Foner, Eric, 81
Foreign Intelligence Surveillance Act, 191
formal modeling, 129
Fort McHenry, 186
Fort Sumter, 79, 132, 185
founders, 8, 10, 20, 25, 26, 35, 99, 100, 108, 141, 235, 236, 239, 241, 247*n*.13, 248*n*.1, 265*n*.28
Founding Fathers, 9, 10, 20, 47, 247*n*.22, 250*n*.14, 255*n*.94, 255*n*.99,
founding, 33, 39, 234, 235, 106
Fourteenth Amendment, 70, 77, 263*n*.12
Fourth Congress, 77
framers, 69, 70, 72–74, 76, 77, 79–83, 125, 132, 182, 186, 239
France, 15, 18, 22, 133, 207, 223, 246*n*.5, 246*n*.9, 247*n*.4, 248*n*.5,
Free Institutions Program at CUNY, 5
free states, 71–74, 77, 79, 80, 82
freedom, 37, 38, 44, 45, 75, 81, 83, 236, 275–277
Frist, William, 126
Frost, David, 184
Frozen Republic, The, 5, 292
fugitive slave clause, 44, 46, 64, 65, 66, 69, 72, 76, 254*n*.89

G

Gallup Poll, 264, 265, 283
Garrison, William Lloyd, 11, 43, 248*n*.2,
Garrisonians, 11, 43, 44, 45, 249*n*.8,
Gaza Strip, 196
General Order Number 100, 193
Geneva Conventions, 191–193, 196
Georgia, 45, 61, 95, 116, 253
Germany, 133
Gilbert and Sullivan's Mikado, 77
Gingrich, Newt, 20
global warming, 129
God, 15, 17, 19, 20, 22, 237, 239, 246*n*.6
Goldsmith, Jack, 278
Goldwater v. Carter, 202
Gonzalez, Alberto, 198
Gore, Al, 29, 87, 88, 92, 93, 100, 105, 107,
    115
Graber, Mark, 69, 291
Great Britain, 133
Great Compromise, 52, 73, 76
Great Depression, 133
Greece, 61
Greens, 112
Gridlock, 121–135, 137
Guantanamo Bay, 140, 192, 195, 196
Gulf War, 220, 279*n*.9

H

habeas corpus, 34, 140, 185–187, 195, 196,
    200, 203, 212, 214, 215, 216, 225,
    279*n*.15, 279*n*.30
Hague Convention, 192
Hamdan v. Rumsfeld, 195, 203, 212,
    281*n*.75, 285*n*.19
Hamdi, Yaser Esam, 196
Hamilton, Alexander, 49, 89, 141, 247*n*.2,
    252*n*.36, 257*n*.28, 258*n*.46
Hamiltonians, 182
Hammond, James Henry, 44, 249*n*.5
Harper, Fowler, 124
hate speech, 34, 153
Hawaii, 116, 131, 192, 246, 263
healthcare, 135, 137, 142, 148
Helvidius, 36
Henry, Patrick, 10, 246*n*.25, 250*n*.19
Heritage Foundation, 198
Hicks, David, 195
Hirabayashi v. US, 192

Hispanics, 19, 90, 100
Hoagland, Jim, 133
Hodges, Albert, 186
Holder, Eric, 199
Holy Trinity, 20
House Judiciary Committee, 202
House of Lords, 18, 34
House of Representatives, 55, 70, 71, 73–
    75, 78, 80, 81, 83, 122, 123, 125–128,
    132, 184, 190, 197, 198, 201, 202, 251,
    262, 276, 285, 287, 293
Houston, 94, 121
*How Democratic is the American Constitu-
    tion?*, 5,246*n*.24, 259*n*.15
Hull, Cordell, 190
Huston Plan, 184

I

Idaho, 116, 246
Illinois, 18, 93, 111, 116
impeachment, 182, 202
Imperial Presidency, 179, 181–205
inclusiveness, 170
Incrementalism, 144, 145, 172
Indianapolis, 94, 249, 267
Iowa, 93, 116
Iqbal, Asif, 195
Iran Contra, 188, 198, 202, 207, 217-220,
    282*n*.81, 282*n*.83, 284*n*.110, 287*n*.41
Iraq, 5, 20, 35, 36, 140, 176, 191, 194, 196,
    207, 208, 210, 216, 222, 223, 225, 228,
    229, 279*n*.9, 281*n*.67, 285*n*.3, 285*n*.7,
    285*n*.14, 286*n*.37, 287*n*.59, 287*n*.62,
    288*n*.71, 288*n*.72

J

Jackson, Andrew, 105, 114, 253*n*.66, 262*n*.2,
    265*n*.28
Jackson, Robert, 189
Japan, 133
Japanese-Americans, 191
Jay Treaty, 77
Jefferson, Thomas, 105, 106, 114, 183, 235,
    253*n*.66, 255*n*.95, 262*n*.1, 265*n*.27,
    265*n*.34
Jeppesen Dataplan, Inc. 200
Jewel v. NSA, 199
Jews, 100
Johnson, Dawn, 126

Johnson, Lyndon B,. 126
Joint Chiefs of Staff, 132
Jordan, 291
judicial review, 70, 128, 149, 163, 170, 172, 174, 181, 197
judicial supremacy, 212
Justice Thomas, 214
justice-related justifications, 155-157, 159, 272*n*.20

K

Kabul, 204
Kansas, 95, 116, 245
Kennedy, Edward M., 124
Kennedy, John (F.), 95, 107, 113, 126, 265*n*.30, 265*n*.31
Kent Weaver, 146 269*n*.8, 270*n*.22, 270*n*.33
Kentucky, 116
Kenyon, Cecelia M., 8, 245*n*.18, 246*n*.22
Key, V.O., 261
Knox, Frank, 190
Korea, 285
Korean War, 195
Korematsu v. US, 192
Kuwait, 229

L

lame-duck, 132, 133, 184
Länder, 18
Landy, Marc, 207, 291
large states, 73, 126
Latin America, 26, 33
Law, David, 126
Lawrence v. Texas, 172
Lazare, Daniel, 15, 292
Leahy, Patrick, 202
Lee, Josh, 190
Lee, Richard Henry, 76
legislative branch, 136, 176, 219
Levinson, Sanford, 5, 25, 27, 135, 136, 147, 247*n*.1, 258*n*.55, 266*n*.1, 268*n*.27, 269*n*.1, 274*n*.3
liberal, 122, 275, 292
liberalism, 25
Libertarians, 112
Lieber, Francis, 187
Light, Paul, 127
Lincoln, Abraham, 69, 71, 80, 132, 141, 208, 235, 256*n*.1, 258*n*.54, 258*n*.62,

258*n*.63, 279 *n*.14, 279*n*.22, 279n,23, 279*n*.24
living Constitution, 198
Locke, John, 208, 278*n*.7
Lord Lothian, 189
Los Angeles Times, 226, 269*n*.16, 289*n*.81
Los Angeles, 94, 259
Louis XVI, 15, 22
Louisiana, 80, 95, 116, 265
Lower South, 184
Lutz, Donald, 121

M

Macedo, Stephen, 274*n*.10, 274*n*.11, 284*n*.127
Madison, James, 10, 69, 126, 49, 57, 60, 72, 73, 89, 90, 106, 110, 114, 130, 135, 147, 197, 235, 236, 247*n*.2, 248*n*.12, 252*n*.37, 253*n*.64, 257*n*.28, 258*n*.46, 259*n*.11, 265*n*.27, 266*n*.39, 268*n*.29
Maine, 116, 246, 263
Majoritarianism, 71, 81, 82, 166
majority rule, 70, 81, 126
Maltz, Earl, 48, 64, 250*n*.20
Manifest Destiny, 182
Manley, John F., 6, 245*n*.3
Marshall, George, 189
Marshall, John, 123, 198
Martin, Joe, 190
Maryland, 44, 62, 116, 186, 190, 256, 263, 266, 291
Mason, George, 57, 59, 60, 61, 66, 106, 251*n*.29, 254*n*.78,
Mason-Dixon Line, 72, 77, 79, 81
Massachusetts, 72, 76, 91, 116, 249, 251, 263, 277
Mayhew, David, 123
McCain, John, 94, 95
McCain-Feingold campaign finance reform law, 140
McCulloch v. Maryland, 266*n*.3
McDonald, Forrest, 8
Medicaid, 139, 144, 270*n*.23
Medicare, 129
Meese, Edwin, 198
Melnick, Shep, 135, 292
Merryman, John, 186
Mexican War, 81
Mexico, 15, 38

Michigan, 18, 93, 116, 263
Middle East, 22
Midwest, 185
military tribunals, 187, 194–196, 198, 200, 203
militia, 185
Mill, John Stuart, 276n.29
Milligan, Lambdin, 187
Minnesota, 93, 116
minority interests, 100
Mississippi River, 183
Mississippi, 95, 116, 183, 255, 263
Missouri Compromise, 80, 81
Missouri, 80, 81, 93, 116
moderates, 81
Mohamed, Binyam, 200
Montana, 18, 91, 95, 116, 190, 246, 263
Morris, Gouverneur, 45, 52, 53, 54, 55, 58, 59, 62, 253n.55,
Mount Rushmore, 183
Muslims, 100

N

Nader, Ralph, 88, 98, 259n.6
Nadler, Jerrold, 202
National Assembly, 18
National Security Agency, 191
National Security Council, 218, 283n.106
Native Americans, 235, 236
Naval Appropriations Bill, 189
Navy, 185, 189, 190, 196
Nazis, 183
Nebraska, 95, 116, 263
Negroes, 45, 73, 74
Neustadt, Richard E., 278n.3
Nevada, 93, 94, 116, 263
New Deal, 198
New Hampshire, 52, 55, 62, 67, 83, 88, 91, 93, 94, 116, 238, 246n.3, 246n.7, 254n.77, 269n.4
New Jersey Plan, 73
New Mexico, 91, 93, 94, 116, 263n.15
New World, 131
New York, 72, 75, 204, 245, 247, 258, 264, 268, 270, 277, 278
New Zealand, 275n.23
Newsweek, 20, 239, 247
Nicaragua, 286
Nicholas, George, 78

Nineteenth Amendment, 239, 241
Nixon, Richard, 105, 107, 109, 111, 113, 184, 204, 263, 265, 270n.10, 279, 284, 291
No Child Left Behind, 124
Non-Detention Act, 203
nonwhites, 19
the North, 72, 73, 77, 79–81, 246
North American Free Trade Agreement (NAFTA), 220, 287n.53
North Dakota, 19, 118, 246n.3, 246n.7,
North Korea, 208

O

Obama Administration, 127, 199–201
Obama, Barack 124, 127, 133, 181, 199–201, 268, 269, 282, 288, 293
Obamacare, 142
Office of White House Counsel, 198
Ohio, 18, 93, 116, 249, 263
Oklahoma, 95, 116, 127, 190, 263
one person, one vote, 130
Opportunity Points, 143
Our Undemocratic Constitution, 5, 135
Oval Office, 128, 181, 202

P

Pacificus, 36
Padilla, Jose, 201
Padilla v. Rumsfeld, 203
Pakistan, 196, 217
Panetta, Leon, 200
parliament, 18, 28, 31, 34, 97, 108, 209, 275n.23
Parrington, Vernon Louis, 6
Paterson, William, 46, 51, 52, 252n.37
Perry, H.W., 124, 267
Pennsylvania, 18, 50, 62, 93, 116, 201, 237, 249, 256
Pentagon, 194, 196, 197
Petraeus, David, 194
Philadelphia Convention, 8, 25, 35, 48, 65, 73, 74, 76, 268n.28
Philadelphia, 34, 46, 48, 51, 75, 76, 77, 183 249n.12, 250n.18, 258
Phillips, Wendell, 10, 43, 44, 45, 70, 246n.26, 248n.3,249n.7, 249n.11, 257n.10
Phoenix, 94

Pinckney, Charles, 57, 61, 78
Pinckney, Charles Cotesworth, 48, 50, 52,
    53, 54, 55, 57, 62, 66, 78
Pious, Richard, 292
Poland, 200
policy congestion, 137
political science, 121, 124, 129, 133, 291,
    292
popular vote, 71, 74
Post-Civil War amendments, 70, 74, 76,
    83, 256n.8
POWs, 193, 199
Powell, Colin, 176
Pragmatism, 17, 96
Preamble (to the United States Constitu-
    tion), 130
prerogative, 183, 185, 187, 188, 193, 198,
    199, 201, 229, 278, 279
President, 29, 71, 72, 74, 80, 81, 83, 87,
    122, 124, 126–128, 132, 181, 182, 184,
    186–192, 194, 195, 197–201, 203, 208,
    213, 223, 235, 236, 264, 282, 285, 291,
    292
prisoners, 183, 187, 191–193, 196, 200
Prize Cases, 186, 279n.26
progressive movement, 6
progressives, 6, 8, 9, 10, 11, 37, 113, 135,
    137
Proposition 13, 22
Publius, 76

                    Q

Quebec, 31, 38, 154

                    R

Rabkin, Jeremy, 5, 292, 176, 245n.1, 281n.76
radical Republicans, 81, 187
Rakove, Jack, 89, 257n.37, 260n.10, 268n.28
Ramsay, David, 78
Randolph, Edmund, 78
Rasul, Shafiq, 195
Rasul v. Bush, 195, 203
ratification, 48, 67, 69, 71, 72, 75, 76, 77,
    78, 79, 80, 110, 131, 132, 209,
    254n.77, 255n.98, 256n.5 257n.37,
    258n.41, 258n.43
rational choice theory, 129
Rawls, John, 170, 241, 272n.25, 277n.50
Reagan administration, 198

Reagan, Ronald, 22, 137, 217, 286n.38
Reconstruction, 6, 70, 74, 76, 78, 79, 81
Red Cross, 196
Renditions, 198, 200
republican government, 70, 129
Republican Party, 70, 189
Rewriting the United States Constitution:
    An Examination of Proposals from Re-
    construction to the Present, 6
Rhode Island, 19, 22, 30, 91, 109, 117,
    146, 237, 246n.3
Richards, Neil M., 273n.40
rights, 70, 76, 83, 126, 132, 152, 192, 200,
    202, 291, 292
Robin L. Einhorn,10, 246n.25
Rockman, Bert, 146, 269n.8, 270n.33
Roe v. Wade, 172
Romania, 200
Rome, 61, 204
Roosevelt, Franklin, 82, 133, 188
Rosenberger, Gerald, 173
Rossiter, Clinton, 20, 96, 188, 247n.12,
    247n.2, 251n.28, 261n.38, 268n.40,
    280n.34
Rotch, Sr., William, 76
Rubinfeld, Jed, 176
Rumsfeld, Donald, 194, 286n.25
Russell Feingold, 268n.44
Russia, 34

                    S

Sabato, Larry J., 292
Sanchez, Ricardo S., 194
San Diego, 94
San Francisco, 94
Sarbanes-Oxley Act, 140
Saudi Arabia, 196
Schatschneider, E.E., 167
Schlesinger Jr., Arthur, 112, 207, 265n.32,
    284n.2
Schroeder, Mary M., 200
Schumer, Charles E., 20
SEC, 191, 281, 283, 284
Second Circuit, 203
Second Reconstruction Act of 1868, 187
Security Council, 133
Senate, 31, 69, 70, 73–75, 77, 78, 80–82,
    125–128, 130–132, 139, 146, 182, 190,
    246, 262

separation of powers, 70, 123, 181–183, 197

September 11, 2001, 195, 212, 214, 215, 282*n*.93

Seventeenth Amendment, 240, 243, 263*n*.12, 268*n*.44

Shogun, Robert, 188

signing statement, 198

Sinclair, Barbara, 125

slave rebellion, 46, 47, 66

slave states, 43,47, 50, 54, 56, 58, 60, 65, 66, 69, 70, 72–75, 77, 78, 80, 81, 249*n*.13, 250*n*.16, 252*n*.41

slave trade, 46, 52, 54, 58, 60, 61, 62, 63, 64, 65, 66, 67, 69, 72, 75, 76, 78, 242, 249*n*.8, 250*n*.18, 254*n*.77, 254*n*.84, 254*n*.87, 255*n*.91, 255*n*.92, 255*n*.95, 256*n*.105

"slave trade" clause, 46

slavery, 11, 43–67, 69–84, 126, 131, 183, 184, 249–251, 253, 255, 291

slaves, 45, 49, 50, 54, 60, 61, 70, 72–76, 78, 83, 235, 254

small states, 73, 91, 130, 131

Smith, J. Allen, 6, 8, 9, 11, 234, 245*n*.5, 245*n*.6, 245*n*.10

Smith, Jean Edward, 125

Snyder, Jack, 173, 277*n*.53

Social Democratic Party, 28

Social Security, 125

Sorensen, Theodore, 278*n*.4

the South, 48, 72, 73, 75, 78, 79, 184, 185, 187, 190, 191

South Carolina, 48, 72–74, 77, 78, 83

South Dakota, 30, 89, 91, 95, 117, 246*n*.3, 246*n*.7

Southern federalists, 70, 75, 78

Southwest, 79, 91

Soviet Union, 133

Speaker (of the House of Representatives), 113, 132, 138, 283*n*.105, 283*n*.109,

Spirit of American Government, The, 6, 245*n*.6, 246*n*.31

stalemate, 137

state conventions, 75, 77, 78, 82, 182, 191

State Department, 202

State Secrets Protection Act, 202

statistical analysis, 129

Steel Seizures, 219

Stid, Daniel D., 245*n*.13

stimulus package, 124

Story, Joseph, 70

"strong form" judicial review, 176

supermajorities, 83

Supreme Court, 80–83, 122, 124, 125, 132, 186, 187, 192, 195, 197, 200, 203, 204, 292

Syria, 196

T

Taliban, 191, 213

Taney, Roger, 186

tax, 46

Tenet, George, 204

Texas, 17, 19, 91, 93–95, 117, 172, 258, 291, 292

Thailand, 200

Thatcher, Margaret, 28

The Constitution: A Pro-Slavery Compact, 10, 44, 246*n*.26, 246*n*.28, 249*n*.7, 249*n*.11, 257*n*.10

The End of Inequality: One Person, One Vote and the Transformation of American Politics, 173, 277*n*.53

The Welfare State that Nobody Knows, 145

Thirteenth Amendment, 45, 69, 70, 72, 75, 76, 77, 78, 83, 252*n*.37, 256*n*.100

three-fifths clause, 16, 46, 47, 50, 51, 52, 54, 55, 57, 58, 59, 64, 66, 67, 69, 72, 76, 82, 242, 252*n*.49, 253*n*.55, 253*n*.66, 256*n*.105, 263*n*.12

Tories, 28

torture, 187, 193, 194, 198, 200, 202–204, 225

Treasury (Department of), 8, 139, 185

Tribe, Laurence, 273*n*.35

Truman, Harry, 133

Tushnet, Mark, 163, 174, 176, 271*n*.1, 271*n*.4, 273*n*.29, 274*n*.6, 293

Twelfth Amendment, 21, 26, 106, 107, 110, 236, 239, 262*n*.1, 262*n*.2, 263*n*.12, 263*n*.17, 265*n*.29

Twentieth Amendment, 132

Twenty-fifth Amendment, 243

Twenty-fourth Amendment, 100, 263*n*.12

Twenty-sixth Amendment, 100

Twenty-third Amendment, 106, 263*n*.12

two-party system, 89, 95, 96, 97, 102, 103, 108, 138, 267*n*.24
Tydings, Millard, 190

U

U.S. v. Nixon, 204
U.S. v. Reynolds, 203
ultra vires review, 151, 271*n*.2, 272*n*.3
undivided governments, 123
Uniform Code of Military Justice, 193
Union, 16, 57, 61, 70, 80–82, 131, 133, 175, 183, 185–187, 218
unitary executive, 191, 198
unitary presidency, 182
unitary theory, 191
United Kingdom, 188
United Nations Convention Against Torture and Other Cruel, Inhuman, or Degrading Treatment or Punishment, 225
United Nations, 133
Upper South, 44, 185
USA PATRIOT Act, 140
Utah, 91, 95, 117, 127
Utopianism, 130

V

Verizon, 191
Vermont, 17, 91, 117, 146, 246, 263
Versailles, 15
veto-point, 122
veto, 65, 74, 75, 79, 81, 122, 123, 128, 129, 133, 143, 198
Vietnam War, 36, 129, 188, 216, 282*n*.83, 285
Vile, John R., 6, 245*n*.2
Virginia Plan, 49, 70, 81
Virginia, 49, 61, 70, 72, 76, 78, 81, 91, 117, 126, 131, 190, 196, 251, 258, 262, 263

W

Waldron, Jeremy, 163, 166, 170, 272*n*.12, 274*n*.1, 274*n*.12, 275*n*.23
Wall Street Journal, 188, 280*n*.36, 280*n*.37
Walsh Amendment, 189
War Crimes Act of 1996, 193
War of 1812, 38
War on Drugs, 20

War on Terror, 20, 96,140, 173, 192, 197, 203, 207, 208, 212, 215, 218, 221, 222, 223, 224, 226, 228, 229, 278*n*.1, 279*n*.10, 281*n*.68, 281*n*.76, 282*n*.78, 285*n*.3, 289*n*.76
War Powers Act, 35, 36, 216, 217, 283*n*.103
war powers, 182, 185, 197, 202
Warren, Charles, 251
Washington, D.C., 246, 250, 251, 255, 278, 279
Washington, George, 60, 106, 126, 194, 236
Washington Post, 283
Washington, 94, 106, 117, 123, 126, 183, 185, 193, 246, 250, 251, 255, 259, 260, 263, 270, 278, 279, 283
Waterboarding, 200, 202, 227
Watergate, 188
"weak form" judicial review, 176
Weldon, Dave, 20
welfare policy, 292
welfare state, 145
West Bank, 196
West Coast Hotel v. Parrish, 273*n*.42
West Indies, 191
West Virginia, 126, 190
Wheeler, Burton, 190
Whigs, 81
White House, ix, 11, 21, 29, 107,114, 127, 139, 140, 145, 187, 190, 197, 198, 201, 211, 225, 261*n*.52, 281*n*.55, 283*n*.105, 287*n*.58, 293
Whittington, Keith, 173
Willkie, Wendell, 189
Wilmot Proviso, 81
Wilson, James, 50, 54, 59, 62, 63, 66, 90, 254*n*.77
Wilson, Woodrow, 6, 7, 135, 136, 225, 243, 245*n*.12, 245*n*.13, 280*n*.33
winner-take-all system, 87, 89, 98, 107, 111, 112, 147, 265*n*.27
Wisconsin, 93, 117, 263
World Trade Center, 21, 222
World Trade Organization, 176,
World War II, 182, 192, 195
Wyoming, 91, 95, 117, 130, 146, 246

Y

Yoo, John C., 198, 201